INDUSTRIAL MARKETING

Sara Miller McCune founded SAGE Publishing in 1965 to support the dissemination of usable knowledge and educate a global community. SAGE publishes more than 1000 journals and over 800 new books each year, spanning a wide range of subject areas. Our growing selection of library products includes archives, data, case studies and video. SAGE remains majority owned by our founder and after her lifetime will become owned by a charitable trust that secures the company's continued independence.

Los Angeles | London | New Delhi | Singapore | Washington DC | Melbourne

INDUSTRIAL MARKETING

Thomas Fotiadis, Adam Lindgreen, George J. Siomkos, Christina Öberg & Dimitris Folinas

Los Angeles | London | New Delhi
Singapore | Washington DC | Melbourne

Los Angeles | London | New Delhi
Singapore | Washington DC | Melbourne

SAGE Publications Ltd
1 Oliver's Yard
55 City Road
London EC1Y 1SP

SAGE Publications Inc.
2455 Teller Road
Thousand Oaks, California 91320

SAGE Publications India Pvt Ltd
B 1/I 1 Mohan Cooperative Industrial Area
Mathura Road
New Delhi 110 044

SAGE Publications Asia-Pacific Pte Ltd
3 Church Street
#10-04 Samsung Hub
Singapore 049483

Editor: Matthew Waters
Editorial assistant: Charlotte Hanson
Production editor: Martin Fox
Copyeditor: Tom Bedford
Proofreader: Christine Bitten
Indexer: Gary Kirby
Marketing manager: Kimberley Simpson
Cover design: Francis Kenney
Typeset by: C&M Digitals (P) Ltd, Chennai, India

Library of Congress Control Number: 2022934596

British Library Cataloguing in Publication data

A catalogue record for this book is available from the British Library

ISBN 978-1-5297-7854-0
ISBN 978-1-5297-7853-3 (pbk)

This textbook is based on the Greek language textbook, *Industrial Marketing* (Siomkos, G.J., and Fotiadis, Th. (2020), *Industrial Marketing*, 1st edition, Nicosia: Broken Hill Publishers). Therefore, a special thanks is owed to Broken Hill Publishers, for their kind permission to exclusively and extensively use and get inspired by the original material of the Greek text, and lay the essential foundation on which this international textbook is based.

To Hermie$_{12}$ – My little rare unicorn, magical, enchanting and full of colors. Radiant, glorious, and bright, full of humor, passionate—an Idol already! We have been waiting for you so long—but it doesn't matter — we are and always will be your biggest fans, our little Diva. The only wish is more time in this life to have a role in all the magic universes you will most definitely create. So proud of you rising star... – Thomas

To my lovely daughters Vic and Zazou, you make me proud every day; to Dad, you introduced me to the world of books, for which I will always be grateful; to Joëlle, we have done well (so far ☺) with our daughters; and to Inna, you mean the world to me – Adam

To my family that always makes me very proud: Stella, Agatha, John, Dimitris-Aristotelis.

To all the thousands of my undergraduate, graduate and doctoral students at the Stern School of Business (New York University), Long Island University, University of Piraeus, University of Macedonia, and the Athens University of Economics & Business, who I had the privilege to teach as well as learn from – George

To my parents Mona and Bengt – Christina

To Angie, Mia, Kostas, and my little Charis for your support and love.

To my father who, watching me read all the time, always complained that "something is wrong with this kid," and to my mother who argued, "that growing up he would overcome it." To my students and colleagues at the International Hellenic University – Dimitris

PRAISE FOR THIS TEXTBOOK

"This is probably the most comprehensive textbook on industrial marketing and supply chain management. It brings together a wide range of literatures and provides readers with a thorough overview of topics pertinent for manufacturing firms and other companies in industrial markets."

Professor Christian Kowalkowski, Professor of Industrial Marketing, Department of Management and Engineering, Linköping University

"A welcome new and innovative book from five well-established and well-published scholars in the field. The complexities of the subject are nicely teased out throughout the book, with excellent use being made of numerous tables and graphs to add extra insight. What I particularly liked was the way in which the book sits at the interface of industrial marketing and supply chain management, and also the way that it uses a range of case studies from around the globe to support the points being made. Definitely a book to add to the shelves of any scholars in the field!"

Peter Naudé, Professor of Marketing, Manchester Metropolitan University Business School, Manchester Metropolitan University

"This new and up-to-date textbook provides a fresh view on industrial marketing. Bringing together established frameworks and latest research insights from two streams of literature, industrial marketing and supply chain management, it develops a unique perspective on the marketing, selling, and purchasing of industrial goods and services. With its chapter on data, information, and technology, and its insights on socially responsible marketing approaches, it offers a timely perspective on the art and science of industrial marketing. Highly recommended!"

Professor Andreas Eggert, Professor of Business and Service Marketing, Marketing Department, Freie Universität Berlin

"The business ecosystems in which companies operate are strongly shaped by industrial relationships. It is therefore fundamental to understand what industrial marketing—as the activity of creating and managing these industrial relationships—covers. This is the objective of this book, which succeeds perfectly in producing an integrated vision of industrial marketing and supply chain management in their essential role of value creation. Therefore, if some chapters seem usual in an industrial marketing book, others are less so (transportation of goods, warehousing, etc.) and all contribute greatly to producing this new vision of industrial marketing. For students, who sometimes find it difficult to figure out what industrial relationships are, this is the ideal book. It will show students the richness of these relationships and the nature of the multiple activities that industrial marketing is made of. For researchers interested in industrial marketing, they will find a very integrated vision of the various themes related to industrial relations, which will allow them to finely situate their research issues. Finally, practitioners will not fail to find in this book the precision of their daily activities in marketing and supply chain management and will fully benefit from the perspectives it offers.

Catherine Pardo, Professor of Marketing, Marketing Department, Emlyon Business School

"This book is a welcome and timely addition to the business and academic community with heightened interest on industrial marketing issues and the increasing importance of supply chain management around the globe. It covers key issues in industrial marketing and addresses the main challenges in the area in a competent fashion and without making it difficult for the reader to follow. The examples, case studies, and vignettes that accompany the book are particularly useful in helping the reader develop a critical understanding of the challenges, realities, and developments in industrial marketing and supply chain management and learn how to appropriately apply related concepts. Highly recommended."

Professor Constantinos N. Leonidou, Professor of Marketing and Business Administration, Faculty of Economics and Management, Open University of Cyprus, and Adjunct Professor, Leeds University Business School, University of Leeds

"I am delighted to recommend this new text which will be suitable for either graduate or undergraduate classes in business-to-business marketing. Professors Fotiadis, Lindgreen, Siomkos, Öberg, and Folinas bring a wealth of experience and scholarship in B2B teaching and research to this book. The business-to-business marketing landscape is rapidly changing with the emergence of new technologies, which have affected all aspects of marketing, from customer research to product innovation, marketing communications, and supply chain and logistics. This text provides a fresh and updated perspective on the issues and challenges currently facing the B2B marketing professional."

Professor C. Anthony Di Benedetto, Professor of Marketing, Fox School of Business, Temple University

"*Industrial Marketing* provides an important contemporary perspective. It is a research and practice informed textbook, which has the potential to become seminal. While the primary audience is undergraduate students in the field of B2B marketing, it also is highly relevant to students in related areas including innovation, entrepreneurship, product management, and supply chain management or logistics. The viewpoints will also be of interest to students in the broader fields of business administration, management, and economics in general. Scholars, researchers, and practitioners working in marketing or logistics will also find this text useful."

Roderick J. Brodie, Professor Emeritus, University of Auckland Business School, University of Auckland

"This enlightening textbook brings together industrial marketing and supply chain management, and this is achieved in a succinct, holistic, and integrated manner. I am impressed by the breadth of topics covered, which reflects successfully the contemporary, dynamic, and volatile business environment. A very much welcomed book, which will support students, scholars, and practitioners in their attempt to understand better the links and interrelationships between industrial marketing and supply chain management."

Professor Michael Bourlakis, Director of Research and Director of the Centre for Logistics, Procurement & Supply Chain Management, Cranfield University

"It is exciting to see the new textbook on *Industrial Marketing* by Fotiadis, Lindgreen, Siomkos, Öberg, and Folinas. In a constantly evolving global landscape industrial markets are key contributors to the global economy. Industrial marketing is cornerstone of any marketers' arsenal. This text covers critically relevant material in a deep and engaging way. This text will equip aspiring industrial marketers with a deep appreciation of the exciting field of industrial marketing and prepare them to make their way in this highly competitive and dynamic field."

Professor Aron O'Cass, Dean of La Trobe Business School, La Trobe University

"This is a comprehensive, contemporary, and well-structured textbook, providing an excellent coverage of the various facets of the industrial marketing process. It offers a balanced combination between theoretical and practical aspects of industrial marketing, while also putting together classic knowledge on the subject with recent developments in the field. Enriched with multiple case studies, practical examples, and useful illustrations, it provides a systematic pedagogic approach that helps to have an all-round and in-depth understanding of the various concepts, techniques, and tools related to modern industrial marketing."

Dr. Leonidas C. Leonidou, Professor of Marketing, Department of Business and Public Administration, University of Cyprus

CONTENTS

LIST OF CASE STUDIES AND VIGNETTES

CASE STUDIES

VIGNETTES

ONLINE RESOURCES

Industrial Marketing is accompanied by online resources to aid teaching and support learning, which are available for lecturers to access at: **https://study.sagepub.com/fotiadis**.

Please note that lecturers will require a SAGE account in order to access the lecturer resources. An account can be created via the above link.

FOR LECTURERS

- **PowerPoint decks** that can be downloaded and adapted to suit individual teaching needs.

ABOUT THE AUTHORS

THOMAS FOTIADIS

Thomas Fotiadis is an Associate Professor of Marketing and Head of the Marketing Laboratory at the Department of Production Engineering and Management of the Democritus University of Thrace. He holds a post-doctoral degree in modern advanced statistical methods for the science of marketing and a PhD in marketing (high technology). In addition, he holds an MSc in business administration, and an MSc in business computing. His first degree is in economic science.

He has more than 22 years of teaching experience at both undergraduate and postgraduate level, in Greek and international universities and higher technological institutions.

Thomas Fotiadis' scientific work has been published in international scientific journals, including the *Journal of World Business*, the *Journal of Tourism Management*, the *Journal of International Marketing*, the *Journal of International Business Review*, the *Psychology & Marketing Journal*, and the *Journal of Applied Business Research*.

He has published more than 100 articles in journals, international conferences, and book chapters. Additionally, he has published *Strategic Marketing for High Technology Products: An Integrated Approach* (Routledge, 2018), *Marketing and Supply Chain Management: A Systemic Approach* (Routledge, 2017), *The Customer Value Chain: Integrating Marketing and Supply Chain Management* (Routledge, 2021), and he has edited and authored numerous scientific books in the field of marketing (in the Greek language).

ADAM LINDGREEN

Adam Lindgreen has undertaken studies in chemistry and physics (Copenhagen University) and engineering (the Engineering Academy of Denmark). He obtained an MSc in food science and technology at the Technical University of Denmark; his eight-month long MSc thesis was undertaken in collaboration with Danida in Denmark and Banco de Semillas Forestales in Nicaragua. He then earned an MBA at the University of Leicester. He received his PhD in marketing from Cranfield University, with 18 months spent at University of Auckland's Business School.

Adam Lindgreen's first appointments were with the Catholic University of Louvain and Eindhoven University of Technology. Subsequently, he served as Professor of Marketing at Hull University's Business School; at the University of Birmingham's Business School, where he also was the research director in the Department of Marketing; and at the University of

Cardiff's Business School. Under his leadership, the Department of Marketing and Strategy at Cardiff Business School ranked first among all research-intensive marketing departments in Australia, Canada, New Zealand, the United Kingdom, and the United States. Since 2016, Adam Lindgreen has been Professor of Marketing at Copenhagen Business School, where he also heads the Department of Marketing. Under his leadership, the department's number of AJG 3 journal articles and that of AJG 4 and 4* journal articles have increased by 925 and 600 percent respectively. Since 2018, Adam Lindgreen has been extraordinary professor with University of Pretoria's Gordon Institute of Business Science where he is also international research advisor.

Adam Lindgreen's publications have appeared in academic journals, including *Business Strategy and the Environment*, the *California Management Review*, *Entrepreneurship and Regional Development*, *Industrial Marketing Management*, the *International Journal of Management Reviews*, the *Journal of Advertising*, the *Journal of Business Ethics*, the *European Journal of Marketing*, the *Journal of Marketing Management*, the *Journal of the Academy of Marketing Science*, the *Journal of Product Innovation Management*, the *Journal of World Business*, *Organization Studies*, *Psychology & Marketing*, and *Supply Chain Management: An International Journal*, among others.

Adam Lindgreen's 31 books include *The Emergence and Rise of Relationship Marketing* (published PhD thesis; 2000), *A Stakeholder Approach to Corporate Social Responsibility* (with Kotler, Vanhamme, and Maon; 2012), *How to Fast-Track Your Academic Career* (with Di Benedetto, Vanhamme, and Nicholson; 2021), *Managing Market Relationships* (2008), *Public Value* (with Koenig-Lewis, Kitchener, Brewer, Moore, and Meynhardt; 2019), and *Sustainable Value Chain Management* (with Maon, Vanhamme, and Sen; 2013).

The recipient of the "Outstanding Article 2005" award from *Industrial Marketing Management* and the runner-up for the same award in 2006, Adam Lindgreen is co-editor-in-chief of *Industrial Marketing Management*. Furthermore, he is co-editor-in-chief of Food and Agricultural Marketing, a series of highly managerially relevant books published by Routledge.

Since 2016, Adam Lindgreen has been a member of the International Scientific Advisory Panel of the New Zealand Food Safety Science and Research Centre (a partnership among government, industry organizations, and research institutions); since 2017, of the Chartered Association of Business Schools' Academic Journal Guide (AJG) Scientific Committee in the field of marketing; and since 2020, of Det videnskabelige Råd for Lex.dk.

GEORGE J. SIOMKOS

George J. Siomkos is professor of marketing at the Athens University of Economics & Business (AUEB). He is also the director of the MSc Program in Services Management (MSM) (www.msmfull.aueb.gr), and director of "Agora" (Market Analysis & Consumer Behavior Laboratory).

He has served as dean of AUEB's School of Business (2013–2021) and the chairman of AUEB's Business Administration Department, deputy chair and chair of the University of Macedonia's

Business Administration Department, and university senate member of the aforementioned universities. He has served as the vice president of the management committee of the University of Peloponnese. For many years he has been a member of the management committees of AUEB's MBA-International and Interdepartmental MBA Programs.

George J. Siomkos holds a BSc (cum laude) in marketing and management, an MBA in finance, an MSc in statistics & operations research, an MPhil in marketing, and a PhD in marketing and corporate strategy, all from Stern School of Business, New York University.

He has taught at Stern School of Business—New York University, Long Island University, the Athens Laboratory of Business Administration, the University of Piraeus, the University of Macedonia, and the Hellenic Open University (in which he has been "Marketing II" module coordinator for 12 years). In 1988 he was a Doctoral Consortium Fellow—American Marketing Association (at the University of California—Berkeley). For his teaching he has received many teaching excellence awards.

His research and publishing interests include: consumer behavior and analysis, customer experience (CX) management, marketing research, services marketing, strategic marketing and planning, and product-harm crisis management.

George J. Siomkos is the author of 12 textbooks in marketing and has published over 80 articles in academic journals, including the *Journal of Retailing*, the *European Journal of Marketing*, the *Journal of Consumer Behaviour*, the *Journal of Business Strategy*, *Long Range Planning*, *Advances in Consumer Research*, *Industrial and Environmental Crisis Quarterly*, the *Disaster Recovery Journal*, the *Journal of Business & Psychology*, the *Journal of Business & Industrial Marketing*, the *Journal of Internet Banking & Commerce*, the *European Journal of Innovation Management*, and the *Journal of Internet Marketing*.

He has served as a member of the organizing and scientific committees of several international scientific conferences as well as a member of the editorial boards of various scientific journals.

CHRISTINA ÖBERG

With a background including leading positions in finance, Christina Öberg obtained her doctoral degree in industrial marketing in 2008 at Linköping University, Sweden. In 2012, she became an associate professor at Lund University, and in 2014, Christina Öberg became the professor/chair in marketing at Örebro University. She was there the director of a research center (Interorg) focusing on marketing, strategy, and entrepreneurship. During her directorship, the center obtained international recognition, and became the most productive center of the Örebro University School of Business.

Since 2021, Christina Öberg has been a professor in marketing at Karlstad University, CTF Service Research Center, a world-leading research center in service and value creation research. She is also associated with the Ratio Institute, Stockholm. The Ratio Institute is an independent research institute specializing in entrepreneurship and enterprise conditions and consists of leading scholars in management, sociology, and economics.

Christina Öberg has been a visiting scholar at several leading universities including University of Bath, University of Manchester, National Tsing Hua University, University of Exeter, Stanford University, Harvard University, University of Florence, and University of Leeds.

Her research interests concern changes in business interactions and ways to conduct business, with mergers and acquisitions, the sharing economy, and the evolution of 3D printing as pronounced examples. In 2021, she received a Best Paper Award at the Academy of Management.

Christina Öberg has published more than 80 journal articles in such journals as *Entrepreneurship and Regional Development*, the *European Journal of Marketing*, *Information Technology & People*, *Industrial Marketing Management*, the *International Marketing Review*, the *Journal of Business Research*, the *Journal of Cleaner Production*, *Production Planning & Control*, and *Supply Chain Management: An International Journal*.

Books by Christina Öberg include *A Comprehensive Guide to Mergers & Acquisitions: Managing the Critical Success Factors Across Every Stage of the M&A Process* (with Yakoov Weber and Shlomo Tarba) and a handful of textbooks in marketing and financial analysis.

With a background in industry, Christina Öberg has continued to interact with the surrounding society in research, consultancy roles, and as a board member. Her board memberships include the Swedish Textbook Association, Nordic Academy of Management, and two private corporations. She is part of the Swedish Competition Authority's Research Council.

She has taught marketing courses along with courses in financial analysis and research design across bachelor, master, and PhD levels at her home universities and in Taiwan, Italy, Denmark, and the UK. She has supervised several PhD students.

DIMITRIS FOLINAS

Dimitris Folinas is a professor at International Hellenic University in the Department of Supply Chain Management. He holds a PhD in applied informatics from the University of Macedonia, Thessaloniki, Greece, and a Master of information systems from the same institution. For more than 20 years, he has held various teaching posts with Liverpool University (UK), the Hellenic Open University (Greece), and the University of Macedonia (Greece), teaching mainly information systems, enterprise information systems, and logistics and supply chain management. He is the author and co-author of over 280 research publications, ten books, and as a researcher, he has prepared, submitted, and managed a number of projects funded by national and European Union research entities such as Attracting Leading Scientists to Russian Educational Institutions, Eurostars Programme, FRS-FNRS. His research interests and working experiences refer to enterprise information systems, as well as logistics and supply chain management and technologies.

ACKNOWLEDGEMENTS

Some of the textbook's case studies and vignettes have been co-authored with colleagues. We would like to acknowledge co-authorship with the following colleagues:

Michael B. Beverland (Implementing a Market Orientation Among New Zealand Ranchers; Industrial Global Brand Leadership).

Mogens Bjerre (Brands Are Affected by Their Context; DSV Introduces the Silkway Express: Fast China–Europe Road Freight; Internal Functions Can Create Value for Customers Too; Maersk: Vertically Integrating the Container Transportation Supply Chain; The Danish Customer Centricity Index Project; Vestas: Capturing the Full Potential of the Service Business; When Sales and Procurement Processes Are Out of Sync).

Martin Hingley (Customer Relationship Management; Implementing a Market Orientation among New Zealand Ranchers; Fourth-Party Logistics; Industrial Global Brand Leadership; Meeting the Fresh Produce Needs of Growing Ethnic Minority Populations; Meeting the Value Needs of Customers; Purchasing Practices; Value Chains and Supplier Perceptions of Corporate Social Responsibility; Value in Marketing; When Purchasing and Marketing Interact: Processes and Integration Tactics).

John D. Nicholson (AI and Programmatic Marketing in Advertising Agencies; Platform-Based Business Model Innovation; Servitization in Business-to-Business Marketing; Supply Chains for the Floriculture Sector in Uganda; Technology-Mindset Interaction in New Product Development).

Thomas and Dimitris would like to thank their former and current PhD students, Efthimios Kokmotos, Aggeliki Konstantoglou, and Anna Maditianou for all their invaluable help and support. Christina would like to thank Lisa Aaboen, John Bessant, Maria Björklund, Hsin-Hui Chou, Enrico Fontana, Gary Graham, Jens Laage-Hellman, Maria Huge-Brodin, Frida Lind, Leon Poblete, Tawfiq Shams, Tommy Shih and Anna Trifilova for joint research in the original work to case studies and vignettes.

Finally, we extend special thanks to SAGE, especially Charlotte Hanson and Matthew Waters, who have been most helpful throughout this entire process.

ROADMAP

This textbook covers some familiar, widely taught, and well-researched subject areas. Industrial marketing and supply chain management are key topics in nearly every business administration course and technology-oriented program, at undergraduate and postgraduate levels. But the vast increases in the size, value, and importance of supply chain management, at a global level, combined with the remarkable impact of industrial markets on the structure, shape, and balance of interrelated economic systems worldwide, have inspired this book as a necessary source of information. That is, industrial marketing and supply chain management drive economies, nationally and globally, and they constitute cornerstones of the shape of international economic and competitive environments. Their influences largely determine prosperity and utility levels, and they are linked to almost every relevant variable contained in global socio-economic webs.

But assessing and forecasting how these influences and related practices will evolve remains extremely difficult for marketing executives. Most industrial sectors are dynamic and volatile, in terms of not just how the firms operate but also the challenging competitive environment. Therefore, with this textbook, we seek to clarify customers' (commercial and industrial buyers') concerns and the factors that inform their industrial purchase decisions. In detail, this textbook covers various development motifs dominated by uncertainty, the need for research and development investments, prototype production costs, and technological standards in the supply chain. We introduce readers to the differences between consumer and industrial markets, the differentiating features of business-to-business (B2B) markets, and what marketing mixes (distribution, promotion, communication, pricing, products) look like in industrial markets. Other topics pertain to the risks associated with adopting innovations and the complex relations involved in the co-creation of value among manufacturers and end users in industrial markets.

In turn, our overall goals are to:

- Help companies move along their own learning curves.
- Give academic researchers a stable foundation for further research.
- Establish applicable knowledge that can apply to various fields and industries.

Accordingly, this textbook is aimed at the following audiences:

- Undergraduate students in the fields of industrial marketing, innovative entrepreneurship, product or management engineering, industrial marketing, B2B marketing, constitutional buying, international buying centers, supply chain management, or logistics. The viewpoints presented herein also may be of interest to students in the broader fields of business administration and management, engineering management, marketing, technology, production engineering, and industrial planning, as well as students of technology and economics in general.

- Scholars, researchers, doctoral students, postgraduate students, and post-doc students in these fields, who may find the unique, cohesive angle presented by this textbook helpful.
- Practitioners working in the marketing or logistics departments of business entities or who work on marketing/supply chain management more generally, such as marketing/supply chain management professionals, logisticians, industrial executives and managers, product management engineers, technology marketers, industrial buying centers, industrial decision-makers, and constitutional buyers, from both the supply and demand sides of an industry.

The material we feature in this textbook capitalizes on current academic standards and insights. We emphasize a wide array of relevant cognitive elements, though the focus remains analytical and in-depth in orientation. Therefore, this textbook provides an introduction to the theoretical background and prerequisites that readers need, if they are to develop a more solid understanding of specific topics. In this sense, a lack of prior knowledge should not be an obstacle to learning from this textbook. The requirements for understanding and applying the key insights are not so demanding as to require prior fundamental knowledge specific to these fields.

We know of no similar texts that, directly or indirectly, address industrial marketing and supply chain management topics together, within a unified content framework. In that sense, this textbook reflects our unique effort to create synergies and novel insights by integrating two important, contemporary, and complementary scientific topic areas in a compact, convincing manner. Rather than myopic considerations, we seek a holistic view by building on a solid scientific and theoretical background that accommodates both scientific areas. Thus we can distinguish specific objectives in each chapter and section of this textbook, but when we combine them, we aim to provide an integrated view of the focal topics discussed.

In particular, we cover the following topics and considerations:

- Business-to-business (industrial) markets differ from consumer markets, which reveals the need for marketers to adopt a distinct approach to conduct B2B operations. This multifaceted context incorporates relevant variables related to industrial marketing and supply chain management, presenting the complex web of interrelations and contemporary competition in a compact yet extensive way.
- The characteristics of different constituents shape industrial markets; we analyze their complex webs of interrelations, with special emphasis on the complexity that stems from the particularities of both the B2B purchase process and the constituent factors that inform the attitudes, behaviors, and perceptions of the players involved.

- We analyze the elements of the marketing mix in detail, adjusted to reflect the setting of industrial markets, so as to provide a useful, consistent roadmap that can guide tactical and strategic decisions.
- In presenting a marketing philosophy on industrial markets, we explain the nature of industrial products to render their classification clear. Strategic consequences arise from the nature of these products; we also consider the role and features of industrial buyers.
- Issues related to distribution and operations in industrial markets and the categories of intermediaries, each with their own advantages and disadvantages, are covered, as are issues related to the design and management of distribution channels.
- Marketing communication in industrial environments has unique characteristics and produces distinct interactions, particularly among industrial salespeople. Thus we can detail the communication process and present relevant marketing tools. Corporate social responsibility also is addressed in this textbook, as it relates to marketing communication.
- We define price, pricing, and pricing methods for industrial products. Price adjustment strategies are possible and can reflect managerial practices; in addition to suggesting a general pricing model, we discuss the role of the Internet in pricing-related decision-making.
- The characteristics of an industrial product, the process for and importance of developing new products, and factors that lead to success or failure are also presented. In analyzing the notion and framework for integrating different departments, we elaborate on the product life cycle and its characteristic stages. Product portfolio analysis also offers a strategic decision-making tool.
- We apply an integrated marketing and logistics perspective to packaging, in terms of the importance and role of sales and operations planning, as well as the uses of CAD-CAM information systems in business processes. Product development approaches that adopt environmentally friendly practices are within the scope of a marketing and supply chain management perspective too.
- Warehousing in industrial markets or of manufacturing products (including material handling requirements) creates some notable challenges for B2B markets. In addition to outlining key parameters for distribution centers in supply chain networks, we offer an extensive discussion on Warehousing 4.0 (technologies, practices, example cases).
- Issues related to emerging trends and philosophies in marketing can be applied to industrial contexts. The notion of interfunctional integration is relevant, as is the application of a systemic approach to meet the specific prerequisites of such forms of integration. It is strategically imperative to create conditions for collaboration by competitors in an industry, while still acknowledging that industrial services are integral to consolidating B2B products.
- Information, databases, online environments, and digital solutions imply channel diversification for promotions and content marketing. Issues related to

internationalization also fall within the scope of our unified examination of industrial marketing and supply chain management. Beyond the importance of information, knowledge, and innovation in high-technology environments, the notion of creating value with customers is highly relevant. These characteristics in turn have notable effects on the formulation of strategies in such environments.

- The principles of marketing, applied to an industrial context, can be implemented in a high-technology context as well. Specific details of high-tech markets and products suggest the need for differentiated approaches. This textbook pinpoints critical variables that can reduce the time devoted to developing new products and services, by overcoming disruptive uncertainties and inefficiencies. Thus, we can outline how a new (high) technology spreads, along with how it gets adopted.

We hope that this textbook stimulates colleagues and students and contributes to their teaching and learning of industrial marketing.

1

APPLYING MARKETING PHILOSOPHIES TO INDUSTRIAL MARKETS

Learning Objectives

- Define industrial markets.
- Understand a marketing philosophy for approaching industrial markets.
- Describe the nature of industrial products.
- Outline the most important approaches for classifying industrial products.
- Recognize the strategic consequences of the nature of industrial products.
- Describe the characteristics of industrial buyers and their roles in industrial markets.

Case Study

Value in Marketing

A key, critical premise of this first chapter is the essential role of marketing for creating value. If customers are satisfied with, or even pleasantly surprised by, the firm's offerings (services, products, or bundles of both), they perceive good value, which can be monetary in nature but also extends beyond just the price paid. When they perceive good value, they are more likely to repurchase from the same firm, to which they even might develop a sense of loyalty and reciprocity.

(Continued)

Such descriptions might seem self-evident. But, the emphasis on value creation actually is quite new. In the past, firms focused more on profitability as their central goal, with little consideration of the outcomes for customers. Their transactional approach to interacting with customers, just once and just to make the sale, in turn prompted these firms to offer standardized products and services, which they could produce more efficiently. Such methods tend to be reinforced in regulated markets and closely controlled distribution channels, as well as when the industry suffers scarce production resources. These conditions are increasingly rare though, even in previously closed economies that feature expanded market liberalization, around the world.

In today's markets, value is not only critical to marketing but also highly relevant to related efforts, such as purchasing and supply management. Furthermore, relationship marketing is the dominant paradigm: firms attempt to attract customers to enter into long-term, mutually beneficial relationships to convince buyers to keep returning. Marketing managers cannot just push products to customers but instead must manage customer interactions as touchpoints within market relationships that in turn involve networks of actors. The products and services on offer therefore need to be customized or even individualized. Table 1.1 lists some key differences between the transactional marketing that previously held sway and the relationship marketing that most of today's successful firms embrace.

Thus, value gets created through and in networks and interactions, such that firms should ensure their offerings provide value to customers, then go further to establish more valuable relationships. By understanding precisely how customers gauge value, firms can create more appealing product, service, and relationship offerings, which they deliver through the most effective means and with the collaborative help of the most relevant actors.

Table 1.1 Transaction Marketing versus Relationship Marketing

Transaction marketing	Relationship marketing
Many alternatives	One of few alternatives
Every deal is a new business, and no-one should benefit from past performances; independent and discrete market exchanges	A deal is part of a relationship, and the relationship is part of a network context; dependent and ongoing market exchanges
Exploit the potential of competition; anonymous and efficient market	Exploit the potential of cooperation; numerous market networks
Short-term, arm's-length distance, and avoid coming too close	Long-term with tough demands and joint development
Hierarchical, functional organization	Cross-functional, process-based organization
Renewal and effectiveness by change of partner, and choose the most efficient supplier at any time	Renewal and effectiveness by collaboration and team effects, and combine resources and knowledge
Buying products; standardized products	Buying capabilities; customized products

Transaction marketing	Relationship marketing
Services only augment the core product	Services are basis for differentiation
Price orientation, strong in achieving favorable prices in well-specific products; marketing is through the 4Ps	Cost and value orientation, strong in achieving low total costs of supply and developing new value; marketing through relationships, networks, and interactions

Source: Lindgreen (2008, p. 5)

Source

Lindgreen, A. (2008), *Managing Market Relationships: Methodological and Empirical Insights*, Aldershot: Gower Publishing.

MARKETING

Marketing places customer satisfaction at the center of its focus and efforts. Through an unwavering commitment to creating conditions that lead to efficient, profitable transactions, marketing aims to provide value (utility or usefulness) to all members involved in a trade or transaction. Marketing comprises an integrated, systematically structured, comprehensive system of business activities, purposefully and conscientiously constructed so that they cover all aspects of the creation, promotion, distribution, and pricing of products.

Integral to a customer-centric approach embodied by marketing, and perhaps its most meaningful form, is its outline of a business philosophy reflected by the "marketing ideology." In contrast with a common view of marketing as a tool or method that firms use to "victimize" its customers, the truth is that for marketing, the customer is integral to business operations, its ultimate purpose, and, in many cases, a partner. This role is particularly evident for industrial customers, for which marketing functions as an approach, a coherent link with buyers, and a way to enhance communication and understanding between the supplier and the buyer. This focus on customer satisfaction, achieved through uninterrupted, unified, intensive, and coordinated efforts involving the entire range of actions and functions of the firm, has come about through multiple stages, involving differing approaches and visions, before arriving at its present form.

Looking Back...

This marketing orientation is the result of an evolutionary course that has led to the "evangelization" of its modern ideology. The common denominator of an earlier perspective was a one-dimensional, parochial approach to the purpose or the reason for the existence of marketing. Those involved in marketing were "contaminated" with the belief that the sole reason to involve marketing at any level was to generate money, to such an extent that marketing eventually became synonymous with trading activities. The prevailing idea, defining all the components and activities involved, could be condensed in a statement of any company's main obligation: to achieve satisfactory performance (in financial terms).

Even intuitively, it is clear that for a firm to grow (or persist as an entity), it needs financial resources, which it must obtain from its profits. Thus, superior financial performance (or efficiency) is indispensable and unconditional. The validity of this argument is well recognized by marketing, so this position became incorporated within marketing's definition. Therefore, the aim shifted: to act as a catalyst (or multiplier) of transactions that generate usefulness for all trading parties, including the focal firm. Never ending attempts to provide satisfaction, according to a strategic, long-term approach to meeting customer needs, also implies reciprocity in the relationship. It accounts for the simultaneous satisfaction of the firm's own (organizational) needs. This bilateral reciprocity resembles a dependent system. If there is a breach, it could mark the end of the symbiotic relationship between the firm and its customers.

However, an uncontrolled desire to sacrifice everything for money, in combination with a one-dimensional pursuit of short-term returns and achievements, can distort strategic, long-term views of marketing (associated with short-term orientations in its design). Milton Friedman, the American economist, cited greed as a powerful machine that is both necessary and effective; what it embodies, however, has fueled economic catastrophes (monetary and debt crises, etc.). This view actually is foreign to marketing, for which the core rationality is the belief that to achieve (long-term) organizational goals, the only option is to satisfy customer needs. Peter Drucker, an Austrian scholar of business corporations, similarly described the purpose of the firm as being to create and satisfy customers.

Achieving goals (financial profit, performance), from a business point of the view, as in Figure 1.1, is dualistic, simultaneously an instrument and a goal. Customer satisfaction is an objective and a prerequisite condition to build a lucrative offer that gives customers an incentive to engage, be involved in, and actively participate in the trading process. At the same time, satisfying customer needs constitutes the ultimate means of achieving the goal of the other participant in the transaction, the business itself, which is to make a profit (or "generate" money through financial performance). The close interdependence and interconnectedness of these objectives is clear: without achieving its aims (by fulfilling the objective of meeting customer needs), the firm cannot survive in the long term and then will not be in a position to address customers' needs. As Drucker observes, money is a necessity, but it cannot be equivalent to the purpose of a firm.

Figure 1.1 Simultaneous Satisfaction of Customer and Business Goals

Therefore, to reflect the marketing ideology fully, it is necessary to include all the components in Figures 1.2 and 1.3.

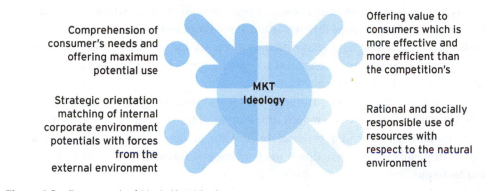

Comprehension of consumer's needs and offering maximum potential use

Offering value to consumers which is more effective and more efficient than the competition's

MKT Ideology

Strategic orientation matching of internal corporate environment potentials with forces from the external environment

Rational and socially responsible use of resources with respect to the natural environment

Figure 1.2   Framework of Marketing Ideology

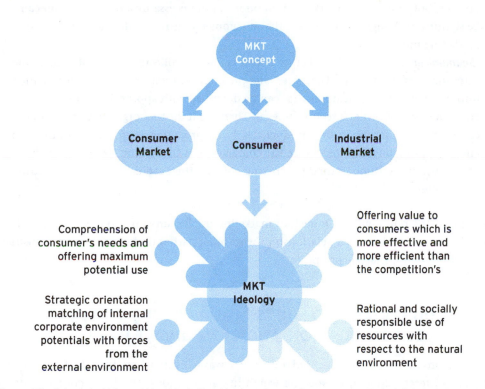

MKT Concept

Consumer Market

Consumer

Industrial Market

Comprehension of consumer's needs and offering maximum potential use

Offering value to consumers which is more effective and more efficient than the competition's

MKT Ideology

Strategic orientation matching of internal corporate environment potentials with forces from the external environment

Rational and socially responsible use of resources with respect to the natural environment

Figure 1.3   Integrated View of How Marketing Ideology Covers Consumer and Industrial Market Needs

Consumer and Industrial Marketing

To differentiate features of the marketing philosophy for consumer versus industrial markets, several elements are particularly effective: rationality expectations, product differentiation, and emphasis on purchasing behavior, marketing techniques, and communication.

- *Rationality expectations*. Consumers often are described as guided by feelings or irrationality, but in industrial marketing settings, customer firms are expected to make rational decisions.
- *Product differentiation*. Consumer marketing benefits from product differentiation; in industrial marketing settings, differentiation alone is not truly relevant. Industrial marketing customers do not prefer a product due to its diversity but rather because a product exhibits better characteristics than existing alternatives or appears more suitable for the uses for which it is intended.
- *Purchasing behavior*. Whereas consumer behavior and purchasing behavior represent two different pillars, both of which require attention from the firm, industrial marketing puts more emphasis on purchasing behavior, because the product's functionality is such an important parameter. Functionality is the fundamental reason an industrial customer decides to purchase and use a product.
- *Marketing techniques*. Consumer marketing often spreads resources across various options, but in industrial markets, promotion is not necessarily a priority. It still can be significant though, to the extent that it complements the application of the wider marketing mix.
- *Communication*. Industrial marketing efforts center on collecting, understanding, and listening to customers' needs, desires, and preferences, then turning this information into product or service features that can be described with appropriate language to guide business efforts at a technical level. Then the industrial organization works to communicate the benefits of a product clearly, by providing appropriate information and prompting buyers to recognize the characteristics that define its superior value. These customers, through their purchasing choices, then can enjoy all that the firm has to offer.

In summary, the philosophy of industrial marketing implies attempts to create, consolidate, enhance, expand, and improve relationships with other parties (industrial or non-industrial) that offer long-term, strategic prospects.

INDUSTRIAL PRODUCTS: APPROACHES TO THEIR CLASSIFICATION AND COMPONENT PARTS

Industrial products can be classified in several ways. Even when they feature varying formulas, different criteria, or specific weighting applications, the basic components of these classifications tend to be quite similar. In describing these components, this section also captures the various perspectives that different available classification models adopt (Figure 1.4).

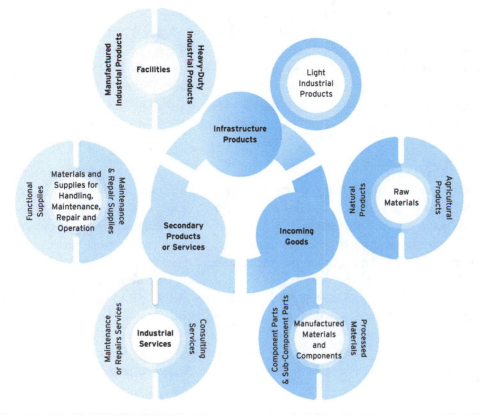

Figure 1.4   The Range of Industrial Products

Industrial Products

Industrial Manufacturing Products

This category refers to infrastructure design and construction, which may include buildings and other large-scale structures such as chemical treatment plants, drilling rigs, or cranes. These infrastructure installations take on a massive scale, with great value, and they are intended to assist production for extended periods of time, without ever becoming part of the final product.

Industrial, Heavy Equipment

These products have large capital requirements and a long expected lifespan. They comprise large machinery and tools such as presses, engines, ground leverage machines, supercomputers, turbines, or trailer vehicles. The products may be developed on special request and made-to-order for the customer, for which these products then may become fixed assets.

The products' life expectancy and capital requirements create significant financial considerations. Their acquisition implies the extensive involvement of prospective (industrial) buyers in the decision-making process. Such purchases often require loans, with partial repayment over the time frame of their life expectancy. Therefore, they demand strategic planning and extensive financial analyses by the buyer. Significant aspects of these products include their perishability, prior to which they must make a useful contribution to the production process, and their lack of integration into what is generally considered the final outcome of their use.

Industrial, Light Equipment

These products comprise auxiliary machinery and tools or even accessories. Compared with the two previous categories, they tend to be considerably cheaper, and their estimated in-service lifespan is shorter. They are fixed assets but not part of the permanent machinery installation; their use is mainly auxiliary to the production process. Lathes, drills, and lifting machines, as well as office equipment such as photocopiers, typewriters, calculators, printers, and computers, are included in this category. Although the products are capital goods, treated as such by firms, both financially and for tax purposes, their precise classification relative to the two preceding categories depends on how they are used in the production process. Usually, light equipment industrial products are standardized and not custom-made, unlike the heavy equipment industrial products used in manufacturing. This greater degree of standardization, in terms of their size and main features, implies the availability of alternative versions, provided by many competing manufacturers.

Industrial Component Materials and Parts

These products are constructions, parts, and subparts of other products that, unlike the industrial product categories, are incorporated into or become part of the final customer product. This category includes small engines and motors, semiconductors, capacitors, integrated circuits, connectors, measuring instruments, batteries, tires, and cables. Their importance for their manufacturers often depends on the persistent needs among buyers for replacement versions of spare parts or subcomponents, so that the production of these parts can be an important or perhaps even the most significant proportion of the manufacturer's income.

Industrial Materials and Supplies for the Handling of Maintenance, Repairs, and Operation

These products have low unit value and do not form part of the finished product. They are used by a wide range of industrial buyers, and the range of needs they cover resembles the uses by private customers. Due to their low unit cost, these products often are purchased in large volumes, so that the buyer can meet its logistics needs over time. A highly competitive supply market is likely available. Factors that diminish choice among the many suppliers then become significant variables, such as reliability, delivery times, and variety. A frequently encountered subdivision in this category of products separates perishable operational supplies like printer ink, toner, stationery, markers, fuel, lubricants, and heating materials from supplies intended to be used for maintenance and repair, such as detergents, cleaning products, light bulbs, or screws.

Maintenance, Repair, and Operating Supplies

These products include materials and supplies used as part of the standard operations of a production process. They consist of consumables for which the cost of switching suppliers is small or non-existent (i.e., there is a wide range of competing suppliers). An intense distribution strategy is usually preferred; the unit cost is low, and purchases are made in small quantities. Examples include various lubricants, cutting machines, cleaning products, cutting discs, and stationery.

Raw Materials

These products come from the natural environment and have not undergone any treatment, other than financial management or transportation. Materials derived from forests, mines, and the sea such as minerals, fish, trees, and crude oil represent the subcategory of natural products. Cotton, cereals, and the progeny of livestock breeding fall within the subcategory of agricultural products. They create a primary link for supporting production chain mechanisms, and for this reason, it is crucial that the supply process for these materials be non-stop, regular, systematic, and continuous in its flow. Depending on the wider economic context of "production" (e.g., financial, legal, competitive, political), transactions of these materials may be governed by the law of supply and demand, which can be more or less influenced, at various times, by buyers and sellers themselves.

Manufactured Materials

This category relies on raw materials and upgrades their value through enhanced refinement processes, such as crushing, shredding, or calibration, or even through a process of classification, such as in terms of their size. Typical examples of such materials include steel, fabric, cement, coal, and petroleum; acids, lubricants, solvents, and motor fuels are essential constituents of almost all productive activities. A relevant difference in "raw" products is the degree of their processing, which allows more processed products to be used as final products. Because these products are not usually highly differentiated, the competition among suppliers is largely defined on the basis of product augmentations, such as technical assistance, delivery method and time, control systems, and modern ordering technology. An important consideration here is to avoid interrupting or disrupting any smooth functioning.

Industrial Services

In the industrial sector, intangible products are not the main consumption focus, as is the case in consumer markets. However, they remain a vital, integral, and critical component.

Services get produced and offered by qualified professionals, ensuring their high quality and thereby safeguarding the harmonious technical and administrative operations of the firm. In addition, services can be classified into two categories, depending on the orientation of the offer: maintenance and repair (e.g., cleaning, computer support, equipment maintenance) or consulting. The latter relates to a wide range of advisory products, such as payroll management, supply chain management, financial advice, accounting, insurance, credit services, market research, data management, and data processing. The great growth of services and their ever-increasing share in the gross domestic product of most developed (and developing) countries, as well as growing demand for specialized skills and competencies, have moved business planning to the forefront when it comes to outsourcing to third parties.

Such services, in industrial markets, can be purchased autonomously or in conjunction with a particular material product, as part of an overall, integrated, expanded set of benefits that adds value to the product proposal. As in consumer markets, the distinctive features of services require a different approach, at least in terms of human resources and establishing perceptions and assurances of a consistent (superior) level of intangible product quality.

Classification Approaches

Most industrial marketing scholars argue that the difference between B2B marketing and consumer marketing lies more in the nature of the customer (who plays a role) and less in the nature of the products. It is easy to understand and accept this point of view, considering that many products are not directed exclusively at individual consumers or industrial buyers. However, some products are marketed entirely to meet specific, distinct consumer or industrial needs. It is the use of the product that distinguishes consumer from industrial products. In this case too, different classification models rely on various components and classification criteria, such that various categories can be organized in different ways. Some example criteria include the cost of acquiring the goods or the way the product is used. But once more, the different approaches feature the same components at their core; they are simply organized differently, on the basis of which criterion each approach highlights. According to the structural components of the original classification we have analyzed, synthetic parameters (industrial products) can be classified into three major categories.

Incoming Goods

The first class of incoming goods describes industrial products that are integrated into (and end up in) final, completed products. Their acquisition cost is an expense during the production process. This category therefore includes raw materials, manufactured materials, and subparts. As shown in Figure 1.5, raw materials include specific subcategories, that is, natural products and agricultural products; manufactured products also can be subdivided into two categories, processed/treated materials and component and subcomponent parts.

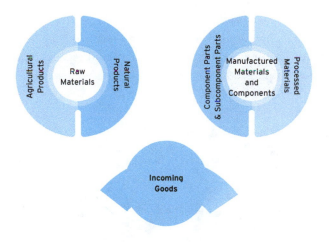

Figure 1.5   Incoming Goods and Their Subcategories

Infrastructure/Foundation Products

The second cluster of industrial products in this classification features infrastructure products, which are goods that are considered capital-oriented. Their cost is depreciated gradually, along with their use, which has long-term implications for the production process. These installations can include foundation products, as well as light industrial products (Figure 1.6). We distinguish two further subcategories with regard to installations, as previously mentioned: industrial construction products and heavy equipment industrial products.

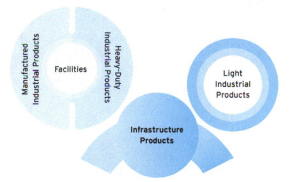

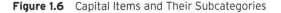

Figure 1.6   Capital Items and Their Subcategories

Facilitating Goods/Services

The third category of facilitating goods/services mainly refers to different types of supplies and services that support business activities. These goods generally are not directly involved in the production process, nor are they part of the finished product. Facilitating goods can be divided into two categories, each with two subcategories (Figure 1.7). Specifically, one axis pertains to materials and handling supplies, maintenance, repair, and operations, which integrate operational supplies on the one hand and maintenance and repair supplies on the other. A second axis refers to industrial services, which comprise maintenance and repair services and consulting services.

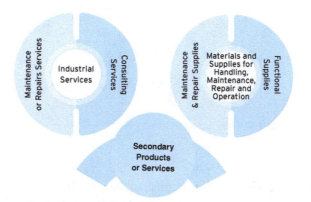

Figure 1.7 Facilitating Goods/Services and Their Subcategories

Classification of Industrial Products by Their Integration Level in the Final Product

As a basic classification variable, Kotler (1991) suggests the degree to which the goods or services are integrated into the final (finished) product. According to this classification, we can identify three levels of integration: full, partial, or none (see Figure 1.8).

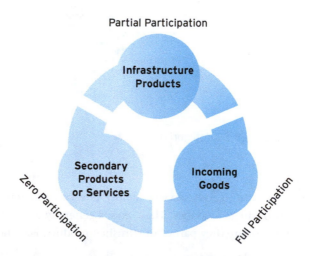

Figure 1.8 Degree of Integration of Industrial Products within the Final Product

Shapiro and Murphy & Enis Approaches to the Classification of Industrial Products

The classification system that Shapiro (1977a) suggests relies on the degree of product standardization as a difference that can define distinct categories. It separates products into fully standardized items, produced according to certain specifications (proprietary products); fully customized products, created to satisfy explicitly expressed needs for a specific and limited purchasing audience (custom-designed products); and an intermediate category that features customized versions of standardized products (custom-built products). This classification system includes services as a separate category, which can offer additional value to any product (through the integration of a benefits/services package, such as counseling or maintenance services), such that it diffuses throughout all three prior categories.

There is another interesting approach which differs from the construction logic and benchmarks; Murphy and Enis (1986) propose a four-pillar classification system that they claim is capable of equally and efficiently describing and separating consumer and industrial products simultaneously. The components of this classification system reflect two criteria, as depicted by Figure 1.9:

- The effort made to ensure that the product comes into the possession of the buyer.
- The perceived risk involved due to a possible error of judgment in the choice of product.

Depending on both criteria, the customer incurs varying costs in the purchasing decision. For example, the effort element includes parameters such as the time and energy spent by the buyer to make a decision, along with the monetary resources required to complete the purchase.

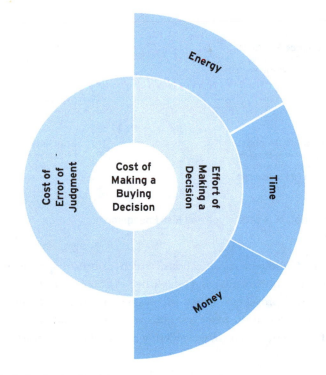

Figure 1.9 The Cost of a Buying Decision

In turn, these two criteria produce four categories that might apply to both consumer and industrial products:

- Convenience products. Require minimum effort by buyers to make their choice, and the risk of making an error in judgment is negligible.
- Preference products. Products demand a higher degree of effort for the choice and also carry a significantly increased risk of error in judgment.
- Shopping products. Both the risk of a wrong choice and the effort needed for the choice and acquisition of the product are higher. This category includes products that represent key equipment and accessories, as well as processed parts that are fully integrated into the final product. A logical consequence and extension of customization is the relative increase in buyers' willingness to become more involved in solving the purchasing problem (exhibited by greater expenditures of money and time resources). It also requires a rational approach, because of the high acquisition cost involved and the greater risk associated with making a bad choice.
- Specialty products. These products feature the highest degree of perceived risk, as well as substantial effort required to acquire them. They include large fixed-capital equipment for a factory and highly specialized services. The high risk and cost convince buyers to invest large amounts of time and energy into making the best choice and reducing the associated risks as much as possible (Figure 1.10).

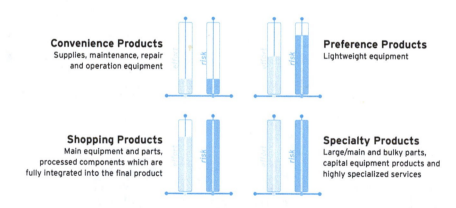

Convenience Products
Supplies, maintenance, repair and operation equipment

Preference Products
Lightweight equipment

Shopping Products
Main equipment and parts, processed components which are fully integrated into the final product

Specialty Products
Large/main and bulky parts, capital equipment products and highly specialized services

Figure 1.10 Combination of Product Type and Risk Engagement

Having highlighted different classifications, which prioritize specific factors that prior authors have considered fundamental and established as criteria, we also note a potential outcome of these various approaches. That is, the evaluation, interpretation, and usage of different approaches likely reveal the perception of the actors who adopt each one, rather than the preferences of competitors. But by considering all the different treatments, it is possible to adopt a more comprehensive approach, based on comparisons rather than distinctions of right or wrong. That is, the differences help broaden understanding, by revealing different perspectives on the same reality.

Overall, existing classification systems emphasize the nature of the products themselves, how they are used in production processes and procedures, and the extent of their incorporation into the final product. Accordingly, they generally focus primarily on the seller's perspective. Murphy and Enis' (1986) model is distinct, in that it takes the buyer's view, using classification criteria related to the concerns and dimensions that buyers regard as significant. Arguably, these two orientations should actually be complementary, such that they "match" supply and demand in an economic theory sense. In combination, the orientations function as valuable sources of multifaceted information for marketing.

What follows is an attempt to outline their implications with regard to their strategic importance and insights for the nature of marketing, to highlight some additional variables that might be influenced by the characteristics of the varying nature of industrial products.

Strategic Implications Related to the Nature of Industrial Products

As noted, the most appropriate way to use different classification systems depends on their particularities, which align with the different criteria that reflect the dimensions of perception and perspective. For a comparative assessment, for example, a classification system based on "more or less appropriate" is preferable over a "better or worse" evaluation. Similarly, to support the choice of a strategic marketing design, decision-makers with more extensive knowledge and information can come closer to formulating and choosing the most appropriate strategy. Starting with the breadth, depth, and quality of information (which may depend on the organizational system itself) offered by classification systems, we highlight some strategic dimensions that emerge from a more comprehensive, component-based approach to the aforementioned models. As we have sought to establish, the degree of customer engagement in each product category varies naturally, so different approaches to the marketing mix are required to provide customization and address each customer case effectively and individually.

Strategies for Infrastructure Products

Regarding industrial products classified as infrastructure, the size of investment required, their long-term nature, their accounting classification as fixed assets, depreciation in terms of time and form, and the way (degree/intensity) they participate in the production process indicate the need for special attention to:

- Building and managing long-term seller–buyer relationships.
- Uninterrupted provision of technological support services.
- Competitive advantages arising from superior technological solutions offered by the product.

- Longer-term indicators (e.g., return on investment versus initial acquisition cost).
- Motivations that may support the purchase decision, involving not only objective parameters (e.g., expected performance of fixed equipment) but also emotional stimulation (e.g., dominance among competitors).
- Personal selling as a dominant and appropriate sales tool.
- Direct distribution channels between the original producer and user to transfer products tailored to the users' needs (custom built), built especially for the users (custom designed), together with less direct, less expensive distribution channels (indirect, featuring more participation by horizontal intermediaries) for mostly or fully standardized products (e.g., proprietary goods).
- The time-consuming, step-by-step process of personal selling, demonstrated through appropriate techniques activated.
- The nature of these markets (costly, long-term), which also means they pose greater risks and require senior executives to take responsibility for decisions.

Strategies for Manufactured Materials and Parts

For manufactured materials and parts, integrated into the product, the challenges for marketing include identifying the specific needs of the diverse range of customers and the product supply parameters required to deliver what a marketing philosophy advocates: superior, effective satisfaction of the buyer's product needs, so that the transaction becomes profitable for all participating parties in the long run. Specifically, if these products are more customized or have a personalized nature, it is critical to:

- Emphasize personal selling.
- Invest in developing relationships.
- Highlight, from the seller's point of view, strong supply chain management skills.
- Adopt a personal sales approach, through which sales staff "eavesdrop" on new markets while also distinguishing the unique needs of different customers.

For processed materials and product parts, usually purchased in bulk, with a high degree of standardization, the important features include:

- Competitive prices.
- Timing and reliability of delivery.
- Accompanying support services.
- Strategic, automated, technological communication and ordering systems. It is possible to complete such processes as routine decisions, with minimal contributions in terms of time or effort, due to the capabilities of modern computing systems and their corresponding software.

- Price as a means to differentiate the product, with particular attention to purchasing incentives.
- The equivalent importance of quality, delivery time, and extra services in terms of the ability to detect and serve different, unique buyers' needs.

Strategies for Materials/Supplies

For the product category classified as materials/supplies, the fully standardized items, with fixed specifications, have a low per unit cost and are not incorporated into the final product. Overall, price competitiveness, consistent and reliable delivery, product signaling, good variety, and appropriate promotional actions that support seller flexibility are critical parameters. In addition, for this type of strategy development, managers should take care to address:

- The role of price. Because materials/supplies are undifferentiated, competition among providers can be fierce. Price can be an effective differentiating factor.
- Investments in the products' non-differentiated character that incorporate additional, desirable benefits and reflect the product core by complementing and reinforcing the benefits of better, more complete, more comprehensive, and timely needs coverage, such as consistent and orderly product delivery or reliability in delivery schedules.
- Approaches other than personal selling, which likely is inappropriate. Cataloging, advertising, and promotions through intermediaries are more relevant approaches.

Vignette

Implementing a Market Orientation Among New Zealand Ranchers

Ranchers in New Zealand who raise sheep and venison have access to a couple of dedicated agricultural cooperatives to represent their interests and provide them with various forms of assistance: Merino NZ (MNZ) and the New Zealand Game Industry Board (NZGIB). These associations also can be sites of contention and debate though, as was the case when forces in broader markets suggested the need for these producers to adopt a market-oriented, rather than purely sales-oriented, approach to selling their wool and venison. A market orientation can produce a wide range of positive performance outcomes, but it is far from simple to achieve, often requiring top-down change processes.

In particular, transitioning into a market orientation generally involves three stages of change, each with its own challenges and benefits. For wool and venison producers, facing declining returns on sales of their products and threats to their market share, MNZ and NZGIB represented contexts in which they could debate the need for change, address the challenges, and ultimately attain the rewards of embracing a market orientation.

(Continued)

Debating the Need for Change and Unfreezing Conventional Wisdom

Both NZGIB and MNZ hosted ranchers who expressed and held firm to some long-standing assumptions about their markets. Despite vast shifts in these industries, they maintained that venison and wool products represented commodity products—a status they regarded as intrinsic and unchanged. Thus, any price trends (even extended periods of diminished prices and returns) were just part of the game: unavoidable, normative, and "natural," even if frustrating. In line with these beliefs, many of these stakeholders maintained a traditional, perhaps outdated view that they had to accept commodity cycles passively, rather than trying to change the rules of the game or seek to obtain additional value through marketing-related tactics such as branding, developing trusting instead of antagonistic relationships with other members of the supply chain, and engaging in future-focused strategic planning.

When the associations raised challenges to these views, they cited the need for change due to the shifting character of markets, both in general and specific to wool and venison products. They proposed widespread changes that would entail adopting customized marketing practices and novel positioning efforts. In their attempt to convince ranchers of the need for such change, these stakeholders built coalitions to garner political and grassroots support, actively identified pockets of resistance, and communicated critical information to various other stakeholders, especially those resisting the change. The emphasis in these communication efforts was on creating a clear, imaginable view of a possible future, marked by a market orientation, in which ranchers developed new customer and network relationships, offered customization, engaged in branding, and thus added value.

Addressing Challenges through Movement

Having raised challenges to existing assumptions, the associations and their senior leadership then had to offer some alternatives. The resulting change programs, designed to encourage members to move toward a market orientation, required strategies that reflected and matched the resources available in the industry, among members. Both associations sought to establish a market-oriented vision and approach that applied to all, or nearly all, of their members.

To achieve this broad acceptance, the two associations realized the importance of influential members as "first adopters" of the market-oriented change, as well as detailed market intelligence. Thus, they conducted extensive research to identify market opportunities, including interviewing key business-to-business (B2B) buyers, before proposing or launching any cohesive strategy. By presenting the results of this market research to association members—using new communication tools, such as a web page, newsletter, industry conference, and regional workshops—NZGIB and MNZ obtained support for the change program in advance, creating a momentum and movement toward change.

For example, the NZGIB gathered information about how US restaurateurs perceived venison, signaling the potential for developing a strategy that would enable ranchers to target their products to high-end US restaurants. Beyond this specific insight, NZGIB's research suggested the need for a dual marketing program that could target consumers and B2B buyers separately.

As a relevant, unique strategy thus started to take shape, the NZGIB showed its members how investing marketing resources into trade programs and collaborating with high-profile chefs and famous athletes could create widespread consumer awareness and interest.

But to achieve this repositioning among consumers and B2B buyers, the industries also needed to reconsider their existing norms and value propositions. A focus on quality became a new tactic, such that the NZGIB developed the "From Pasture to Plate" program to minimize the stress of the slaughter process on deer, so that buyers could be assured that stress hormones were not interfering with the quality and taste of the meat they purchased. Similarly, MNZ's "Fleece to Fashion" program assigned responsibility to ranchers to affirm that they took a responsible approach to raising and shearing their sheep. In line with these production-related guarantees, as methods for building brand value, the associations embraced sustainability principles as likely sources of additional value. However, the approaches that each group took to establish this positioning differed, in some instructive ways.

For MNZ, the goal was to get its members and channel buyers to collaborate in identifying mutual challenges and possible solutions. It recommended complete transparency throughout the supply chain, to create shared understanding that all parties in that supply chain would benefit from a consistent supply and consistent prices, which in turn could support the proposed brand program. In parallel, MNZ sought to expand its membership, to include a wider range of potentially interested stakeholders and provide full openness to them as well. For NZGIB though, representing a larger industry that spanned multiple product lines (deer can be processed for meat (venison), velvet (antler powder used in traditional Asian remedies), leather, and other body parts (hooves, tails, and sexual organs also used in Asian remedies); the Cervena program (a farmers' program that brands quality New Zealand farm-raised venison) only covered the highest quality meat, while markets were still required for lower quality cuts), the primary goal continued to be increasing prices at auction. This narrow focus seemingly ignored the potential that revised pricing mechanisms offered, with regard to facilitating branding efforts.

Accordingly, MNZ achieved greater success, measured in several ways: members expressed revised beliefs about supply chains and relationships, and more ranchers entered into fixed contracts with large B2B buyers, which supported greatly enhanced stability and predictability in the market. Due to the continued reliance on auctions, members of the NZGIB instead suffered ongoing inconsistencies in prices and supply levels, which undermined the ranchers' brand promises and relationships with key buyers.

The approach embraced by MNZ also appeared effective at convincing other supply chain members, such as garment manufacturers and retailers. In the past, retailers wielded substantial power, such that they issued demands and pulled products through the supply chain, and they were loath to give up such power. By emphasizing quality, value, and sustainability in transparent ways, though, MNZ attempted to convince these powerful partners to start demanding New Zealand Merino wool specifically and to these partners' benefit. By also working with the garment manufacturers to ensure consistent supply of the high-quality raw materials, all the parties realized advantages from their collaborative strategic planning.

(Continued)

Despite these differences in tactics, the communications shared by both associations revealed some notable similarities, in terms of a shift in tone. Rather than argumentative, they became educational; rather than just top-down, they grew more collaborative, to encourage widespread support for the programs through the active involvement of various stakeholders. Rather than focusing just on the challenges, they started to cite small successes, including positive feedback from buyers. Finally, rather than only trying to convince members that the new strategy would work, they could point to actual positive outcomes to legitimize the project and secure further resources (e.g., compulsory levies from members, who frequently sought to reduce any such fees). With these convincing arguments and evidence of legitimacy, they could implement the strategies comprehensively and ensure they remained in place, to secure ongoing strategic advantages.

Confirming Continued Benefits by Refreezing

To solidify and institutionalize the lessons and strategies adopted in the previous phase, NZGIB and MNZ each adopted several methods, systems, and goals:

- Shared feedback on market-oriented efforts.
- Identified and communicated successes.
- Remained on message.
- Presented artifacts, stories, and myths to celebrate market-oriented values.
- Offered rewards for market-oriented behaviors.

Such efforts were both internal and external to the supply chains. For example, to reinforce market-oriented values, the associations' public relations efforts sought to raise ranchers' profiles among various stakeholders, whether by celebrating their recent achievements, providing educational information about new programs they had adopted, or seeking to persuade others to commit to programs by supporting those ranchers.

Some differences arose between the cases though, reflecting the distinct approaches to customization versus standardization. Recall that MNZ embraced customization for buyers, and accordingly, it established feedback systems that enabled ranchers to adapt their offerings to individual customers' needs. In contrast, the venison ranchers remained subject to a standard, one-price schedule that prevented dynamic pricing.

These distinctions also were evident in the associations' quality improvement efforts, in which MNZ exhibited a more extensive approach. That is, NZGIB members continued to use an existing, generic feedback system that made it difficult to react promptly to any demand-driven shifts. But by developing a new type of feedback system, MNZ helped ranchers identify unique demands and make ongoing improvements to their products. This new system included changes to the criteria for grading wool; previously, there had been no means for buyers to identify the regional source of wool or receive any scientific proof of its quality. Furthermore, because the old system did not include any feedback loop, farmers also did not know what those buyers really wanted from them, nor were there sufficient educational resources to show them how improved farming practices could enhance the quality of the wool they produced. When MNZ invested in a central grading facility, it meant that ranchers could shear, package, and grade each fleece individually, so buyers knew precisely what they were receiving in each bag of fleece. Every product was linked to an individual farm and animal, so ranchers could bale wool of similar quality and provenance and set prices for each bale, then justify those prices with clear evidence of its quality.

On the basis of these efforts, and the benefits they provided, MNZ actively communicated about the causal link between market-based activities and market-based success. In the face of such evidence, ranchers more broadly embraced a learning orientation, driving the quality of the market-oriented outcomes even higher. The virtuous cycle soon produced new innovations, developed in collaboration with buyers, such as Zealander, Opossum Wool, and Denim Wool product lines. A novel auction system, designed to create interest in wool rather than just to set prices, even featured a "finest wool" competition.

Perhaps because the NZGIB never developed systems that could specify, identify, and demonstrate the benefits of its change program, its communications instead exhibited a troubling shift, away from the educational tone it had adopted during the second stage and toward more critical communications. But the inability to alter or revise the traditional price-based auctions limited the market-oriented benefits available to deer ranchers, because these methods continually undermined their relationships with other supply chain members—especially key buyers.

Insights for Managerial Practice

If managers seek to apply the lessons that emerge from these two cases, they might start by applying a three-stage model of change, as a sort of roadmap for implementing their own market-oriented change processes. Clearly, they should adapt it to their own situation; if a firm already has identified and accepted some market-oriented values but is struggling to implement them in practice, it arguably can skip to the second and third stages.

But, regardless of the unique situation, these cases show that managers must identify and leverage the inputs of a very wide range of stakeholders, both within and beyond their firm boundaries. At the start, marketing managers must convince employees (including non-marketing staff and top leadership) of the value of the change effort, to build coalitions and ensure support over time.

Finally, the examples of MNZ and NZGIB show marketing managers that developing a market orientation means addressing the firm's culture, learning, systems, and structures, all together and consistently. Therefore, they should take the initiative to develop clear and helpful educational materials, design reward systems that truly incentivize market-oriented behaviors and innovation, encourage unusual and creative collaborations, and build clear feedback loops that demonstrate the links between actions and outcomes.

Source

Beverland, M.B., and Lindgreen, A. (2007), "Implementing market orientation in industrial firms: A multiple case study," *Industrial Marketing Management*, 36(4), 430-442.

Industrial Buyers

Industrial markets are product/service markets not intended for individual consumption, either used as capital goods or incorporated into the production of other products, usually by large governmental or non-governmental enterprises or institutional public or private buyers. Because of the way such industrial customers use these products, this element represents the most distinctive variable for differentiating industrial marketing from consumer marketing. In addition, industrial customers can be divided into three major categories (Figure 1.11).

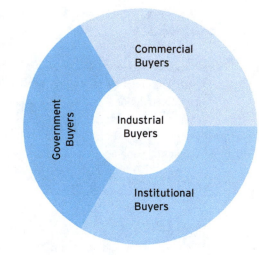

Figure 1.11 Classification of Industrial Customers/Buyers

Each category in turn has distinctly identifiable characteristics. By undertaking a close characterization of these particularities, we provide a more detailed view of dimensions critical to marketing too.

Commercial Buyers

These buyers include manufacturing enterprises and construction companies, transport firms, service providers, specialized professional groups or manufacturers, and reseller trading firms, including both wholesalers and retailers. They are for-profit companies. The substantial diversity of buyers participating in this category—a motley crew, to some extent—thus is clear. A further categorization also could take place on the basis of their different market goals and motives (Figure 1.12) of users, dealers, and original equipment manufacturers.

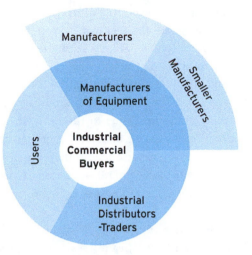

Figure 1.12 Industrial Commercial Buyers and Subcategories

Users

Assuming their intention to buy, users in this category are commercial firms. They buy goods and services that they either consume or incorporate into finished products, such that the purchases eventually lose their identity and are not discernibly detectable in a final product. These buyers focus on products/services that help them make products or provide services that subsequently will be directed to industrial or consumer markets.

The purchased product, such as motor fuel, gets integrated by the user, such as an urban transportation service provider, in the final product of intercity transportation services available to customers, who might be private consumers (e.g., a student traveling from Athens to London) or industrial customers (e.g., the bulk shipping of packages and mail delivery by the postal service). Although used to provide the service, the product is not considered distinctly traceable. In another example, a weaving machine, purchased by a shirt manufacturer, gets incorporated (through its functional use, not consumption of its composition) into the final product of a shirt, sold to consumers for their personal use or to a hotel chain to provide employees with uniforms.

Industrial Traders and Distributors

These buyers are commercial firms (intermediaries), whose business activity entails purchasing industrial goods and reselling them. They are essentially wholesalers/distributors of industrial products, such that they facilitate the transfer of industrial goods from the seller to the buyer/consumer, functioning like an intermediate link. In addition, distributors represent businesses with a commercial nature; they can take ownership of the goods they trade and transport, but they also may function mainly as agents. In other words, even if they are in possession of the product, they may not have ownership of what they distribute.

Although their efforts have minimal impacts on the formulation of the product, distributors and intermediaries essentially build around this utility. Even if not obvious most of the time (e.g., technical support services for a corporate computing center are useful but rarely acknowledged explicitly), their work adds value to the product. Two main forms of their offerings produce benefits that might not be immediately perceivable but still are essential and crucial. That is, intermediaries (1) increase the profitability of transactions by reducing the actions required for them to take place, and (2) facilitate transactions by providing more rational economic management in terms of the quantity and varietal differences between sellers and buyers.

With regard to the first contribution, intermediaries can condense the overall production process (and corresponding upstream/downstream webs of socio-economic relationships). In a practical sense, to complete any transaction, each seller would have to interact with each buyer. By adding intermediaries into the equation, the number of contacts needed to complete a transaction decreases radically.

For the second feature, fundamental principles of micro- and macro-economics emphasize the inherent incompatibility between sellers and buyers, universally applicable to consumer and industrial markets. On the one hand, most sellers and firms seek to produce and sell large quantities of the products they offer, a position reinforced by a wide range of dimensions. For example, greater production/sales volume implies more favorable trading terms with suppliers, lower fixed costs, faster learning curves, and, ultimately, economies of scale that support a lower cost per unit of manufactured product. Compelling evidence of these claims is available in the significantly higher prices of custom-designed products that entail monopsony purchases, relative to somewhat standardized products that have undergone processing or refinement to accommodate the needs of a limited group of buyers (custom built), relative to fully standardized products (Shapiro, 1977a). On the other hand, industrial buyers want to purchase a wider range of products to meet their production process needs, completely and in an integrated way, rather than committing their liquidity and financial resources to purchasing large quantities of one type of product that only partially covers their needs.

This incompatibility (quantity–variety) acts as a barrier to profit maximization and profitability by these trading partners; it can be overcome by mediators, through their intermediation and service provision. They act as likely quantity inverters of variety, serving both buyers and sellers. We present the role, contributions, and marketing types of distributors in more detail in the next chapter, but here, we identify several features that provide added value to products and that therefore should be perceived by distributors as forms of competitive advantage:

- Quick, up-to-date, immediate knowledge of customers' needs and suppliers' capabilities and characteristics.
- Reliable, valid, and timely extraction, organization, and use of customer and supplier information, to achieve better segmentation and targeting, as well as more rapid service.
- Flexibility to change and adopt new technologies.
- Resource-saving capabilities that translate into savings and lower transaction costs among stakeholders (intermediaries produce benefits through the effective application and use of specialized knowledge, know-how, modern technological infrastructure, specialized equipment, and operational processes).
- Faster, better, cheaper: although each dimension of this triptych may take a different weight, depending on the type of industrial product or buyer, all three factors together (even with trade-offs across them) constitute axes of a competitive edge.

Original Equipment Manufacturers

These industrial manufacturing enterprises buy component parts and equipment to incorporate into their own end products, sold under their own name. We make a distinction based on the buyers of their products: other industrial buyers or end consumers. The consumer market mainly consists of post-purchase sales of component parts or equipment that can replace, repair, or upgrade a previously sold product (using integrated accessories/equipment).

For example, an industrial mobile phone manufacturer might purchase device component parts like screens from other industrial companies, then incorporate them into its own finished, branded product. These screens, as autonomous products, can also be sold simultaneously in after-markets, such as to private consumers. In this B2B scenario, depending on the purchase context (product, user, use), the roles of the large industrial phone manufacturer, the smaller industrial screen manufacturer, and the industrial buyer and industrial seller can be clearly assigned. But the partners also might function as industrial manufacturers (and sellers) in after-market business-to-consumer transactions.

Even claims to be "larger" or "smaller" might be questionable. A mobile phone also might represent a component-based industrial construction that gets incorporated into another product, so the roles of the industrial buyer and seller change in this B2B market. The separation of larger and smaller industrial manufacturers also raises the point that large manufacturers are fewer in number but larger in size, and they powerfully shape market conditions and variables. An important observation, with strategic implications, is the high degree of concentration that distinguishes these businesses, both geographically and by size. Smaller industrial manufacturers need to be more flexible and capable of adapting their products to the particular conditions and needs of the market segments in which they operate.

Finally, the varying roles in the industrial commercial buyers category are not impermeable; their barriers often are indistinguishable or variable, depending on the specific object, the orientation of their production activity, and the intended purpose of each product for each customer. It would be more consistent, purposeful, and strategically probable for us to describe the category not with absolutes that separate the participants but rather by focusing on common ground across their activities, reflecting the context of each buying situation. Their roles are not mutually exclusive.

Institutional Buyers

These buyers are public or private foundations such as schools, educational institutes, libraries, universities, research institutions, hospitals, or clinics, with for-profit or non-profit natures. According to their categorization (Figure 1.13), these buyers might be financed or controlled by government agencies, in which case their purchasing behavior is determined or limited by the political environment and local legislative framework. But privately held institutional organizations tend to be managed like firms, and their purchasing needs sometimes exceed those of the publicly controlled or non-profit institutions.

Figure 1.13 Institutional Buyers

Whether public or private, for-profit or non-profit in nature, institutional industrial buyers tend to be staffed by highly educated, specialized, and qualified personnel, and they offer prestige. Their structures generally support functioning by organized segments of markets within the institution. A common approach integrates participants (institutionally) into buying processes, seeking to foster understanding and acceptance of the market advantages. To make their way through the maze of bureaucratic procedures and mechanisms imposed by government agencies, they usually adopt a procedural protocol that governs transaction and procurement processes. These processes also can be specific and diverse among organizations. Thus, what is particularly important is to understand the complexity that emanates from the wide range of diverse needs of those involved in the purchasing process.

Governmental Buyers

This group of buyers comprises local government organizations, government services, public enterprises and organizations, the defense industry, and so forth. They need nearly all categories of products and services. As in the case of institutional customers, though to an even greater extent, political parameters and regulatory legal frameworks define the decision-making environment and govern purchasing processes.

The supply of goods/services mainly occurs through two channels: open tenders or negotiated contracts. The use of one or another form is dictated largely by the product features. The former method is effective for products with a high degree of standardization, such that the main distinction among them (and thus the dominant selection criteria) is the price level. Although price also is a relevant variable for negotiated contracts, it does not constitute a notional difference or selection criterion. The products under negotiation are also more complex: they must meet specific performance and safety requirements and possess a set of desirable characteristics. Depending on the buyer, they may be more or less customized.

Overall, the emphasis should be on personal selling and sales promotion, the use of more direct distribution networks, the provision of reliable after-sales support services, the development of strong long-term interpersonal relationships, and competition in terms of the acquisition price, though not a one-dimensional view of full equivalence for the initial acquisition cost.

Vignette

The Danish Customer Centricity Index Project

A pilot research effort, undertaken by the Customer Agency, Copenhagen Business School, and Confederation of Danish Industry, aims to analyze how five Danish business-to-business (B2B) firms achieve customer centricity through their in-house efforts, then compare those findings with evidence related to how customers actually experience consumption from those firms. With this unique approach, the researchers hope to gain deep insights into customer centricity and especially how firms themselves think customers perceive their customer centricity initiatives. With such evidence, the results should offer B2B firms clearer recommendations for achieving the commercial potential of adopting a customer-centric approach.

Customer centricity once was considered just "nice to have." But positive, well-differentiated customer experiences now represent a vital competitive advantage, in a wide range of industries. Firms that exhibit customer centricity can realize increased customer retention, more sales to customers, increased customer intake, and reduced costs—that is, various commercial rewards that are high on most firms' strategic wish lists but are also notably difficult to realize.

(Continued)

Thus far, the collaborative research project has produced six notable insights:

1   Firms' abilities to differentiate themselves by offering better customer experiences are significantly correlated with those firms' growth, relative to their main competitors.
2   To attain 3 percent higher growth than competitors, firms need to achieve a 10 percent improvement in four forms of customer centricity execution:
    i   Vision and goals.
    ii   Management and culture.
    iii Processes, insights, and services.
    iv   Customer-driven innovation.
3   The feeling that customers take away, after being in contact with the firm, is the most important element of the overall customer experience.
4   Only one-third of customers agree that firms make it clear what kind of experiences they are trying to give customers.
5   Fewer than half of customers sense that firms focus on customer experiences at touchpoints that these customers consider important.
6   Only 55 percent of customers believe that firm employees they encounter "are passionate about delivering good customer experiences."

These external perceptions are interesting on their own, but the evidence gathered from employees adds even more salient insights. Employees who address customer needs and resolve their problems are more satisfied, and stay with the firm longer, which helps the firm avoid the struggle of constantly having to find qualified employees.

Beyond this relatively consistent finding, though, three problematic contrasts arise in the views expressed by managers and employees of the firms, which might hinder firms' ability to deliver the experiences customers really want:

1   With regard to whether exhibiting customer centricity informs promotions and rewards, 60 percent of managers agree or partially agree that employees should focus on customers to achieve promotion or rewards, but only 20 percent of employees in the customer-facing roles indicate that they have encountered such incentives.
2   Perceptions about whether existing operational systems can deliver good customer experiences also vary, such that almost 90 percent of top managers believe their customer-facing systems enable employees to deliver good customer experiences efficiently, but this perception emerges from only about 60 percent of the employees.
3   Showing some agreement, 70 percent of both employees and managers believe they "go a long way to give customers good experiences." However, only 47 percent of customers agree with this claim.

The project results affirm that customer centricity pays off: more customer centricity equals more profits. As additional key lessons for managers, the research shows that they must model the behaviors they want from employees, by prioritizing customers all the time, not just when deals are being signed. Ultimately, it is the frontline employees who ensure and enhance good customer experiences and relationships.

Source

Bjerre, M., and Jensen, P.A. (2017), *The Danish Customer-Centricity Index*, Copenhagen: Confederation of Danish Industry.

2

DIFFERENTIATION CHARACTERISTICS OF INDUSTRIAL MARKETS

Learning Objectives

- Establish a framework of the characteristics that differentiate industrial markets from consumer markets.
- Define the strategic implications of the distinctive characteristics of industrial markets.
- Understand the impact of specific characteristics on the formulation of a marketing approach.

Case Study

When Purchasing and Marketing Interact: Processes and Integration Tactics

For a firm to create value, it needs the contributions of both its purchasing and marketing functions, but beyond just contributing their expertise, these two functions need to integrate their efforts to ensure clear alignment, both within the organization and externally,

(Continued)

with the broader business environment. The latter, external interactions have received far more attention in research to date, which notes how organizations deal with their customers or their suppliers. By using strategic insights gathered about these external relationships, it also may be possible to establish recommendations for achieving efficacious, productive, internal relationships between purchasing and marketing functions that reflect strong integration efforts.

One such recommendation, by Toon et al. (2016), produces the framework in Table 2.1 that describes both contextual factors that influence the integration of purchasing and marketing and the managerial approaches required to achieve these outcomes. That is, they specify three types of influential dynamics: structural dynamics that refer to the nature and type of exchange links and reveal the mechanics governing interactions; human dynamics and trust or norm-based behaviors that create patterns in exchange processes; and situational dynamics, or the series of factors that determine how interactions between functions take place. With regard to managerial approaches, Toon et al. also identify three types:

- *Transactional* managerial approaches prioritize already known cost or quality criteria, such that they mainly apply in less complex settings and do not demand substantial innovation.
- *Integrative* managerial approaches instead attempt to build interfunctional teams to encourage regular communications and thereby align each function's unique goals with the strategic pursuits of the organization as a whole, while also accommodating the priorities of each exchange partner.
- *Co-management* is neither transactional nor relational, in that it leverages managerial systems to assign tasks and confirm accountability, without monitoring but also without relying on relational capital. Rather, interactions are planned, and roles and responsibilities are clearly delineated. It thus offers an efficient bridge between purchasing and marketing functions that can support strategic goal harmonization.

To identify the best internal configuration for their organization and organizational context, managers might turn to the descriptive classifications in the table and adopt the integration approaches that best match their situation. In particular, moving beyond the benefits of integration for value creation, managers should acknowledge the potential for integration types across value chains to determine organizational performance: with a strong internal alignment with strategic goals, the firm can deliver customer value more effectively.

Table 2.1 Process-Interface Framework for Marketing and Purchasing Integration

Forms of Dynamics	Theoretical Manifestation	Managerial Approach to Purchasing–Marketing Co-Ordination		
		Transactional	**Integrative**	**Co-Management**
Structural Dynamics	Exchanges based on "formalization, joint planning, and team work" (Homburg et al., 2008).	Preexisting work and market systems (e.g., competition), exert positive effects on clusters in the value chain, with particular applications to integration along the value chain and external to the organization (Teller et al., 2015).	Internal functions are co-located and a set of exchange processes are interwoven.	Co-management systems are internal and use organization-wide knowledge-sharing architectures. Co-management measures may be more successful if extended to more upstream and downstream zones (Wagner & Eggert, 2015).
Human Dynamics	Trust in exchanges emerges through "information sharing" and communication that reflects cultural norms (Blois & Ivens, 2006).	Knowledge exchanges are typically predetermined by contracts. Communication is less frequent than in integration or co-management approaches, and it is mostly formal.	Information is shared in an ongoing process, into which both purchasing and marketing feed. This iterative value creation process features continued knowledge exchanges and adjustments (Toon et al., 2012)	Co-management facilitates the structured inclusion of upstream and downstream external value chain agents to bring about exchange-based adaptation in the process (Viio & Grönroos, 2015)

(Continued)

Table 2.1 (Continued)

Forms of Dynamics	Theoretical Manifestation	Managerial Approach to Purchasing–Marketing Co-Ordination		
		Transactional	Integrative	Co-Management
Situational Dynamics	Goal orientation, physical location, institutional power arrangements, and cross-functional knowledge (Flynn et al., 2010; Griffin & Hauser, 1996; Wind, 2005).	Shared goal orientation assists in value delivery to customers. For example, a dual orientation on customer and supply bases provides strategic assets from which the organization can attain advantages (Ziggers & Henseler, 2015).	The co-location of internal functions and adoption of singular goals supports organization-wide strategic goals. Power is not exercised internally, and cross-functional knowledge develops through the close interaction.	Physical proximity and integration incentives can facilitate co-management, leading to effective information sharing and aligned decisions (Gonzales-Zapatero, 2015).

Source: Toon et al. (2016, p. 77)

Source

Toon, M., Morgan, R., Lindgreen, A., Vanhamme, J., and Hingley, M.K. (2016), "Processes and integration in the interaction of purchasing and marketing: considering synergy and symbiosis," *Industrial Marketing Management*, 52(February), 74-81.

SPECIFIC CHARACTERISTICS FOR DIFFERENTIATING INDUSTRIAL MARKETS

Various efforts to outline key dimensions or develop a framework have created foundations for defining the differences between industrial and consumer markets. This chapter presents relevant characteristics and differences, in an attempt to explain them as comprehensively as possible.

Derived Demand

The term *derived demand* refers to a situation in which industrial market demand is generated, followed, captured, or produced as a result of consumer demand. The building blocks (products and services) that comprise products we characterize as industrial products then become (more or less directly) part of a finished product, aimed at meeting consumer needs. Thus, consumer demand for products determines industrial demand. The very term "derived" indicates the great dependence of one factor (industrial demand) on the other (consumer demand).

However, this description is accurate only to the extent that industrial customers express demands for resources they need to carry out and complete the production of products and services geared to meet the needs of end consumers. To be more conceptually precise, it might be more appropriate to adopt the term "demand chain," because derived demand can be analyzed on the basis of its immediacy, measured by the number of separate chain reactions that must take place before demand from end consumers creates demand effects in industrial markets. Consumers' demand for goods and services that meet their expectations can kick off a mechanism that gets mobilized (and motivated) through to a final link. This mobilization is like a demand flow, continuously and sequentially transferred, not a one-way reflective act that takes place between just the consumer and the business.

We also can distinguish direct versus indirect derived demand, according to the magnitude of the sequence and repetition of the phenomena involved in the creation of demand, until the point at which the consumer need is finally satisfied. Thus for example, consumer demand for cars is not a direct, demand-derived feeder of mining companies that extract steel, unless we simply choose to accept this general convention, for the sake of easier comprehension. But a more detailed, accurate approach would acknowledge that consumer demand for cars feeds a chain of dependent, demand-driven sequences through multiple industrial companies in the production chain, before reaching the mining company. This indirectness of the (derived) supply chain—at least in industrial market fields—is due to the existence of different roles (industrial buyers) and areas of activity in the production process, which represent transmitters of the derived demand. That is, defining some industrial firms as transmitters (of demand) reflects that, relative to end consumers, they make distinct contributions to the production process by performing their own work, for which they have needs that drive demand back, toward their own suppliers.

Returning to the car industry, the mining company likely cannot produce (within its own discrete production framework) engines to meet derived demand, so it transfers demand for engines to other industrial manufacturing companies (which have their own corresponding objects in the discrete production process). Thus, in parallel with its production activity, the company provides a coherent transfer and translation link in the demand chain for component parts, representing the backward trend that started with consumer demand. That is, the mining company is both a receiver/object of derived demand and its carrier.

With this rationale, we can describe derived demand as a well-orchestrated sequence that features a set of immediate (derived) demand challenges between two dependent parties (in terms of needs coverage). The flow of derived demand dynamically aggregates smaller subsets of induced direct (derived) demand between production activity objects. The nearest or most immediately perceived, in terms of covering consumer demand, are downstream activities. Actions perceived as more indirect – whether because they occur in an initial phase of the production process, exhibit a low degree of conversion in the product, or experience time restrictions in their production or transportation needs – are instead upstream activities.

It would be easy to overlook the complex nature of derived demand though. The threshold at which consumer demand converts into derived demand does not necessarily occur on some set barrier between consumers and industrial enterprises. A consumer who buys a car does not see the car itself as addressing a need but rather regards it as a means to meet a need (e.g., transportation). Thus, even consumer demand for the car itself, as a product, is generated.

To avoid losing sight of the overall picture, Figure 2.1 illustrates the relationship between consumer demand and industrial generated demand.

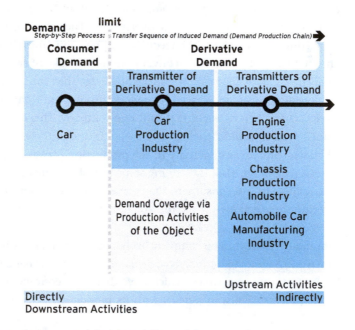

Figure 2.1 Integrated Approach to Interrelations of Components and Building Blocks that Describe the Flow of Demand

Generated demand (for the industry as a whole) is also an outcome of expectations developed in the industrial sector, which strives to capture, predict, and prepare the industrial machine to meet consumer demand. These expectations could be detailed in similar mechanisms with psychological and proactive elements. As powerful economic leverage mechanisms, those expectations need to be taken seriously.

The close interdependence and web of interrelations within generated demand chains can make it seem like a coalition of industrial buyers, who create a market to channel their products, mobilize the constituent variables of demand, or stimulate more consumer demand. Creating and developing a new consumer market is the most common example of industry involvement in creating private demand, such as for introductions of novel products characterized by substantial innovation, technology, originality, and modernity.

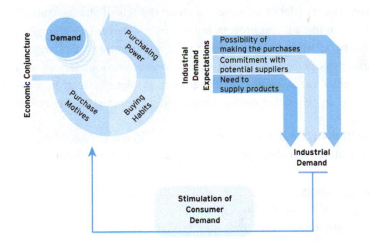

Figure 2.2 Structural Factors, Interpretive Framework, and the Feedback Process of the Demand Circuit

Accelerator Effect

By describing derived demand as a flow, involving a series of (derived) supply chain challenges, we can make the magnitude of the correlation and degree of influence and interdependence among different actors clearer. Intuitively, it is easy to understand and accept that an increase in the quantity of passenger cars demanded by private consumers likely translates into increases in (generated) demand in the steel mining industry. However, other variables complicate this mechanism. In particular, the percentage change in the consumer demand and downstream activities differs from the rate of change in derived demand in upstream industries, due to two factors that combine to create an accelerator effect: time and the expectations of each participating actor that functions as the transmitter.

In the previous section, we briefly noted the concept of expectations, and in Figure 2.2, expectations offer an interpretive filter. The receiving end of derived demand, such as the industrial producer, expresses expectations. Along the upstream path forged by the demand factor, information transmitted across industrial structures does not contain the same percentage of variation that is directly received. It reflects the percentage change in demand, interpreted according to the transmitter's expectations, experience, and industry-recruiting capabilities. It pushes this interpretation to other industrial suppliers/manufacturers, so that they can meet the needs of their own production process.

Let's assume that (consumer) demand for cars varies by X percent. Rationally, information about this generated demand gets transferred to Y automobile manufacturer. For Y to meet needs in terms of cars, but noting the changing rate of demand received as generated (consumer) demand, Y should function as a transmitter and move this information to more upstream actors. The transfer of information about the rate of change embodied in generated demand might seem like a linear process, but if Y faces a percentage change in demand in the range of X percent, to meet generated demand, it does not need to change its orders equivalently or by exactly X percent. Rather, it should consider various factors, such as production capacity. If Y needs Z car assembly robots per shift, it might forecast how durably stable the percentage change in generating demand will be and then take alternative actions:

- Increase shift hours (from 8 to 10 or 12 hours).
- Increase the number of shifts per 24 hours (e.g., two or three 8-hour shifts instead of one or two).
- Hire assembly robots.
- Outsource part of the production.
- Upgrade existing robots to increase their productivity.

Even if there had been no intervention on the rate of change in demand by an interpretive filter, the generating demand does not necessarily spread across the whole spectrum of industrial manufacturers and suppliers to reach the most upstream activities.

Consider another, refined example in the automobile industry. Last year, consumer demand was in the range of 1,000 units (cars). The main industrial activity of Y automobile manufacturer requires one assemblage robot for every 50 cars produced. Thus, in the last year, Y used 20 robots to meet demand. Considering last year's demand, Y decides to buy two new robots this year, to replace those scheduled to be retired (i.e., they no longer contribute to the production process due to depreciation or age). Despite no change in the demand for cars (zero percent change), Y's (derived) demand in the robot manufacturing industry would be on the order of two units.

Now suppose that the demand for cars increases by 20 percent. In that case, Y needs to produce 1,200 cars to cover the additional demand, such that it would need an additional four robots (4 robots × 50 cars = 200 cars = coverage of additional demand). Adding them to the two robots to replace out-of-date versions, the percentage change in demand increases to six, and the percentage change in generated demand for robots is around 67 percent.

With all other factors remaining stable, due to the "passage" by the first transmitter, the percentage change has gone from 20 to 67 percent. Multiplier effects (e.g., percentage increase or percentage decrease in consumer demand) occur throughout the flow production of generated demand, as a result of the accelerator effect. In turn, expectations and forecasts strongly determine administrative decision-making mechanisms.

Predictions that growth (or recession) will exhibit constant rates of change, their length, or their continuity over time in the same direction, obtained through a specific expectation and forecasting perspective, create important expectation-forming parameters. They also inform strategic choices among the alternatives for capacity management. These options can cause further distortions in the generated demand, because they influence, irrespective of size, the outcome of the accelerator.

Finally, the time needed for generated demand to reach industrial buyers increases as it flows to more upstream production activities. This loss of time implies that generated demand has passed through more transmitters, been processed more times through expectations/forecasts and strategic and administrative decisions, and ultimately may be very distant from the size, timing, or substance of the originally expressed consumer demand.

As a whole, the accelerator effect, along with other parameters that influence its power and dynamics, makes it extremely risky to accept the generated demand for downstream industrial enterprises as equivalent to the generated demand for the upstream industries, especially with modern, simultaneous options. In this very simplified example, we ignore heterogeneities in preferences though.

Market Concentration

An important characteristic of industrial markets is the high degree of concentration in demand. The degree of concentration in industrial markets (cf. consumer markets) indicates that customers are not scattered. However, it also signals diversification in the industry, depending on the market in which it is measured. One metric, proposed for objective comparisons of different degrees of concentration, is the concentration ratio, equal to the combined size of the market shares held by the (few) large companies operating within it. Therefore, the degree of concentration for market X is the sum of the market share of the three or four largest players active in that specific market.

Two main dimensions relate to the extent of concentration. One reflects the consumer side and emphasizes that a high degree of concentration is inextricably linked to the existence and development of monopoly powers. In economic terms, it implies greater possibilities and opportunities for inter-operational agreements that might drive product prices higher. This distortion—that is, the large gap between terms and conditions governing the market in free (perfect) competition—arises due to the existence of a small number of companies that individually (or together) have a dominant share of the specific market. Beyond their obvious mutual pursued and served interests, price-level conspiracies are easy to adopt and handle, because the few market players (cf. nearly infinite numbers of companies in a perfect competition environment) can easily and immediately engage in (illegal) background consultations to set a price level that enables the simultaneous realization of their mutually accepted profit maximization goals.

As a result, the economic efficiency of the structural parameters of an industry is undermined. In practice, a monopoly means higher price levels but also fewer choices for consumers. The reduced range of options available could lead to artificially increased consumer brand loyalty, which in turn might act as a disincentive for developing innovative solutions with sufficient intensity and frequency.

In any game, the more powerful, strong, and capable the competitors are, the more intense and creative their competition becomes, and the more profitable the match becomes for the audience, relative to the price of the ticket. The same logic applies to industrial markets. Some industrial roles entail providing products/services to other industries. In monopsony situations, a small number of specific (highly concentrated) industrial enterprises "shop" from other industrial manufacturers that provide (small or large) equipment and supplies. Those industrial actors that enjoy large portions of the consumer market then become the largest (or even sole) buyers from some industrial providers. Therefore, concentration, which refers to consumer market share, also may be indicative of the concentration of purchasing power within industrial markets.

Physical proximity is another dimension of concentration that can be expressed according to the "cohabitation" of industrial enterprises in specific geographical areas, mainly to reap the benefits of more direct access to raw materials or energy. Other factors might also encourage them, as a means to create economies of scale (infrastructure, transport, productive capacity). Physical concentration also could refer to the level of industrial enterprises engaged in commercial activities with similar products (shopping malls) or similar service centers (brokerage, law, financial).

International Character of Industrial Markets

The international character of industrial enterprises is well established; most export companies are industrial companies. The transaction value of industrial markets in developed economies also reaches more than twice the value of the corresponding consumer markets. Although entering global markets and accessing international settings entails peculiarities and difficulties, it can be facilitated by internationally accepted models, specifications, and standards for quality, composition, and technical characteristics.

Because of the composition of other specific characteristics (e.g., derived demand, purchasing criteria of industrial buyers), international industrial markets also do not depend much on restrictions, which instead refer mainly to criteria related to consumer demand (e.g., religion, language, cultural environment). Distinct, necessary levels of know-how, technology, proximity to energy resources and raw materials, and specialization all intensify the concentration differential too, when manufactured products are exported to wider international markets that, without corresponding resources or economic structure, cannot produce them on their own.

In recent years, international trends have seen the removal of trade barriers and restrictions, enhanced liberalization, and expanded free trade zones. Such shifts can facilitate the introduction and greater activity of smaller businesses, but they simultaneously enable mobility by larger ones. Strategic partnerships, mergers, and acquisitions also appear to have increased. The removal of trade restrictions and the presence of various strategic alliances prompt even more concentration in many industrial sectors. For example, a favorable environment achieved through direct access to wealthy rural areas with plentiful natural resources or unobstructed supplies of cheap labor creates access to new markets and the prospect of alternative strategic partnerships.

Financial Products

Consumer and generated demand fluctuations both require flexible, immediate access to capital through modern, alternative forms of credit and financial instruments. Consider the example we use to describe the accelerator effect. The automotive manufacturer Y considered various alternatives to deal with the percentage change in demand and in its derived size. But when downstream industry players encounter derived demand, what is the rational choice? Should Y purchase more equipment to cope with the change in demand (increase), or should it adopt a more flexible approach? Finding an answer requires exploring various dimensions (borrowing rates, borrowing convenience, loan repayment time, company balance sheet structure, financial circumstances) and their configurations to forecast outcomes and make a decision.

Some novel financial products aim to meet consumer needs, and these alternative funding programs can be helpful for addressing fixed, non-technological, mechanical, equipment, and industrial needs, such as leasing, factoring, and forfeiting. These offerings provide substantial flexibility. For example, leasing allows the firm to retain capital it can use to acquire other production equipment or to support other uses. The total cost usually is less than the total cost of borrowing, and the repayment is in the form of rent. There are also tax benefits, because leasing is a company expense. Thus, the company can update its equipment and the technology it uses at a fast pace. Next, factoring is a long-term agreement that includes the prepayment requirements of the industrial customer, thereby increasing the working capital; a variant called forfeiting instead meets export needs by providing guarantees.

Complexity of the Purchasing Process

The high degree of complexity of purchasing processes in industrial markets, compared with consumer markets, is reflected and underlined by the many management positions that are staffed by professionals who specialize in industrial markets. This complexity stems from multiple factors, each with distinct weights in terms of affecting processes.

Industrial products themselves are complex, often appear highly specialized, and require expertise to be both manufactured and purchased. Furthermore, they may be characterized by technological variables that must be codified before being incorporated into the product as a solution for the focal need, then decoded on the buyer side to clarify the benefits and encourage a purchase decision. Another factor pertains to the financial stakes involved. Transactions have great monetary value, but even beyond the large amounts of money being paid—and the correspondingly large risks and consequences of a bad choice—the strategic consequences of purchasing choices are immense.

As complexity continues to increase, more people become involved in the process of solving the industrial purchasing problem, and the organization exerts a formal influence as well. Recognizing who is involved in the purchasing process, including the relative weight of their knowledge, the influential power they bear, their role, and the criteria they apply, thus are equally important factors, which again increase the complexity of the purchasing process. Next, the complexity of the process reflects the diversity of functionally specialized views that each person adopts. Organizations, especially large ones, have many features in common with the societies in which they operate; to some extent, they are microcosms. A commonly accepted goal is to operate according to a set of rules, which ensure smooth cohabitation and overall progress toward mutually beneficial outcomes, so that individual members can achieve their own organizational goals. Similar to social structures, these symbiotic interrelationships and combinations of different capabilities should support the mutual organizational goal. But, trivially and arbitrarily, this is often relegated to being a second priority, influenced by functional expediency or self-motivation, through less formal or official channels.

When industrial buyers are organizational structures, they also can differ from one another, which calls for a different, and in certain cases, more personalized approach. The broader environment in which industrial actors operate may also vary considerably, with corresponding implications. Relationships are more personal and direct, and promotional messages must emphasize, in each individual case, that the offering being sold is a unique and individual solution, tailored to the needs of each individual industrial buyer, not just some product. In addition, the elapsed time between the implementation of the marketing programs and the response from the industrial buyer makes it difficult to evaluate buying process effectiveness. The time-consuming character of this process also constitutes an expression of the degree of complexity.

Product Complexity

In industrial markets, a serious risk—one that can irreversibly undermine the benefits of a customer-centric approach and thus the conception, design, implementation, and effectiveness of achieving organizational goals—lurks in the lack of importance attributed to communication.

But a key source of competitive advantage in industrial markets is the technical, technological, and construction characteristics that industrial products feature, and a foundation and further enhancement of a robust technological background is a cornerstone of innovation, as well as a prerequisite or necessary condition for excellence. The recorded history of leading organizations in their field of activity often reveals an emphasis on both the creation/maintenance of a strong technological base and an overall orientation of resources toward enhancing and exploring existing skills, abilities, and advantages.

A technological orientation, emphasis on innovation, persistence in construction, technical capabilities, and an emphasis on research and development (R&D) are necessary conditions for the creation of a backdrop of superior organizational performance and the promise of excellent value. But these conditions are not capable of doing the job alone. A more integrated approach regards the concept of the product as a whole, not just its economic, technological, and technical features that offer mutual benefits. Thus, it also entails the development of a network of customer relationships. To make these relationships more visible, the critical contributions of marketing are required.

A focus on products exclusively also implies a failure to understand a basic principle: A product merely offers an excuse to reach out and develop a customer relationship. Value for customers is the main goal, so the organization must focus on its efforts and actions, along with the orientation of its strategy. The contributions of marketing to formulating and implementing the organizational orientation also have greater significance in industrial marketing contexts. A marketing orientation needs to be adopted without restraint, as an irreplaceable feature for extracting and heeding the needs of industrial customers.

Due to the technological complexity associated with meeting this need, corresponding levels of complexity are also incorporated into the product, in terms of the level of understanding and finding ways to meet needs. Effective, timely, and accurate heeding of key parameters, components, and dimensions of the need relate directly to products' capacity to function as effective solutions to (purchasing) problems. The department responsible for establishing coherent communication links and information bridges between the organization and the purchasers is marketing; its contribution and participation is undeniably critical. The problem begins if just a partial and fragmentary perception of the product exists. As an entity, the product is defined by its ability to meet the customer's needs; in the absence of that ability, the product does not exist as an autonomous or self-supported concept.

Overall, for industrial organizations to achieve a sustainable competitive advantage, the focus must be on the customer. Technological superiority is easier to translate into excellence if this superiority combines with the ability to interpret complex needs and the adoption of a suitable marketing orientation. Simultaneously adopting these guidelines constitutes a safe, integrated method to create the means to satisfy (product) needs, as well as achieve and maintain competitive excellence.

Vignette

Vestas: Capturing the Full Potential of the Service Business

As the world's leading name in wind turbines, Vestas already owned the largest installed base of more than 25,000 turbines that produce 60 GW of power. However, producing and selling the actual turbines offers limited potential, leading the firm to pursue greater servitization of its products, by selling the output the turbines produce, rather than just the machines themselves.

This vignette outlines a collaboration between Vestas and its customer Ørsted in the wind turbine market, in which Vestas seeks to move from selling wind turbines to customers to setting up a partnership in which it installs, operates, and maintains the wind turbines. Ørsted pays for the power output that the wind turbines produce.

By building its capacity beyond an existing, product-based business model, Vestas believes that:

We should be able to get more efficiency from our scale in services from doing things consistently in the same manner across the globe. We have therefore also decided to create a new service organization... to get increased focus and transparency on the service business, and here we need to leverage the largest installed base.

It thus plans to increase its service business by more than 30 percent of total revenues. In addition to its strong product-based foundation, Vestas can leverage its carefully developed, industry-leading computing capabilities that gather massive data about both weather and the performance of its constantly monitored wind turbines. These big data, featuring global wind flow patterns, and the complex analytical models that Vestas subjects them to in turn, provide customers with valuable advice on where to install wind turbines for their own purposes.

Although Vestas commits to monitoring and optimizing the performance of the individual turbines it sells, such desired servitization outcomes are difficult to attain, in both the short and long term, suggesting the need to address critical questions related to:

- Ensuring managerial support, from both top management and sales and operations managers, to maintain the strategic servitization focus.
- The investments required to develop and implement services and solutions, such as developing subscription-based business models.
- Changing firm mindsets and capabilities, to focus on selling and delivering services and solutions. For Vestas, this step was easy, as it is an add-on, not a total change of the full business model; the firm still produces wind turbines.
- The strategic effort needed to capture the potential of an already existing installed base, that is, tapping into already sold turbines and taking over the operation of these. For Vestas, this could be a totally new revenue stream.
- How to develop new key performance indicators and align incentives to integrate the sale and delivery of products with services—thus far, this has been the biggest challenge for Vestas.

- Coordinating and aligning new product development efforts with new service developments.
- Customers' involvement in development processes turned out to be crucial, which is essential to servitization; otherwise, the newly created services might not match the customers' needs.
- Creating enough flexibility and adaptability to enable customization and thereby meet customers' distinct and diverse needs and priorities.
- Finding ways to leverage insights into customers' needs to formulate attractive value propositions. For a customer like Ørsted, this has been an opportunity to free up capital that it can invest elsewhere.
- Enhancing the quality of the service provision to match increased customer expectations, which for Vestas have continued to grow over time.
- How to design service-level agreements to balance risk versus reward, even in interactions marked by information asymmetry. For Vestas, it has been a learn-as-you-go experience as opposed to a fully planned process (like Vestas traditionally would do).
- Developing trusting relationships to support Vestas' investments in customer-specific competencies.
- Geographical and cultural distances that may influence globally distributed networks of service partners. Initially, the transformation primarily has taken place in Denmark, minimizing potential cultural distances.

Source

Avlonitis, V., Frandsen, T., Hsuan, J., and Karlsson, C. (2014), *Driving Competitiveness through Servitization*, Copenhagen: CBS Competitiveness Platform.

Departmental Interdependence

The characteristics that constitute the particularities of industrial markets can also act as a roadmap that places appropriate emphasis on the design and implementation of marketing strategies. A common denominator is that all these dimensions require finding and selecting the most effective ways (strategies, methods, practices, tools) to approach and satisfy the particularities of buyers within their particular environments.

Interdepartmental collaboration approaches inherently recognize and seek to leverage the strong interdependence of operational departments (intra-corporate) in industrial enterprises. Such collaboration has emerged as a critical contributor to achieving organizational goals, but it has also gained increasing significance in the context of industrial enterprises, especially those that adopt a customer-centric orientation. In turn, relevant marketing decisions are based on a multifaceted, multidimensional, integrated framework that offers a precise understanding of customers and their needs. A customer-centric philosophy should be expressed and implemented with greater intensity so that other features can be dealt with effectively.

Due to the more emphatically defined role and importance of customer-centric perceptions, which reflect the particular context of the features, interdepartmental collaboration becomes a goal, as well as a necessity. It can be defined as the symbiotic interrelation of two or more operational departments of an organization, whose aim is to produce an advantage for the organization that is greater than the sum of the benefit that each functional part could produce independently and without contact, cooperation, or feedback with one another. Essentially, interdepartmental collaboration is a dynamic, interorganizational process of combining, coordinating, and integrating the efforts of different operational specializations, to gain a deeper understanding and more effective satisfaction of the needs of (industrial) customers and thereby achieve corporate goals.

In its specific role, the functional competence of marketing entails listening to and heeding the needs of customers. In an industrial context, it requires a more personalized approach, because the buying process is so complex. Furthermore, marketing executives are charged with acting as coherent links between the organization and customers, conveying important information to and from their employing organization. Both of these dimensions become utterly useless though, no matter how efficiently or accurately the marketing department has accomplished its stated mission, if no one is paying attention. The functional alignment of specialized functions as a means to achieve expressed goals is not possible if information is omitted or displaced by the organization's decision-making algorithm.

The alienation of departments and functional deviations from a common, organizational objective also may be due to barriers (e.g., differences in various specialized knowledge backgrounds, perceptions of different business parameters), as well as short-sighted considerations that lead to the promotion of unilateral, segmented goals or even personal gain. But dividing specialized, functional capabilities prevents competitive advantages from being generated.

Good communication/collaboration and departmental interdependence can catalyze the transformation of information analysis into critical success features, such as building satisfaction of an expressed need or producing a personalized and integrated solution that responds to the specific needs of specific customers. A deep understanding of the whole range of needs cannot be a one-way street for industrial firms though. Each functional department makes a contribution, reflecting its implementation of the functional orientation, which is key to delivering value to customers. The functional departments can adopt integrated communication and feedback orientation and then systematically exploit the functional specializations and capabilities of other operational departments.

For example, R&D is functionally responsible for translating needs into tangible product features, specifications, and technical characteristics. If it seeks to address the specific characteristics of industrial markets by converging and aligning its activities with the marketing department's efforts, a strong foundation exists for matching the product to the specific target market. In essence, the R&D department configures product creation, based on an expressed need (previously detected and transferred by the marketing department), and determines the elements of its composition. Ignoring such interdependence across departments implies a lack of strategic orientation and constitutes a gap in the overall picture. Finally, a great degree of functional interdependence or cross-sectoral coordination may be an endogenous variable that defines a marketing orientation.

Number of Customers

Unlike the consumer market, in industrial markets, customer identification and recognition can be done rapidly, with the use of fewer or simpler tracking mechanisms. This characteristic is associated with the high degree of concentration, as previously discussed. That is, concentration reduces the number of customers (or potential customers), as well as the fragmentation and segmentation of the markets, which can be separated into sections with special, distinctive attributes.

The number of customers may relate to the construction parameters of markets, which again could be linked to demand or particular components of buyers' requirements for the (distinctive) products they need. It also likely reflects the weight of importance of each requirement, related to the use for which the products are intended. Demand for magnetic resonance imaging (MRI) machines in a small country like Greece is likely limited to a few dozen, similar to demand for some valuable, rare, strategically important material, with a limited or specific range of uses and possibly high-risk extraction, processing, transport, and integration processes. Thus for example, uranium tends to be traded in monopsony-type markets in a particular continent or oligopolistic markets worldwide.

Even if the norm of a limited number of customers is violated, identifying remaining customers is easier in an industrial market than in a consumer market. For more widely used products, such as computers, (industrial) buyers might be greater in number, compared with the few buyers of MRI machines, but they still can be relatively easily identified.

In the matrix in Figure 2.3, we attempt to map industrial markets on two dimensions, which relate to and are derived from the broader set of the characteristics of industrial markets.

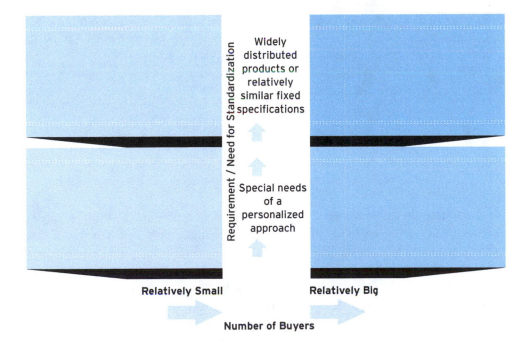

Figure 2.3 Mapping Matrix of Industrial Markets Based on Standardization Requirements/Number of Buyers

In terms of practical consequences due to the existence of the characteristics of industrial markets, we observe the more certain advantages for the industrial manufacturer. Promotion activities can be harmonized more easily and better aimed at target markets; market research is more subtly taken for granted. The R&D department can adopt specific orientations and seek to enhance competitive advantage by aligning the organization's specialized capabilities with the dynamically improved effort to satisfy specific customer needs.

Overall, the pool of knowledge and experience available in a limited market can be expanded constantly, to the mutual benefit of business partners. But when focused on the disadvantages, an opposite argument could emerge: in some circumstances, the frequency of innovations correlates negatively with consumers' trust.

If commitment remains safe and unchanged, organizations would not have much incentive to generate new innovations. A (relatively) small number of buyers and a (relatively) small number of sellers transact with a smaller range of options, reinforcing their long-lasting relationships, with less (overall) demand from all industrial buyers (and less motivation) for innovation to industrial manufacturers (as a whole). Furthermore, it is almost always the case that a small number of customers are at risk of overreliance and low risk spread, due to reasons that may also alter demand. Therefore, there is an indirect link between buyer–seller interdependence and the role that some customers may play.

Significance of the Customer

In describing the particularities that constitute industrial markets as a distinct field, individual clients have special significance, due to two key features:

- Individual customers are usually few in number in each industry.
- The relatively few orders received by industrial organizations are compensated for by the volume of each order and thus its large value.

This market structure in turn has relevant implications for the relative strength, bargaining power, and opportunity costs of changing existing partnerships or replacing partners. It also implies a monopsonistic setting, such that customers gain an edge over industrial firms in defining the balance of not just their relationships but also the status quo surrounding the sales process.

In particular, the customer enjoys special attention from the organization, expressed as a readiness and willingness to tailor the products it manufactures to match the customer's requirements perfectly. Such narrow targeting inevitably reduces the producers' or manufacturers' ability to appeal to other potential customers, such that they may grow dependent on their targeted customer and lose bargaining power. They even might go beyond product adjustments and make changes in their organizational structure to conform to the customer's preferences and perform more effectively for a particular customer.

In industrial markets, attention to specific customers thus is fraught. Customers have ready options to choose other suppliers, and the resulting potential of greater competition due to the market structure represents an important determinant of the behavior of industries toward their markets.

Vignette

Strategizing in Industrial Markets

Industrial markets are characterized by interdependencies among parties. The degrees of these interdependencies depend on the percentage of the supplier's revenues provided by a particular customer, the extent of adaptations by both customers and suppliers to each other during their repeated exchanges, and the specificity of their resource investments. Accordingly, interdependencies might be nested within business relationships, but because suppliers and customers also form business relationships with other parties, networks of interdependencies actually develop, such that each company's strategy depends on the actions and reactions of various other companies, strategizing in parallel.

When perceived in relation to other companies, strategies might be described as:

1   Complementary: The strategy involves doing what other companies do not, which contributes to the realization of their strategy. It is relatively easy to attain, because other companies have no reason to resist it.
2   Shared: Many companies together form a strategy to compete as a network level with other networks. Firms sharing the strategy assume shared goal realization, but external firms might exhibit other, potentially negative reactions.
3   Copying: A company acting in a way similar to other companies may seem harmonic, but it often evokes competition.
4   Company-rooted: Some companies ignore how others are likely to react or how they strategize. This blind strategy rarely can be realized in its initial form. Other companies react in ways not foreseen by the strategizing company.
5   Challenging: Even if aware of the interdependencies, reactions, and strategies of other companies, a firm might seek to shake things up and create change in its interdependencies. The reactions are expected, though perhaps not their precise form, and the goal is to break away from past customers or suppliers to form new business relationships.

Figure 2.4 illustrates connections among the five strategies, according to the extent to which they conform with or confront existing interdependencies and whether reactions affect the possibility to realize the strategy extensively or to more limited degrees.

(Continued)

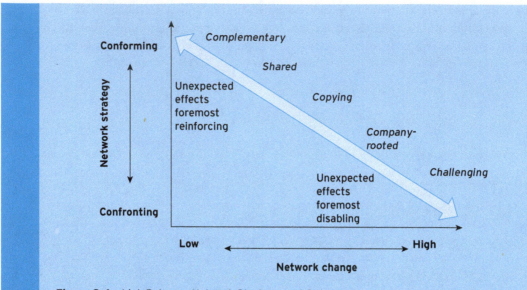

Figure 2.4 Link Between Network Strategy and Outcomes

Source: Öberg et al. (2016, p. 126)

Source

Öberg, C., Shih, T., and Chou, H.-H. (2016), "Network strategies and effects in an interactive context," *Industrial Marketing Management*, 52, 117-127.

Relationships Between Buyers and Sellers

The conditions and structure of industrial markets indicate the orientation or even the nature of relationships between sales organizations and buyers. Although these two elements represent a foundation on which to build relationships, they are not the only influences; other considerations need to be considered as well. For example, acknowledging different influences, even opposing ones, may offer a reliable, comprehensive framework for understanding and describing current circumstances and their consequences, mutually for both sellers and buyers.

In general, more stable relationships and links that persist over the longer term serve the purposes of buyers. By exhibiting consistent preferences and purchasing behavior, they can pursue closer contacts and develop them with greater frequency, requiring intensive efforts by sellers that then reinforce the buyers' dependency on the sellers. At the same time, the buyer likely develops dependency on the seller, reflecting its ability to offer various benefits, such as:

- Reliable product delivery schedules.
- Extra services, such as unscheduled product deliveries.

- Continuous and uninterrupted flows of supplies.
- Reliable and timely maintenance of the buyer's equipment, especially if the purchased product is integral to its production process.
- Timely and valid provision of know-how, as required for the product being sold.
- Favorable payment terms.
- Modern automated systems to receive and process orders.
- Critical information sharing, pertaining to:
  - Competition.
  - Consumer market trends.
  - Industrial market trends.
  - Existing and new products.
  - Price trends.
  - Changes in technology.
- Adaptation.
- Customer-specific knowledge.

These sources all contribute to a cooperative relationship based on interdependence, which achieves a long-term, stable equilibrium rather then imposing a one-sided influence. The closeness, duration, and frequent recurrence of such a partnership depend on a web of mutually beneficial goals. Furthermore, longevity and stability signify a distinct mindset, in which making a sale is not the ultimate goal but is merely a moment in time, when the means of achieving the true goal (a long-term relationship) exist. Acquiring knowledge and accounting for deeper needs are prerequisites; they also are the core of customer-centric thinking. As relational marketing proclaims, the relationship with the customer does not end with a sale, which actually is just the start. Most interpersonal relationships are not based on ongoing negotiations or the current portfolio of resources that each party contributes. Instead, they require a mutual understanding of each party's needs and mutual recognition of their interdependence. It is natural for collaborating and conflicting interests to arise within a cooperative framework, and their simultaneous satisfaction may be mutually exclusive. Yet it also must be noted that competitive rather than antagonistic trends usually prevail in relationships.

Further development of a quasi-symbiotic relationship can be the starting point for developing strategic coalitions. If an inert climate is created, there are no expressed desires to replace the supplier; instead, the nurturing and fostering climate encourages further loyalty and trust.

Reciprocity in the Relationship of Purchase and Sale Agreements

Reciprocity is a logical, expected development in such a relationship, reflecting the reasoning underlying it. With reciprocity, the boundaries of the trade extend beyond cooperation, while depending on it, and interdependence gets confirmed and enhanced. Through the rotation of roles, reciprocity generates countervailing benefits for buyers who simultaneously function as sellers, in that they leverage and exercise their bargaining power to secure some level of sales in advance while demonstrating loyalty and commitment to existing relationships with suppliers (who are also their clients). This role reversal might entail a corresponding reversal in bargaining power and dependency. If all dependencies remain balanced, then an interdependence regime persists, ensuring a healthy, mutually beneficial relationship dominated by the logic of cooperation–competition rather than antagonistic conflict.

Thus, if reciprocity emerges and is nurtured in close cooperation, such that both parties work toward mutual advantages, it produces benefits and synergies for both organizations. Otherwise, unbalanced bargaining power and a relationship based on the unequal distribution of dependencies develops, with detrimental effects on both the marketing toolbox and the underlying philosophy.

Demand: Axes, Dimensions, and Elasticity

The derived demand mechanism in industrial markets acts as a regulatory factor that also indirectly affects other determinants of demand. For example, a demand parameter that has an important role in consumer markets is price elasticity. The law of supply and demand exerts axiomatic power (with a few exceptions, such as Giffen goods, which are goods that people consume more of as the price rises) on the inverse relationship between the quantity demanded and the price: the higher the price, the lower the quantity demanded, and vice versa. Demand elasticity, as it relates to value, also affords greater precision and clarity to the contradictory relationship. It refers to the amount of change in the quantity demanded of a good, as a result of a change in its selling price. In other words, demand elasticity reflects the intensity of the reaction of a buyer (in accordance with the law of supply and demand), as manifested in the quantity demanded after a change in price. Demand is elastic if the percentage response, as a change in the quantity demanded, is greater than the percentage change in the price. Conversely, if a percentage change (increase/decrease) in the price (independent variable) causes a smaller percentage change (decrease/increase) in the quantity demanded (dependent variable), it indicates relative rigidity, and demand in terms of price is considered inelastic. Thus the law of supply and demand indicates the direction of the relationship (inverse); the magnitude of the demand elasticity in terms of price describes how proportionate (or disproportionate) the inverse relationship is.

In consumer markets, elasticity indicates the degree of consumer freedom, because the quantity demanded is an indicator of dependence or the importance of the product in demand. For example, demand for medicinal products is inelastic, because their importance for buyers is so great that even a price increase would not be reflected proportionally in a reduction of the quantity demanded.

The factors that affect demand elasticity in terms of price differ somewhat in industrial markets, which feature, almost as a rule, demand inelasticity. As we discussed when describing derived demand, the expression of demand in industrial markets is largely secondary and indirectly driven by demand for consumer products. A price reduction for products that industrial buyers purchase is neither a necessary nor a sufficient condition that might disproportionately trigger increases in the quantity demanded. Therefore, price demand in industrial markets tends to be inelastic; the price of the products does not have a decisive role. Rather, the market is dominated by consumer demand and the transfer of the outcome. If we combine such demand, as reflected in consumer markets, with the heavy dependence of industrial demand on consumers, we deduce that price demand elasticity strongly affects the corresponding size of industrial markets.

Using the logic of the arguments used to establish the power of the generated demand, we can also anticipate that elasticity in industrial markets depends indirectly, or as a secondary result, on the transfer of influences in consumer markets. If consumers are resilient/inelastic in their quantity demanded for any price changes, then beyond derived demand (expressed in corresponding actions in industrial markets), the elasticity in industrial markets will be affected too. For example, if the price of a finished product on the consumer market changes, and consumers react as expected (with a decrease/increase in the quantity demanded, in accordance with the law of supply and demand), proportionately or disproportionately, by changing the demanded quantity, then a chain reaction in the industrial market should be triggered, featuring:

- A corresponding change (reversal) in the quantity demanded of industrial products by industrial purchasers (decrease/increase), due to derived demand, which acts as a conduit for the transfer of the power of the supply–demand law from the consumer to the industrial market (according to particular characteristics that describe the derived demand).
- Some corresponding degree of elasticity or inelasticity, in light of possible distortions that might arise due to limitations and particular features of the transfer process from the consumer to the industrial market (consistent with the characteristics of derived demand).

Therefore, existing price demand elasticity in consumer markets is clearly useful for defining and interpreting the corresponding elasticity in industrial markets, such that it qualifies as a robust tool for interpreting the price of products sold in industrial markets. If we were to isolate all other factors, such as the impact of industrial demand on consumer demand in terms of price, we might invoke parameters that can converge to form a picture of firmly inelastic demand in relation to industrial markets, such as the nature of industrial products, their contribution to the cost structure, and how they are attributed:

- If industrial products fall into the category of large facilities, their constant per unit cost for each product produced is subject to depreciation.
- If industrial products are component parts or cheap raw materials, the value of their monetary cost is a very small fraction of the total cost of the final product.

The degrees of freedom for buyers, in terms of cost, thus appear substantial, contributing to the inelastic demand that they express toward the price. From an alternative view, industrial buyers simply do not have the luxury to stop buying (or to buy in smaller quantities) the products they need to facilitate their own production to cover expressed consumer demand, regardless of prices.

Therefore, either the price of products sold in industrial markets is obsolete as a variable to determine demand elasticity, relative to its effects in the consumer market, or else the characteristics that govern industrial markets dictate that price does not have a decisive role. But excluding price from the variables that appear likely to affect demand would be misguided. Even indirectly, the price of products sold in industrial markets intrudes and influences the cross-elasticity of demand, defined as the degree to which purchasers indicate their readiness and willingness to change (increase/decrease) the amount of another product they purchase, when the price of the product that they prefer changes (decrease/increase). If price increases, and they seek to replace its demanded quantity with another product, they engage in substitution. If the market features nearly perfect, fierce competition, with products that are very similar or undifferentiated, substitution is particularly likely, unless other features exist to enhance the value of the focal product (e.g., delivery services, automated ordering systems).

The factors that affect demand in industrial markets also reflect the possibility of complementarity. Complementary products exist when demand for one product increases (decreases), and that shift leads to a similar increase (decrease) in the demand of another product. This aggregate variable informs overall demand in industrial markets.

Furthermore, demand depends on the international activities of the industrial players, regardless of their country of origin or the economic framework from which they originate. That is, industrial markets are closely linked and dependent on factors that extend well beyond local or national borders. Consequently, they must engage in continuous, systematic collection, updating, and analysis of information to identify relevant parameters and determine the importance of their impacts on the business.

The need to monitor the environment and trends on an international scale also stems from the nature of the demand generated. Industrial organizations follow emerging consumer demand, as it gets transmitted to them (with distortions). If the expressed demand for consumer products increases, retailers react by increasing their inventory, and then organizational buyers follow this downstream trend to increase their upstream demands of industrial organizations.

Due to such dependency, some proactive mechanisms exist. Industrial market participants monitor and evaluate the complex environment, but they also might intervene vigorously by reacting to and also shaping current developments. Many international organizations develop marketing programs for consumer markets, designed to attain more effective control and an ability to define key market factors. A well-known airplane manufacturer markets air travel to consumers in its effort to increase orders for its aircraft from airlines, for example.

Life Cycle of Industrial Products

A product life cycle reflects its performance on specific measures, such as revenue and profits for the business. The values of these two parameters over time can signal distinct life cycle stages, each of which can be linked to particular marketing strategy elements and requires special attention with regard to the organizational design. Metaphorically, the life cycle mimics the life courses of living organisms: birth, development, maturity, and death. Just like living beings, products access the different stages at varying speeds (e.g., how quickly they shift from one stage to the next) and spend varying amounts of time in each stage. Industrial and consumer products tend to exhibit different life cycles too.

Overall though, the introduction stage is quite long. The product needs time to become known and for its features to be tested, evaluated, and adopted as acceptable, relative to the needs it seeks to satisfy. The long duration of the introduction stage also means that for quite some time, the product cannot cover its own expenses, and it generates negative profits or losses. Industrial products require substantial investments and resources, such as for R&D, which can take years to complete. Therefore, upon their introduction into the market, low recognition and a low rate of adoption are deeply problematic, because such conditions mean the company cannot cover its expenses. Even once they enter later stages, industrial products tend to remain in each stage for longer than consumer products, due to the relatively more stable purchasing trends of industrial buyers, who are slower in shifting their preferences than consumers are.

DIFFERENCES BETWEEN INDUSTRIAL AND CONSUMER MARKETING

In Table 2.2, we map some pillars of differentiation between consumer and industrial markets; we also detail some specific characteristics that arise across each dimension. The table reflects the hierarchical structure of the background or analytical approach that underlies each dimension, detailing the differentiated dimensions and their parameterization (level/degree or value). The three sections of the table group the attribute differences into (1) structural differences in the market, (2) differences in purchasing behavior, and (3) differences in marketing practices. We reason that differences observed between industrial versus consumer markets in the first section (market structure) affect those in the next two sections (purchasing behavior and marketing practices), and differences in purchasing behavior also give rise to and create the need for differentiation in the marketing practices adopted in industrial versus consumer markets.

Table 2.2 Industrial Marketing Differences in Relation to Consumer Marketing

Dimension	Industrial Marketing	Consumer Marketing
Differentiation in the market structure		
Nature of demand	Produced	Immediate
Demand volatility	Higher volatility	Lower volatility
Demand elasticity	Lower elasticity	Higher elasticity
Reverse elasticity	More common	Less common
Nature of customers	Greater heterogeneity	Less heterogeneity
Market fragmentation	Greater fragmentation	Less fragmentation
Market complexity	Greater complexity	Less complexity

(Continued)

Table 2.2 (Continued)

Dimension	Industrial Marketing	Consumer Marketing
Market size	Higher total value	Lower total value
Number of buyers corresponding to each seller	Small	Large
Number of buyers per market segment	Small	Large
Relative size of the buyer versus the seller	Often similar	The seller is much larger
Geographical concentration	Often concentrated	Usually scattered
Differentiation in purchasing behavior		
Influences to make a purchase	Many	Few
Trading cycles	Often long duration	Usually short duration
Value of the transaction	Often high	Usually low
Complexity of the buying process	Often high	Usually low
Level of buyer–supplier interdependence	Often high	Usually low
Level of professionalism in the market	Often high	Usually low
Importance of relationships	Often high	Usually low
Degree of interactivity	Often high	Usually low
Formal, written rules	Common use	Unusual use
Diversification in applied marketing practices		
Sales process	System sale	Product sale
Personal sale	Extensive use	Limited use
Use of relationships	Extensive use	Limited use
Promotion strategies	Limited, customized for the customer	Mass market
Internet presence	Higher level	Lower level
Branding	Limited	Extensive, sophisticated
Market research	Limited	Extensive
Segmentation process	Simplified	Complex
Level of knowledge/awareness of competitors	Low	High
Level of product complexity	Higher	Lower

Source: Adapted from Brennan et al. (2014)

3

SUPPLY CHAIN NETWORKS FOR MANUFACTURING PRODUCTS

Learning Objectives

- Introduce supply chain management.
- Define industrial supply chains.
- Understand the difference between supply chain and logistics system management.
- Introduce the key decisions underlying supply chain management.
- Identify the key players and strategies in an industrial supply chain.
- Describe logistics processes in an industrial supply chain.

Case Study

Purchasing Practices

To obtain necessary materials and keep supply chains flowing, purchasing and supply chain managers engage in one-off transactions, but they also build collaborative supply networks. Which is better?

That might be the wrong question. Both transactional and network exchanges are necessary and effective, for different suppliers, products, and contexts. Thus the real question is not which one but rather when and in what proportion?

(Continued)

Broadly, we might distinguish between a primarily transactional supply management approach from one that mostly emphasizes network coordination and ongoing relationships. In the former case, the purchasing firm aggressively sources what it needs by continuously searching for the best deal, new suppliers, and alternative options. In the latter case, purchasing managers aim to position their organization strategically within a wider network, in an effort to gain benefits that way. Transactional purchasing represents a traditional, conventional approach; relational practices are increasingly common. Of course, they are not mutually exclusive.

Furthermore, either of these options can take place electronically or interactively. If they make purchases electronically, organizations use the Internet, one-to-one, and one-to-many technologies to create and mediate exchanges with suppliers. In contrast, interactive purchasing involves interpersonal interactions of employees with individual suppliers.

Thus we can define four purchasing practices, in line with an instrument introduced by Lindgreen et al. (2013) to measure organizations' use of transaction purchasing, electronic purchasing, interactive purchasing, and network purchasing. They lead to significant differences in the buying organization's links and interactions with its suppliers, as detailed in the eight formative indicators (and the general indicator) we list in Table 3.1 that characterize and determine the various practices. Simply contrasting pure transactional versus pure relational purchasing would be overly simplistic and obscure key performance outcomes that reflect organizations' relative emphases on mixes of various purchasing practices.

Table 3.1 Indicators for Purchasing Practices

Aspects	Transactional Perspective	Relational Perspective		
	Transaction Purchasing	Electronic Purchasing	Interactive Purchasing	Network Purchasing
Purpose of exchange: When dealing with our direct suppliers, our purpose is to:	achieve cost savings or other financial measure(s) of performance (monetary transactions).	create information-generating dialogue with many identified suppliers.	build a long-term relationship with specific supplier(s).	form relationships with various organizations in our supply market(s) or wider purchasing system.

Aspects	Transactional Perspective	Relational Perspective		
	Transaction Purchasing	Electronic Purchasing	Interactive Purchasing	Network Purchasing
Nature of communication: Our communication with direct suppliers can be characterized as:	our organization using undifferentiated communications with all suppliers.	our organization using technology to communicate with and possibly among many individual suppliers.	individuals at various levels in our organization personally interacting with individual suppliers.	senior managers networking with other managers from a variety of organizations in our supply market(s) or wider purchasing system.
Type of contact: Our organization's contact with our direct suppliers is:	arm's-length, impersonal with no individualized or personal contact.	interactive via technology such as the Internet.	interpersonal, involving one-to-one interaction between people.	across firms in the broader network (from impersonal to interpersonal contact).
Duration of exchange: The type of contact with our direct suppliers is characterized as:	transactions that are discrete or one-off (i.e., not ongoing).	technology-based interactivity that is ongoing and real-time.	interpersonal interaction that is ongoing.	contact with people in our organization and wider purchasing system that is ongoing.
Formality of exchange: When people from our organization meet with our direct suppliers, it is:	mainly at a formal business level.	mainly at a formal level, yet customized or personalized via interactive technologies.	at both a formal business level and informal social level on a one-to-one basis.	at both a formal business level and informal social level in a wider organizational system/network.

(Continued)

Table 3.1 (Continued)

Aspects	Transactional Perspective		Relational Perspective	
	Transaction Purchasing	Electronic Purchasing	Interactive Purchasing	Network Purchasing
Managerial intent: Our purchasing exchanges are intended to:	find new suppliers and the best deal (i.e., low prices).	create two-way, technology-enabled data exchanges with our suppliers.	develop cooperative relationships with our suppliers.	coordinate activities among ourselves, suppliers, and other parties in the wider purchasing and supply system (e.g., second-tier suppliers, key customers, service providers, other organizations).
Managerial focus: Our purchasing strategy is focused on issues related to:	the purchase item and its price.	managing IT-enabled relationships with many individual suppliers.	one-to-one relationships with suppliers or individuals in supplier organizations.	the network of relationships between individuals and organizations in our wider supply system.
Managerial investment: Our purchasing resources (i.e. people, time, and money) are invested in:	specifying products, negotiations, ordering, and expediting activities.	operational assets (IT, website, logistics) and functional systems integration (e.g., purchasing with IT).	establishing and building personal relationships with individual suppliers.	developing our organization's network relationships within our supply market(s) or wider purchasing system.

Aspects	Transactional Perspective	Relational Perspective		
	Transaction Purchasing	Electronic Purchasing	Interactive Purchasing	Network Purchasing
General indicator: Overall, our organization's general approach to our direct suppliers (of product-related items) involves:	using aggressive sourcing (continuously search for new suppliers) to obtain and purchase items at the most favorable conditions.	using the Internet and other interactive technologies to create and mediate data exchanges between our organization and our suppliers.	developing personal interactions between employees and individual suppliers.	positioning the organization within a wider organizational system or network.

Source: Lindgreen et al. (2013, pp. 76-77)

Therefore, using the relevant indicators, Lindgreen et al. (2013) suggest four clusters of organizations that adopt distinct emphases on the various purchasing practices, which they label "transactional," "interpersonal dyadic," "interpersonal network," and "integrative relational." The transactional cluster scores high on the transaction purchasing index and low on electronic purchasing, interactive purchasing, and network purchasing. The integrative relational configuration cluster scores low on the transaction purchasing index and high on the electronic, interactive, and network purchasing indexes. Then the remaining two clusters both achieve medium scores on the transaction purchasing index. The interpersonal dyadic configuration scores high on the interactive purchasing index but lower on the electronic purchasing and network purchasing indices. The interpersonal network configuration has a high score on both interactive purchasing and network purchasing but a low score on the electronic purchasing index.

In a sense, the transactional and integrative relational configurations oppose each other. Considering their medium scores on the transaction purchasing index, both the interpersonal dyadic and interpersonal network configurations represent intermediate options. In addition, the integrative relational configuration outperforms the others on marketing and financial performance indicators, as well as on supplier quality, and then it also outperforms the transactional configuration on delivery reliability and supplier on-time delivery. Across all four configurations, we note that organizations tend to use more interactive and network purchasing with suppliers of direct inputs but more transaction purchasing with suppliers of indirect inputs.

(Continued)

Overall then, all buying organizations manage portfolios of supplier relationships, some of which are more transactional and others that are more relational or networked. These dynamic shifts are the key to understanding and predicting success in purchasing practices.

Source

Lindgreen, A., Vanhamme, J., Raaij, E., and Johnston, W.J. (2013), "Go configure: The mix of purchasing practices to choose for your supply base," *California Management Review*, 55(2), 72–96.

INTRODUCTION TO SUPPLY CHAIN MANAGEMENT

The supply chain supports collaborative relationships with other businesses and organizations, such as suppliers, producers, wholesalers, and retailers. A broad definition holds that "The supply chain is regarded as the network of organizations or companies involved, through continuous and two-way interactions, in processes that add value to the products/services provided to the end customer" (Ballou, 1999, p. 198), such that supply chain management (SCM) must entail the set of approaches or efforts to integrate producers, suppliers, and carriers in ways that enable products to be produced and distributed, in the right quantity and quality, at the right time, to the right place, at the lowest overall cost (Simchi-Levi et al., 2003). In a supply chain network, materials, information, and money all flow, from the supply of raw materials to the delivery of the finished products to the end user, as indicated by Figure 3.1.

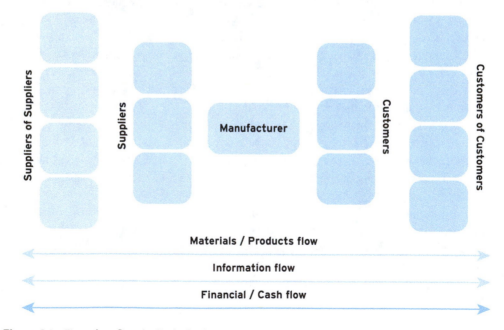

Figure 3.1 Flows in a Supply Chain System

The flows at each level span relationships of more than just two business units; potentially, they include all involved business units. The key stakeholders (supply chain links) are not just the suppliers and customers but also the organizations that provide required services. Figure 3.2 depicts a simplified supply chain network with its corresponding costs.

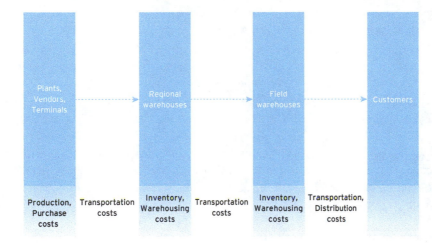

Figure 3.2   Participants and Costs in a Supply Chain System

Many challenges exist for effective SCM, which must pursue the success of the entire supply chain system (network), not just of a single link or a single business. The total cost is greater than the sum of the costs of the individual components; it includes shipping, storage, inventory maintenance, in-store and warehouse shipping, and order handling, as well as building and machinery costs, to name just a few. The problem intensifies if reducing one cost might cause the increase of another cost. For example, reducing storage costs might mean increased transport costs. The relationship between cost increases and service levels is also not linear and can even be exponential.

The conflicting goals, within each business and across businesses in the supply chain, also raise challenges. For example, the firm's production department prefers to manufacture the same product in large quantities, even if doing so increases stock levels and places more pressure on the warehouse department. In the wider supply chain, producers prefer high production levels, but wholesalers and retailers try to keep their stocks low, and at the same time, shipping companies want to establish fewer routes that involve large quantities.

Finally, members of the supply chain often participate in multiple chains, each of which operates as an open system comprised of the main supply (inbound logistics), production, and distribution (outbound logistics) subsystems. To achieve set objectives, it is essential to coordinate these various subsystems.

Vignette

Supply Network Management in Smart Cities

Smart cities rely on technological solutions, such as the Internet of Things (IoT), to support and facilitate local production, consumption, communication, and exchanges within the town. In addition to developing new cities, information communication technology can be introduced to existing cities. Several outcomes are likely with regard to supply chains.

In particular, the IoT allows for surveillance, data capture, and digital coordination, which in turn suggest new business opportunities and ways of organizing. Big data also might encourage entirely new solutions and business opportunities. For example, big data about how inhabitants move around a city may provide input for city planning and can inspire innovations. Supplier networks will likely gain importance, due to the increased levels of complexity and connectivity associated with distributing competences and resources across multiple suppliers, which in turn work together to create customer offerings. Enabled by information technology, for example, production might be distributed among different suppliers. Then the flow of goods would resemble not a chain, from raw material to customers, but a grouping of multiple parties at and among various supply chain positions.

Source

Öberg, C., and Graham, G. (2016), "How smart cities will change supply chain management: A technical viewpoint," *Production Planning & Control*, 27(6), 529-538.

WHAT IS DIFFERENT IN INDUSTRIAL SUPPLY CHAINS?

In industrial markets, designing an efficient, effective supply chain is highly complex. The objective is not different (increase the level of service provided at lower costs), nor are the key strategic axes (create value-added products, through innovation or improved products and services introduced to the market). But several characteristics distinguish industrial supply chains from their consumer counterparts:

- The design and production of a new product requires collaboration by many businesses, even at the earliest stages. These businesses may be geographically dispersed. For example, to produce a simple t-shirt, the design might come from Italy, the fabric is supplied from Indonesia, the buttons come from Egypt, and the sewing is done in China.

- The production process requires specialized knowledge and equipment at all stages of the product's life cycle (e.g., R&D, engineering). Consider software development companies: in almost all cases, their objectives are to reduce time to market, introduce innovative products, reduce product life cycles and waste, provide customized products and services, reduce environmental impacts, and maintain low stocks. The very nature of these industrial products requires specialized knowledge and infrastructure to achieve these goals.

- Relations among businesses can be "win–win" if they engage in simultaneous risk sharing. An automobile manufacturer might demand that a shock absorber manufacturer provide the best possible quality and reliability, because its success will pass through to other supply chain members. Cooperation also may be needed with a proximal link in the supply chain, and for industrial markets, an integrated chain is needed to establish information transparency across the entire chain. If a hardware failure occurs for a specific model or batch of cars, the automaker needs to know who has bought them, as well as which supplier is responsible for the problem.

- The environment features substantial complexity and uncertainty. In modern networks of many businesses, political, economic, and social events can affect the smooth running of various processes. When social unrest exists, especially in international supply chains, it can have detrimental impacts on the procurement, production, and distribution of industrial products.

- Outsourcing is particularly applicable in industrial networks. Partners with specialized know-how, experience, and advanced facilities can represent critical success factors.

- The evolution of industrial networks in the past 50 years began with mass production; key industries adopted vertical integration efforts: rather than create strategic networks during the oil shocks of the 1970s, they focused on individual logistics processes (e.g., transport, procurement, storage) and efforts to reduce operating costs. But supply chain relationships have also reflected emerging trends in consumer markets. Industrial firms adopted collaboration to produce customized products that would meet customers' specific requirements. In addition, lean production and market globalization prompted industrial actors to pursue closer cooperation with suppliers, whether located nearby or far away. A powerful driving force was new technologies, which have helped integrate business processes and provided the foundation for new business models for e-commerce.

- Logistics and supply chain executives must account for many variables and factors to make key decisions from the first moment of a product's life cycle, such as make-or-buy decisions. The dynamic nature of collaborative networks and the technological developments underlying new products together force industrial networks to gather large volumes of data, as well as use specialized tools, to make their decisions.

Thus, SCM aims to unify and manage core business processes across the entire supply chain, not simply to integrate processes at the various stages of the supply chain (i.e., for a single business). To understand SCM for the purposes of this text, we focus on the logistics system of a business.

Vignette

Supply Chains for the Floriculture Sector in Uganda

Uganda's floriculture sector is among the three largest in that country's economy, with a net worth of around £3 billion in 2018 (Asoko Insight, 2021). To ensure its continued flourishing and growth, logistics and speed to market represent key considerations, due to the innate perishability of cut flowers. These considerations in turn demand an effective physical infrastructure that can support rapid transport to overseas markets. But Uganda's supply chain historically lacked critical mass and capabilities in several areas, including cold transportation, breeding, and propagation methods to develop plant strains that were best suited to local growing conditions. It was falling behind Kenyan and Ethiopian floriculture sectors, which had achieved more advanced flower production and export expertise.

But a major highway project, which included the Entebbe-Kampala Highway (supported by financial aid and construction expertise from China), together with the development of a logistics hub at Entebbe International Airport, has catalyzed growth in the sector since 2018. The resulting supply chain design prioritizes export, mainly to Europe, including submissions for auctions in the Netherlands and other world centers of floriculture excellence. Moving beyond their existing supply chain relationships with established growers and partners in the Netherlands, Ugandan flower suppliers have also been leveraging their growing knowledge of cold transportation, locally adapted plant breeds, and new markets to build connections with geographically diverse actors, such as from China and Russia. In exploring new markets, the sector is also addressing its historical overreliance on the dominant supply chain linked to the Netherlands.

These new international relationships and supply chains with China and Russia are also creating some new markets; burgeoning demand for cut roses in China has become particularly notable (CGTN, 2020). Local Ugandan growers thus can protect their livelihood from European shocks while avoiding some restrictions imposed by European regulations regarding pesticides and environmental protection. These expansions promise to feed on one another too, such that growers are finding new value-added options related to distribution (e.g., cold transportation) and to R&D (e.g., investing in local versions of existing plant breeds, such as roses or chrysanthemums). They are also undertaking some speculative experiments with plants that have not previously been grown commercially. Potentially, the supply chain could even develop into a self-contained manufacturing cluster that can supply various overseas markets. Furthermore, growth in this sector appears promising for addressing rural unemployment among working-age Ugandan adults (18-45 years), especially among women (Newvision, 2020).

LOGISTICS CHAINS AND SUPPLY CHAINS

According to the definitions in the previous section, logistics and SCM in industrial markets are very broad, covering a wide range of planning, implementation, and control activities performed by the organization (e.g., procurement, strategy, material handling, packaging, distribution channels, locating distribution centers, technology, recycling, purchasing, transportation, inventory control, and customer service). Each company designs, implements, and controls various functions (e.g., supplies, materials handling, demand forecasting, inventory, order processing, geographical location of plants and warehouses, warehousing, packaging, transportation, spare parts and repairs, customer service, handling of product returns, recycling and collection of waste) in its efforts to transform the raw materials obtained from suppliers into finished products to market to customers. More generally, each company uses all its available resources (physical, financial, human, information) to optimize the cost/profit ratio, increase production flexibility, and ensure effective product delivery (flexible time and place), as well as meet the specific needs of customers. These efforts then strengthen the relationship and connection with customers, enabling enhanced service provision and competitive advantages, as indicated by Figure 3.3.

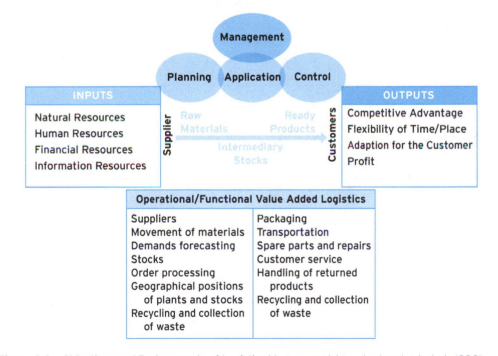

Figure 3.3   Objectives and Environments of Logistics Management (see also Lambert et al., 1999)

Logistics management involves the design of four main business functions: demand planning, supplies/procurement planning, production planning and scheduling, and transportation planning (Table 3.2).

Table 3.2 Basic Business Functions in Logistics Management

Function	Definition and Key Actions
Demand planning	Process of forecasting demand for products/services. A more accurate forecast improves the services provided to customers, while reducing costs that can arise from uncertain demand.
Supply/ procurement planning	Planning process to meet market demand based on available resources and stock levels. Meeting supply/procurement requirements ensures that safety stocks are at an appropriate level.
Production planning and scheduling	Planning and scheduling process for examining available resources and devising an optimal production program based on the constraints imposed by the limits of reality. This process can automatically adjust production plans if some suppliers are unavailable or a key product is not available (inactive).
Transportation planning	Design process for optimal, economical methods for transportation and distribution, taking into account constraints such as date/time of receipt or the type of transportation.

To understand the concepts of logistics management and SCM, consider the dairy industry. In Figure 3.4, dairy cooperatives collect raw material (milk) from small and large dairy producers and supply required packaging materials, which they source from a large manufacturing industry that produces this packaging material. The packaging firms obtain their raw materials to manufacture packages from other manufacturing plants, received and stored in their warehouses. The dairy cooperatives also maintain warehouses to store milk, raw materials, and packaging materials separately. Their production process (pasteurization) creates finished products, which must be packaged and stored in another warehouse for finished products. These products can then be offered to customers and consumers, through a distribution network that includes wholesalers (who distribute the products in specific geographical areas) and retailers. Each business entity (milk producers, cooperatives, packaging materials producers, dairy industry, wholesalers, retailers) has its own logistics system, of varying sizes. Furthermore, the various departments of each firm—procurement, warehousing, production, quality control, transportation, distribution, returns—work together to fulfill orders and demand. In this chain, as in many others, many players appear, but they adopt only two key roles: supplier and customer.

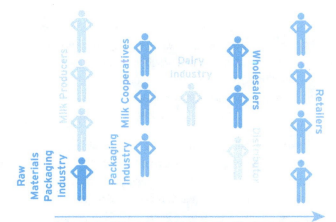

Figure 3.4 Example of a Supply Chain

Logistics management mainly focuses on managing this system to integrate and coordinate the components that constitute the logistics system. SCM instead pertains to managing, coordinating, and integrating the logistics systems of the various members of the supply chain.

Vignette

Meeting the Fresh Produce Needs of Growing Ethnic Minority Populations

In a global era, people living far from where they grew up often seek out and expect to find little reminders of home, like herbs and vegetables grown in the fields and sold in the local stores of their origin country. Supply chains and networks arguably can serve these demands too, because they can provide a dedicated channel for ethnic minority groups to find and purchase the various exotic or specialized produce they seek.

Hingley et al. (2010) identify clear latent demand for vegetables normally grown in temperate climates (e.g., sweet Pakistani carrot, pak choi cabbage, okra, pumpkins, squashes) among ethnic minority populations in the UK West Midlands area. But challenges to the local production of such foods, as well as network integration barriers, seemingly keep the strong, local, entrepreneurial ethnic minority population from accessing the products. The barriers took a few forms, according to Hingley et al. (2010):

(Continued)

- Price sensitivity, which dictates channel sourcing and market development.
- The reliance of foodservice businesses on wholesale traders, as gatekeepers of their access channels, market information, and product availability, who in turn represent overseas agencies and thus resist local and regional supply options.
- Cultural biases that separate rural (predominantly white) growers from (predominantly Asian) wholesale intermediaries and retail foodservice businesses.

A solution might emerge from technological innovations and new distribution formats. For example, specialty markets created by produce growers have enabled them to find innovative food platforms that do not depend on the supermarket sector or demand high-volume, low-value sales through wholesalers. Farmers' markets, direct sales, and Internet ordering also offer promising options, an example established previously by rural produce innovators. Direct delivery of specialty products can occur through box subscriptions, such as when meal services develop creative and ethnically diverse recipes (e.g., Hello Fresh, Gousto). This latter channel offers the added advantage of creating a broader customer base for traditional ethnic foods and dishes (as well as organic, vegan, and environmentally responsible foods).

These creative and innovative alternatives help reveal how traditional, linear supply chains can become constraints. Rather than being restricted to their "assigned" channel, growers, trade intermediaries, retailers, and foodservice outlets can seek more diverse connections, such as between ethnic farming communities and mainstream business networks. Various innovative networks (e.g., collaborations by micro-innovators, Internet ordering and delivery of niche specialty foods, platforms to showcase innovative products, adding "farm shops" or farmers' markets to urban settings or even roadside service stations) already have established new markets and connected previously separated supply chain players. When consumers worried about the COVID-19 pandemic more actively sought alternatives to mainstream, in-person retail shopping (Lopes de Sousa Jabbour et al., 2020), Internet and mobile technology formats gained even more promise for food supply innovators, while also encouraging wider collaboration among specialists within food networks.

Source

Hingley, M.K., Lindgreen, A., and Beverland, M.B. (2010), "Barriers to network innovation in UK ethnic fresh produce supply," *Entrepreneurship and Regional Development*, 22(1), 77-96

INDUSTRIAL SUPPLY CHAIN: KEY DECISIONS

Key Players

An industrial supply chain consists of two distribution networks. The distribution network for consumer products starts with the manufacturer and finishes with the end consumer.

The distribution network for industrial products starts with the producer and finishes with the buyer, as shown in Figure 3.5. The producer in the first network is the industrial customer in the second.

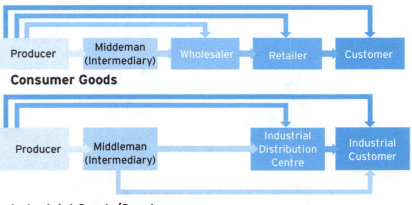

Consumer Goods

Industrial Goods/Services

Figure 3.5 Distribution Networks in a Supply Chain

In detail, a producer/industrial customer manufactures materials (raw materials, semi-finished products, finished products). In many industrial sectors (e.g., automotive), manufacturers have great purchasing power, but in others (consumer products in retail sectors), recent market trends have led to a shift in power toward retailers. The wholesaler is an intermediate link. Wholesalers generally rely on their own warehouses and fleets of vehicles. In some industries, such as pharmaceuticals, wholesalers control distribution and wholesale sales. Then the retailer is the last link in the distribution chain. Its financial ability and size usually determines its degree of influence over other members of the supply chain. For example, large retail chains maintain distribution centers that function as distribution warehouses for products. Goods obtained from different manufacturers and suppliers remain in these warehouses, and the retailers use their own transportation resources to deliver products to their stores. An intermediary might facilitate these processes between producers and wholesalers, often on a per-market or -country basis. An industrial distribution center collects and distributes large quantities of products to many businesses.

Thus, two types of distribution channels can be distinguished, depending on whether they include intermediaries: a direct channel, with products shipped directly from the producer to the customer, or an indirect channel, in which one or more intermediaries move products between the producer and the customer. The presence of intermediaries can facilitate and reduce the cost and number of transactions, which represent value-added services, but they also tend to increase the selling price of the product.

Vignette

Making Suppliers CSR Compliant

To achieve corporate social responsibility (CSR) in its business operations, it is not enough for a supplier to adopt sustainable production processes in-house; it also must control other suppliers upstream in the supply chain. Although suppliers are held responsible for the entire supply chain, such responsibility can be difficult to ensure. For example, many suppliers simply aim to control the sustainability of the next party upstream, then assign it the responsibility to check the next step, in a domino effect of responsibilities.

Another option involves nominations of sub-suppliers. In a study of the Sri Lankan apparel industry, Fontana et al. (2021) describe how large branding houses select sub-suppliers and designate which parties their direct suppliers may use to obtain their goods or raw materials. Although this approach allows branding houses to exert more control over suppliers and sub-suppliers, it imposed substantial pressures on the direct suppliers; they become "sandwiched" between the branding houses and their sub-suppliers, and they may seek good enough, rather than optimal, performance. The direct suppliers also complain that they knew better which sub-suppliers are reliable and responsible, so the branding houses' efforts appeared more like an attempt to gain power over the direct suppliers.

Source

Fontana, E., Öberg, C., and Poblete, L. (2021), "Nominated procurement and the indirect control of nominated sub-suppliers: Evidence from the Sri Lankan apparel supply chain," *Journal of Business Research*, 127, 179–192.

Strategies

Defining strategies for an industrial supply chain usually starts with a choice about what kind of relationship the manufacturer will develop with other members of the chain, which might range from occasional transactions to long-term strategic partnerships (Figure 3.6). Table 3.3 describes each relationship type in more detail.

Figure 3.6 Relationship Types in an Industrial Supply Chain

Table 3.3 Relationship Types in an Industrial Supply Chain and Key Characteristics

Relationship Type	Description
Occasional transactions	An occasional transaction represents the simplest relationship between two parties (supplier and customer) in consumer and industrial distribution channels. It has three key features: • Short time horizon. Both parties understand that there is no prospect for a future partnership. It is obvious that the supplier has low priority for the buyer, and changing suppliers is easy, without much cost for either party. The resulting lack of trust may hinder the exchange and information sharing. • Standardized, widely consumed products and services, on offer by many suppliers. • Focus on price, lead time, and quality of the offered products or services as performance metrics. Any change in the latter two factors leads to a change in the first factor (win-lose relation).
Regular transactions	In industrial supply chains, customers might order the same products and services repeatedly from the same supplier. The supplier's goal is to increase revenues, generally not with profit margins but rather through increases in sales volumes. Two key characteristics emerge: • The prospect of new orders and potential for a partnership in the future increases suppliers' interest and efforts in serving the customer. Repeated transactions create a climate of trust. • Performance metrics prioritize key logistics functions, such as the degree of responsiveness or lead times.
Short-term partnerships	If many customer orders are required, but the supplier fails to exhibit reliability on its own, they might enter into short-term contracts and agreements, leading to partnerships. The contract period is usually between one and three years. Their link enhances customer service while supporting win-win and lose-lose relationships.
Long-term/strategic partnerships	A successful long-term partnership features interdependence, trust, and information exchanges. It has one goal: to develop solutions that benefit both parties, such that one party's success passes through to the other party (win-win). This relationship takes on strategic dimensions, and decisions are made mutually, by the management of the collaborating parties. They commit to the relationship, due to their obligations, dictated by the terms of the agreement, but also their common goals.

Another strategic decision in industrial supply chains pertains to the adoption of a push or pull production philosophy. With a push strategy, the manufacturing firm knows that demand exists for a specific product, and it is in a position to calculate this demand with some degree of precision. Such scenarios often exist for branded products, as well as when historical sales data, continuous monitoring of the market, and effective customer relationship management with specialized information systems support good predictions. The manufacturing company produces and stores products, then pushes them to the market in a timely manner (make-to-stock production). If it cannot anticipate demand, or if the product requires too many resources, the manufacturing company instead might produce products once it receives orders. The order thus pulls production (make-to-order, assemble-to-order, order-to-order) (see Table 3.4).

Table 3.4 Production Strategies

Strategy	Details
Make-to-stock (production and storage)	By maintaining stocks for immediate delivery, this strategy can minimize corresponding time costs. It is feasible for standardized products with high production volumes and relatively accurate demand forecasts, or if the company produces a single product for a particular customer that orders large enough volumes (small variety, large quantity). The key priorities are consistent quality, on-time delivery, and low costs.
Make-to-order (custom-made production)	The product is manufactured according to the customer's specifications in small quantities, and the process starts after an agreed order, which prompts purchases of the materials. The competitive priority is the customization element; typical examples include construction companies and automakers.
Assemble-to-order (production/assembly of customized products from relatively few components)	Similar to the make-to-order strategy, as soon as a customer places an order, the assembly process creates the product by combining standardized, semi-finished products, for which the company is known, in large quantities. The manufacturing process should be efficient to keep costs low; the assembly process should be flexible enough to produce different products. Typical competitive priorities are fast delivery time and customization.
Order-to-order	This strategy is adopted by retailers rather than manufacturing companies. Upon receipt of a customer order, the company orders the product from the manufacturing company or distribution center. An example is the pharmaceutical supply chain.

4

ORGANIZATIONAL BUYING PROCESS, BUYING RELATIONS, AND BUYING BEHAVIOR IN INDUSTRIAL MARKETING

Learning Objectives

- Understand the key parameters of the industrial market.
- Define the context in which relationships between industrial buyers and sellers form.
- Outline the determinant variables that shape the behaviors of industrial buyers and sellers.
- Identify the nature of the relationships that determine the buying situation.
- Develop models of organizational purchasing behavior and understand how they can be constructed.

Case Study

Who Decides on Buying?

Organizational buying normally involves several company representatives on both supplier and customer sides. They perform various functions, at different organizational levels, and they often meet to negotiate deals with counterparts representing comparable organizational levels (Figure 4.1). As they get to know one another, buying also may become a habit, rather than the result of a careful evaluation of offerings.

(Continued)

In addition, procurement professionals often try to increase the focus on the business side of buying and reduce the power of suppliers. With preferred supplier strategies, the procurement manager negotiates with some set number of suppliers, seeking the best price. For example, the manager might interact with three suppliers, each of which offers a catalog of products with pre-negotiated prices. None of these suppliers is ever certain of getting the order. In addition, the procurement manager does not need to be part of every deal but can delegate some choices to more operational levels.

For suppliers, the goal has been to design more comprehensive offerings, which can help them sell more while also increasing the customer's dependence on them. Furthermore, more expansive offerings, such as those that integrate service offerings, increase the day-to-day interactions by representatives of the customer and supplier companies.

Comparing these two strategies, we note that both the supplier and the customer try to gain power over the other party, though in very different ways. The supplier tries to increase its relational connection with the customer; the customer aims to minimize it. The supplier tries to make the customer buy as much as possible from the supplier; the customer tries to spread its purchases across multiple suppliers.

Despite these differences, the two methods might align at an operational level, as long as the specific supplier is one of the ones the customer has identified as a preferred supplier. This designation implies that the supplier has been around for some time or at least has built some strong connections with the customer firm. In either case, these features should reduce the motives of the customer company to change to a different supplier. Thus, we note that operational decision-makers might base their decisions on parameters other than price; decisions at the operational level often reflect habit and personal connections; and intricate strategies attempted to gain power over a counterpart can fall quite flat, especially if trust exists in the counterpart.

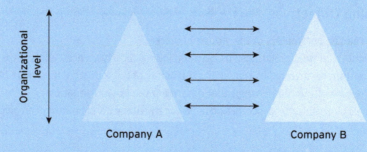

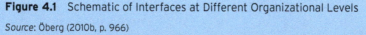

Company A   Company B

Figure 4.1 Schematic of Interfaces at Different Organizational Levels
Source: Öberg (2010b, p. 966)

Source

Öberg, C. (2010b), "What happened with the grandiose plans? Strategic plans and network realities in B2B interaction," *Industrial Marketing Management*, 39, 963–974.

GENERAL FRAMEWORK OF RELATIONSHIPS BETWEEN INDUSTRIAL BUYERS AND INDUSTRIAL SELLERS

The relationship between buyers and sellers in industrial markets is based on three pillars:

1 A high degree of interdependence.
2 Dedication to the relationship, such that they exhibit no drive to replace each other.
3 Mutuality and reciprocity.

These pillars reflect the broader context of the characteristics and particularities of industrial markets, evolving according to the type and quality of the interface over the course of their professional activities and interactions.

Due to the high degree of concentration, the derived demand, the nature of the products, and the size and frequency of the transactions, interactions tend to be direct and personal. Long-term, stable, close relationships develop, featuring collaborations and provisions of assistance. The partners try to resolve problems together and approach their counterparts' needs comprehensively, beyond standard boundaries of organizational responsibilities and duties. Within such relationships, the successful completion of a buyer's organizational objectives depends on the successful achievement of the seller's organizational objectives, and vice versa.

The term *inertia* represents the natural consequences of a long-term relationship characterized by a high degree of interdependence, in which the parties enjoy substantial relationship satisfaction. In this sense, inertia stems from devotion that develops in buyer–seller relationships, and it deters the possibility of change or termination of the relationship. Inertia also requires the creation of loyalty, as a prerequisite, which tends to arise from objective benefits, such as a partner's ability to achieve technical standards, its reliability and consistency in meeting business needs, and its professionalism or know-how. These factors can also be reinforced by other, more subjective motivational forces, such as effective relational management efforts. Commitment must not be parochial, and it must have the power to trigger, to be compatible and aligned, and to be tried and tested by all members' devotion, first and foremost, in the very company that employs them, and whose interests they serve and defend.

Thus, rather than a short-sighted approach that temporarily satisfies the needs of one party more than the other's, interdependence, commitment, and inertia in relationships function to induce alignment of and dedication to a broader framework of long-term goals. This interdependence and inertia framework also comprises reciprocity.

ORGANIZATIONAL PURCHASING PROCESSES

Transactions in organizational markets follow a step-by-step process, such that an organizational purchasing process consists of distinct, successive stages. Each stage entails decisions that lead to a particular outcome, and the final decision outcome reflects the entire set of processes. Accordingly, each stage also comprises definitions, partial solutions, and decisions. Once it ends, the next stage begins, subject to the parameters established by all previous stages. The significant dependency across stages produces an interconnected decision-making sequence, comprised of each individual stage. In other words, each stage configures the process by specifying (and limiting) any subsequent decision; each stage also can be a critical point of interest that functions as a filter, defining the increasingly limited set of alternative actions possible in the stages that follow.

The dynamic nature of this process means that the stages might be condensed, in terms of their time requirements, whether that means completely skipping some stages or tackling them in parallel. These decisions also depend on the dynamic conditions that inform each stage, from both within and outside the organization. Depending on the nature of the purchase decision, the external influences, the required number of stages, and the time each stage requires, the process will take varying lengths of time. If a similar purchase process or stage already has been completed in the past, or some critical decision variables remain stable, the solution might be achieved through a relatively quick, routine decision. If the organization also gains substantial experience with such decisions, it likely creates an efficient decision process and structure. In this case, even significant changes in the internal or external environment, which lead to temporary or permanent interruptions, likely can be dealt with effectively, because the well-structured decision process offers insights.

Even if some stages might be completed quickly or skipped, their significance remains, as does the value of their contribution to the overall process. That is, each stage is important, even if it gets skipped in some situations, because it transmits critical information and involves evaluations of relevant issues, which contribute pieces to the overall puzzle of the final decision.

An organizational buying process usually begins with the realization of a problem. Despite the generally negative meaning ascribed to this term, a "problem" is not necessarily unpleasant; it might involve the recognition of an available, unexploited opportunity. Perceiving a need or opportunity then should initiate processes to solve this purchase problem. The resulting mechanisms and procedures function to determine, for subsequent stages, potential solutions to the problem as they relate to product offerings (e.g., who, how much, when). In this process, the concept of a product is linked to the capacity to address a need or address an opportunity. A product is anything that can lead to such outcomes. Once the status and acquisition parameters of such a product can be identified, it can be developed to overcome a deficit, meet a need, or provide a better benefit, in ways that enhance the organization's competitiveness and standing.

To identify a need or opportunity, this first stage might involve searches of the internal or external organizational environment. If a need is realized, it activates mechanisms to identify relevant product attributes, characteristics, and properties. At this point, an axial frame forms (whether intentionally or not) that specifies and restricts the options for addressing the need (e.g., supplier selection, market timing, quantity). For example, a need to acquire high-tech equipment produces considerations of the specific properties and specifications required, almost by default at the earliest stage, which then excludes some potential options, such as suppliers whose products do not feature the desired attributes.

The second stage involves a general description of the characteristics that constitute a satisfactorily acceptable solution, and the third stage seeks a detailed specification of the characteristics the product must have. These stages thus build on and extend the first stage; their duration might be long or short, and they can also occur in parallel, depending on the parameters established in the first stage.

The fourth stage centers on identifying alternative suppliers that might meet the firm's clearly expressed need. In collecting and evaluating alternative proposals in the fifth stage, the firm invests some level of energy and time, according to the importance of the choice for its performance. If it already possesses most of the relevant information, for example, it might merge this stage with the fourth stage. But if instead the organization faces a complex, difficult purchase decision, the fifth stage likely is separate and extensive, such as when the decision requires involvement by top executives or specialized experts who intervene actively in the process.

Following the selection of the supplier, the sixth stage involves drafting a timetable and specific terms of an agreement regarding estimated delivery times and required quantities. The seventh stage provides a critical evaluation of the whole process. It offers choice safeguards; if a chosen supplier fails to meet the buyer's requirements, the buyer can return to an earlier stage and reconsider its options.

Through this purchase process, organizations aim to apply various relevant filters to achieve a rational decision, in a dynamically changing environment. Such careful applications of the framework are necessary, considering the importance of the decisions for the survival of organizations.

FRAMEWORK FOR ESTABLISHING RELATIONSHIPS BETWEEN INDUSTRIAL BUYERS AND SELLERS

As noted, industrial markets result from, contribute to, and derive from strong dialectical relationships between buyers and sellers. The relationship therefore constitutes an endogenous variable that informs, more or less directly, the formulation and definition of each other variable that defines industrial marketing. The character, nature, consistency, consequences, duration, durability, strength, and complexity of relationships can take disparate values and reflect a vast range of combinations (e.g., from simple transactions to assemblies of complex strategic alliances). But regardless of these variations, as a cornerstone for industrial markets, the buyer–seller relationship shapes expectations and thus the market overall.

Strategic choices also reflect the relationship form. For example, choosing the nature and complexity of the product to offer depends on the technical, economic, and personal features of the buyer–seller link and their high degree of involvement. In a strong interdependence framework, the relationship produces conditions of stability, security, and predictability within a particular environment, along with mutually strategic implications. Due to the central strategic importance of relationships in industrial markets, the focus shifts: from the product or a broadly defined market to a network of relationships including the buyer–seller link.

These relationships start from individual interactions of two enterprises, which encompass a range of dimensions and various levels of communication, negotiation, processes, and techniques to exercise influence, achieve operational sales or post-purchase support, and deal with countervailing markets. The available choices depend on strategic choices of a type of relationship; they also reflect cost–benefit comparisons of various relationships, to determine which are worth investing in, according to a relational marketing approach.

In industrial markets, buyer and seller roles often are adopted by groups, but a binary relationship approach is still relevant. It is an essential component of more complex social dimensions that develop through ongoing transactions. It also defines the frame for different roles in this relationship, such that the diverse dimensions are reflected. Accordingly, we examine the expectations of each party, related to each role they perform, as they reflect their respective interpretations and tendencies.

DETERMINANTS OF BUYER BEHAVIOR IN INDUSTRIAL MARKETING

Several factors determine how industrial buyers perform their roles and thereby can predict their attitudes and responses relative to sellers:

- Personal needs/motivations.
- Organizational needs/objectives.
- Confidence or perceived risk of the purchase decision.
- Stage of involvement in the purchasing process.
- Extent of exposure to promotional activities.

Needs (personal and organizational) drive behavioral actions; they evoke motives to address them. As the foundational motivations, needs influence the perceptions that develop about a situation. The proper and timely recognition and decoding of needs then creates the pretext for understanding where attention will be focused and the significance they evoke.

In distinguishing personal and organizational needs, we propose that organizational needs are a subset of social needs, reflecting their transfer to an organizational environment. They motivate behavior and action by highlighting the social needs of other relevant stakeholders. In contrast, personal needs should evoke a primary awareness and perception of the existence of a product that might resolve them. Selling effort by a seller is unlikely to be meaningful before the buyer realizes its own organizational and personal needs. Then needs start a chain reaction of practical activities, such as the chances that the seller tries to arrange a meeting to highlight specific points and present key information, and then the magnitude of the impact of such efforts on the purchase decision.

Another relevant factor pertains to the degree of confidence that buyers possess, which directly affects their perceptions of the risk associated with the buying decision. Such perceived purchase risk can also exert a separate influence, though its intensity tends to reflect decision-makers' confidence in their abilities.

A buyer's exposure to information about the product represents an equally important influence. Impersonal, commercial information exerts different effects than personal communication; the latter tends to be more effective for shaping and improving the buyer's attitude toward the product. That is, impersonal, commercial information transmitted through sales-oriented sources is unlikely to evoke a strong positive attitude toward the product. Still, industrial buyers are simultaneously influenced by both sources of information, as well as insights they can glean from the assistance and trading procedures they encounter. Furthermore, buyers might be affected by a range of relevant information, such as advertising messages or interactions with other stakeholders. The weight assigned to these different sources of information, when used to evaluate or reflect on decision options, strongly influences various stages of the buying process, in line with the product life cycle. In the step-by-step decision process, with its various questions to address, buyers need diverse information and access to a range of sources of information. Depending on the stage, the importance of each source and type of information varies, creating dynamic abilities to address their informational needs at each stage of the decision-making process.

FACTORS DETERMINING SELLER BEHAVIOR IN INDUSTRIAL MARKETING

Just as certain variables shape the role of industrial buyers, we can identify a comparable—and somewhat symmetrical—set of factors that shape the role of industrial sellers. These agents represent the sales organization, such that they tend to take on similar work tasks. The key factors informing their roles include:

- Personal needs.
- Organizational needs of their employer.
- Confidence in their ability to sell.
- Ability to understand their roles, responsibilities, the distribution of power, and jurisdictional limits at different stages in the purchase process, reflecting the different roles within the buying organization.
- Ability to sense other stakeholders' expectations of how the seller should perform its role.

The complex roles required of the seller can reflect conflicting or competing influences that in turn produce confusion and ambiguity. Such climates hinder the effectiveness of the selling system. Regarding others' expectations of sellers, relevant stakeholders likely develop these ideas through their interaction with the seller. In industrial buyer–seller interactions, each party must perform its expected duties, through a recognizable role-play that reflects the other parties' own behaviors and expectations. Social dimensions shape the role-play, by channeling prejudices, behaviors, value systems, and beliefs to influence the perceptions of the players performing the roles.

Expectations in turn derive from two main sources: corporate reputations and stereotypes. First, as signaled by source credibility notions in communication theory (Webster, 1991), the reputation of a source of information, such as the information the industrial seller provides by fulfilling an expected role, can affect how that information is received. Sellers who represent organizations with strong, positive reputations are more likely to receive a favorable response by performing their roles. In turn, sellers who perform their roles well further enhance the reputation, credibility, and image of the company they represent. Therefore, sellers' reputation, credibility, and effectiveness in performing their work roles depend on the credibility of the organization they represent. If that organization instead suffers a weak or negative reputation, such that its credibility is questionable, the expectations of the seller might be similar in valence. A possible risk arises with an extremely strong reputation for credibility on the part of the selling organization though, in that it might create disproportionate or unrealistic expectations for the sales representative.

Second, stereotypes filter the perceptions of sellers, such that buyers and other stakeholders likely expect a conventional, stable, and simplified approach to the role of an industrial seller. These expectations might vary with the prior experience of each industrial buyer, such that their subjective perceptions and applied stereotypes reflect the sum of a system of overall perceptions they have developed over time. In practice, stereotyping often produces an expectation that sellers will adopt fully sales-oriented roles, determined to exploit the buyer. But such stereotypes can hinder effective communication, because they lead buyers to erect barriers and express resistance to sellers' efforts.

Beyond these general influences, the roles that sellers take depend on the organizational structure around them. In this sense, organizational sellers operate in a gray area, between their company and the wider environment, and they function as bridges, communicating information, assistance, and feedback to and from the business and the environment. Their counterparts—namely, industrial buyers—operate and function in similar conditions. Therefore, the activities, responsibilities, and roles adopted by each actor reflect some common points shared by each business and the wider environment.

But at this interface, sales representatives take on a distinct and dual helping role, in relation to the company's efforts to meet the needs of industrial buyers. They listen to potential buyers and share this information with their employer, to help it derive and build a solution, in the form of a product offering. At the same time, they present this derived solution to industrial buyers representing their company. Through this two-way communication, a role performed by the industrial seller, the firm confirms and reinforces its customer-centric orientation, which is a necessary prerequisite for achieving corporate goals. For example, the industrial seller's receptivity to expressed customer needs clarifies the selling organization's perceptions of the buyer's requests, proposals, and demands.

Considering some common points for industrial sellers and industrial buyers, we note that for the sellers to perform their roles effectively, they might need to blur the lines between their organization and the environment, and this tendency may be reinforced by the way sellers perform their roles. That is, many corporate sellers spend most of their work time interacting with their "peer" representatives from the purchasing companies, often in close physical proximity. The relative lack of time and proximity shared with other members of their employing organization can lead to greater psychological distance and a loss of a sense of corporate identity—which might be replaced by adopting the corporate identity of the buyer company.

This shifted identification might be beneficial for understanding the buyer's problem and needs, but it can be deeply problematic when it comes to sharing and disseminating that customer information back to their employer. If the sales representative comes to take on a buyer identity, the sales organization's suggestions and requirements might seem irrational or opposed to the needs, goals, and strategies of the client company. Salespeople who express such concerns might gain a reputation as "heretics" within their own company, evoking suspicion among their colleagues. Although often necessary, simultaneous roles as transmitters and receivers of information, to and from the buyer and seller organization, often result in difficult, conflicting, or even mutually exclusive role expectations.

Adding to the challenges, salespeople also encounter competitive expectations that arise from stereotypical perceptions and the characteristics of the employing organization. Due to their dual roles, they might even face ambiguous expectations from both sides of the interaction in which they serve as bridges. For example, stakeholders at higher management levels in the seller organization need to establish their expectations of the individual seller clearly, consistently, and in a way that matches the organizational objectives overall (i.e., achieving one does not undermine the other). Otherwise, the role conflict suffered by the sales representative may be exacerbated.

In addition, top managers, who establish corporate expectations overall, must ensure that their own expectations are compatible with the expectations expressed by purchasing organizations. If they conflict, regardless of which role the sales representatives prioritize, they ultimately will suffer confusion about how they should be performing their roles. They would have no choice but to use their own judgment in evaluating incompatible or conflicting expectations, then prioritize and choose their activities, to reflect some expectations of their roles, likely in a way that facilitates the transaction. But the unstable, inaccessible, or incompatible expectations ultimately are likely to frustrate these important bridges, to the extent that they may stop trying to perceive buyers' needs or support the success of their employer.

Similar to industrial buyers, sales representatives seek to meet personal needs and achieve organizational goals; their confidence in themselves, usually gained through prior experience, background knowledge, education, or personality traits, is important for these actors too. Finally, the effective execution of a sales role requires sales representatives to understand conflicting expectations not just across buyer and seller organizations but also within the purchasing organization. Resolving the potentially conflicting expectations of the members of a buying organization can lead to success, so this effort constitutes a likely sales behavior.

Vignette

Customer Relationship Management

Customer relationship management (CRM) is an attractive concept that remains difficult to implement, especially for organizations that struggle to realize their own vision. In particular, some firms have trouble identifying the stage of relationships they have entered into with their business customers. To address such common concerns, Lindgreen et al. (2006) suggest a practical tool that can help managers identify and prioritize the most critical CRM aspects.

The application of their proposed approach to a case organization—one that operates in a competitive, business-to-business domain and achieves substantial success in providing lighting solutions to the automotive industry—reveals ten different CRM areas: customer strategy, customer interaction strategy, brand strategy, value creation strategy, culture, people, organization, information technology, relationship management processes, and knowledge management and learning.

In developing extensive lists of scale items for each area, Lindgreen et al. also established a systematic ranking, such that each area encompassed 11 scale levels (0-10). The minimum level 0 represents an immature, unsophisticated CRM structure; the maximum level 10 implies the CRM program is both mature and well-managed. Table 4.1 offers an example of the ranking for the customer strategy area in this vignette.

Table 4.1 Scales for Relationship Management Areas

Level	
0	We sell our goods to customers who are willing to buy. We have no criteria in place to select customers.
1	We have a customer strategy to select customers. Someone in our organization is responsible for this strategy.
2	We define customer strategies, which mainly are focused on acquiring new customers.
3	We base our customer strategies primarily on the needs of prospective and existing customers, rather than on (potential) customer lifetime value.
4	We analyze the lifetime value of individual customers to understand their importance to our organization. Different approaches, including activity-based costing, are used to calculate the value of individual customers.
5	We rank customers by their value to define customer segments. Customers with similar lifetime value are allocated to the same customer segment.

Level	
6	We set clear business objectives for each customer segment. We develop a corresponding value proposition that is consistent with these objectives, such as our selling and pricing strategy. In each segment, customers have the same lifetime value, but they can be differentiated by their needs.
7	We build and develop relationships with our most valuable customers. We continually analyze their potential, and we take actions to transform unprofitable customers into profitable ones.
8	We retain our most valuable customers by understanding loyalty drivers and introducing appropriate value-adding propositions. Moreover, we know why some customers defect and how to win them back. We increase customer retention by offering value-adding propositions.
9	We meet the specific needs of our customers, and our value propositions regularly exceed their expectations. We build unique relationships with our most valuable customers. Our customers prefer to do business with our organization rather than our direct competitors because we excel in creating value-adding opportunities. We review our customer strategy continually.
10	We develop excellent customer strategies, which create customer trust and commitment and drive our profitability growth. We are the top strategic supplier for our most valuable customers. To develop the most value-added goods and services in the marketplace, we collaborate closely with our customers to exchange knowledge.

With this tool, managers can assess the implementation of a CRM program by their own firms. An easy option is to create a scorecard that reflects the findings of the assessment tool, perhaps depicted as a radar diagram that is easy to present electronically and adjust as needed. Regardless of the preferred format though, firms can use it to monitor their CRM program implementation, promptly and constantly, both in general and with regard to target outcomes for specific customer segments. Whether the organization is failing to meet this target or even surpassing it, the tool provides a basis for a focused, strategic decision about how to allocate resources more effectively. When the case organization that participated in Lindgreen et al.'s study adopted it, the tool quickly took on a critically important strategic role.

Source

Lindgreen, A., Palmer, R., Vanhamme, J., and Wouters, J.P.M. (2006), "A relationship-management assessment tool: Questioning, identifying, and prioritizing critical aspects of customer relationships," *Industrial Marketing Management*, 35(1), 57-71

RELATIONSHIP BETWEEN INDUSTRIAL BUYERS AND SELLERS AS A DETERMINANT OF PURCHASE

The construction, maintenance, and enhancement of buyer–seller relationships over time inform their types and the transaction process they undergo. Determining the time horizon is necessary to establish objective targets on each side, that is, the outcomes required to call the relationship finalized and a success. These targets also need to be weighted and balanced, reflecting the range and scope of the processes involved and the rate of their completion. In turn, the buying context can form.

Different expressions of industrial buyer–seller relationships reflect the diversity of their strategic orientations, duration, and targets. An effective way to approach this vast diversity is to categorize the different relationships by duration. A transactional, circumstantial relationship has a short term; a relationship based on more solid foundations and planning lasts for a strategic and longer term. In Table 4.2, we present three configurations that describe varying intensities of buyer–seller engagement. The features listed in this table indicate and reflect the length of the relationship too.

Consider simple transactions to start. The contact is a circumstantial phenomenon, and if an automatic recurrence of a transaction or one-time purchase occurs, it would involve purely procedural efforts. The products are fully standardized, similar to other offerings or even perfect substitutes. Therefore, price emerges as a key determinant of the transaction outcomes. The buyer's perceived risk is relatively minimal; the high degree of product standardization reduces concerns about potential fluctuations in product performance, and if a buyer needed to switch suppliers, the costs would be minimal too. The parties do not make any commitments, so their relationship, such as it is, involves only procedural transactions, such as product delivery or payments. The simple processes that define this relationship are standardized, though rivalry can arise during price negotiations. Most interactions between the buyer and seller focus on reconciling their diverging expectations of the selling price, which is also largely a procedural issue (especially when tendering procedures are automated).

This simplistic relationship changes if either party begins to expect that it will develop into a more stable, long-lasting form. If this motive to alter the relationship and move to a more stable state involves only one side of the relationship, the equilibrium becomes unstable. The two sides' disparate relationship aspirations prompt disproportionate investments in the relationship, a situation that is likely to lead to discontent.

But if both parties prefer to move along the relationship continuum, even if their motives differ in intensity, the strategic orientation can shift. In this case, some common interests/goals likely have emerged, revealing the parties' interdependence, such that they see the possibilities of more solid, long-lasting, cooperative structures. This common ground and pursuit of mutually beneficial goals creates the defining feature of the relationship. Although price remains important, it falls in priority, behind other relationship characteristics, such as a long-term goal of better product quality. This outcome might be achieved through reliable product delivery and reduced total costs, both of which can encourage closer cooperation. Among the needs that encourage the creation of strategic relationships, the need to supply a more complex or specially tailored (and thus differentiated) product, available according to the requirements of a particular buyer, likely is primary. Such an approach requires bilateral investments in the construction and maintenance of the relationship (and its termination would evoke similar costs). Even within a network of interdependencies, the efficiency of the suppliers likely remains relevant. In addition, a monopsony relationship with one affiliated supplier would be rare.

Moving farther along the spectrum, we find strategic alliances: stable, timeless, and complex relationship forms. The degree of mutual dependency between the buyer and seller reaches its highest level, which could even evoke joint ventures. This logical development upgrades any relationship forms that emerged previously. Mutual commitments, with a long-term strategic perspective, might manifest as takeovers, mergers, or even consortia, such that two parties to a transaction become partners. Their transactions therefore transform into internal interactions, reflecting their merger and integration. Still, the determinants of the relationship start with individual efforts, with varying intensity, to address specific needs. Long-term, strategic relationships require greater intensity, which in turn can increase the tension between the involved parties. In particular, both sides need to disseminate strategic information, participate actively in product design efforts, enhance the functional interfaces (e.g., adopting just-in-time systems), invest in automated ordering systems, or pursue multilevel relationship building and development.

Although all these efforts, channels, and processes incur correspondingly higher costs, the cost–benefit analysis likely shows that the high costs can be offset by the long-term improvements in quantities sold, product quality and reliability, service provision (e.g., delivery time), and costs. These outcomes reflect the notion of an expanded product.

Moving along the continuum, from procedural, repeat-purchasing processes to the emergence of strategic alliances, the factors converge as follows:

- The degree of dependence on market forces is significantly reduced.
- The interdependence of the trading parties increases.
- Rather than supply or buy the product, the parties create strategically complete and integrated new formats.

Table 4.2 Continuum of Industrial Purchasing Cases

Industrial Purchase Cases	Simple Transaction	Stable Long-Term Relationships	Strategic Alliances
Parameters			
Bureaucracy size	Minimum to non-existent	Moderate	Large
Dependence on market forces	Complete	Moderate	Minimum
Existence of non-differentiated products	Perfect substitutes	Some adjustments to needs of the buyer	Complete adaptation to the needs of the buyer
Market type	Perfect competition	Oligopolistic competition	Monopsony

(Continued)

Table 4.2 (Continued)

Industrial Purchase Cases	Simple Transaction	Stable Long-Term Relationships	Strategic Alliances
Administrative costs	Minimum to non-existent	Moderate	Large
Investing in the proximity of the relationship	Minimum to non-existent	Moderate-significant	Immense
Perceived risk	Minimum	Moderate-significant	Immense
Cost of switching supplier	Minimum to non-existent	Moderate-significant	Immense
Obligations, prerequisites	Minimum to non-existent	Moderate-significant	Immense
Perception of time horizon in the relationship	Short term	Medium-long term	Long term
Kind of relationship	Occasional/procedural-handling content	Long-term strategic payouts	Strategic
Relationship independence	Immense	Moderate	Minimum to non-existent
Main concerns/goals	Price, cost of product	Product quality, availability, reduction in overall cost	Total systemic improvement of quality, cost, reliability, availability
Functional interface/integration	None	Small	Large
Product complexity/composition	Minimum	Moderate	Large
Importance			
Product price	Large	Medium	Small
Cost of product	Small (buyer) Large (supplier)	Moderate (buyer) Large (supplier)	Large (buyer + supplier)
Quality of product	Small to medium	Large	Immense
Reliability of delivery, availability	Large	Large	Immense
Product enhancement support services	None	Medium to large	Immense
Overall cost approach	None	Medium to large	Very important

Industrial Purchase Cases	Simple Transaction	Stable Long-Term Relationships	Strategic Alliances
Strategic system integration process	No	Not at all to a little	Yes
Orientation to industrial buyer functions	Supply	Supply	Product creation

ORGANIZATIONAL PURCHASING BEHAVIOR MODELS

The BUYGRID Model

The buying circumstance (or buying situation) refers to parameters that exist at a specific moment and that provide the structure for the variables that inform the purchase decision. For example, significant, long-term decisions usually involve mobilizing more complicated, time-consuming, and complex processes and include more participants. The time requirements then increase to complete the process, due to the heightened information needs and increased number of criteria used by decision-makers, whose perceptions in turn are based on their prior experience with relevant decision-making cases. Thus, the overall purchasing approach likely varies significantly with their level of previous relevant experience. If previous experience with the purchase process is similar and rich, it implies decision-makers have dealt with similar concerns, processes, and decisions in the past. In this case, the prior experience may take on such powerful influence that it represents the determining decision factor, rather than the product on offer.

Noting this situation, Robinson et al. (1967) propose a typology to link the relative experience of industrial buyers to the purchase process. They assert that the magnitude of prior experience constitutes a decisive factor in shaping the conditions that then define the purchase context. In turn, they predict three types of purchasing contexts, each of which reflects and relates to different levels of relevant purchasing experience.

New Buying Task Situation

In this case, there is a complete absence of previous relevant experience. The need or problem to be resolved and relevant variables define the decision-making process, without any input from existing knowledge or experience. Therefore, decision-makers have an urgent need to gather and process significant amounts of information to inform their perception and awareness of alternative solution options. The goal is not necessarily greater volumes of information though; rather, key considerations pertain to where and when the information can be collected. Active, systematically structured information collection efforts should start in the earliest stages, at the moment the demand becomes clear. To achieve differential advantages, the organization can establish its ability to produce viable solutions as soon as needs arise. By pursuing proximity and immediacy with primary sources of information, it can also test out alternative solutions and exhibit its effective, proactive approach.

The new buying task situation features a lack of any clearly structured or documented selection criteria, as well as the absence of any clear preference for a particular solution. It thus demands an extended solution process. The high levels of uncertainty inherent to these situations can be intensified if the strategic importance of the choice and its long-term consequences are greater. When the product on offer also entails substantial technical complexity or is provided by new suppliers without any reputation information, uncertainty surrounding the evaluation of alternatives grows exponentially. In response, decision-makers might rely on strategic considerations, such as relevant financial ratios or the company's business skills and capabilities. The long-term financial position of the organization relates to its competitive advantage and survival in the long run.

Finally, special attention must be devoted to the information transmitted by the organization. Contacts should be collaborative, such that they establish some degree of familiarity among other parties with the organization's behavioral characteristics, personality, or the atmosphere of decision-making centers. With a client-centered approach, the organization can attend to dynamically evolving needs, evaluate them according to the context, and identify appropriate solutions.

Direct Repurchase (Straight Rebuy)

For a direct repurchase, the organizational buyer's experience is significant, achieved due to its constant, repeated demands. It has little need for new information, because it already has gathered and recorded pertinent information to evaluate various alternatives and make choices. These insights are included in the existing knowledge pool and processes of the organization. Finding and evaluating new alternatives would be redundant and potentially unprofitable, without significant benefits for facilitating improved evaluations. Rather, to resolve the problem, the buyer relies on a routine and applies existing criteria to complete the purchase process. The existing choice pillars have been tested and validated over time; they also might have evolved through the process of developing preferences for specific products or suppliers.

Some variations may arise though, with relatively little importance in terms of defining the product purchase and proportionally minimal amounts of required information. For a less important product, for example, variations might arise in procedural completions of simple processes, such as shipments. For more important products to the business (e.g., accessories or components incorporated into the final product), even if they are subject to repeat purchases, the buyer might reconsider a range of alternatives. The cost also determines the execution of the procedure.

But over repeated cycles, order processing often becomes a reflexive, automated process. The presence of prior knowledge and experience, as well as well-structured weighting, evaluation, and selection criteria, free up administrative resources that are then redirected to addressing other strategic issues. As a result, the implications differ for suppliers that have already made sales and those that might be preapproved affiliates but have not been the selected supplier yet. For the previously selected suppliers, the goal is to strengthen the relationship and reassure buyers that they made the right selection. If they can detect new needs and respond promptly to them, these suppliers likely enjoy a strong and persistent relationship, encouraging longevity and cooperation.

However, for suppliers that have failed thus far to make a sale, the situation is a challenge. Even if buyers reconsider their alternatives, they usually do not encounter sufficient motivation to switch, because doing so does not offer enough benefits to offset the costs. It already feels secure with its existing knowledge, information, and choice structures, and its prior decisions already have been tested and validated. Disrupting this routine and switching from a tried-and-tested situation to a less-known one, involving unknown parameters, is risky. They lose the ability to predict possible outcomes, consequences, and extensions with confidence. Due to this perceived risk, inertial forces encourage acceptance of the status quo. To alter it, a previously non-chosen supplier must persuade the organization of the distinct benefits it could offer. This painstaking effort offers uncertain final outcomes. Therefore, a supplier that wishes to enter into a collaboration with a buyer might propose redesigning the process, to make inertia less appealing, by offering evidence of significant rewards that could result. Such an effort likely requires the supplier to take on the role of the buyer organization to demonstrate convincingly how its needs have changed or why its existing needs demand different weighting and responses. Revealing a gap that exists, then showing how it can overcome them effectively, gives the seller a window of opportunity and a chance to cooperate with the buyer.

Modified Rebuy

In this case, decision-makers have significant purchasing experience, but they also believe they can reap significant benefits by reconstituting or re-evaluating the range of alternatives and collecting additional information. This belief might stem from various triggers, such as reduced costs to acquire a product or service, improved product or service quality, and new options for extending key or complementary features. These developments drive explorations of new opportunities for collaboration and might allow for breakthroughs in a repetitive, routine purchasing process. Then the depth, breadth, and intensity of the resulting modifications reflect the strategic orientation and long-term, satisfactory coverage of needs.

If these two factors exhibit only temporary variation, investments in modifications probably are limited and based on an equally limited database. The range of alternatives will be relatively narrow. But if the firm encounters a significant, strategic, long-term shift, it would require a more active role, greater engagement, and expanded collections and analyses of information. Industrial buyers then might seek to expand their pool of alternatives to ensure as many suppliers as possible can meet their long-term needs; this option also strengthens the buyers' bargaining position. The degree of uncertainty increases and becomes measurable.

In turn, a supplier's appropriate course of action—or strategic orientation—differs with the proximity of their relationship with the organizational buyer: whether it is already included among the organizational buyer's active partners or even is its directly accessible default option. If the supplier has joined the close circle of already selected partners, its goal is to encourage an immediate repurchase, such as by understanding the benefits the organizational buyer might perceive from renewing or replacing its existing suppliers. Detecting causes that drive a buyer to consider a change, which also are likely to evoke immediate responses from existing supplier partners, can support troubleshooting to deal with conflict. Corrective actions and reorientation to achieve a better understanding and then meet organizational needs would helpfully redefine the relationship, especially in the event that suppliers have lost a clear view of buyers' needs.

In contrast, if suppliers are not existing or approved affiliates, their objective is to encourage redeployments and then convince the buyers to evaluate them as potential alternatives. Here, a proactive approach is even clearer: knowledge of the conditions, environment, competition, and existing or emerging needs of the organization all determine the readiness and ability of the potential supplier to cooperate with the purchasing organization.

The Anderson, Chu, and Weitz Model

Anderson, Chu, and Weitz (1987) investigate organizational buyers, emphasizing the relationship of emerging and novel data with information needs, and then their consideration of new alternatives. All three factors can define different buying circumstances (situations/cases). The findings confirm a strong correlation between new data and desired/required information levels, and then the degree of analysis undertaken by decision-makers. In contrast, the alternatives to be evaluated do not appear to correlate with these variables. Therefore, it appears that only new data and information needs define organizational market circumstances. With this research, the authors could map the shape and structure of buying centers, depending on the type of cases they manage. A proposed classification includes two groups of buying centers. First, some buying centers mostly encounter new market projects and purchases. In terms of their structure and features, they can be characterized as follows:

- Large in size, involving many stakeholders.
- More rigid and slower decision-making processes.
- No clear or defined image of needs or the suitability of potential solutions for these needs.
- Main priority is to find an acceptable solution at a low price.
- Open to the objective, sound consideration of non-cooperating or unapproved (current) suppliers.
- Less inclined to favor already cooperating and approved suppliers.
- Affected to a greater degree by technical staff of the organization.
- Assign less weight to the inputs of purchasing agents of the organization.

Second, other buying centers are more likely to experience repeat purchases or modified rebuys, such that their characteristics diametrically oppose the preceding parameters.

The Webster and Wind Model: Factors That Influence the Organizational Process of Purchase Decisions

In an attempt to develop an integrated framework of perception and understanding of the forces that influence purchase decisions in organizational markets, Webster and Wind (1972a) identify four variables: environmental, organizational, social influences and the buying center, and individual.

Environmental Variables

Environmental variables have a formative influence on information, rules, the value system, and the operating conditions and environment in which organizations operate. These influences get exerted through the (macro, generalized) external environment, such as political, social, economic, and governmental actors, as well as by the (micro, immediate) environment, as represented by suppliers or competitors. The resulting environmental influences comprise social, political, legal, economic, technological, and environmental variables. They are not static and instead change rapidly. Due to the permeability across these boundaries, they feature mobility and diffusion of influences. Any imaginary line, linked to communication or exchanges or clear definitions of the nature of the variable, disappears. Even if the timing, type, and size of the influence might be distinct, the very nature of the variable reflects the synthesis of multiple influential environmental variables. Detecting and tracing these types of influence is difficult, yet they are crucial to the organization, because they define the context within which buyer–seller relationships form and develop.

Particularly important influences that require careful consideration relate to economic and technological forces. An organization must constantly seek a clear view, challenging its own perceptions and broadening its assumptions, with regard to the market. It needs sensitive perceptions of consumer demand as well, to design its upstream production process. It should acknowledge the potentially international range of these interests and influences. Not all financial parameters are equally relevant to all types of organizations, but they exert some direct or indirect impacts on any organization's ability or its willingness to negotiate. Technological variables mostly affect organizational productivity and capabilities. The pace of technological change informs the qualitative and quantitative composition of the groups that the organization establishes to carry out the purchase decision-making process. Beyond team-based organizational structures, technology changes can influence the process adopted. According to Weiss and Heide (1993), in turbulent environments marked by high rates of change, organizations engage in more intensive exploration but invest less time in research, because of the relationship between profitability (gained from technology) and the corresponding investment in research effort to acquire its benefits. Time-consuming processes are costly.

Organizational Variables

The model recognizes four groups of organizational variables: technology, structure, goals/objectives, and participant. These four organizational subsystems interact to determine the organizational functions and clarify the objectives, attitudes, information requirements, and assumptions involved in the purchasing decision. Depending on the individual purchase situation, a particular subset of variables might be selected and applied to define the composition and function of the buying center. For example, the organizational structure consists of communication, power, rewards, prestige, and workflow variables. Within the communication subsystem, four functions (commands and instructions for information, influences, persuasion, and integration) affect members of the buying center individually, as well as the buying center as a group, to inform the purchase decision-making process. The power subsystem instead determines the strength of the members of the organization involved in the buying process, reflecting their ability to make decisions or exercise influence over other members. Then the reward subsystem determines remunerations for particular behaviors and interacts with the power subsystem to determine the limits of responsibilities of some members to evaluate and reward others. The prestige subsystem assigns distinct roles to members of the purchasing center and defines acceptable behaviors within those roles. Finally, the workflow relates to the procedures followed in purchase and decision-making processes.

Figure 4.2 Schematic Representation of Organizational Variables

In Figure 4.2, the group of organizational goals/objectives variables also comprises three dimensions. The goal-setting factors are defined by the step-by-step purchase process, as we described previously. A very important dimension pertains to the degree of concentration, which affects how buyers perform their duties in various ways. In particular, it determines the power relationships between purchasers and administrative personnel at higher levels in the hierarchy, who are responsible for organizational purchases across the enterprise; it establishes the level of formality that will govern the user–buyer relationship; and it specifies the channels of communication. Finally, the degree of concentration can determine (geographical) locations of employment and influence the sense of loyalty toward other members of the organization.

Social Influences and the Buying Center

Webster and Wind (1972b) argue that the buying center is essentially the organization's way of shaping a buying situation, which they define as a conscious perception that an organizational problem can be solved through a purchase action. Thus the buying center is made up of all the members of the organization involved in the buying process, due to their participation in the purchase process. The role of each member reflects the respective expectations pertaining to that role; the expectations of that role are defined by behaviors adopted within the role. It also shapes the network of relationships among roles within the buying center. Group processes result from interactions of activities and emotions; they arise in narrowly defined contexts for carrying out organizational tasks but may also relate to organizational achievement. Therefore, the buying center seeks to rationalize and manage the organizational purchasing problem; perhaps as a byproduct though, it also pursues more distant organizational goals, while encouraging the individual and group development of its members. Thus, a highly complex web of interconnections across roles, goals (organizational and personal), and participant characteristics forms (Figures 4.3 and 4.4). The external influences (e.g., environmental variables), organizational variables, and leadership of the group contribute to these roles and the center's operations as well (Figure 4.5).

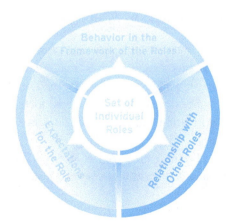

Figure 4.3 Set of Individual Roles

Achievement of Individual Goals

Personal Characteristics

Nature of Leadership

Achieving Organizational Goals

Structure of the Buying Center Team

Organizational Variables

Environmental Variables

Figure 4.4 Formulation Variables for the Nature of Buying Center Functions

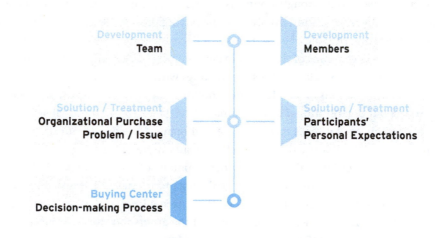

Figure 4.5 Results of Decision-Making Processes

The roles within the buying center include (Webster, 1991):

- *Users*. These members of the organization come in the most direct contact with the outcome of the purchase decision process, that is, the product/service.
- *Buyers*. Charged with authority and responsibility for the execution of the purchase.
- *Deciders*. Members who choose a particular supplier, product, and brand.
- *Influencers*. Contribute information and help formulate the criteria on which decisions are based.
- *Gatekeepers*. They control and manage the direction, size, type, and recipients of information.
- *Initiators*. By highlighting and demarcating the purchase status, their role is covered by the definition itself.

Some members of the buying center may take on more than one role. As illustrated in Figure 4.6, the expectations, purposes, and perceptions of such members who take on multiple roles influence the practices of the buying center, such that they are shaped by their roles within the organization too, along with their backgrounds and responsibilities.

Both practical and theoretical approaches also suggest other moderators of the composition and function of buying center variables. For example, the size and degree of complexity of buying centers tend to increase and include more functions, across different levels of the organization, when the degrees of uncertainty, originality, complexity, and investment of the purchase situation, as well as its importance for the organization, increase. Some researchers also propose clearer definitions of the dimensions that characterize the structure of buying centers and their interactive relations. For example, Johnston and Bonoma (1981) define vertical involvement as the number of organizational (stakeholder) members that influence the buying center and maintain communication channels with it. Lateral involvement refers to the number of distinct functions, segments, and sections of the organization involved in the purchase process; extensiveness describes the number of people in a communication network. Next, connectedness describes the development of interfaces of two members of the buying center among the set of potential interfaces. Finally, centrality is the total number of incoming and outgoing communications linked to the buyer, weighted by the total number of participants in the buying center.

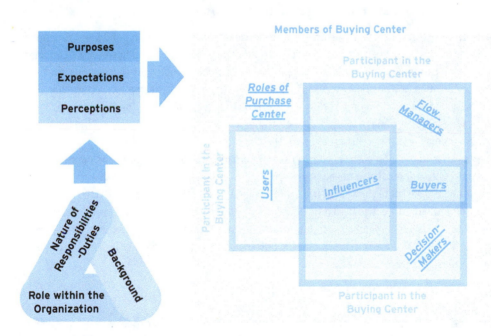

Figure 4.6 Buying Center: Role Mapping, Effects, and Relationships

Individual Variables

Each type of organizational behavior is expressed and enacted by individual behaviors. Decision-making, actions, and the definition of (purchasing) issues can be congruent and constituent of a wide range of often heterogeneous factors, but they ultimately are carried out by humans. Therefore, the buying process is strongly influenced by individual motivations, needs, and desires. A reciprocal employee–employer relationship offers a reliable interpretive tool for perceiving links and interrelations of individual goals with organizational goals. Individuals choose to work in an organization, motivated to meet their individual needs. Organizations use rewards to mobilize employees' behavior in ways that lead to desired organizational goals; rewards function as coherent links between individual needs and organizational requirements. The cohesive web of individual perceptions shapes employees' performance, and the way they assume their roles, within the frame of participating in the buying process, is valuable. Accordingly, the focus of sales campaigns should be members who make the decisions, not the vague notion of the "organization." Finally, in this organizational framework, collective decisions emerge from the combination of individual decisions and corresponding negotiations, discussions, and proselytizing, which evokes a shift in perspective toward common ground.

Vignette

Internal Functions Can Create Value for Customers Too

Value creation for customers is usually the responsibility of the marketing and sales functions of the firm. But quantifying value creation can be cumbersome, especially when we consider that it may reside with sales and marketing but can also be found in other functions, such as finance, logistics, and customer service, to name a few. Consider, for example, the close dialogue that arises between a firm and its customers during a delivery process. The focus moves away from sales and marketing to logistics and customer service. Thus, all customer-facing functions clearly can play a part in value creation for the customer.

But what about non-customer-facing functions? In particular, procurement might offer a relevant context in which to develop stronger ties with key accounts. At Maersk for example, procurement does more than serve the firm in which this function is embedded. Members of its procurement department seek to provide value outside the firm, such as by allowing customers to join Maersk's procurement contracts to achieve substantial volume discounts (sometimes even larger than Maersk's), such that ultimately the savings to Maersk increase as these partners increase the total volume and value of the contract they adopt.

Source

Bjerre, M. (2021), Interview with Henrik Larsen, CPO, A.P. Møller-Mærsk Group.
Morgendagens Salg (2020), Results from the research project. Retrieved 16 June 2022 from www.morgendagenssalg.dk.

5

THE MARKETING MIX: DISTRIBUTING INDUSTRIAL PRODUCTS

Learning Objectives

- List the marketing functions involved in distribution.
- Categorize intermediaries in a distribution channel.
- Elucidate the advantages and disadvantages of using intermediaries.
- Explain different types of distribution channels.
- Outline the key issues in transactions with intermediaries.
- Describe the requirements for effective distribution channel design and management.
- Understand the role of the distributor from different perspectives.
- Analyze distribution efficiency.

Case Study

Fourth-Party Logistics

Who needs fourth-party logistics (4PL)? Traditional third-party logistics (3PL) implies that an external provider offers logistics services to a dedicated client. But with 4PL, the external provider manages the overall process, which might involve multiple sellers and buyers, by combining a wide range of process, technology, and management services. In this arrangement,

(Continued)

all the parties contribute by sharing their available assets, such as systems capability, strategy development, and process re-engineering skills. Employees of buyer or seller firms might even physically relocate to the logistics provider's offices. Then the logistics provider, functioning like a tactical partner in the supply chain, leverages its existing knowledge and locates specialists to provide any expertise or capacity that it does not have immediately available.

Such complex, advanced supply chains have started to emerge in the UK grocery retailing sector, reflecting its long-standing tradition of innovating logistics and supply chain management practices. Hingley et al. (2011) detail issues related to horizontal collaborations based on their exploratory investigation of retailers, suppliers, and logistics providers in this retail sector, with a particular focus on 4PL providers, then offer some illustrative examples in a subsequent publication (Hingley et al., 2015).

Those studies can help us answer the question that opens this case. Figure 5.1 contains a typology of logistics collaboration, based on intensity and complexity features. At low levels of complexity and collaboration intensity, a transactional 3PL relationship may suffice, but if distribution complexity increases, a relational 3PL arrangement appears more appropriate. When collaboration intensity reaches a high level, 4PL arrangements are likely necessary, so that the provider can engage in physical distribution management on an arm's-length basis for customers, which may entail a comprehensive approach or else specialist input, depending on the level of complexity.

Hingley et al. (2011) also find that suppliers and logistics service providers offer divided opinions about the management and operational capacities of 4PL. Some logistics service providers express great confidence in their ability to manage such processes—enthusiasm that may have resulted from their existing operational efforts on behalf of a major grocer. In these efforts, the 4PL providers establish storage and national distribution of a significant range of products, and they also demonstrate their willingness to outsource as required.

But the logistics service providers also acknowledge that other firms tend to be wary and protective, rather than collaborative, because they fear the potential losses of business that could result from working together with competitors. Such concerns suggest the need for clear safeguards to facilitate 4PL collaboration; system transparency appears particularly relevant. Overall, suppliers seem to suspect that 4PL could disrupt their dynamic relationships with retailers. Another critical consideration is trust: some logistics service providers seek to establish trusting supply chain relationships but face resistance. The other participants worry that if they share their proprietary knowledge, they will be subject to exploitation. Among suppliers, the trust gap also manifests in suspicions that the logistics providers or retailers might use 4PL to generate extra profits, at the suppliers' expense.

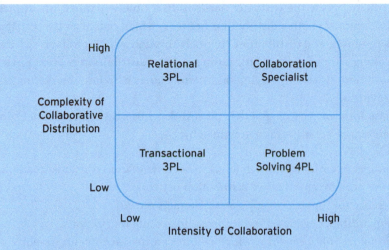

Figure 5.1 Proposed Typology for 4PL Collaboration

Source: Hingley et al. (2011, p. 319)

Sources

Hingley, M.K., Lindgreen, A., and Grant, D.B. (2015), "Intermediaries in power-laden retail supply chains: An opportunity to improve buyer–supplier relationships and collaboration," *Industrial Marketing Management*, 50, 78-84.

Hingley, M.K., Lindgreen, A., Grant, D.B., and Kane, C. (2011), "Using fourth-party logistics management to improve horizontal collaboration among grocery retailers," *Supply Chain Management: An International Journal*, 16(5), 316-327.

DISTRIBUTION, DISTRIBUTION NETWORKS, AND COMPETITIVE ADVANTAGE

With a product offer established and finalized, the firm must next pursue two main goals: introduce the product offer and its uses to existing and potential customers and then make the product available to these customers, at a place and time that is convenient for them. To meet the first goal, firms engage in promotion and communication with customers, such as by using personal sales or advertising. To meet the second goal, they must develop distribution processes and design appropriate systems.

Distribution must be understood as a process, which requires availability and reliability in the supply procedures as essential enterprise objectives in an industrial environment. This process also contributes to the marketing mix, because it ensures that the product is available in the place the customer needs it, in a timely manner. In turn, the distribution process comprises both a distribution network, which organizes the distribution of the company's products, and distribution channels through which products get transferred to customers along various paths. Thus, ultimately, the distribution process links production with consumption, usually by relying on intermediaries who form marketing channels and logistics providers.

The precise form of each distribution process depends on the environment in which the industrial enterprise competes, as determined by:

- The number of customers, which tends to be fewer than in consumer markets and thus limits the need for an extensive distribution network.
- A preference for suppliers to approach customers directly.
- Larger quantities, negotiated by businesses to execute transactions.
- Substantial technical expertise, which requires greater investments, resource allocations, training processes, and physical installations.

These factors define the number of intermediaries required to cover market needs, but they also structure the relationship between the supplier and those intermediaries. Unlike consumer markets, industrial relationships between suppliers and intermediaries tend to be closer, involving greater dependence, such that intermediaries make the supplier's product offer available to consumers and frequently add value to it, such as by adapting the offer to a consumer's precise wants and needs.

Added Value

In industrial markets, the distribution process provides a means to add value to the product offer, relative to the value provided by competitors. For example, if intermediaries provide faster delivery or efficiencies that lower the price of the product offer, they add clear value (see Figure 5.2). An effective distribution strategy thus exploits the value-adding capabilities of all involved intermediaries; well-designed plans can grant the business a sustainable competitive advantage.

Benefits Package   Distribution   Added Value

Figure 5.2 Distribution Enhances Product Value

Relationships with Other Functions: Consequences of Distribution Planning

The distribution process—as a business function and an element of the marketing mix—is not independent and should never be treated as such; it functions in relation to other elements of the marketing mix. To formulate a successful distribution strategy, a harmonious, collaborative atmosphere must support clear communication with other departments: sales, which provides accurate data to support efficient distribution planning and predict demand-related variations; production, which keeps distribution informed about when the products will be ready to ship; financing, to ensure distribution has the monetary resources to keep the distribution channels running; and so forth. Then this effective distribution strategy can support an effective marketing strategy overall, through cooperation across the firm.

The result should be a sustainable competitive advantage, based on several foundations. A well-run distribution process reduces the time required to complete orders. It can reduce overall costs, such as by achieving economies of scale through appropriate order processing and coordination. Finally, it can make better, more efficient use of the organization's existing assets. But on the flip side, a poorly designed, discontinuous, or ineffective distribution strategy—whether due to its design or implementation—will create serious problems, ruining the firm's reputation for reliability or even creating legal issues. Such detriments to the firm's credibility and market image are likely to lead to financial losses.

Push and Pull Strategies in Distribution

With a push strategy (Figure 5.3), the intermediary is central. Through personal sales efforts, it drives demand back to all levels of the distribution channel. In addition to generating demand, the intermediary is responsible for meeting demand when it encounters strategic pulls. Therefore, the entire marketing mix needs to be adapted to match the intermediaries' role, accounting for the supplier's dependence on them. Such push strategies, sometimes referred to as selective distribution, tend to be more common in industrial markets.

Figure 5.3 Push Strategy

With a pull strategy (Figure 5.4), the intermediary is more passive. By performing advertising and personal sales activities that target consumers directly, the supplier business takes the initiative to drive product demand. A pull distribution strategy usually involves a wider, rather than selective, range.

Figure 5.4 Pull Strategy

BASIC MARKETING FUNCTIONS FULFILLED BY INTERMEDIARIES

Distribution management and strategic planning aim to deal with the challenges of managing the resources and operations that are integral to a distribution channel. Such operations require resources (monetary, human). In turn, the need for intermediaries in a distribution network stems from the activities they perform to add value to the supplier company's product offer, including reducing the cost burden on that company. Yet due to the value that each intermediary adds to the product offer, the final price of the product often can increase. Maximizing the value for customers while minimizing the cost to the supplier is nearly a guarantee of success for an intermediary that can deliver it. Furthermore, a reliable intermediary frees the supplier to focus on its core operations and specialties, to the benefit of its ongoing operations.

Customers express varying demand levels, though the desired product quantity tends to be more consistent in industrial markets compared with consumer markets, whereas the variety of products requested might be greater. On the whole, the intermediaries reconcile existing offers with the demands generated by client companies. In so doing, they actually create more efficiency than is possible with direct channels, in which the supplier transfers the product offer immediately and directly to the customer. For example, the intermediary might perform the following marketing operations in a distribution context (see Figure 5.5):

- Purchasing: Ownership of the product is attained by the intermediary, so it also takes on the risk of a potential failure to make a final sale and earn a profit. The intermediary must purchase products from the supplier, and then it is responsible for reselling them.
- Sales: The intermediary searches for potential customers, makes contact with them, and then promotes the product offer to encourage a sale.
- Stock: The intermediary usually collects products from a plethora of suppliers and makes them available in limited bulk volumes, with a wide variety.
- Segmentation: Because an intermediary maintains a wide range of products in its stock, beyond any one supplier's offerings, it grants customers greater access to product offers that are more likely to meet their needs. If the intermediary receives a large quantity of products, it also can divide that quantity into smaller sets, to help ensure the products are resold.

- Mixing: It combines available products into groups, which reflect customer needs. An intermediary might gather a variety of commonly associated products from different suppliers to create a valuable solution to customers' needs.
- Financing: By providing credit to customers, as well as reducing stock, storage, and maintenance costs, the intermediary facilitates the exchange process. It makes the needed investments to maintain stocks and extend credit to customers.
- Warehousing: Suitable storage areas protect products from damage or deterioration, to prevent losses, then make product transportation and distribution easy and efficient. Because many products are installed in a specific, often central location, they are nearly immediately available.
- Evaluation: The intermediary can perform inspections, checks, and quality evaluations of products received from a supplier, to protect its reputation for quality among consumers.
- Transportation: The physical flow of products throughout the distribution network needs to be managed. This intermediary role is often referred to as the logistics function.
- Feedback: Because intermediaries are in close contact with markets of suppliers and of customers, they gain access to a wider range of data and information, such as product availability, product quality, competitive conditions, and customer needs. With these insights, they can contribute to the strategic planning process in ways that improve various stakeholders' performance.
- Risk: Intermediaries accept the uncertainty or risk of not making a profit from the distribution of products, in which case they would not be fully compensated for their purchases from suppliers. Moreover, risk arises from keeping stocks of products that may become damaged or obsolete.

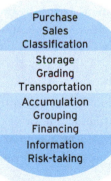

Figure 5.5 Marketing Functions During Distribution

TYPES OF INTERMEDIARIES IN THE INDUSTRIAL BUSINESS FIELD

Industrial business environments generally contain distinct types of intermediaries that contribute to the distribution network. Their presence can support marketing goals, because these intermediaries manage some transactions between suppliers and customers, as we detail in this section and depict in Figure 5.6.

Agents/Representatives

Representatives are distinct in that they do not acquire (physical or legal) ownership of the products. They tend to be highly specialized in the geographical area they cover or the categories of products they promote. Their contracts with a supplier define these restricted geographical areas or product mix, as well as the specific commission rate they will earn on any sales made. Representatives can market products from different companies, but usually they must avoid working with multiple direct competitors. Thus, their product assortment should include complementary offerings.

The use of representatives as intermediaries involves several advantages. In terms of maintenance of the distribution network, there are no large inelastic fixed costs; for distribution efforts, the costs are variable. Therefore, the supplier can maintain complete control over the marketing strategy to be implemented, including pricing decisions. Representatives also tend to develop a strong understanding of the particularities of the area for which they are responsible, which in turn can reveal important market gaps, predict emerging market conditions, and clarify the requirements of different consumers.

However, the use of representatives could be unnecessary or even harmful, especially when sales volumes increase, such that the cost to maintain a sufficient number of representatives likely becomes excessive. Representatives also tend to have limited technical expertise, so they might not provide much service or support to product buyers. Because they emphasize sales volume, representatives are not necessarily focused on sharing product offers with the most value for customers or that meet the strategic goals set by the supplier; they might direct most of their energy to product offers that generate the most revenue for them.

Brokers

Similar to representatives, brokers do not take physical or legal ownership of the product. Their primary role is to facilitate a transaction (or negotiation) between a supplier and a buyer. This function might be activated by a request from either side, then terminated once the negotiation finishes. Thus, brokers' relationships with clients tend to be relatively short-lived.

An advantage of using brokers as intermediaries stems from their ability to access a vast communication network, which they develop to reach businesses of interest. Brokers usually have a good sense of the market in which they operate and are aware of existing norms, as well as supply and demand trends. With well-developed familiarity with relevant products, the broker provides ready access to information pertaining to the product or the market.

A disadvantage of using brokers as intermediaries is the added cost because brokers also have to make a profit from the partnership.

Industrial Wholesalers

Unlike the two previous groups, the intermediaries in this case take physical and legal ownership of the product. Industrial wholesalers purchase products with the intention of selling them to companies that will incorporate them into their products, use them in their production process, or sell them to other distributors. Because this category of intermediaries performs most of the marketing functions in a distribution network, they sometimes are referred to as full-service intermediaries. If wholesalers cater to specific businesses, they represent the subcategory of general trade wholesalers. More generally, they can be categorized according to the range of products they carry, as general merchandise wholesalers or limited/specialty line wholesalers. The former offer a product assortment with a shallow depth; the latter establish an assortment of products with narrow breadth and greater depth. The biggest disadvantage of wholesalers is that high capital is required in terms of infrastructure, equipment, staff, etc.

Drop Shippers

By moving products from the supplier premises to the buyer premises, drop shippers help process the order. They do not hold or use their own facilities to store products, so the amount of operating costs they incur is lower. These limited service intermediaries tend to market high volume products sold without packaging (e.g., building materials, minerals, oil), which often are costly to ship, load, unload, or store, so they actively work to avoid such costs. However, sudden stock shortages are one of the most common problems sellers have with drop shippers. Other problems include more issues with customer service.

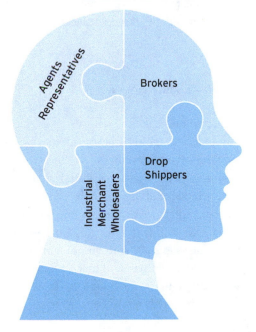

Figure 5.6 Types of Intermediaries

Advantages and Disadvantages of Using Intermediaries

Building on the specific benefits and detriments associated with each type of intermediary, this section lists first the overall advantages of using intermediaries, and then the overall disadvantages (Figure 5.7).

Advantages

Intermediaries as a general class provide the following benefits to suppliers:

- Additional sales staff on hand, as well as customer reach, to complement any efforts by the supplier's own sales teams.
- Extra visibility for product offers.
- Elimination of costs linked to low volume orders.
- Access to customers in particular locations, especially if the supplier operates remotely.
- Stock retention capabilities.
- Physical distribution of products, often immediately, due to closer proximity to end users.
- Information required to support promotional efforts (e.g., mailing lists).
- Networks through which the supplier can showcase and also promote its image.
- Facilitation of sales of product types and sizes that are difficult for the supplier to handle alone, such as seasonal offerings, such that the supplier does not need to hire additional sales staff during a busy season.
- Unique knowledge of and dedicated sales experience in specific markets, which also implies the existence of dedicated networks of contacts.

Disadvantages

Intermediaries impose the following limitations on suppliers:

- Loss of control over the distribution channel.
- Need to train, oversee, support, and monitor intermediaries' activities and functions, which demands additional operational resources.
- Potential loss of flexibility in sales efforts, such as offering price discounts. Intermediaries might not know whether such discounts are possible, or they might be overaggressive in promising discounts to ensure higher sales volumes for themselves.
- Need to coordinate internal sales staff with efforts by intermediary salespeople.
- Difficulties motivating external sales staff, who do not work directly for the supplier and thus will be responsive to different motives and incentives than internal sales reps are.
- Potential for external sales representatives to adopt their own tactics, which may not align with the supplier's preferred methods; these differences often reflect the conflicting interests of each party.

- Challenges in defining appropriate remuneration or commissions to offer to sales agents, internal and external, to avoid cannibalization and encourage cooperation.
- Potential need to identify the intermediary in promotional materials.
- Demands that the supplier adapt its operations or philosophy to match the intermediary's norms and approaches to ensure full exploitation of sales and marketing potential.

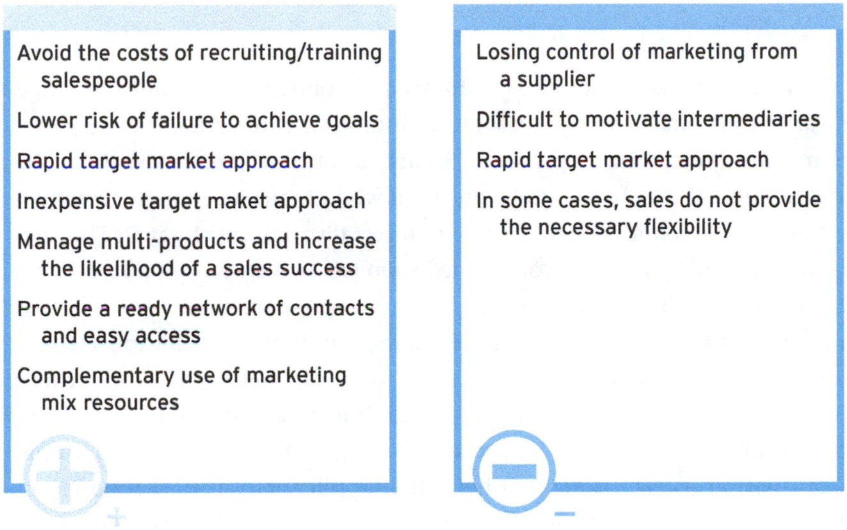

Avoid the costs of recruiting/training salespeople	Losing control of marketing from a supplier
Lower risk of failure to achieve goals	Difficult to motivate intermediaries
Rapid target market approach	Rapid target market approach
Inexpensive target maket approach	In some cases, sales do not provide the necessary flexibility
Manage multi-products and increase the likelihood of a sales success	
Provide a ready network of contacts and easy access	
Complementary use of marketing mix resources	

Figure 5.7 Advantages and Disadvantages of Using Intermediaries

TYPES OF INDUSTRIAL DISTRIBUTION CHANNELS

Industrial distribution channels generally can be classified as direct or indirect (Figure 5.8).

Direct Distribution Channels

In channels in which the supplier comes in direct contact with the customer, it can effectively personalize the distribution strategy, through close collaboration and communication. The flow of the product offer (which might include both material goods and services) along the distribution channel is completely controlled by the supplier's own marketing efforts. When suppliers adopt direct distribution channels, they usually serve a relatively small number of industrial buyers, experience high geographic concentration, and enter into high-value agreements that include highly complex product offers.

Consider the case of capital goods, for example. The sales process usually entails approaching the customer directly, because this product offer features complex, technical details that need to be explained to customers, and the company is most qualified to provide such explanations. These processes may be expensive, but what customers of capital goods generally are seeking is support, including installation by well-qualified engineers, intimately familiar with the product. In addition, customers may require extended, complicated post-purchase support. Thus, a direct distribution channel enables the supplier to promote and provide its own strengths and capabilities.

Indirect Distribution Channels

Indirect channels can take a multitude of forms and configurations, and the range of these channels varies from small to large, though for industrial enterprises, this range tends to be shorter than those for consumer products. Regardless of their precise specifications though, indirect distribution channels tend to be preferred when there are enough customers to serve that they cannot be accommodated by a single, direct distribution channel. They may also be more actively adopted by resource-constrained suppliers, which cannot afford to hire a huge sales force or maintain their own inventory and warehouse operations.

Beyond these sorts of constraints that encourage indirect distribution channels, some benefits also underlie this choice. For example, they can help companies enter new and unfamiliar markets, in which the supplier lacks necessary experience and knowledge. Intermediaries also reduce the risk associated with growth efforts, by providing relevant information about the new market that helps the supplier craft its product offer more effectively. Even in existing markets or for standardized product offerings such as raw materials though, suppliers might not want to provide extensive customer service, so the use of intermediaries can provide a link to customers, without requiring the supplier to engage in non-core operations.

Indirect distribution channels require careful considerations of how to ensure the intermediaries' commitment to the project, as manifested in their contributions and investments of operational resources, throughout the distribution channel, as well as their willingness to coordinate with other channel members to ensure coherent flows of information. Ideally, strong integration of the individual functions would create a type of joint venture, such that the overall distribution structure functions like its own organization.

Figure 5.8   Direct and Indirect Distribution Channels

Multichannel and System Approaches

A pluralistic multichannel system (Figure 5.9) involves the use of many different channels to approach the market, such that each channel takes responsibility for different products or product groups. The associated targeting then pertains to distinct market segments. A monolithic multichannel system instead comprises both indirect and direct channels, which the company establishes to gain access to a customer base. The members of each channel adjust the functions they perform, depending on their client group. This structure provides good flexibility and integration among channel members.

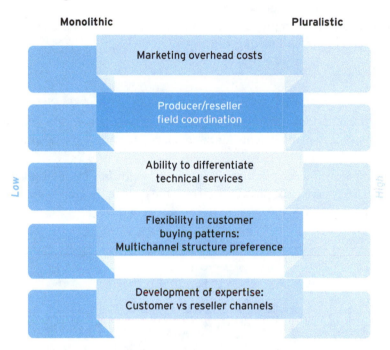

Figure 5.9 Different Multichannel Approaches to Distribution Systems

Source: Adapted from Brennan et al. (2014)

Activities in Indirect Channels

When suppliers select indirect distribution channels, they expect the intermediaries to undertake the following activities (Figure 5.10).

Communication

All communication activities with the target customers are managed throughout their geographical distribution. Communication can be achieved through the use of advertising as a tool, but even more so through the use of executives who make up the sales staff while being responsible for the task of establishing and managing contact with customers, as well as receiving orders from them.

Interventions in Product Offers (Modifications or Assemblies)

Depending on the item, some kind of intervention may be required to adjust the product provided by the supplier. Its components can be modified or used to assemble a new product that meets customer-specific requirements, for example.

Facilitate Product Supply

To ensure product availability, especially for local demand, intermediaries need to maintain sufficient stocks and then provide valuable resources to facilitate trade, such as advice and guidance on product features or product selection, commercial and logistics support, credit or financing, order processing, and product delivery.

Maintenance and Repair Services

If suppliers and their customers are located far away from each other, intermediaries should take on the role of maintenance agents for the products, holding them in locations that are closer to the customers.

As these expectations indicate, indirect distribution might not be appropriate for service providers, which likely need to be physically present and close to the consumer to ensure ready service availability.

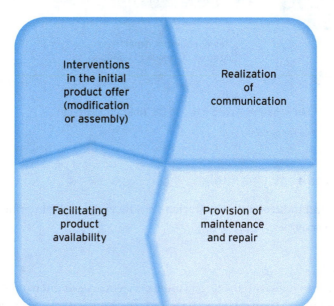

Figure 5.10 Intermediate Activities During the Implementation of an Indirect Distribution Channel

Industrial Electronic Distribution Networks

Electronic commerce resulted from advances in information technology and related tools (personal computers, information systems, the Internet). The affordability and benefits thus created sowed a fertile ground for exploiting the potential of industrial enterprises and prompted many of them to create new channels. In particular, electronic distribution channels help reduce the cost of intercompany transactions. In this new channel format, new types of (electronic) intermediaries have also emerged, whether traditional forms that took on electronic elements or new forms. Thus, we define three basic types of electronic intermediary systems (Figure 5.11):

- Seller system. The seller has an electronic trading system, which buyer businesses can use. Depending on the sophistication of the process developed by the vendors, well-configured websites can establish appropriate settings and adjustments to meet the needs of individual buyers.
- Buyer system. Tailored websites maintained by the buyer allow sellers to submit offers. This process makes sense if the buyer has particularly high requirements, such as in terms of the volume of supplies or the purchase amount required to satisfy its production process. In this system, the buyer likely takes the initiative in terms of initiating communication, and a relationship may develop with the supplier business.
- Intermediary system. Here, the philosophy shifts between the two preceding ones. The purpose of such systems is to facilitate the approach of the supplier and selling businesses (and vice versa) but also to enable their own transactions among themselves.

Figure 5.11 Electronic Intermediate Systems

KEY POINTS WHEN SELLING TO INTERMEDIARIES

Some key points associated with selling to intermediaries, after the distribution channel has been determined, are as follows:

- Confirm the intermediaries can maintain appropriate stock levels, in expected and safe conditions.
- Provide on-site support to ensure employees of the intermediary sell and distribute the product properly.
- Design and evaluate training programs, to cover topics such as technical issues and product details, as well as sales skill capacity building.

- Consider whether to establish parallel direct and indirect channels, which may help direct intermediaries' efforts.
- Engage in joint efforts to achieve sales, as needed.
- Conduct advertising campaigns, public relations, and promotional procedures to establish and maintain a reputation and brand name for the product, among both intermediary representatives and end customers. Such efforts might involve joint efforts too.
- Undertake marketing planning to coordinate multiple intermediaries that might be operating in the same distribution channel.

Even if intermediaries ultimately acquire roles similar to customers of the supplier or even partners with it, the conditions must be shaped strategically to ensure long-lasting, harmonious relationships. Such efforts can lead to a deeper understanding of how the distribution process works and inform better operational decisions.

DISTRIBUTION CHANNEL DESIGN

Improving the distribution process by design can significantly reduce cost burdens. Such reductions might even be greater than the optimization costs that accrue at other operational levels. In addition, because the distribution process is dynamic and constantly changing, design and revision efforts need to be ongoing too. Decisions made in the past, related to the design of a distribution channel, may need to change, especially if new information and data emerge during a process, as well as to reflect altered balances of responsibilities or power due to their evolution over time.

In this sense, we can describe the process of designing a distribution channel metaphorically as similar to the construction of a building with different parts, which together and individually are indispensable to keeping the building upright and to withstanding time and environmental conditions. We detail the elements of such design efforts, as illustrated abstractly in Figure 5.12, next.

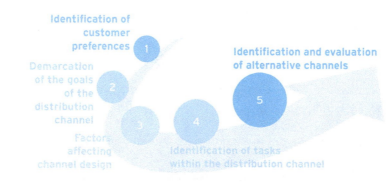

Figure 5.12 Design Elements of an Industrial Distribution Channel

Source: Adapted from Tomaras (2009)

Identification of Customer Preferences

From a marketing perspective, the customer must take center stage in the design process. Designing an industrial distribution channel requires accounting for industrial customers' preferences, such as the types of intermediaries they like to use or the channels they choose to activate. Just as a construction designer must know whether the buyer wants a house, an apartment building, or an office space built, the parties responsible for designing the distribution channel need to understand what customers value and how to match their preferences. By using customers' shopping habits and preferences to inform the distribution channel configuration, it is also possible to align the design with the goals of the supplier. This supplier must ensure that the comments and instructions provided by the customer are taken seriously, such that they become integral to the framework of the building itself, to demonstrate the supplier's willingness to comply with customers' demands.

Demarcating Distribution Channel Goals

The objectives the distribution channel is designed to achieve reflect the desired results that the company establishes, which might be financial factors or otherwise. Just as a building designed for commerce differs from one designed to house people, the purpose and objectives of the distribution channel can differ; in turn, they need to align with the planned business and marketing strategies. However, the organization must take care, because goal setting can conceal cost elements that may be more or less perceptible and observable. Nor should the company assume that, just because it has not found any challenges to its operations yet, they will not arise later. Buildings need to be able to withstand extreme weather conditions, even if no big storm has hit the area lately; similarly, distribution channels need to be designed to ensure they can achieve their objectives, even if conditions change radically.

Complicating this element is the potential for the various goals embraced by each business to differ, depending on each party's needs and strategic orientations. Yet the distribution channel design process also offers a unique opportunity to define clear objectives, such as ensuring a means to market the product directly to buyers, reducing the costs of operating the channel, increasing brand name recognition in the market, optimizing feedback procedures, determining competitive prices for the product, and ensuring the smooth physical flow of products.

Factors Affecting Channel Design

Factors from the market, competitive conditions, and the wider environment can influence or obstruct channel design. Some of them might be controlled, but not all of them can be, and their potential effects can be more or less intense. Although there are a vast number of potentially influential factors, we detail four broad categories here:

- Geographic dispersion of customers: If there are many customers, spread across a large geographical distribution, it would be illogical to implement a direct distribution channel. If geographical concentration is greater though, shorter distribution channels might be optimal.
- Product characteristics: Expensive, complex products might benefit from direct distribution channels, which emphasize the contributions of the supplier company's expert staff. A product's life cycle stage also can affect distribution channel designs, such that a product in its early life cycle (introduction and development phase) may need a more direct approach, to introduce and explain it to customers. As it matures though, the use of indirect distribution channels may become more appropriate.
- Competitive characteristics: If a distribution channel confronts stringent competition, the supplier must make a critical decision: use intermediaries in an existing competitive configuration or find new agents without relationships with competitors.
- Operational resources and capabilities: The size and capabilities of the business also determine its preferred distribution channel. A large-scale, high-capacity business likely can afford to implement a direct sales distribution channel, effectively support its own sales staff, maintain storage areas, and develop effective handling systems, for example. A small, resource-constrained company instead might need to rely on more experienced, knowledgeable intermediaries.

Identification of Tasks Within the Distribution Channel

For a channel to be efficient and effective, the tasks it encompasses must also be specified. Similar to designs of elevators in buildings, these tasks represent the processes by which the channel meets both strategic organizational goals and customer needs. In defining these tasks, the channel needs to be broken down into a series of activities, to clarify what actions to take and their order of priority. Then it becomes possible to make decisions about which members of the channel should be assigned which activities, to achieve a fair sharing of responsibilities across the channel.

- With regard to the purchase decision task, the elevator might go to the very top: Executives should take the responsibility if the purchase is critical to the organization, infrequent, poses a significant risk, or requires a very high price. In this case, a direct channel is likely preferable. But mid-level managers might take over the purchase decision task for purchases that feature little market risk, low costs, and greater frequency. In these cases, intermediaries may also be more effective, from both financial and service-level perspectives, such as when the transactions involve automatic straight rebuys or slightly modified rebuy decisions.
- It is necessary to find the most efficient means—depending on the nature of the problems an industrial product is meant to solve—to serve the customer. The product offer must address the customer's expressed needs; the service and delivery functions must be carried out quickly, which may require using intermediaries.

- The decision of how many intermediaries to include depends on the company's positioning strategy, the markets it has identified as targets, the marketing mix it has formulated, and the characteristics of the product (specific features). Then the distribution policy must match these elements, because any discrepancy might cause problems with respect to product usage and perceived image (among channel members and end users).

There are three main types of distribution policies: intensive, selective, and exclusive distribution. First, intensive distribution is designed to maximize product availability in the market; this option does not impose any particular requirements or increase the knowledge and competence required of intermediaries. Rather, it implies the inclusion of many intermediaries that differ from one another to cover the widest market possible, in line with the distribution channel design. In the case of selective distribution, if the target market embodies specific characteristics or the supplier needs to establish a clear image and reputation, aligned with specialized preferences and purchasing habits, a selective distribution strategy can create criteria to ensure all the chosen intermediaries have the qualifications preferred by the target market. Finally, an exclusive distribution strategy implies that only one intermediary has the right to distribute the product offer, as least in each market. The chosen intermediary should have a strong image of its own, based on its extensive knowledge, resources, and competencies, so that its promotion of the product offer confirms or heightens its appeal. Exclusive distribution is a powerful means of establishing an organization's position.

Identification and Evaluation of Alternative Channels

Identification

At this stage, the designer needs to identify available distribution channels and make appropriate decisions to configure those channels. The first major decision pertains to the length of the channel, as represented by the number of intermediaries (i.e., number of levels)—similar to a decision about the number of floors a building should contain. This channel length determination establishes distribution intensity, which distribution policy alternatives are available, and the distribution channel mix. The resulting scope of the indirect distribution channel also depends on the level of product risk, purchase frequency, delivery requirements, necessary technical advice, and services required to support the product offer.

Then the next key decision pertains to the type of intermediaries to include in the distribution channel, as previously outlined (e.g., representatives, drop shippers). The choice of optimal intermediary types depends on the characteristics of the different types and the tasks they might be able to perform, as established during prior channel design stages. Another important factor is the number of heterogeneous target markets the supplier wants to reach, which likely differ in their purchasing habits and preferences.

To identify suitable candidates to include in the distribution channel, channel designers might review the competitive arena and existing intermediaries. They could also gather information from government agencies. Suitable candidates likely participate in trade fairs and industry events too. Having identified such candidates, the organization must apply clear, unambiguous criteria to evaluating them (Figure 5.13), such as the potential intermediaries' available business resources, other product offers, marketing opportunities, and willingness to adopt and commit to achieving the previously set channel objectives, as well as the financial position of the prospective intermediary, the reputation or image it has built in the market, its type and level of specialization, the geographical area it covers, and its sales or support capabilities.

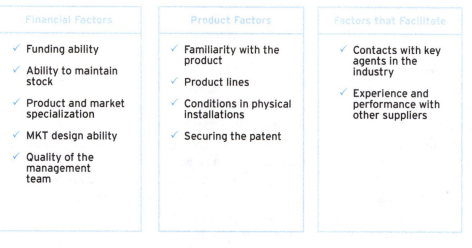

Figure 5.13 Evaluation Factors for Selecting Intermediaries

Source: Adapted from Cavusgil et al. (1995)

In addition to selection procedures adopted by a supplier, the distribution channel design process involves intermediaries' choices. They evaluate prospective supplier partners, to decide whether they want to distribute its product offers, according to the criteria listed in Figure 5.14.

A third key decision pertains to the number of channels to include in the distribution mix and the extent to which it will rely on multichannel distribution systems. This decision mostly depends on whether the multiple markets targeted by the distribution channel differ in their purchasing preferences and the extent to which products in different life cycle stages can be serviced by a single network.

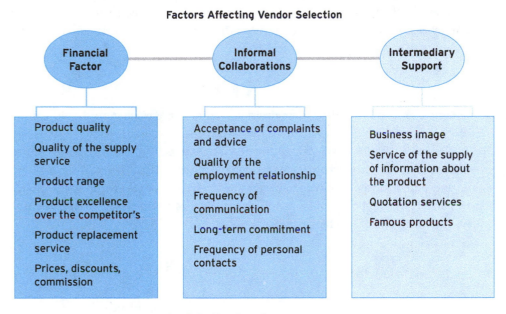

Figure 5.14 Evaluation Criteria for Selecting Suppliers

Source: Adapted from Shipley and Prinja (1988)

Some frequently used distribution channels include sole or area distributors, stockers, commission agents, dealers, and retailers. Other alternatives are private stores or franchising. Some newer options that also might function as effective channels are telemarketing, teleshopping, and Internet shopping. Along with determining which channels to include, decision-makers must consider whether their use should be simultaneous, so that they function as complementary (cf. competing) channels. If multichannel distribution systems with hybrid marketing channels can be established, they promise great efficiency and low costs, due to:

- Undifferentiated sales flow: The business can deliver its products to a target market using multiple distribution networks.
- Differentiated sales flow with product differentiation: The firm can market different products through different channels in the same target market.
- Differentiated sales flow with target market differentiation: The business can market its products through each channel that addresses a different target market using multiple distribution networks.

Such systems can lead to sales expansions, greater market coverage, and better adaptation to the specific requirements of the target market. Of course, they also impose heightened control and evaluation demands. Resolving conflicts among competing intermediaries that are seeking more customers, sales, or scope of action can also be very difficult.

However, the advantages of this approach can be better exploited, and its challenges overcome, with the use of advanced IT. Although it may be easier to manage the simultaneous efforts of multiple channels with IT, some problems remain thorny, such as coordination across channel elements, conflict resolution within the distribution networks, and monitoring the effectiveness of each component of the network.

Evaluation

Once the design process has settled these decisions, an ongoing evaluation should consider all the selected alternatives. Such evaluations can be difficult, because they rely on a snapshot of a particular place and time, even though the relevant inputs (e.g., sales volume, cost data, expected sales) are inherently dynamic and evolving. Collected data can reveal the evolution over time and potential trends, but the image captured in any single snapshot will change, sooner or later. The best choice today may be completely different from the one identified yesterday, and it will also likely change tomorrow.

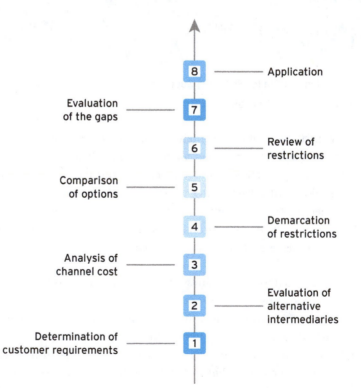

Figure 5.15 Evaluation of Alternative Distribution Channels

Source: Adapted from Stern and Sturdivant (1987)

If the channel design process suggests adapting existing structures to a new situation, it represents a relatively easy process. But if the company needs to redesign all its structures, it has to explore more available alternatives. To derive a general approach to such evaluations of the suitability and attractiveness of alternative channels, please refer to Stern and Sturdivant's (1987) model (Figure 5.15). In this approach, some ideal channel exists that perfectly meets the client's needs, but a more viable channel might also exist, and the existing channel might differ from both of these. By considering these three channels (ideal, viable, existing), the evaluation might reach three possible conclusions:

1 The channels are identical. In this case, nothing needs to change, and the focus should be on keeping the situation stable by managing any complaints or outside disruptions.

2 The existing channel and viable channel are similar but not ideal. The business should investigate and perhaps address its limitations, assumptions, and formulated goals, because the approach it seeks does not appear realistic.

3 The channels differ significantly. Here, the firm needs to reconsider the relative positions of the channels. If the viable channel sits between the ideal and existing versions, the existing channel can be upgraded, which does not necessarily affect previously set goals.

Furthermore, channel evaluations should rely on quality as well as quantity. Certain parameters—such as the degree to which the business can maintain control over the channel, "hear" the market through the distribution channel, or adapt channel elements to respond to changes during system modifications—contribute significantly to effective evaluations of alternative channels.

Even after selecting and evaluating various channels, the designer's work is not done. To ensure proper operations and appropriate adaptations to emerging environmental changes, it must establish control procedures that keep the distribution channel operating as effectively and efficiently as possible. Finally, the business needs to resolve daily issues, a function more commonly known as distribution channel administration.

In Figure 5.16, some of the critical points of the vendor selection process are depicted.

Vignette

How 3D Printing Is Reshaping Supply Chains

Additive manufacturing—or 3D printing—as a technological development implies that a customer can print goods, rather than buy them from a supplier. But it also challenges several positions in a supply chain. Additive manufacturing can consist of rapid prototyping or rapid manufacturing. Rapid prototyping alters the innovation process, such that solutions can be printed early to evaluate them as full-scale, three-dimensional products. Rapid manufacturing instead allows

(Continued)

products to be printed on demand, such that firms can avoid having to buy spare parts and instead print them as needed.

In addition to speeding up the design and manufacturing of goods, additive manufacturing might allow goods to be manufactured with different structures (cf. solid materials), take different forms (e.g., more organic than conventional mechanical parts, printed in one piece rather than requiring assembly). From a supply chain perspective, internalizing production can decrease the need for upstream suppliers and logistics services. Moreover, manufacturing techniques based on powder or thread-based printing, derived from drawings, would eliminate the need for some types of tools, obtained from specialized suppliers. This development should shorten the supply chain, lead to more of its activities being internalized by the manufacturing firm, and support greater customization. Scholars thus identify an overall shift, from a supply chain to a demand chain, as a key consequence of additive manufacturing.

Source

Öberg, C., and Shams, T. (2019), "On the verge of disruption: Rethinking position and role— The case of additive manufacturing," *Journal of Business and Industrial Marketing*, 34(5), 1093-1105.

DISTRIBUTION CHANNEL ADMINISTRATION

The goal of distribution channel administration is to ensure that the distribution network always runs smoothly. Such operations might identify specific intermediaries with which to cooperate, engage in efforts to attract them, conduct training, and resolve any conflicts or disputes. Because the necessary process of selecting intermediaries can and should be repeated, administration efforts can help optimize distribution channel staffing or fill any gaps due to prior rearrangements. Failing to administer the distribution processes carefully can lead to diminished customer satisfaction or undermine relationship trust, as well as damage the reputations of the involved parties.

Enrolling Intermediaries

To become intermediaries in a distribution channel, candidates might be recommended by customers, agents, other businesses in the market, or specialized media for an industry. The supplier then should assess whether the goals it has set align with the goals and strategies of these independent companies. Only if they align can the companies cooperate effectively within the distribution channel. If candidates are judged suitable for joining the distribution channel, such that a working relationship is promised, it becomes necessary to clarify partnership terms and define how that relationship will develop, to avoid misunderstanding

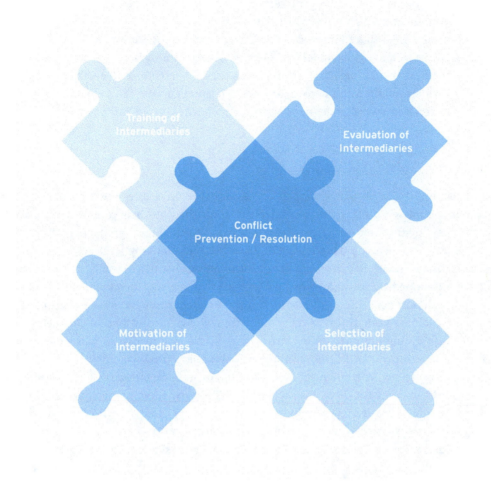

Figure 5.16 Focal Points for Optimal Vendor Selection

and friction. Partnership terms should specify the type of products to be delivered and the type and level of services available to customers. In addition, the level of remuneration and support the intermediary will receive from the supplier must be clear, along with the geographical boundaries of its operations and its jurisdiction over customers that might be considered key accounts for certain areas. The detailed terms of the cooperation should be documented in writing, from the beginning of the relationship, to exclude any possible ambiguity with respect to the rights and obligations of each party.

In addition, supplier-driven incentive methods should provide clear motivation for the intermediary, such as in the form of appropriate remuneration that reflects prevailing market conditions and competition, so that it offers fair compensation for the activities conducted and the magnitude of the effort made. Non-financial incentives may have meaningful effects too, such as training to share know-how about product offers, providing ordering or inventory management technologies and tools, protection of each intermediary's area against incursion by competitors that are also in the distribution channel, or cooperative advertising. Such actions can create conditions to improve the level of relationship trust and encourage cooperative efforts, even if the supplier develops a strong dependence on the intermediary.

Intermediary Training/Support

Providing appropriate training and support to intermediaries in a distribution channel is particularly important when the product offers are distinguished by their complexity. Detailed knowledge held by the intermediaries—about the characteristics of the product and its use, as well as the services that accompany it—is essential. Therefore, the supplier needs to offer such support, to ensure the effective operations of the distribution channel, as well as provide incentives for the intermediary to work toward achieving learning goals. Incomplete or inaccurate information can hurt both sides, by undermining the coherent form and image of the product offer that should have been displayed consistently throughout the distribution channel.

Here again, training support and incentives to motivate intermediaries to devote greater effort (or more resources) and commit more to the supplier's products might take financial or non-financial forms. The financial incentives might include attractive commissions or increased profit margins for those that achieve certain goals. Guarantees of exclusivity are also financial tools, because they promise the intermediary that it is the only source of the product in the market. In terms of non-financial resources and assistance, the supplier might provide assistance in efforts to sell to specific customers (e.g., negotiate agreements), share useful data and information (e.g., market research information), and provide marketing communications support. Perhaps the most important source of motivation though is the development of a collaborative working relationship, in which both companies negotiate areas of agreement: joint planning at a strategic level to define the intermediaries' responsibilities for certain customers, tasks, and products; ensuring understanding and appreciation by acknowledging the intermediary's efforts; regular communication, including exchanges of both information and interpersonal contacts; and confirmation that the supplier is committed to a long-term relationship.

Evaluation of Intermediaries

A control procedure is also required within distribution channels, designed to monitor and evaluate intermediaries' performance. Evaluation in a distribution channel administration context primarily focuses on compliance with the conditions established at the start of the cooperation. It also might include measures of the results the intermediary actually achieves.

Through such evaluations, the supplier can identify any "weak links" in the distribution channel. If inadequacies or capability gaps become evident, they should be addressed immediately with training or support processes. However, some relationships may need to be terminated, even within the framework of cooperation created by distribution channels.

Relevant evaluation criteria in distribution channels (Figure 5.17) might refer to the extent to which each intermediary contributes to channel operations and addresses the related needs and challenges. Other measures could gauge the level of commitment shown by an intermediary and its compliance with the norms and guidelines established for the channel. Its ability to adapt its practices to manage the product offers effectively might also be evaluated. Other metrics should assess the level of satisfaction customers express.

An audit and evaluation process in turn can establish a common course, shared by multiple enterprises within the distribution channel. Any necessary corrective actions can be clarified and changes made, such as to the terms of the agreement or the jointly set channel objectives. Even acknowledging the possibility of such adjustments though, the goals have been set to motivate both sides toward optimal performance in their cooperation and continuous self-improvement. In turn, these goals must be ambitious but also feasible; unrealistic goals can act as a deterrent to effort. Ultimately, each intermediary should want to work with the supplier to achieve set goals; if not, altering these goals might lead to improved operations in the distribution channel.

Figure 5.17 Evaluation of Intermediary Performance

Source: Adapted from Kumar et al. (1992)

Control in the Distribution Channel and Intra-Channel Conflict

Control in relationships between businesses and coordination of their activities might rely on different methods. For example, coordination in a distribution channel might result from exhibitions of power by one relationship party, arrangements established through prior agreement, or instruments based on trust.

The first option, involving power, might arise in channels in which one firm has significantly more resources than the others, such as a strong reputation or a recognizable product. This power may accrue to either side of the relationship. If the supplier is more powerful, it might insist that intermediaries devote more effort to their product offer, then determine the rewards and support it will grant. If intermediaries have the power, such as due to their ability to move substantial product volume or quantities, they might insist on access to more extensive markets—which also might make it easier for the supplier business to access fragmented and dispersed customer groups. However, when power gets imposed on weaker members of a chain, it has negative implications and becomes a source of conflict. If a strong company seeks to persuade and positively influence its channel partners to encourage coordination across channel operations and define a fair distribution of the outcomes, it might increase the satisfaction of all participants and limit conflicts.

The second option is based on agreements that detail the cooperation among the members of the channel. Such agreements should cover 13 key points, such as the products to be distributed, the outlets, the level of supplies, the necessary costs, stock carrying, the freedoms and power that intermediaries possess, promotion and sales support, and post-sale service. For example, in franchising agreements, the parties must establish the functions and procedures that each side will carry out and set the policies to which they are both subject, as well as define the type and amount of remuneration they receive.

A third option assumes that coordination in operations and relationships within the channel lead to trust among participants. Continuous communication and collaboration tend to produce norms and behavioral patterns, which also shape the participants' expectations and contributions. To build trust between members of a distribution channel, collaborative communication thus can be a useful tool, which also tends to increase engagement and perceived coordination. For example, a trust-based process might feature the following components:

- Frequent communication between channel members, through all available media.
- Continuous dialogue and two-way communication.
- Formal policies that address and guide processes for communication.
- Influence tactics that highlight the value of achieving and prioritizing shared goals.

The ideal of collaborative communication is increasingly embraced in many industries that seek to shift from a competitive logic to collaborative relationships among members of the same distribution channel, yet it is not necessarily appropriate or applicable to all market conditions or relationships.

If efforts to coordinate fail, or communication between channel members cannot restore a balanced relationship, conflicts arise. Of course, conflicts are difficult to eliminate altogether; they might result from minor disagreements or fights over important topics. Rather than trying to avoid them completely, the parties should seek to reduce the number or intensity, as well as establish methods to resolve them promptly. Channel members should be trained to address severe conflicts.

One such option is to develop proactive responses and prevention procedures, which are relatively easy to implement, at low financial and time-related costs. Moreover, the risk associated with implementing preventive measures is minimal. A key prerequisite for such efforts also involves harmonious communication between channel members, as noted previously. Such communication—whether formally established through structures or informally realized through interpersonal, day-to-day interactions by members of the channel—should reflect common perceptions and understanding by members of the channel, with regard to their cooperative norms and shared channel objectives. These elements create good conditions for cooperation and coordination. In turn, coordinated activities, information exchanges, and resource sharing can enable change without creating too much conflict.

In a multichannel setting, segmentation of the target markets might reduce the risk of conflict among intermediaries. Such segmentation could be based on geographical data, industry type, customer size, or product groups. Another option is to institute control mechanisms, such as through forward integration, impositions of power, or enforcing contractual obligations in an agreement (e.g., as for franchising).

To identify causes of conflict, and thus to seek to eliminate them, channel administrators should track behaviors that appear to be "symptoms," heralding an impending conflict. But the goal should never be to resolve just the symptoms or dismiss actual problems as symptoms. In both these cases, the underlying cause and problem will reappear, with negative consequences. Instead, in identifying the causes of a conflict, administrators might find underlying issues such as:

- Observed differences between the objectives, interests, or strategic approaches of the supplier and the intermediaries, which might lead to misunderstandings.
- Disagreements over which product lines the intermediaries should manage.
- Limitations imposed by multiple distribution channels or competitive behaviors when different channels are granted responsibility for the same tasks.
- Poor performance, whether relative to the expected performance of intermediaries or the expected support from suppliers.
- Reactionary responses from an intermediary to instructions issued by the supplier, with regard to the sales process or product promotions, especially if the supplier experiences some loss of power in the channel.

These causes might lead to two main types of conflicts: between the supplier and the intermediaries or else among the various intermediaries in the channel. The former represents vertical conflict, which is more common. The supplier likely prefers to service key accounts itself, which limits the intermediaries' access and responsibility, as well as their revenues and satisfaction with the channel. To avoid such conflicts, the design of the remuneration and rewards systems and the precise terms of the cooperation should account for such frustrations and actively attempt to ensure channel members believe they are being treated fairly.

The latter form, or horizontal conflicts, stem from two major causes. First, a poor distribution channel design allows multiple distributors to compete for the same area of responsibility, so they waste operational resources to compete with one another. To resolve this cause, rational channel designs should identify the optimal number and allocation of intermediaries in particular areas, which might even entail exclusive distribution agreements, assuming this approach adds value to the product offer. Removing an intermediary that engages in persistent conflict or offers a minimal contribution is also possible. Second, if it applies an aggressive distribution policy, the intermediary might extend into an area assigned to another intermediary in the same channel. The supplier then needs to make clear that such behaviors are unacceptable, contrary to set agreements. If such suggestions are not effective, the next move is to sanction or remove the non-compliant member from the channel. It is up to the strongest member of the channel to exercise such coercive power to ensure its proper functioning and harmonious cooperation among members.

Finally, it should be noted that conflicts within a channel are not always catastrophic. Friction can be a springboard for changes and revisions to the channel structure, in ways that might make it more effective and efficient. Then the members might establish closer, cooperative bonds that diminish their sensed need to act competitively against one another.

SUPPLIER AND INTERMEDIARY PERSPECTIVES ON RELATIONSHIP ISSUES

Intermediaries and suppliers appear to have different views on the role of intermediaries in the distribution channel. Therefore, we provide comparative lists of their distinct viewpoints here, which managers and executives might use beneficially to gain a better understanding of both sides, help limit conflict, and encourage the enhanced performance of the distribution channel. In particular, the following topics appear contested, due to the different viewpoints:

- Direct contact and selling by the supplier with an intermediary's customer.
- Failure by the intermediary to manage the customer relationship, according to the supplier.
- The required stock levels the intermediary should maintain.
- The intermediary's non-exclusive supply of the supplier's range of products.
- Changes to the number of intermediaries and overlapping areas of responsibility.

Intermediary Perspective

Many intermediaries regard themselves as independent entrepreneurs, proud of their industry activities and role in the economy. They highlight their ability to achieve sales, supply a wide variety of products, and serve customers. Notably, intermediaries regard customers as their "own," so reaching and serving them represents the service they provide to the supplier.

They also cite their acceptance among customers as a strength. But they consider themselves customers of various suppliers, free to decide which products to carry and promote. In turn, they assess suppliers according to product quality and availability, the support they provide, and their ability to service orders accurately and predictably. Finally, intermediaries tend to be customer-oriented rather than supplier-oriented. They acknowledge suppliers' attempts to establish a good product image but remain committed to their belief that their primary responsibility is to meet customer needs.

Supplier Perspective

Suppliers perceive intermediaries as members of their organization, in terms of sales and physical distribution, so they express disappointment with their lack of management capacity or depth, inadequate financial management, and inability to anticipate managerial succession. Even if they appear financially successful, these channel members appear indifferent to innovation or best management practices. Thus, suppliers assign them small accounts and ask them to perform physical product delivery, but they retain large accounts, sales, and technical support for themselves. Similarly, the sales representatives employed by the intermediaries tend to be dismissed as simple "order-takers," without the ability to identify new customers (due to their lack of information or interest in market research) or aggressively promote new products. Their main function is to provide a requested product, at the right place and time, to customers. Another source of supplier disappointment involves inventory levels: they believe intermediaries should be fully stocked at all times, which is not possible. The suppliers also believe that customers are theirs, so they are unwilling to share information about the market and individual customers with intermediaries.

DISTRIBUTION EFFICIENCY

To achieve efficiency in distribution channels, ongoing analyses should cover the following topics:

- Sales Data. Analyzing sales data can reveal the level of homogeneity in the market in which the distribution channel will operate, as well as purchase patterns that might relate to customers' geographical locations, product types, or quantity considerations. In addition, sales data might reveal significant dates, distributions of sales across consumers, and items that require longer or shorter stock maintenance (i.e., high or low stock terms). This analysis helps to make decisions about transactions in markets with low sales volume.
- Sales Fluctuations Due to Product Characteristics. This analysis aims to identify fluctuations in sales, which is important at the distribution level. Product characteristics that induce such fluctuations can then guide the design of a distribution network that anticipates them.

- Sales Fluctuations Due to Time, Volume, Location, and Volatility. This analysis can inform the design of distribution processes, such as to achieve the required delivery time of the product at the desired levels.
- Inventory Maintenance Functions in Relation to Business Needs. Detailed knowledge of the functions related to inventory maintenance (security stock, stock needed to cover fluctuations in production) can inform calculations of the optimal desired level of inventory retention.
- Costs of Physical Distribution. Cost studies provide a measure of the efficiency of the distribution process.
- Alternative Distribution Channels and Methods. Regardless of which distribution channels have been selected and configured, both their selection and the methods used must be regularly reviewed. Any changes in production techniques, the products themselves, or the underlying technology must be evaluated to confirm their efficiency in relation to the dynamic conditions.

6

SUPPLY CHAIN TRANSPORTATION OF MANUFACTURED PRODUCTS

Learning Objectives

- Introduce transportation in industrial supply chain management.
- Identify the features, challenges, and opportunities of the physical distribution of manufactured products.
- Gain familiarity with transportation means and systems.
- Understand the combined transportation paradigm.
- Describe Transportation 4.0 practices and technologies.
- Define the difference between supply chain and logistics system management.

Case Study

Maersk: Vertically Integrating the Container Transportation Supply Chain

The goal for AP Moller Maersk's integrator strategy was to transform the firm into a comprehensive, customer-facing, door-to-door logistics service that earns significantly greater profits. To achieve these broad, challenging goals, Maersk CEO Søren Skou, speaking at Maersk's Capital Markets Day, explained that the firm was ready to build three divisions with strong synergies among them, based on a customer focus that would drive value creation through digitalization:

(Continued)

Today, we are rapidly transforming our A.P. Moller Maersk in line with our strategy. We have come far, but we are not yet done. We continue to see a significant opportunity in the market for global end-to-end logistics and are confident that we can continue to deliver value. Maersk's value creation model will link Logistics and Ocean through customer synergies, and Ocean and Terminals through financials and operational synergies. And, while Ocean and Terminals are expected to deliver steady returns, Logistics and services will be the major profit drivers (gCaptain, 2018).

Accordingly, Maersk combined its three regional carrier brands (MCC Transport, Sealand, and Seago Line) under a single firm: SeaLand-A Maersk Company. The simplified naming structure sought to increase brand recognition and ensure clarity of choice for customers.

To support its growth, Maersk also invested around US$1 billion in capital expenditures over two years, which it complemented with mergers and acquisitions to build capabilities and progressively scale up the business. It specifically sought firms that fit with its strategic geographic footprint, already had an established customer base, and appeared scalable. As Vincent Clerc, CEO of Ocean and Logistics at Maersk, further explained, "All three of the acquisitions that we have done so far do fit this model, and the acquisitions that we will have in the future will continue... to have to live [up] to these three litmus tests," so that the company could "move gradually to larger targets" (gCaptain, 2018).

The three acquisitions to which Clerc referred were deals involving Vandegrift (2019), Performance Team, and KGH Customs Services (both in 2020). In describing these past acquisitions, Clerc clarified how they fit with the firm's overall M&A goals, such as when he referred to the Performance Team acquisition by noting, "The purpose and the strategic rationale was to move from a network, which was essentially based on port-side flow logistics, and to move from that flow logistics into omnichannel fulfillment and e-commerce capabilities that we could scale up" (gCaptain, 2018).

Maersk's strategy also prioritizes end-to-end logistics. It hopes to use its technology to book shipments, its warehouses to fulfill orders, its logistics network to make deliveries, and its ships to carry freight. It has laid out this strategy clearly, such as in its 2019 annual report, which contained the explicit recognition that ocean transport will remain a central part of its business, but growth in land-side logistics would help it become an end-to-end integrator (see Figure 6.1).

In contrast, most shippers still have highly fragmented supply chains with multiple providers across the various steps. Orchestrating movement among these partners can be complicated, especially when trying to deal with imbalances, so for Maersk, "Our winning aspiration is about leveraging our unique set of capabilities to bring about a disruptive offering that can change this paradigm... We call it truly integrated logistics" (gCaptain, 2018). As Clerc explained, Maersk wants full accountability for a shipper's supply chain, because "The advantage is that basically at any time, we can get our hands on the cargo, we can prioritize the access to capacity, change the outcome, affect what is happening for customers in a way... that firms that do not have this direct operational control cannot do" (gCaptain, 2018).

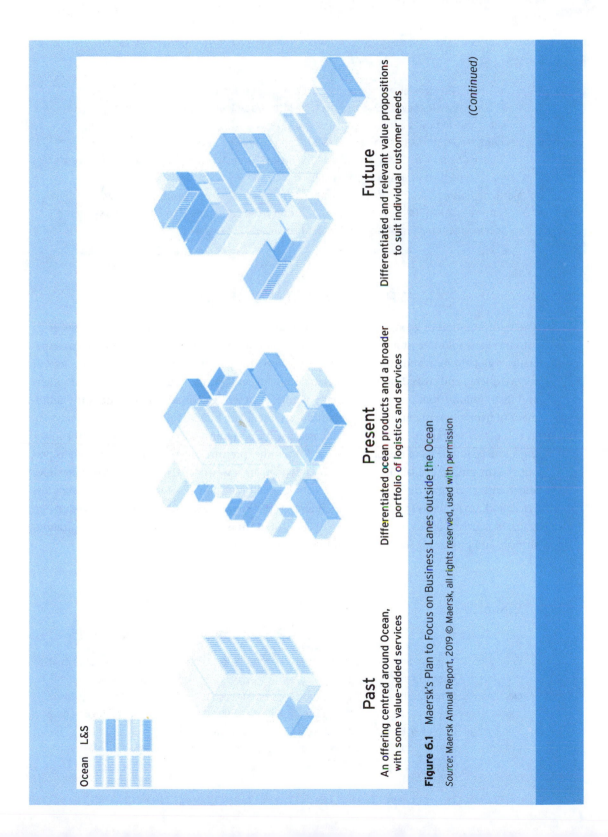

Past

An offering centred around Ocean, with some value-added services

Present

Differentiated ocean products and a broader portfolio of logistics and services

Future

Differentiated and relevant value propositions to suit individual customer needs

Ocean   L&S

Figure 6.1   Maersk's Plan to Focus on Business Lanes outside the Ocean

Source: Maersk Annual Report, 2019 © Maersk, all rights reserved, used with permission

(Continued)

Sources

gCaptain. (2018), "Maersk announces latest step in business integration strategy," *gCaptain*, 19 September. Retrieved 16 June 2022 from https://gcaptain.com/maersk-announces-latest-step-in-business-integration-strategy.

Leonard, M. (2021), "Maersk pursues M&A for end-to-end logistics, moves to 'larger targets'," *Supply Chain Dive*, 12 May. Retrieved 16 June 2022 from www.supplychaindive.com/news/maersk-mergers-acquisition-ocean-shipping-logistics/600027.

Maritime Gateway. (2021), "Maersk accelerates transformation to integrated service," *Maritime Gateway*, 12 May. Retrieved 16 June 2022 from www.maritimegateway.com/maersk-accelerates-transformation-to-integrated-service/.

TRANSPORTATION OF GOODS

The transportation of goods, particularly raw materials that support production processes or go into products sold to customers, represents an important determinant of business success, especially as globalization and international trade increase the pressing demands for both the level of service offered and costs. That is, raw material sourcing and transport (from one point to another) and distribution (from one point to many points) represent global activities, as does the fulfillment of demand in manufacturing organizations (including building products to specifications). In this global setting, the Internet is vital, because it can minimize overall costs while still ensuring a satisfactory level of customer service. Yet another pressure on suppliers and customers pertains to the limited availability of necessary resources and raw materials. Together, these pressures and trends highlight the great need for well-designed transport networks that can ensure low prices and timely delivery, while also maintaining strict stock control at every stage of production, from the sourcing of raw materials to the delivery of the finished product, through transportation, storage, and processing stages, whether in proprietary or third-party installations.

Vignette

DSV Introduces the Silkway Express: Fast China–Europe Road Freight

When, in 2021, a container vessel became stuck in the Suez Canal for ten days—a route that accounts for approximately 12 percent of all sea transport in the world—it became abundantly clear how dependent shipping firms are on this passage. Suddenly, it was also obvious: trade routes between Europe and Asia require free flows in the Suez Canal, and this dependence on a single route is highly risky, especially in the COVID-19 era, when there is no business as usual. For example, passenger flight cancellations put pressure on air freight, causing capacity constraints.

A new intercontinental road bridge between China and Europe promises a reliable alternative. In addition to quick transit times, of 14-18 days, at costs much lower than air freight rates, DSV Silkway Express offers valuable flexibility. Furthermore, unlike air, rail, and sea freight operators, DSV collects cargo precisely when it is ready from the shipper, so customers do not need to think about closing and cut-off dates for specific vessels, rail, or air schedules. The goods can be moved seven days a week, and multiple pickup and delivery locations are possible. Furthermore, customers have the flexibility to reroute goods during the journey.

Security is a top concern and priority. DSV works solely with trusted partners to ensure that goods arrive at their destination safely, and all trucks are sealed and equipped with GPS tracking, so customers can follow the orders on a dedicated site. Security fees are included in transport costs, which cover rest stops at secure gated parking lots (Figure 6.2).

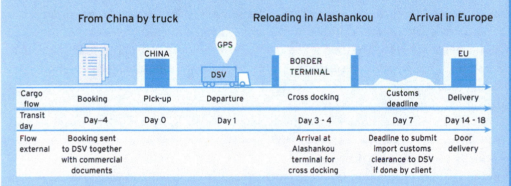

Figure 6.2 Duration and Steps of the Silkway Express

Source: DSV, all rights reserved, used with permission

Sources

DSV (2020) *DSV Introduces Fast China-Europe Road Freight*. Retrieved 16 June 2022 from www.dsv.com/en/about-dsv/press/news/com/2020/10/dsv-introduces-fast-china-europe-road-freight.

DSV (n.d.) *DSV Silkway Express–Try Our Alternative to Air Freight*. Retrieved 16 June 2022 from www.dsv.com/en/our-solutions/modes-of-transport/road-transport/dsv-silkway-express.

EXTERNAL TRANSPORTATION FEATURES

The physical distribution of manufactured products, as one part of the supply chain, involves delivering products to consumers at the right place, space, and time, in the right quantity and at the right price, but also at the lowest possible cost—that is, the key objectives of supply chain management. Even if other logistics processes (inventory management, production support, supplies, information flow) work perfectly, the efficiency of the physical distribution determines the overall image and success of a production business.

Historically, supply chain structures included the transfer of products (raw materials and semi-finished products) from the factory to local warehouses and wholesalers, then distribution to production points or points-of-sale, achieved by maintaining many larger warehouses, with ever-increasing amounts of stock and substantial operating costs. Today, the supply chain is characterized by factory-powered central warehouses that distribute (consumer and industrial) products directly to points-of-sale and supply local warehouses or wholesalers. As a key advantage, this direct distribution of high-demand items from the central warehouse to retail outlets reduces overall logistics costs.

Among the new trends evident in supply chain organizations, we note several as particularly influential. First, direct delivery from the production point to the point-of-sale, without warehousing, is notable for industrial products (e.g., bricks, cement) and large consumer product orders. This structure generally does not include low volume, low sales products though, due to the high costs involved. In those cases, producers still need to use external partners or wholesalers. Consider supermarket chains, which represent key accounts for many production units. The chains use their own warehouses to supply stores, which are themselves supplied by other suppliers. In this case, the point-of-sale is the warehouse, not the supermarket. The warehouses store products in large volumes, though some products might move directly from the production or processing unit to supermarkets. If the supermarket chain, as the customer, is relatively small though, suppliers might maintain their own warehouses. Otherwise, a logistics service provider would need to act as an intermediary (especially for storage and distribution).

Second, direct distribution from the production plant to retail and wholesale outlets has eliminated some central warehouses and transformed others into distribution centers, such that their purpose is to provide supplies received from the production plant directly to retail, wholesale, and local warehouses. This option helps reduce stocks and fast-track product movements.

Physical Distribution of Manufactured Products: Challenges and Opportunities

Supply chains for manufactured products are global. The production plants are located far away from the points-of-sale. The benefits of obtaining raw materials, semi-finished, or finished products from international sources are numerous, and expanding into new markets is a strategic goal of most businesses. For example, manufacturers entering global markets aim to exploit economies of scale in terms of procurement and reducing costs. As new global suppliers enter the market, companies can benefit significantly from low-cost procurement and greater flexibility in their supply chains, such as by seeking competitive bids from suppliers around the world. Relying on alternative supply sources also provides greater security when an existing source fails to offer adequate service, speed, quality, or quantity. Thus many businesses maintain offshore suppliers for the bulk of their purchases (mainly due to lower purchase costs) but keep relationships with local suppliers to address unexpected increases in demand or delays in regular long-distance supply flows.

Such global activities also raise specific challenges and risks for today's businesses. Research into the difficulties surrounding international supply chains for manufactured products confirm some of the most prevalent challenges experienced in real-world practice: (1) lack of visibility across the supply chain, (2) forced scheduling of long-term horizons, (3) demand volatility, (4) multiple channels for market and product distribution, and (5) volatile situations in many parts of the world.

First, transparency is an ongoing problem in global supply chains. The dropping of borders and liberalization of economies have allowed for complex supply chains; business information systems and the enormous spread of the Internet have intensified the challenge of managing vast amounts of information. Improving visibility at all stages of the supply chain, including suppliers, logistics services, transport providers, distributors, and resellers, but also customers and any other global stakeholder, can also enhance flexibility, by enabling more rapid responses to changing demands in various markets worldwide.

Second, an international supply chain for manufactured products demands longer-term planning for the business logistics system. In turn, the global supply chains automatically become exposed to more risks to their smooth operations, because the diversity and complexity of resource management leaves them more vulnerable to such risks. In addition, global supply chains usually extend over greater geographical distances and longer time gaps, with different characteristics, pricing conditions, and so forth.

Third, factoring the fluctuating customer demands over seasons and longer periods of time into the risks adds substantially to the challenges associated with managing production and transport of manufactured products over long distances to meet demand. Such concerns become even more arduous due to the volatility of commodity prices and road, sea, and air transportation costs. Together with rising labor costs in many countries, profit margins might come under pressure, reflecting the increasing costs throughout the supply chain.

Fourth, consumers can make purchases through multiple channels, which creates demand for multiple distribution channels. About three-quarters of all companies use four to five modes of transport to meet demand. Manufacturers, traditional retailers, and wholesalers are compelled to maintain large storage facilities and high stock levels near metropolitan centers; online stores, online markets, and drop shippers must cooperate more closely with logistics providers.

Fifth, geopolitical, economic, and social factors (natural disasters, wars, currency fluctuations, work cultures) also contribute to these difficulties. They demand significant flexibility and investments in modern technological solutions, along with specialized human resources in the international supply chains. Finding reliable partners in many countries, which differ widely, is a difficult task; monitoring the performance and financial stability of all the organizations involved in the supply chain represents an ongoing challenge. At the same time, the lack of common international regulations and standards for logistics procedures, such as safety or risk management rules for international transport, packaging regulations, and labeling requirements, mean that some practices must vary from country to country.

To address such expansive and unavoidable challenges, along with activism pressures and competition for global business, most businesses recognize the need to develop collaborative networks that integrate processes and information flows, to achieve and share in mutual goals, benefits, and risks. Advances in technology are essential for enabling supply chain leaders to manage the challenges, so they also invest in new Internet technologies and telematics applications. Such tools can support decision-making processes for better supply chain scheduling, more accurate demand forecasting, efficient resource and production planning, appropriate stock levels, and appropriate methods of transportation. The Internet-driven supply chain of the future is likely to function as a digital supply chain network, facilitating communication among companies, logistics service providers, corporate networks, and online markets so that the entire supply chain network can immediately regulate its members' inventory, orders, and production capacities.

The contributions of logistics service providers cannot be ignored either, for firms that seek to derive the benefits that arise from outsourcing. Their need to reduce costs drives businesses to outsource part of, or even all, production and operational activities to external partners. This process is not limited to assigning subcontractors to manufacture components; it also includes the provision of services. Thus, it can lead to relocations of different functions to other parts of the world.

TRANSPORTATION MEANS AND SYSTEMS

A simplified description of transportation establishes that a shipment requires a sender, a receiver, and a carrier (means of transport). In reality, the transportation process is much more complex and detailed, involving many parties and actors, as Figure 6.3 illustrates.

The main categories of companies involved in transportation systems are as follows:

- Carrier, owners of transportation means. In this category, the simplest version of transport, companies provide their own vehicles or lease them out for a fixed period (e.g., ship chartering). They can range from a small truck to a fleet of ships. Key advantages are lower prices and direct relationships with the carrier (especially for small businesses). However, their services are restricted in terms of the transportation project (e.g., delivering only in Germany) and auxiliary services (e.g., not able to handle customs clearance).

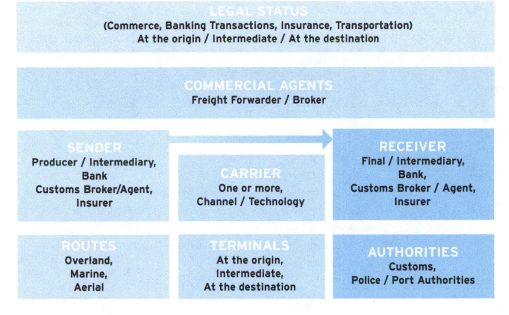

Figure 6.3 Component Parts of the Transportation System

- Agents. This term reflects the mainly transactional character of companies that collaborate with the previous category of carriers to undertake specific tasks (e.g., customs, freight charges, bills of lading). A shipping company without its own offices in an area might assign an agent to act on its behalf there, then proceed with setting up a branch.

- Freight forwarders. Freight forwarders are not carriers in the absolute sense of the term; they purchase transportation space in a wholesale form, from among various means of transport available, then resell it. In addition, freight forwarders offer a range of auxiliary services (customs clearance, inland freight forwarding, warehousing) that they combine with the freight transport. Their services can apply to full shipments with containers or trucks, as well as small quantities for transport (e.g., pallets), which agents do not provide. By buying wholesale shipping space, major freight forwarders can achieve much better prices than each shipper would individually.

- Brokers. This entity arranges, by reward or commission, the transfer of goods. Businesses choose brokers for a variety of reasons but especially when they lack the necessary experience, time, or staff to complete the shipment themselves. Shippers with minimal transport support can use brokers to negotiate fares, overseas transfers, and other processes that the shippers cannot complete alone. In these cases, brokers replace the transport department of the carrier. They mainly perform maritime transport by conventional ships (cf. containers).

Means of Transportation

The different means of transport or carriers can be classified into five categories, the main features of which are presented in Table 6.1.

Table 6.1 Main Modes of Transport and Characteristics

Means of Transportation	Main Characteristics
Road transport	• Used to transport smaller quantities of raw materials and finished products (cf. rail transport). • Door-to-door service providers do not perform intermediate loading or unloading stops but offer high frequency and availability of services, high speed, and facilitation services. • Unable to handle and transport all types of chartering, often due to highway safety restrictions.
Rail transport	• Used for the transportation of raw materials (e.g., coal, chemicals, timber) and low-value industrial products (e.g., food, paper, timber products). • Economical mode of transport for medium to long distances and when speed is not a critical factor for remote production units. • Low speed. • Risk of damage due to vibration movements.
Marine transport	• Main means of transport for offshore industrial production units. • Low speed. • Double load handling. • Catalytic effect of weather conditions. • Application of modern technology has improved its reliability. • Relatively low freight losses and destruction costs. • One of the cheapest ways to transport bulk cargo over long distances and in large quantities.
Air transport	• High speed, especially for long distance coverage. • High cost. • Time-consuming procedures for loading and unloading goods. • Time delays likely at airports. • Ability to carry large-sized freight due to the construction of specialized cargo aircraft. • Provision of better freight security services. • Advantageous for transporting products of high value or with large weight ratios, as well as sensitive products and products with high seasonal demand.

Means of Transportation	Main Characteristics
Pipeline transport	• Provision of small-scale services. • Mainly used for the transportation of crude oil and refinery products. • Slow movement of products inside the pipeline, offset by the constant product stream, 24 hours a day, 7 days a week. • High pipeline capacity. • Low risk of product loss and damage. • Availability of the pipeline is limited only by competitive uses by other carriers.

Then in Table 6.2, we compare the five modes of transport on the basis of specific criteria.

Table 6.2 Comparative Table of Means of Transport

	Road	Rail	Aerial	Marine	Pipeline
Project Coverage	From Point to Point	From Terminal to Terminal	From Terminal to Terminal	From Terminal to Terminal	From Terminal to Terminal
Cost (compared with other means)	Moderate	Low	High	Low	Low
Number of competitors	Large	Very small	Medium	Medium	Very small
Range of products that can be transported	Large	Large	Medium	Great	Very limited
Ability to carry loads per shipment (in tons)	10-25	50-12,000	5-125	1,000-250,000	30,000-2,500,000

TRANSPORTATION 4.0 AND E-FULFILLMENT

The technologies and practices introduced by the 4th Industrial Revolution (or Industry 4.0), related to the day-to-day operations of logistics systems, mainly pertain to operational areas of storage, transport, and distribution. Particularly for transport and distribution (i.e., Transport 4.0), they entail the development of telematics applications. *Telematics* refers to the combined use of telecommunication and information technologies and applications that allow for (1) the exchange (sending/receiving) and storage of data across information systems connected through telecommunications networks (e.g., real-time image transmission by road cameras to a central traffic control office), and (2) functions and commands to be performed remotely (e.g., deactivating a car alarm).

Consider industrial plants, which collect relatively small volumes of information from each workstation but need rapid transmission of that information. The information technologies used in these production spaces reflect a completely different philosophy and cover completely different needs than those found in offices. With greater experience with information gathering efforts in the production space, various machines have evolved to operate together, such as barcode readers, data acquisition stations, programmable logic controllers, and interconnected device control stations (e.g., scales, barcode printers).

Telematics applications in the logistics sector often focus on the transportation and distribution of products, and fleet management in particular. Many applications and systems are available on the market (sometimes called intelligent transport systems) that enable (in real-time):

- Automatic vehicle positioning.
- Problem detection on the vehicle or any of its systems.
- The ability to navigate the vehicle.
- The safety of drivers and vehicles.
- Monitoring the status of the goods.

The use of telematics systems also means that logistics officers and transport service providers of companies that have their own fleet can control the activity of their vehicles, drivers, and goods from a computer screen, at any time and any place.

Automatic Vehicle Location Identification

Managing a fleet of vehicles allows firms that carry passengers and distribute goods on a daily basis to know the precise location of each vehicle on a digital map. There are many examples of such applications in everyday life, for both freight and passenger transport. The key technology for automatically positioning a vehicle is the global positioning system (GPS), which consists of a grid of 24 satellites, all at the same height from the surface of the Earth, such that they cover its entire surface. Satellites transmit specific signals, retrieved from the receptors/receivers (antennas). These antennae can be placed in a device (mobile, personal digital assistant) or vehicle. Through data recovery, it is possible to calculate the latitude, longitude, and altitude of the device or vehicle, as well as the speed with which it is moving; these calculations require signals from at least four satellites. If antennae are connected to computer systems and digital maps, the position and speed of any vehicle can be accurately and easily determined.

In turn, a company with its own fleet of vehicles that distribute products can track the routes and stops made by each vehicle in real-time. It can anticipate the time of arrival of the vehicle at the next stop and when it will return to operation after completing its distribution task. With this information, the company can plan optimal routes for the next distribution, control for any deviations from the schedule, and achieve a more efficient distribution system. Furthermore, such efforts should reduce fuel consumption (due to the more rational use of transport and selected routes), as well as the risks associated with delivery tasks (e.g., theft, driver safety, cargo protection). Thus, GPS enables companies to achieve their goals of increasing the level of service provided to its customers (greater reliability) while reducing their operating expenses (minimizing distribution costs).

Vehicle Troubleshooting Identification

A useful application of telematics in freight transport is the real-time recognition of any problems that may arise across the different modes. In many cases, this application can save lives—a pressing concern, considering the many tragic accidents that historically have been associated with moving cargo, overloading, and mechanical issues. Telematics applications and systems can provide information about vehicles' conditions, such as the amount of fuel and oil or the engine temperature. Telematics using radio frequency identification (RFID) technology also can immediately inform the driver of any problems with the goods being transported. That is, RFID tags attached to products can transmit real-time information about the products' condition. Labels and sensors also can be placed inside the truck to record temperature or humidity levels.

As these descriptions make clear, telematics can be invaluable for the transport of products in cold supply chains, such as frozen foods. Sensors inside refrigerated trucks can continuously measure the temperature of the storage space and warn both the driver and traffic logistics offices if they rise above the desired levels. Such considerations are even more pressing for transports of hazardous loads such as liquid fuel, explosives, flammable materials (gas, liquid, or solid form), radioactive materials, or oxidizing, toxic, or infectious substances. Alarm motion sensors on the inside or electronic sealing on the outside can also ensure the safety of goods, especially high-value goods.

Autonomous Vehicle Navigation

Autonomous vehicles can travel on the road without a driver. They use systems of sensors, cameras, and radar, together with a software program that seeks to simulate human driving behavior, to perform driving functions and monitor traffic conditions throughout the journey. The technology underlying autonomous vehicles is complex, and many factors must be taken into account for the safe and autonomous movement of a vehicle. Accordingly, thus far autonomous trucks have not achieved the ability to carry thousands of tons of goods on the open road. But standalone trucks and robotic systems are integrated into modern warehouses, especially distribution centers. They supplement or replace human resources by transporting goods within the warehouse, then loading and unloading the various modes of transport.

Driver and Vehicle Safety

Telematics technology offers a wide variety of applications and systems that can enhance road safety. The e-call service is notable in this sense: all new vehicles, especially freight vehicles, are equipped with devices that automatically send out an emergency signal (e.g., the 112 European emergency call number) after an accident, prompting more immediate responses from emergency services. Inside vehicles, various systems record data related to vehicle safety, such as road hazards, road conditions (accidents, maintenance work), weather conditions, speed limits, or motionless points on the road, and can then alert the driver accordingly.

Monitoring Goods' Status

Fleet management supported by telematics can achieve real-time vehicle (or fleet) tracking, journey recording, vehicle and route map displays, and vehicle and route reporting, all of which help businesses improve their productivity, reduce operating costs, and comply with applicable laws. Navigation is usually a function provided by vehicle fleet management information systems, which offer a general overview of pertinent media, itineraries, and customer orders. Most such systems feature direct communication with drivers, working with other information systems maintained by the business, to monitor and control the entire order processing procedure. Through such collaboration, they achieve order completion and accurate identification of transported goods.

A critical effort involves choosing the best route to take, to complete the shipment or distribution of goods successfully and in the shortest possible time. This effort must also account for factors such as the volume, weight, and value of the goods; their particular requirements in terms of storage and handling; specific customer needs for delivery times; and existing time and geographical constraints.

Incoterms®: Standardizing Global Transportation Systems

All international transportation raises a critical question: for an international freight shipment, when precisely do the risks and costs transfer from the seller to the buyer? The International Chamber of Commerce (CCI), located in Paris, published a series of international rules in 1936, under the name Incoterms® 1936 (INternational COmmercial TERMS), seeking to establish an answer. It defined Incoterms® as "the trading terms contained in the main body of a freight contract, clearly describing the seller's and buyer's basic obligations and responsibilities in relation to the delivery of the goods, the transfer of risks, and the payment of costs during the movement of the goods from the supplier's warehouse to the final destination agreed."

To adapt these rules to evolving commercial practices, the original 1936 rules have been amended in many ways; the current Incoterms® are from 2020 (replacing the 2010 version). Notably though, Incoterms® are optional: these standardized, recognized norms can help actors avoid differences in international transportation. By referring to an Incoterms® trading term in their contracts, buyers and sellers reduce the uncertainty that tends to arise in international transactions, due to the different trading practices and interpretations from country to country.

Incoterms® that determine the point at which risks transfer from the seller to the buyer when transporting goods are valuable. The risks include loss, theft, or (partial or total) destruction of the goods. By defining the point of transfer, the parties to the transaction (i.e., seller and buyer) recognize the need for appropriate measures to address these risks; Incoterms® help specify who bears responsibility for such measures and the respective costs (e.g., shipping costs, taxes, import duties), as well as which party should prepare and deliver the necessary documents and, finally, undertake logistics processes such as packaging, labeling, marking, loading, and unloading the goods or containers.

In Incoterms® 2020, we find 11 terms, divided into four groups that reflect the obligations of the supplier:

- Group E (starting with E), which includes the term EX Works (EXW).
- Group F, which includes the terms Free CArrier (FCA), Free Alongside Ship (FAS), and Free On Board (FOB).
- Group C, which includes the terms Cost and FReight (CFR), Cost Insurance and Freight (CIF), Carriage Paid To (CPT), and Carriage and Insurance Paid To (CIP).
- Group D, which includes the terms Delivered At Place (DAP), Delivered at Place Unloaded (DPU), and Delivered Duty Paid (DDP).

The classification is not random; it features increasing degrees of liability for the seller. Moving from Group E to Group D, the seller's liabilities increase. Table 6.3 specifies which procedures each party (seller or buyer) undertakes for the 11 terms.

Table 6.3 Seller and Buyer Obligations, Incoterms® 2020

Group	E	F			C				D		
Term	EXW	FCA	FAS	FOB	CFR	CIF	CPT	CIP	DAP	DPU	DDP
Transportation mode	(*)	(*)	(**)	(**)	(**)	(**)	(*)	(*)	(*)	(*)	(*)
Warehouse	S	S	S	S	S	S	S	S	S	S	S
Export packaging	S	S	S	S	S	S	S	S	S	S	S
Loading charges	B	S	S	S	S	S	S	S	S	S	S
Delivery to port/place	B	S	S	S	S	S	S	S	S	S	S
Export duty and taxes	B	S	S	S	S	S	S	S	S	S	S
Origin terminal fees	B	B	S	S	S	S	S	S	S	S	S
Loading on carriage	B	B	B	S	S	S	S	S	S	S	S
Carriage charges	B	B	B	B	S	S	S	S	S	S	S
Destination terminal charges	B	B	B	B	B	B	S	S	S	S	S
Deliver to destination	B	B	B	B	B	B	B	B	S	S	S
Unloading at destination	B	B	B	B	B	B	B	B	B	S	B
Import duty and taxes	B	B	B	B	B	B	B	B	B	B	S

Notes: S: Seller, B: Buyer. *Any transport mode. **Marine transport.

For certain Incoterms®, such as CPT, CIP, CFR, and CIF, the place specified differs from the place of delivery; it signifies the destination for which the shipment has been paid.

Why are there so many terms? They reflect the specificity and unique requirements of the various goods, as well as the particularities (customs procedures, infrastructure) of the departure and destination countries. Another consideration is the seller's (in)ability to transport the goods or the limited availability of different means of transport, for at least one of the parties.

In conclusion, Incoterms® constitute a protocol for good commercial practices, directly related to the sale, transport, and insurance of goods being transported, as well as indirectly related to other processes such as customs and banking. The regulatory scope of Incoterms® is minimal, in that it only refers to certain issues, namely, the determination of the rights and obligations of the trading partners with respect to the delivery of the goods and the transfer of risks. Incoterms® do not address other equally important matters (e.g., consequences of a failure to comply, exemption in the case of failure to complete the delivery), which need to be settled between the parties through the application of relevant law, which should be agreed in advance to govern the contract.

7

THE MARKETING MIX: PROMOTION AND MARKETING COMMUNICATION CHANNELS FOR INDUSTRIAL PRODUCTS

Learning Objectives

- Understand the characteristics of marketing communication and related interactions.
- Define the communication process.
- Describe marketing communication tools.
- Understand the importance of corporate social responsibility in the context of marketing communication.
- Define an industrial salesperson, including the elements and concepts related to staffing an industrial firm to ensure sales potential.
- Outline the process of personal selling.
- Recognize the issues related to the planning and design of industrial sales.

Case Study

Industrial Global Brand Leadership

Branding tends to be less emphasized in business-to-business (B2B) than in business-to-consumer (B2C) markets, despite the notable potential for brands to support strategic differentiation and thus sustainable competitive advantages. Thus, industrial firms should actively build their global brand identities in ways that highlight their ability to meet customer needs, such as on the basis of five relevant brand capabilities:

- *Relational support*: By creating and managing relationships, B2B brands can establish promises to customers that help those relational customers understand and commit to the brand. If relational capabilities are the main plot of the brand story, firms likely establish a consistent, global image that also can be adapted to specific markets and customers.
- *Coordinating network players*: If a brand can create a well-aligned network, it reinforces its powerful position to leverage its own brand value. It also likely induces a pull effect through the channel by creating demand.
- *Leveraging brand architecture*: A brand architecture encompasses multiple brands, each of which has a well-defined role within the portfolio. By establishing this capability, the brand can coordinate marketing efforts and decisions related to brand extensions, deletions, or additions. A clear brand architecture can also manage competing demands related to standardization versus adaptation.
- *Adding value*: The value of a brand goes beyond performance benefits. For example, component brands, which have their own images, contribute valuably to the final branded product, especially by establishing capabilities that might benefit the customer.
- *Quantifying the intangible*: Even if their offers are mostly intangible, firms might seek to quantify their performance aspects, such as with market metrics that clearly specify brand value. For example, by measuring results and brand performance, they can inform their brand-building programs. To estimate the relative worth of a brand, the firm should determine the incremental increase in price a customer would pay for a branded product, compared with an equivalent but unbranded product.

These identity promises in turn demand five capabilities at the organizational level:

- *Entrepreneurial*: To stay successful in the long term and reinforce its position, a brand must take an entrepreneurial outlook and remain active in the market, such as by finding and gathering input from lead customers, as well as questioning existing assumptions about their current business practices.
- *Reflexive*: When they develop a true learning culture, firms can better anticipate change, encourage risk taking, focus on ongoing value creation, monitor customers and competitors, question long-held beliefs, and learn from both mistakes and successes.

- *Innovative*: Three main types of innovation can reinforce a brand's identity: product, process, and marketing.
- *Brand-supportive dominant logic*: To build brand-supportive dominant logics (i.e., how managers think about the business and allocate resources), the firm's culture and structures must reflect the brand. This logic should also encourage internal ownership, using well-designed rewards, training, hiring policies, communications, and systems that ensure consistent delivery.
- *Executional*: Whether launching new products and campaigns, managing relationships, adapting to current and new customers, or entering and growing new markets, an executional capability ensures implementation, often by balancing competing demands.

As recommended by the study that introduced these categories, simple corporate identities are insufficient; what firms need are rich brand identities and strong business reputations for being able to provide solutions in global markets. Naturally, such richness demands multiple, coordinated, firm-level capabilities that contribute to dominant logics that prioritize the brand identity. To convince various internal functions to participate in brand positioning and other marketing initiatives, managers perform internal marketing and education related to the importance of the brand; those efforts should be reinforced by a human resource control system that is designed explicitly to ensure buy-in.

Source

Beverland, M., Napoli, J., and Lindgreen, A. (2007), "Industrial global brand leadership: A capabilities view," *Industrial Marketing Management*, 36(8), 1084-1093.

COMMUNICATION

Business-to-business (B2B) communication functions to provide customers with specific details about the product offer by the seller company. In industrial markets, this information often includes more technical content. Furthermore, relative to business-to-consumer (B2C) communication settings, an industrial branding strategy tends to entail significantly reduced costs, perhaps because the communicated content is designed to clarify the practical value of the offering and provide realistic benefits. For B2C branding, a more prominent goal is shaping consumers' preferences by creating awareness and positive images of the product, brand, or firm.

In addition, purchasing behaviors vary, as noted previously, such that the number of industrial buyers tends to be limited, and the products contain many technical features. Therefore, communication in industrial markets must clearly outline and detail the specific, technical advantages of the product offer and its capacity for satisfying the buyers' specific needs, whether those pertain to cost reductions, production optimization, or quality enhancements.

In turn, industrial branding strategies should reflect segmentation and targeting based on the different needs of industrial buying groups. In industrial markets, a single solution offer that can satisfy the needs of every buyer is extremely rare.

Although industrial buyers tend to emphasize practical utility, they are still heterogeneous with regard to their corporate values and can still be influenced by affective appeals. Sellers must ensure they have a thorough understanding of how buyers make decisions; concepts such as trust, security, and peace of mind can strongly influence the buying process. If the seller connects with a buyer on the basis of these emotional appeals, it might also evoke greater interest and increased attention. That is, sellers should identify the buying rationale but also any social or psychological considerations that buyers express.

Vignette

When Sales and Procurement Processes Are Out of Sync

In a funnel depiction of sales processes, the seller takes the initiative and drives potential customers, and these customers respond. The procurement process does not fit with this visual metaphor though, especially in B2B markets in which procurement is highly specialized, and procurement staffers are experts in their specific marketplaces and the sellers in them. Furthermore, in B2B settings, these customers rarely are individuals; the buying center or decision-making unit instead includes multiple people, taking on several roles.

Such a buying center might request information before offering the possibility of a contract to a few potential sellers, at which point the customer firm already has advanced in its decision-making process. The information it needs thus pertains to in-depth insights about how the supplier can meet the buying company's needs, along with relevant trade-offs of price, quality, or service. In this version of the seller–customer relationship, the seller's ability to understand how the buying center has prioritized and reached its perceptions of price, quality, and service is crucial. Furthermore, the procurement and purchasing process moves ahead of the sales process; procurement has already begun, even before potential suppliers are contacted. Two important implications follow:

- Sales joins the process late and needs to come up to speed quite fast.
- Information about products, services, and solutions must be easily accessible to potential customers, even before they request such information.

Sources

Bjerre, M., and Ulrich, T. (2021), *Sales Governance: The Future of Sales Management*, Copenhagen: The Value Footprint.

Bjerre, M., Johansen-Duus, H., and Ulrich, T. (2019), *Virksomheder kan sælge mere, hvis de gør som et Tour de France-hold*. Retrieved 16 June 2022 from https://videnskab.dk/forskerzonen/ kultur-samfund/virksomheder-kan-saelge-mere-hvis-de-goer-som-et-tour-de-france-hold.

Marketing Interactions in Industrial Business Environments

Communications strategies aim to confirm that the messages the sender wants to send are received accurately by the right recipients. This effort is particularly complicated in industrial settings, so it likely demands a holistic approach, spanning external, internal, and interactive marketing elements related to the business, the customer, and colleagues (e.g., employees, partners). Figure 7.1 illustrates these correlations and the various marketing interactions that take place.

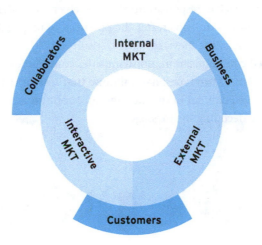

Figure 7.1   Branding Triangle

Source: Adapted from Kotler and Pfoertsch (2006)

External marketing involves pricing, distribution, and promotion processes that accompany a product offer, along its path to the customer. Internal marketing pertains to training and motivation processes, such that the firm transfers its core values to affiliates. Both processes are controlled by the focal business, but interactive marketing instead is shaped by internal marketing. In this holistic conceptualization, all three approaches are equally important, essential components of the broader strategic approach to communicating the company's message. Therefore, when formulating a holistic, corporate communication strategy, the components must also be consistent, because only then can the message that the business wants to communicate be clear and shared by all forms of its marketing and communications.

COMMUNICATION MODEL

As depicted in Figure 7.2, the communication process consists of the following components:

- Source: This origin of the message seeks to establish its own perceived credibility.
- Message: The content of the communication.
- Encoding: A process by which the message takes an appropriate form so that it can be perceived by recipients.

- Transmission: The process by which the content of the message moves from the source to the recipient, through the use of some medium.
- Receiver: A buyer that receives the content of the message being transmitted and then uses its resources to perceive it.
- Decoding: A process of reverse coding, through which the message becomes perceptible and comprehensible. It is not enough for receivers to get the message; they must understand the content as it was intended.
- Feedback: The source receives responses from the receiver about the message, which continues the communication and creates the potential to make adjustments to the communication process or the message being transmitted.
- Noise: In stage-based communication, noise impedes communication or limits its effectiveness. It consists of two types: natural noise that interferes with the senses and thus alters the perceived content of the message, and conceptual noise, which includes errors in encoding or decoding the message.

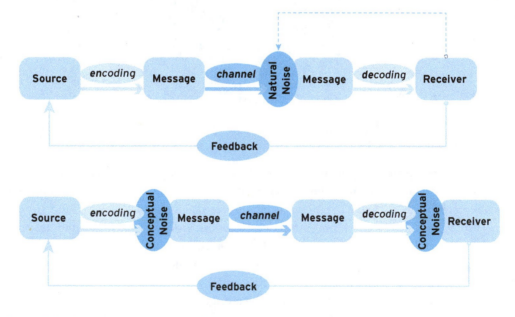

Figure 7.2 Communication Model and Noise

Source: Lasswell (1950) and Gerbner (1956)

MARKETING COMMUNICATIONS TOOLBOX

Businesses use a range of tools to manage communications with customers (existing and potential) and provide information that can encourage their awareness and acceptance of product offers. Although some of these tools are consistent across consumer and industrial markets, they take different weights and priorities within the communication mix. Industrial enterprises rely particularly on personal sales, direct marketing, public relations, trade shows and demonstrations, advertising, and sales promotion. In contrast, whereas product packaging is a relevant element of the marketing mix in consumer markets, due to its capacity to convey messages and information and shape the purchase decision at the moment the customer considers the product in the store, it is less pertinent to industrial products.

To build brand equity, the communications mix should be addressed holistically, because every element helps define the communications strategy and represents a useful tool. Therefore, marketing executives seek a good balance, to use the various tools in combination through effective resource allocations that produce greater overall results than the individual use of each tool can—an approach known as integrated marketing communications. In turn, the customer can develop a single, coherent image of the business and brand.

Promotion Strategies

Two main types of promotional strategies are pull and push formats (Figure 7.3). A pull strategy aims to generate demand from the buyer's side, usually with advertising. It tends to be more effective for lower priced products or fast-moving goods. A push strategy instead encourages buyers to make purchases, often through personal selling processes, and it generally applies to high-quality, high-priced products with complex features.

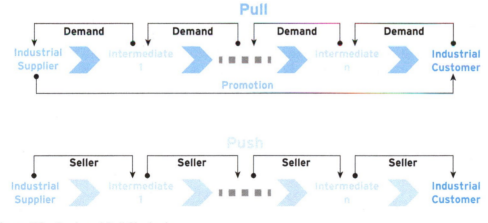

Figure 7.3 Push and Pull Strategies

Personal Sales

Personal sales involve direct, two-way communication with potential customers, designed to get them to place orders. Because the number of customers in industrial settings is relatively limited, and they often need to purchase larger quantities and request expanded forms of support, personal sales is very relevant. The communication can be customized and tailored to each customer's needs. In many cases, personal selling leads to close, long-term, profitable relationships between the seller and the buyer. The seller gains in-depth knowledge of the buyer's needs, as well as marketplace conditions. However, personal sales tend to incur increased costs, such that they may absorb a large proportion of the budget the business has available to communicate with consumers. Still, they are highly effective, with powerful effects on the image that customers develop of the selling firm and critical implications for the customer relationship.

Direct Marketing

Direct marketing aims to spark customer interest in the product offer, using materials such as direct postal mail or email, telemarketing, catalogs and newsletters, the Internet, and other direct communication channels with customers (existing or potential). Some definitions include personal sales as a form of direct marketing, but we separate them, to clarify the particular relevance of the related practices in industrial environments. Modern communication technologies have allowed interactive and more immediate forms of direct marketing, such that businesses can assess customers' responses to these communications. Such expanded capabilities of direct marketing have encouraged its growing use, even in settings in which customers appear to reject traditional forms of advertising. Its appeal stems from its ability to adjust messages to ensure the intended meaning is conveyed, in ways that support relationship maintenance with customers. Finally, direct marketing is particularly cost effective. Thus, direct marketing can be an important solution for industrial businesses that seek to reach customers easily and also allow them to reach the seller easily, because the small size of the market means that finding and communicating directly with a specific customer segment tends to be extremely important.

Public Relations

In a public relations process, the business follows a methodological plan to communicate its message to reach various stakeholders and enhance its image, through some combination of sponsorships, press materials, and so forth. The firm seeks to leverage the prestige, credibility, or authenticity linked to the promotional means for itself, such as gaining a reputation for stellar performance by connecting its image to that of a champion in an athletic domain. Such messages are often popular with wide audiences, including potential customers who avoid contact with direct sellers or advertising. To manage public relations effectively, the business must keep constant track of trends and customer attitudes, which is part of the reason that they can become very costly. Furthermore, the business lacks complete control over the publicity created by public relations, so it must undertake careful planning to increase the chances that the conveyed message is appropriate and likely to appeal to buyers, despite being indirect. Ultimately, public relations are cornerstones of efforts to establish credibility for the business message, because they increase familiarity with the brand name and, ideally, evoke positive connotations of the firm.

Trade Fairs and Exhibitions

Trade fairs and exhibitions help make the name of the business known and build the interest of relevant buyers, within a limited time and space. Unlike other methods for collecting relevant information quickly, trade fairs give customers access to many potential suppliers, at relatively low costs, so they can compare different product offers efficiently. Because of the potential significance of agreements reached during professional trade fairs, balanced against the substantial costs of participating in such events, sellers need to take great care in selecting events, to maximize the outcomes for any given budget. A seller can increase the returns on its investment if it ensures the visitors to the trade fair represent viable customer prospects and then crafts an offer that fits their needs.

Advertising

Advertising is "the placement of announcements and messages in time or space by business firms, nonprofit organizations, government agencies, and individuals who seek to inform and/or persuade members of a particular target market or audience regarding their products, services, organizations or ideas" (American Marketing Association, 2022). Regardless of the media used, advertising must have a clear message, directly related to the product offer, along with meaningful appeals to customers. In industrial settings, advertising is relatively less effective than in consumer markets, because professional business buyers tend to adopt rational purchasing processes and know precisely which features they want in the product, which they seek to obtain at the moment they need it. Thus impulsive or emotion-based purchases are rare. Still, advertising can signal core brand values, (re)stimulate demand, and reduce the time required to complete the sale. Furthermore, whereas mass advertising can quickly become expensive, and perhaps too costly for industrial sellers, some more specialized, alternative forms are less expensive. For example, a seller might combine personal sales with advertising tactics, as well as define clearly targeted audiences, to maximize the benefits of both investments.

Notably, the advertising planning process features clearly defined objectives, specific time horizons, and efforts to ensure consistency across all elements of the marketing mix. Thus advertising managers define the target audience carefully (in terms of size, geographic distribution, customs), design the content precisely, decide which media to use, and schedule how often and for how long the message appears. The content should contain all the information necessary for the buyer (e.g., technical, financial) to recognize the product offer as unique and valuable. For the choice of media, relevance to the audience is a central consideration, though industrial enterprises tend to emphasize written forms of mass media and also use electronic media to spread the information more widely. Frequent or extended displays of advertising can be effective but also quickly extend to overexposure, creating a risk of saturation. If competitors are not sharing frequent advertising messages, it can benefit the focal firm's efforts. Finally, evaluations before and after the implementation of a promotion plan, combined with replenishing efforts, can identify and resolve points needing corrective action, such as through questionnaire pre-checks, focus groups, social media surveys, and monitoring.

Sales Promotion

Sales promotions seek to increase the value of product offers on the market over time, such as by providing economic incentives, discounts, or a trial period. They may be relatively less effective in B2B settings, where buyers already know what product offers they need, but sales promotions can still be pertinent in transactions with retailers, distributors, or other channel members. For example, by offering retailers economic incentives, sellers might get their products better shelf placements. The incentives can include simple discounts, regardless of the quantity sold, for a specific time frame, or they might establish quantity thresholds, such that the wholesale price is lower if customers buy larger volumes. Another option is cash rebates, provided once customers reach some predetermined amount of purchases. Finally, some discounts are linked to the product units sold by a channel intermediary (bill-back, scan back, sales drive).

COMMUNICATION AND CORPORATE SOCIAL RESPONSIBILITY

Businesses can signal and communicate about their corporate social responsibility (CSR) if they engage in fair, socially responsible, sustainable practices, in terms of their innovation, production, and promotion. Socially responsible practices can influence consumption behavior; in turn, social responsibility norms strongly influence business functioning, due to their potential impacts on the company's reputation, philosophy, and values. Communication strategies formulated to present such CSR therefore should reflect the actual corporate CSR culture, which can establish the necessary conditions for a strategic competitive advantage. When these communications align with the needs and concerns of customers, employees, and the wider public, the firm can build strong ties with all these entities, especially if its communications are transparent and reflect its accountability. If the communication succeeds, and the business establishes its reputation as a good corporate citizen, it can have substantial competitive benefits. Communication and promotional efforts that tend to align with CSR, as in Figure 7.4, include the following:

- Cause promotions: The business supports a cause with promotional efforts to raise awareness of it.
- Cause-related marketing: Certain activities, such as donations for a specific purpose, are linked to business performance issues.
- Corporate social marketing: Campaigns aim to change observed behaviors in a positive way.
- Community volunteering: Time allocated by employees or partners to support a cause.
- Corporate philanthropy: Making donations or in-kind contributions, such as provision of services or corporate resources.
- CSR business practices: Adoption and implementation of business attitudes, philosophies, practices, and investments that lead to both environmental and social prosperity.

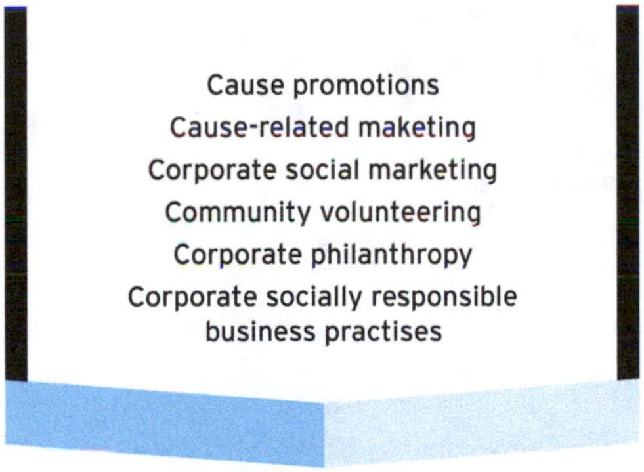

Cause promotions
Cause-related maketing
Corporate social marketing
Community volunteering
Corporate philanthropy
Corporate socially responsible
business practises

Figure 7.4   Corporate Communication and Social Responsibility

Categories of Industrial Sellers

Depending on the activities they undertake, sales staff can be categorized as follows (Figure 7.5):

- Order takers: Contact existing customers to receive their orders, usually for standardized products. Increasingly replaced by more cost-efficient technology options (e.g., specialized information systems).
- Missionary salespeople: Present product offers to an intermediary that can influence customers to make a purchase (indirect sale); often used in chemical, pharmaceutical, and beverage sectors.
- Trade sellers: Work to circulate consumer products through networks of wholesalers and retailers, to increase overall sales among all buyers. Establish long-term relationships dominated by trust. Often act as consultants in terms of promotion and marketing of the product.
- Technical/institutional sellers: Take all necessary steps, from identifying a potential buyer to executing the sale, then providing a range of services, such as counseling and consulting to find more effective solutions.

Figure 7.5 Categories of Industrial Sellers

Motivation of Staff for Industrial Sales

The stringent requirements of sales jobs and the circumstances in which this work takes place, as reflected by demands to balance the needs of customers and the employing seller firm, can prompt anxiety, discomfort, and general dissatisfaction among sales staff. Therefore, the employing company must create conditions, structures, and processes to provide appropriate incentives that encourage industrial sellers to achieve better performance and efficiency.

Vignette

Value Chains and Supplier Perceptions of Corporate Social Responsibility

With CSR initiatives, organizations seek to address the social and environmental impacts of their business operations, ensure the ethical behavior of business partners, manage relations with wider sets of societal actors, and achieve social legitimacy. In global value chains (GVCs), some of those partners and societal actors include suppliers in developing countries, which may require assistance in achieving the codes of conduct imposed by the buyers, as lead firms in the supply chain.

In particular, buyer-imposed codes of conduct and directives—whether developed by the buyers themselves or ethical sourcing and multistakeholder initiatives—demand that suppliers implement the listed demands—many of which may be incomprehensible or practically impossible for these actors. In the garment industry, for example, outsourcing of production to developing economies such as Myanmar is common, but many of the suppliers have only recently been introduced to the notion of CSR. The ongoing transition and changing position of Myanmar in the global economy also continues to inform how garment suppliers might make sense of and implement CSR.

On the basis of an investigation of this supply chain, Bae et al. (2021) propose a typology of various GVC governance modes (captive, modular, market relations) and embeddedness forms (societal, network, and territorial), as recreated in Table 7.1. If suppliers are subject to captive governance by buyers, they adopt CSR approaches that match those buyers' norms and values (i.e., societal embeddedness). They also reveal substantial network embeddedness, such that they lose connections to local norms and practices for work or employment. If instead suppliers experience modular governance, their CSR views still reflect the norms and values of buyers, but their network embeddedness in the buyer's GVCs is weaker, so suppliers remain territorially embedded, even as they practice more CSR. Such territorial embeddedness is particularly strong for suppliers that have been in operation since before Myanmar transitioned to a semi-authoritarian democracy. Finally, suppliers subject to market-based governance tend to embrace CSR activities that signal greater territorial and societal embeddedness in the local context. These operators tend to be small-scale, easily replaceable suppliers, so their network embeddedness is minimal; they are only loosely integrated into the buyer's GVCs and feel less pressure to engage in CSR dictated by those buyers.

Table 7.1 Supplier CSR Based on GVC Governance and Embeddedness

		Buyer Governance Mode		
		Captive	Modular	Market-based relations
Embeddedness Type	Societal	Supplier CSR reflects societal embeddedness with buyers, accepting codes of conduct and social audits.	Supplier CSR reflects societal embeddedness with buyers but also with suppliers themselves, which can create contradictions and supplier discontent.	Supplier CSR mainly reflects their own societal embeddedness, local to the country of production.
	Network	Suppliers are tightly integrated into GVCs of their buyers, which provide exclusive sourcing relationships in return for demonstrated code compliance.	Suppliers are less tightly integrated into GVCs.	Suppliers are loosely integrated into GVCs.
	Territorial	Suppliers are somewhat territorially unembedded from the country of production.	Suppliers display greater territorial embeddedness in the country of production.	Suppliers are territorially embedded in the country of production.

(Continued)

This framework suggests a way to pose and address fundamental questions about the effectiveness of buyer-driven CSR paradigms in GVCs. Can suppliers, facing cutthroat competition on a global level, as well as international buyers determined to exploit them to achieve lower operating costs, really be expected to achieve social responsibility?

Source

Bae, J., Lund-Thomsen, P., and Lindgreen, A. (2021), "Global value and supplier perceptions of corporate social responsibility: A case study of garment manufacturers in Myanmar," *Global Networks*, 21(4), 653-680.

THE PROCESS OF PERSONAL SELLING

Sales goals need to be determined in advance and customized, so that they appeal to the entire sales team and reflect the specific characteristics of each sales opportunity and each individual salesperson. These targets might refer to a certain level of sales (value or quantity) or development of the customer base, as well as a desired level of quality provided to customers. Regardless of what the goals target though, they must be specific, realistic, comprehensible, feasible, and acceptable to all sales staff (Figure 7.6).

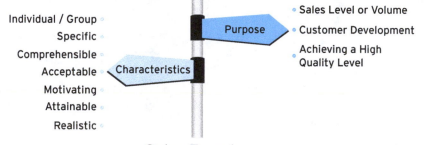

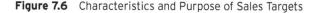

Figure 7.6 Characteristics and Purpose of Sales Targets

Once goals have been set, the next step is to map specific sales areas, which can provide more insights into which sales program the salespeople should adopt and which moves they should make, including how much time they should devote to potential customers (Figure 7.7). Distributing sales staff to area zones also can ensure full market coverage, across the greatest possible range, in the most economical fashion. The best distribution acknowledges each salesperson's existing abilities and skills, as well as their particular preferences.

With appropriate analyses, the company can decide whether to expand its own sales team or outsource these efforts. If it decides to build up its own sales team, it also needs to determine how many sales staff to hire: greater numbers might increase coverage, but they also increase the associated costs, reduce the income attributable to each salesperson, threaten to undermine satisfaction among the sales staff, challenge collaborative coworker relationships, and increase the likelihood of layoffs.

Figure 7.7 Intended Goals of the Demarcation of Sales Areas

Each of the eight stages of personal selling (Figure 7.8) consists of specific features:

- Prospecting. This phase consists of identifying and evaluating potential customers. A company might seek to find new customers if it has lost existing customers or suffered an interruption of the relationship, but also to continue developing and enriching its business clientele.
- Pre-approach. In this phase, the salesperson gathers all necessary information about the customer's needs and the necessary actions to be effective during the sales process.
- Approach. During the initial, direct contact of the seller and the customer, the customer's first impressions form, based on the efforts by the seller, so the seller seeks to stimulate the customer's interest, provide motivation for the customer to attend subsequent presentations of the product offer, and help the customer make a logical transition to the next steps in the process.
- Presentation. Assuming the previous phase has been successful, the seller seeks to persuade the potential customer of the quality, reliability, and appropriateness of the product offer, as well as establish the solvency and reliability of the company. The seller should outline the characteristics of the product offer and the benefits it can provide, with a simple, comprehensible approach, avoiding too much technical analysis or detail.

- Trial close. Having determined how close the potential customer is to entering the purchase process, the salesperson might continue the presentation to address any hesitations, doubts, and objections from the buyer's side.

- Objections. The seller must be prepared to respond to objections from the buyer, with ready information but also an appropriate attitude and behaviors that can win over the customer. Patience is important, though the seller also must be able to manage the buyer's objections to overcome concerns and move on toward the purchase.

- Agreement. The actual purchase takes place. The fine details are identified, and any procedural elements that accompany the completion of the purchase are addressed.

- Follow-up. Once an agreement exists, the seller must ensure that its product is delivered as promised, then continue managing the customer relationship over time by providing post-purchase services, gathering feedback, and identifying and meeting new customer requirements with new, appropriately tailored product offers. The ultimate goal is to encourage the customer to remain loyal to the relationship, which increases the seller's profitability both directly (increased sales) and indirectly through a stronger brand image. It also diminishes the risk of customer churn and its negative consequences.

Figure 7.8 Process and Stages of Personal Selling

Source: Adapted from Tomaras (2009)

DETERMINING THE NUMBER OF SALES PERSONNEL REQUIRED

To determine the size of the sales staff (Figure 7.9), one popular method involves calculating the total costs of sales and their allocation, divided by the amount allocated to the annual salary of each salesperson. The result determines the number of sales staff that the business can support financially. Another option proposes adding salespeople to designated sales areas, guided by the balance between the marginal profit resulting from this addition and the associated costs. This method requires access to a large volume of information that the organization can analyze in making the necessary calculations. A third method takes workloads into account. Once the organization has identified the customers it hopes to serve, as well as the number of visits they will need to agree to a purchase, it can define the number of visits required throughout the year. With information about how many visits a salesperson can accommodate, it can then determine the number of salespeople to employ to fulfill all the necessary sales visits.

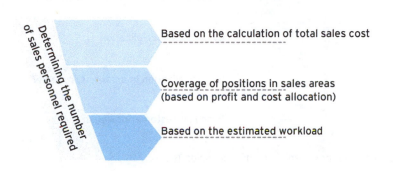

Figure 7.9 Estimating the Required Number of Sales Staff

CRITERIA FOR ORGANIZING SALES PERSONNEL IN INDUSTRIAL ENTERPRISES

The organization of the sales team depends on the product assortment the company offers (breadth and depth), the configuration of its distribution network, the geographical configuration of sales areas, and the segments of the market that it is targeting (Figure 7.10).

- Geographical specialization: If a salesperson covers a specific geographic area, they promote the whole range of the business's products to any customer in that area. This method reduces travel time and can exploit the particularities of the area; it also avoids disputes among salespeople over responsibility for the area. However, it can be challenging to serve diverse customers, regardless of category, that just happen to be located in proximity, as well as have a good familiarity with all of the company's products.
- Product specialization: Specialization in a product category or line is effective if the products are very technically complex or differ significantly. Salespeople then focus on familiar products that they specialize in; they therefore neglect the rest.
- Market specialization: With the customer as the focus, this method effectively classifies them and then, for each category, assigns a sales team, as is appropriate when there are significant differences in purchasing behaviors and requirements across these categories.
- Customer power: Specific sales executives might be entrusted with the responsibility of making contact with businesses with great (negotiating, purchasing) power, to ensure better service, closer communication, and coverage of their special requirements.

None of these forms needs to be applied individually; mixed applications are common, to reflect the unique features of each market.

Criteria for Organizing Industrial Sales Teams

Based on geographical specialization

By product specialization

By specialization in a paritcular market

Based on customer power/size

Figure 7.10   Criteria for Organizing Industrial Sales Teams

8

THE MARKETING MIX: INDUSTRIAL PRICING

———— **Learning Objectives** ————

- Define the terms "price" and "pricing."
- Understand the pricing strategies applied to existing and new products and their characteristics.
- Identify cost analysis issues.
- Analyze methods for determining the price level of an industrial product.
- Outline the strategic decisions associated with price adjustments.
- Identify and diagnose incorrect management practices with regard to pricing.
- Create a generalized pricing model.
- Clarify the role of the Internet as a novel environment for pricing decisions.
- Outline the unique strategic pricing issues related to online environments.

PRICE AND PRICING

The concept of price is quite different from the concept of cost. The value assigned to a product in an industrial environment is an indication of the benefits it offers. Along with the benefits, the price reflects the magnitude of the sacrifice (at an economic level) required of the supplier to be able to deliver the benefits associated with an offering. Moreover, the price defines the producer company's capacity to make a profit and to fulfill its own competitive goals (see Figure 8.1).

Figure 8.1 Price as Reflected by the Business Activity

As the supplier formulates a price level for its product offering, it simultaneously—and inevitably—communicates messages about the features the organization has managed to incorporate into the product (e.g., physical characteristics, intangible features), the marketing strategy that the supplier company has adopted (in relation to the particular product and/or specific customer), the competitive conditions in the environment, and the overall value that the product offer promises to provide to the customer.

To understand the function of industrial pricing though, it also is necessary to recognize that any price formulation is a constituent and a consequence of multiple effects (Figure 8.2), emanating from various factors that form the operations and decisions of the supplier company, and then with relevant implications for the client company.

Determining the Price Level: Benefits and Sacrifices

The variables that reflect the supplier company's perspective should determine benefits that the customer can expect to enjoy. These customer-perceived benefits shape the value of the particular product offering (Figure 8.3), based on the offer itself and its uses (e.g., technical details, technology incorporated), along with the services provided to support the product and cooperation or interactions with skilled employees of the supplier company, all of which contribute to resolving any issues the customer needs addressed.

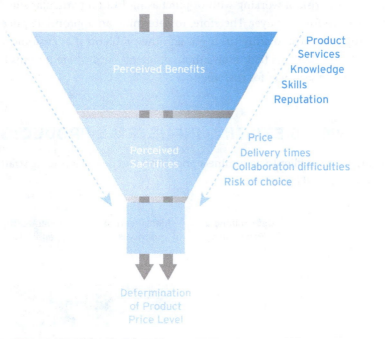

Figure 8.2 Price Formulation, Based on Perceived Benefits and Sacrifices

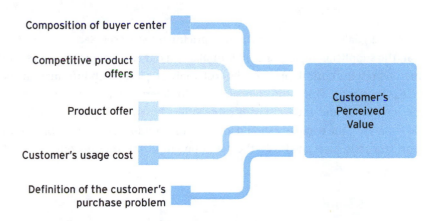

Figure 8.3 Perceived Value from the Customer's Point of View

Source: Adapted from Webster (1991)

Other customer-related factors represent perceived sacrifices, made to obtain and consume the desired product offering. The price sacrifice should be offset by the perceived benefits the customer anticipates, in the form of value gained from the total package of product benefits.

Another sacrifice required of customers involves the execution of the order and subsequent delivery considerations. If customers regard dealing with a particular supplier as particularly difficult, such as due to its poor supply chain or information systems management, stringent credit policies, or lack of collaboration, advancing along these stages may appear like a sacrifice too. Finally, the risk of working with or purchasing from a particular supplier represents a perceived sacrifice for the buyer. Therefore, to determine an appropriate price for a product offering, the supplier must identify the needs and the problems that customers have, how its offering can establish benefits that resolve those problems, and where it needs to facilitate the process to reduce the sacrifices for customers.

PRICING EXISTING INDUSTRIAL PRODUCTS

In more detail, for a supplier to determine a price level and devise a pricing strategy, it must go through several stages (Figure 8.4).

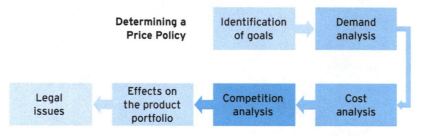

Figure 8.4 Designing Pricing Policy

Source: Adapted from Avlonitis et al. (2008)

First, the desired goals to be achieved through pricing must be set. Second, once the objectives are clear, the supplier company should formulate an overview of prevailing demand conditions, which represents critical input for the cost analysis, along with information about the competitive environment. Third, the company should determine whether (and how) a focal product offer combines and interacts with other offers by the company. Fourth, following these detailed analyses, the company should identify any pending issues and concerns, including legal considerations, associated with the development of this product offer.

Identification of Goals

To formulate a pricing policy, the firm's price targets must align with the broader organizational objectives, according to an overall strategy. The decision of which price level to establish for a product must also reflect a series of central, critical objectives, together with relatively minor but still important goals (Figure 8.5). The primary objective is to achieve a basic return on investments made to produce the requisite supply of the offering. Another objective is achieving desired market share; survival and competitive advantages are further main objectives. Secondary objectives or goals for pricing processes might relate to competitive functions, such as managing relationships across the various channels linked to the organization's product line. In combining these goals, a pricing strategy might aim at different outcomes, such as attaining some certain level of economic efficiency, gaining a greater share of the market, or responding to challenges posed by competitors. Its implementation thus reflects the formulation of multiple goals, which might not always be well balanced or might even come into conflict. But as long as the objectives are clear to all stakeholders (i.e., functional members of the supply chain that must work together), the expected results should be aligned with choices formulated in relation to the other elements of the marketing mix.

Figure 8.5 Purposes of Pricing

Analyzing Demand

Focus on Customer Needs

The supplier organization should establish likely uses of the product offer, along with predictions of customers' expectations related to those uses. With these insights, the supplier can better gauge which price level will produce sufficient perceived value for the customer to seek out and acquire the product offering.

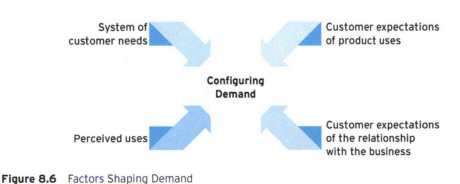

Figure 8.6 Factors Shaping Demand

The Demand Analysis

Analyzing demand for the product offering and the target sector, as in Figure 8.6, helps determine expected sales volume (monetary value and quantity). As we have noted repeatedly, industrial markets are composed of relatively fewer customers, but these limited numbers do not necessarily make analyses easier. Rather, the multiple uses available for most offerings complicate the process; in particular, the analysis might need to extend to other sectors, with potentially distinct structures. For such an approach, market segmentation efforts can identify potential target markets and the value propositions to provide them, which in turn constitutes valuable information for demand estimation efforts. A segmentation process in turn requires secondary data, whether provided by businesses or gathered through sector-based studies, which can also inform demand analyses. Finally, the application of complementary methods (qualitative and quantitative) is often required to identify trends and make forecasts, as well as account for varying scenarios.

Contributions of Experience and Science

Experience and instinct, or a "gut feeling," often guide business decisions and frame the preceding types of analyses. But experience and instinct are not sufficient to achieve robust decision-making, particularly when we consider the inherently dynamic character of wider competitive environments. Therefore, decision-makers need scientific evidence to guide their analyses, actions, and decisions (Figure 8.7).

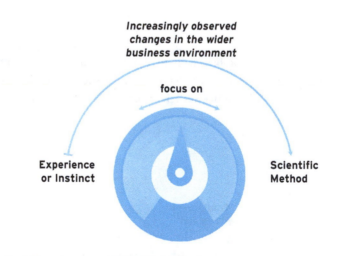

Figure 8.7 Instinct/Experience and Scientific Method

Analysis of Market History

Estimating demand can benefit particularly from analyses of historical data related to the market. Various statistical methods can support such efforts, to ensure the conclusions that emerge are objective, though such approaches cannot achieve appropriate predictions in conditions in which the data and the environment keep changing.

Market Tests

Sampling is a process of selecting an appropriate segment of the market, such that the resulting sample represents the characteristics of the overall market. By applying alternative test pricing scenarios, an analyst can assess market responses to changing price levels, then predict the impacts that similar pricing decisions would have for the market as a whole. Businesses with access to larger markets usually can apply this market test method more effectively, because they have the flexibility and means to select different samples, as well as the operational resources required to perform such analyses.

However, for a particular category of industrial products, this methodological approach is inapplicable, that is, domains in which the products are not available, so they cannot be integrated into experimental, alternative pricing scenarios, or those in which the specificity or complexity of the production processes for the focal products (e.g., heavy-duty equipment, installations) would make the application of the method overly burdensome.

Elasticity of Demand

As the price level of the product offer changes, the quantity demanded varies. Demand flexibility represents the magnitude of the difference, and it informs the resulting demand. Its calculation is complicated, involving the vast number of parameters that can combine to affect demand, of which the price is just one component. In some cases, demand for a product offer decreases (increases) when its price level decreases (increases), such that the direction of these changes can even match.

To establish a demand elasticity parameter, the supplier must understand its offering relative to those of its competitors. If the differentiation between them is minimal (from customers' perspectives), demand elasticity should increase; if this differentiation is strong, demand elasticity likely decreases. A more precise determination of flexibility requires the use of statistical methods, techniques, and tools.

Cost Analysis

Controlling for the costs borne by the business is also necessary to evaluate different pricing parameters. The goal of this sort of analysis is to determine a minimum possible price level for the product offering; using this value, the supplier can apply a cost-plus pricing method, based on the profit margin it seeks to achieve, to establish a stable price percentage. That is, the total cost incurred by a business consists of a substantial variable element, depending on production performance or sales, as well as the wider market, competition, and the existence of substitute products, so a percentage approach can be effective, to keep pace with changing overall costs and ensure a consistent profit margin.

Classification of Cost Elements

We note three broad categories of cost elements that confront industrial enterprises:

1   General industrial expenses, which cannot be attributed to individual products but refer to the range of a business's activities; they are not based on any production or performance factors.
2   Direct costs associated with the production of a particular product.
3   Indirect costs, which may be associated with the production of one product but may also be linked to the production of a wider set of other products.

Experience Curves

Also known as learning curves (Tomaras, 2009), experience curves reflect the tendency for the costs borne by an enterprise during an initial production period to be higher, then decrease over time. As time goes by and the business continues its operations, it gains more experience and knowledge about production processes, which should reveal ways to make them more efficient. Accordingly, when designing and implementing a pricing strategy, the business should explore all options for leveraging its experience and include these ideas in its cost analysis. To capitalize on experience curves, the business needs to enrich its pricing analyses and algorithms to reflect the experience it has gained.

Break-Even Analysis

Another analysis aims to determine the level of production and amount of sales required to ensure the supplier breaks even or makes a profit from expected sales (Figure 8.8). Such an analysis relies on the formula $BEP = CT / [PU - CV - U]$, where BEP is the level of output at the break-even point (production units), CT is the total cost (monetary units), PU is the price per unit of product (monetary units), and $CV - U$ is the variable cost per unit of product (monetary units). Applying this formula reveals the final price per product unit—as long as there exists some forecast for achieved sales volumes (in product units)—at which sales will be profitable. Because a break-even analysis covers a specific, selected pricing policy and offers a restricted view of the results, businesses would need to apply different possible scenarios and break-even points (i.e., through a sensitivity analysis) to get a more complete picture.

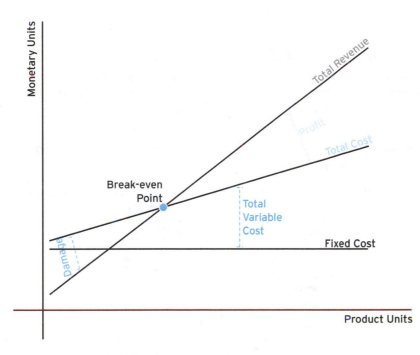

Figure 8.8 Break-Even Analysis Graph

Competitive Analysis

The competitive environment largely determines the highest price that an organization can set, so each organization should analyze these conditions to formulate its pricing policy. In particular, it should investigate the pricing policy applied by its competitors and the characteristics of their product offerings. Then it can turn to its own strategic goals. Finally, it should anticipate the likely responses of competitors to the implementation of its own chosen pricing policy. Such assessments demand various kinds of data, which the organization can access through market research efforts, reviews of annual reports and websites published by competitors, and its own experience and knowledge in the market. In addition, the strategy should reflect the strengths of the organization in relation to its competitors, as well as its strategic pursuits.

Notably, an analysis of the competitive environment should not be limited to identifying pricing conditions and selecting some appropriate price among competing products, which the focal firm can "borrow" and apply to its own offerings. Instead, the analysis should aim to explore possibilities for properly differentiating the organization with the price it sets. The insights sought through the competitive analysis might include price but should also address distinctive product features, services, and distribution characteristics. Then the organization can increase its profit margins, through pricing and other matched strategies.

Consequences for the Company's Product Portfolio

To formulate a specific pricing policy, in reference to a particular product offering, the firm also needs to identify the potential impacts on other products in its portfolio and their sales. The risk of cannibalism is salient here; this term refers to a situation in which one product generates a stronger market response than another product in the same firm's portfolio, such that the latter product loses sales. This outcome is usually unintended and undesirable, because it limits the market share and sales of the company as a whole, despite improved sales of the stronger product (see Figure 8.9).

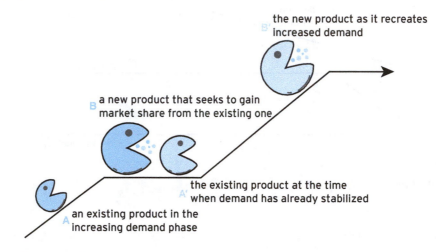

Figure 8.9 Market Cannibalism

Source: Adapted from Landis, S. (2013)

Legal Considerations

The company's activities have legal implications too, both within each jurisdiction in which it operates and on a global level. Various legislative regulations pertain to pricing.

METHODS USED TO DETERMINE THE PRICE LEVEL

Figure 8.10 lists several different pricing approaches.

Calculating the Price Level According to Costs

Two common pricing methods differ in the extent to which they include production costs when calculating the final price for a product. The appeal of these methods is their reassurance that the companies can achieve some set level of profit. We outlined the cost-plus method previously; it increases the price by a certain percentage margin over the costs incurred (or expected) for some production level, which then establishes the desired level of profit. Another option is the mark-up method, which sets a specific price level to ensure the predetermined profit level, earned with the sales the product is expected to generate. The company does not account for production costs with this method.

Figure 8.10 Pricing Approaches

These methods may sound easy to implement, which is largely because they ignore specific market conditions, data, and dynamics. Among the dynamic features excluded from these methods, we note the level and nature of competition, the presence of alternative or substitute products in the market, and price differences of products that have reached different life cycle stages. Furthermore, both competition and customers (and their needs) shape the axes of perceived value that the product can offer, which also cannot be accounted for with a strictly cost-based approach. Nor do these methods give companies a means to learn the price level that customers would consider fair.

Still, despite these limitations, the costs borne by the company in its productive activity must be addressed. The various partial elements that constitute costs must be analyzed carefully, to ensure their appropriate management. Having achieved a clear image, the cost can provide a reference point, or lower desired limit, on the price being formulated.

Calculating the Price Level According to Demand

An alternative approach acknowledges market conditions that shape demand for the product. By determining and predicting this demand, based on customers' perceptions of the product and its value, as well as of competitive offerings, a company can try to match these perceptions by varying the price level with prevailing market conditions or the features of each target segment, as well as the distinct potential uses of its product offer. A higher price level likely is justified if the product offer represents a critical solution (and offers more benefits) in relation to a particular usage setting. This strategy likely works best if the supplier company actively seeks and appeals to customers who are likely to adopt different uses. It can also be beneficial when parallel or specialized distributors enter the distribution channel. Conversely, if the customer approaches the supplier company and asks for a price, this strategy might not be effective.

To implement a price differentiation strategy, the supplier must be aware of and incorporate the pricing of competitive products, as well as their specific uses. If it can do so, pricing becomes an effective tool in the marketing toolbox, taking on a critical role in the overall marketing strategy. However, this strategy may also increase the risk of aggressive tactics in customer negotiations, in terms of customers' purchasing behaviors and expressed demand. For example, when customers also function as suppliers of other companies, they may be prone to impulsive, somewhat instinctive pursuits to maintain existing conditions or constantly achieve cost reductions throughout the distribution channel. Such concerns are especially problematic for suppliers that have invested to develop product offers with greater value. To overcome this challenge, the supplier company can institute procedures to train customers, including the consumers at the end of the value chain.

Calculating the Price Level According to Competition

If a focal firm relies on the price levels set by competitors to set its own pricing policy, it likely seeks to ensure its pricing is competitive, while still acknowledging its own costs and the likely reactions by competitors. Beyond just the price, the company must compare the characteristics of its product offers with those of its competitors, in terms of perceived utility or desired features; even though the specific circumstances in which the offering will be consumed and used are important, they usually are not integrated into the method for calculating price levels.

Accordingly, the risks of this method can be disproportionately large. It creates the potential for pricing wars, including successive price reductions by all competitors in the market, that ultimately damage all the companies involved by undermining their profitability levels. Even if it does not go so far as a price war, basing operations and activities on competitors is likely flawed, due to the inherent differences between different actors in a market. Repeating and mimicking a pricing strategy implemented in a competitive environment is never a guarantee of success. However, it may be a reasonable solution for young companies that have not yet developed their own marketing capabilities, as a way to maintain a pertinent orientation toward its pricing policy.

PRICING FOR NEW INDUSTRIAL PRODUCTS

The pricing process is particularly critical for new product introductions.

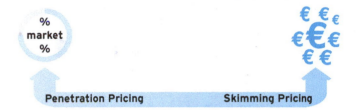

Figure 8.11   Alternative Pricing Strategies for New Products

In such conditions, two pricing methods dominate (Figure 8.11): penetration and skimming. Often expressed as diametrically opposed, and depicted as the extremes of a straight line, these strategies can define the position of the company. With penetration pricing, the company sets low prices to increase sales volumes, gain rapid market share, and strengthen the position of its products. With a skimming strategy, by choosing a higher price level for its product (cf. competitors'), the company seeks to increase its short-term profits from selling the specific product. Both methods can be stand-alone implementations, but an appropriate mix of methods may be optimal; this mix then can be adjusted according to the product life cycle phase. Choosing a different method to apply on a case-by-case basis may offer the best solution to the price level selection challenge.

Managing and Adjusting to the Chosen Pricing Policy

Strategic Discounts

Some companies offer strategic discounts, within the context of their broader pricing strategies, to alter the price levels of their products temporarily and produce a sale, while still maintaining their other, strategically defined goals. Several types of strategic discounts are available (Figure 8.12), which companies can choose among, according to their strategic goals:

- Volume discounts: These discounts establish different discount classes, depending on the volume of sales to the customer, which could be based on the quantity of products or their monetary value. The level of this discount often increases with greater sales volume.
- Cumulative bulk purchase discounts: With a philosophy similar to that for volume discounts, these strategies segment classes of buyers on the basis of cumulative purchase data over time (e.g., quarters, semesters, years).
- Time payment discounts: Some discounts increase depending on how quickly the customer pays. In contrast with a delayed payment, an immediate payment thus earns a price reward. An alternative approach involves credit margins, provided by the supplier to the customer.

Categories	Characteristics
Volume purchases	Scale of discounts based on volume of purchases per order
Cumulative volume of purchases	Scale of discounts based on volume of purchases for total orders over a period of time
Payment time	Scale of discounts based on repayment time

Figure 8.12   Categories and Characteristics of Strategic Discounts

The choice of which discount to offer may depend on factors such as:

- Conditions of the market environment.
- Practices adopted by competitor companies.
- Costs associated with the product.
- Original product prices.
- The nature and elasticity of demand for the product.

Short-Term, Tactical Discounts

Along with strategic discounts, another tactic involves providing regular, short-term discounts for some predetermined period. In this case, as long as the firm's long-term objectives are not harmed, the discounts can effectively promote adoption of the product, as well as address cash flow problems.

Bidding Contests

Forms

Bidding contests, also known as tenders, are usually applied by public, common interest, or non-profit organizations, to find a supplier that will charge them the lowest possible price to obtain a product offering. The contests might be open and informal, such that tenders are submitted orally, or closed and formal, such that clear procedures are followed and all tenders are announced at the same time.

Strategic Options for Participating in Bidding Competitions

Taking part in a bidding contest requires significant resources. For the supplier, the decision to participate should reflect its careful consideration of whether it can actually and realistically meet the obligations arising from entering into such an agreement. Because of the strategic importance of this option, management should only agree to participate in a bidding contest (and, by extension, potentially provide the offering) if doing so would support its specific, clear, and unambiguous strategic goals. Such goals might include greater profitability, increased sales volume, access to new markets or activities, efficient utilization of the company's resources and production capabilities, exploiting its potential, developing its reputation, or simply survival. Depending on its primary goals, the company then should establish the necessary conditions and procedures to enable it to formulate and submit a reasonable proposal to the bidding contests it considers relevant.

The criteria for evaluating bids as relevant should also be formulated in advance. They might be objective or subjective, but each company should establish its own unique parameters to evaluate whether to participate in a contest. In addition to establishing key criteria, the company needs to assign them various weights, according to their importance for determining whether the company submits a bid. This weighting procedure tends to reflect the subjective judgment, experience, and knowledge of managers. Ultimately though, they must base the decision to submit a bid on the company's ability to manage and meet the needs of the customer that posted the bid, in the most objective way possible.

For the various bidders seeking the right to undertake a project, it is difficult to know what price level will be established by their competitors. Therefore, each company should explore the competitive environment and try to determine which goals its competitors seek to satisfy when they pursue a particular bidding competition. With such insights, the focal firm can determine the relevance of winning a particular bid, such as by offering a lower price than it expects competitors to demand. With these insights it can develop a specific pricing strategy to implement, in the context of its participation in a bidding competition.

Management Errors in Pricing in Industrial Enterprises

In some cases, managers make the wrong choices in determining the price level a product, reflecting several possible misconceptions (Saavedra, 2016):

- Price manipulation to increase sales. When the goals refer to a certain sales volume, the company's decision-makers might choose to cut prices to reach it, a practice with significant consequences, such that it is known as "discounter's syndrome" (Figure 8.13). A manager suffering from this syndrome reduces prices to achieve a specific sales volume and initially enjoys some profits, but this positive outcome creates a false portrait. Over time, as these "benefits" accrue, the company reaches a point that it is selling below its cost, and it suffers losses (rather earns profits) on each unit produced/sold. For industrial companies, in transactions involving high-volume orders, the threat to their revenues is high. Once created, such a situation is difficult to rectify; by the time the company does so, competitors may have responded by lowering their prices, so it faces an even more detrimental situation.

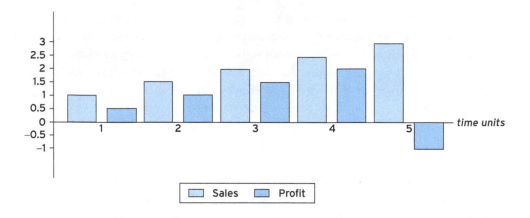

Figure 8.13 Discounter's Syndrome

Source: Adapted from Saavedra (2016)

- Price manipulation to make use of production capacity. In markets with stable inflation rates, industrial companies might use price levels to ensure stable production levels. Pricing managers then might decide to lower the price level, at specific points in time for a period, but they often fail to foresee the impacts of these choices in the medium or longer term. In the short term, it appears beneficial, especially in relation to sales volume goals (e.g., monthly quotas). Raising the price level is not as feasible in an industrial environment, because customers usually reach an agreement for a certain (fixed) price level (especially in environments with constant inflation). Agreements that establish price level stability can guarantee—at least to a certain degree—stable costs for customers. However, if inflation is not stable, supplier companies might determine the final price according to factors that affect the cost.
- Prices drop even if the product offer performs well. In a price war, competitors with superior offerings might promise lower prices than those with low value offerings, as both a proposal and a solution. It helps the sales staff demonstrate the superiority of the specific product offer by invoking more trials. Companies that design and deliver superior product offers that meet specific use cases thus require well-trained, well-prepared, specialized sales staff.

General Model of Price Determination for Technical Products

The theoretical model of methodical, step-by-step approaches for determining price levels in Figure 8.14 is based on the measurable benefits the product offer provides, in terms of the kind of problem it aims to solve. Applying this model requires an initial market segmentation, based on the kinds of uses the product is designed to cover (end-user level). Without such segmentation, based on the benefits provided to customers, pricing becomes very difficult. Otherwise, the pricing parameters would be limited to cost data. Although the model is general, it needs to adjust to respond realistically to the creative and productive efforts committed to making the offering available.

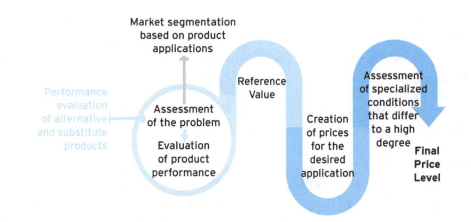

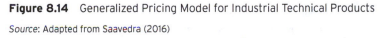

Figure 8.14 Generalized Pricing Model for Industrial Technical Products

Source: Adapted from Saavedra (2016)

Reference Prices

A company can set a reference price and use it to create price lists for standardized products. This price provides a basis for pricing any other products it provides on demand (order). It generally represents a "safe" solution if the supplier cannot achieve a well-informed pricing decision for a product. Most companies recognize a price range for setting prices, and the reference price should fall within the zone created between them, as in Figure 8.15. Its exact position will vary according to the requirements of different customers and the needs of the supplier company.

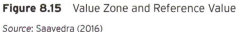

Figure 8.15 Value Zone and Reference Value

Source: Saavedra (2016)

One method used to determine a reference value is value-based pricing. It reflects the principle that a better product offering should be priced higher. To apply this method in an industrial environment, some requirements must be met:

- The company must have sufficient, comprehensive, accurate information about customer needs that can shape a clear picture of the problems the customer seeks to address. Value-based pricing also supports greater quantification and expressions in monetary units.
- With these insights, the company should compare its product offer with competing or substitute versions, as well as the option the product is designed to replace. In all cases, performance differences should be expressed in monetary units.
- The difference in (monetary) value for the performance of the product offer and the price attributed to it should be greater than the corresponding difference for the competitive offer. As expressed by Anderson and Narus's (1999) inequality formula, ΔPerformance(PO) = Performance(POR) – Performance(POC), where POR is the product offer that needs a price set (reference product offer), and POC is the competitive product offer. Each side signals the benefits that customers could receive, expressed in monetary units (value to customers). This approach can also use Performance (X), or the monetary value attributed to the overall performance of product offer X, calculated using metrics for customer needs, which may be related to the functionality of the product offer, its features, or even accounting sizes. Finally, the Price (X) is the price for product offer X; for the focal business, X = (POR) is the dependent variable. This value is expressed in monetary units.
- The company is required to determine whether the customer purchase is to prepare for a new project or to replace part (or all) of its existing equipment, technology, and/or services that it provides. In the former case, the company should apply the preceding formula, together with relevant criteria, to compare its product offer with those of direct competitors or substitute products. Changing the form of the equation, we can also derive the following relation to assess differences in the product offers of different suppliers (Figure 8.16):

If ΔPerformance(PO) = Performance(POR) – Performance(POC), then ΔPerformance(PO) > Price(POR) – Price(POC).

If instead the purchase is a replacement, the strategic marketing plan of the (industrial) company should involve a comparison of the current product offer it receives and the technology currently being used by the customer, while also evaluating competitive offers or substitutes. The version of the original inequality in this case becomes (Figure 8.17):

If ΔPerformance(PON) = Performance(PON) – Performance(CTC), where the companies' product offers are N = 1, 2, with respect to the technology used by the customer (CTC), then ΔPerformance(PO1) – Price(PO1) > ΔPerformance(PO2) – Price(PO2).

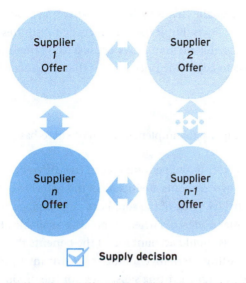

Figure 8.16 Comparison of Offers from Different Suppliers (New Projects)

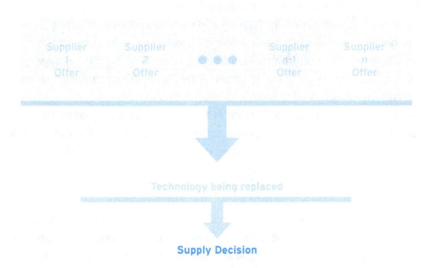

Figure 8.17 Comparison for Replacing Existing Technology

Despite these calculations though, customer preferences may differ; if they decide product A is superior to B, customers likely will choose A. Or perhaps the customer has formed a long-term relationship with the provider of product B, which reduces perceived risk and makes the outcomes more predictable. A supplier also might offer a customer-friendly credit system or payment policy, along with a strong market presence.

The magnitude of the inequality tends to decrease when the product offers being compared relate to commercialized products. But if new products or substitutes are involved, the differences increase. The value of this method arises because the same inequality can be used by different types of suppliers to adjust the price level of their product offerings effectively.

Mistakes When Applying Value-Based Pricing

Many possible errors accompany the implementation of value-based pricing methods:

- The comparison must refer to the performance of the different product offers overall, but many times, only two elements are included: the perceived cost of the customer's problem and the monetary value of the supplier's performance. This limited view ignores the process the customer undergoes when comparing available alternative product offers. The focal business should account for all the benefits that competitors offer when formulating and presenting alternative solutions to consumer problems.
- Comparisons also often ignore existing substitutes for the product offers. An excessive focus on direct competition is myopic, which may risk the company losing its market share as it relates to specific uses of its product offering.
- The method requires information about substitutes of the product offer, along with useful insights about potential threats that may arise.
- In some cases, companies only include certain variables when measuring product performance, when instead they must derive a broader set of features or functions that more accurately reflect both their own and competitors' offers. If the company lacks a clear view of all the uses the product offer is intended to cover, this mistake will likely be inflated and intensified.
- Another error arises from the application of this method in a general market. Differentiating prices according to product uses is not effective if the product is available to the general public or is distributed through third-party intermediaries.

Restrictions on the Use of Value-Based Pricing

Value-based pricing requires sufficient time and effort to gather and evaluate extensive and accurate information. It does not offer the convenience of fast, rough referential prices. It is time-consuming and laborious; for companies that sell many different products, it becomes virtually impossible to apply the method thoroughly in all cases. A value-based pricing solution might apply to some subset of the product portfolio though, even if the company maintains list prices for its other products. Beyond the restrictions based on the time available to fulfill the required conditions and the type of costly information needed, another limitation of this method stems from its application. For example, if a focal firm relies on the selling price set by a competitor, but that competitor has determined its price using a different approach, it may distort the value-based pricing calculations and create a misalignment of the reference price. Finally, this sophisticated method demands well-trained, dynamic staff who can market to customers by emphasizing the benefits of various uses of the product, while also justifying the chosen price. Achieving this capacity requires them to understand the philosophy underlying this method too.

E-Industrial Marketing and Pricing Policies

The Role of the Internet

Technological developments shape all facets of business activity. Whether through the evolution of processes, techniques, or tools, change is always a precursor to something else. For example, the proliferation of the Internet has prompted changes in infrastructure, communication, connection speeds, and other technical features that in turn affect business activities and transactions. Perhaps most notably, the Internet and related developments have significantly reduced the costs of serving existing customers. Through interactive communication with industrial customers, suppliers can reinforce their focus on the anticipated and expressed needs of their customers. It also is easier to extract, collect, and process data, then draw useful conclusions about customers' purchasing behavior and expressed needs. The process of acquiring knowledge about the target audience also expands into this new channel.

With this greater information, the producer company can better customize its product offer, adapting it to the needs and requirements of each customer. Of course, the company can personalize its marketing procedures, which in turn tend to be more effective in attracting sales. One such element reflects the ease with which the company can disseminate information about its products through the Internet. The extensive, accurate, available information on the Internet provides a greater level of detail, even at a technical level. Assuming the company manages this expanded information by offering specially designed interfaces to communicate with customers, it likely meets customers' expectations, which then contributes positively to their satisfaction.

Digital Marketing and Industrial Businesses

For digital marketing in the industrial environment, early developments involved electronic data interchange (EDI), which establishes a link between a customer company and each of its supplier companies. Through this connection, they can exchange data and information of interest to both parties. Along with offering such solutions though, EDI also incurs increased costs, and the information that should be exchanged is not always transparent.

For e-commerce, suppliers create well-structured websites to present their products, then enter into separate transactions with each customer. Another version instead concentrates transactional business groups in one electronic market, to take advantage of using the Internet to provide product information but also increasing the transparency in the process and reducing the costs per transaction. These transactional groups might be groups of suppliers, intermediary groups, or customer groups. Many suppliers seek to address the wide-ranging geographical distribution of their customers with products that meet a wide range of their needs. Intermediaries can more effectively connect customers with specific suppliers. Customers instead prefer to present a single image of the supplies they need, so that they can achieve better cooperation agreements with suppliers but also relative uniformity in the policies that suppliers implement when pricing their products.

Web Auctions

In the case of web auctions, customers set a starting price for a product they want, and the suppliers respond by adjusting the price level to come close to their expectations. To win over customers, suppliers must have strong knowledge of the cost level being shaped, as well as be able to support the product once the sales process is concluded. This process can often save substantial money for the purchase of the desired product. However, to implement it, both parties must be able and willing to make substantial investments. For suppliers, these investments largely determine the desired level of the sales price, together with market conditions. Buyers can not only save money but also gain a chance to approach suppliers that they might previously have been unable to reach, for whatever reason.

Pricing Strategy and Online Business-to-Business Transactions

Managing Price Levels in the Digital Arena

A strategically important pricing consideration is whether prices should be the same for online and physical transactions. Taking a broader view of the competitive environment, pricing offered for online transactions can affect the outcomes of transactions involving other products and offline interactions. Yet the affordability and ease of access provided by the Internet represents a relevant consideration too, as does the amount and type of information available, so that buyers can learn more about product offers that interest them. If a company decides to make its product available online and set an "e-price level," this price may be higher or lower than the price charged offline for the same product, largely due to the levels of competition online, which are growing in both size and intensity. Furthermore, the use of the Internet reduces the need for some intermediaries, so the cost of moving products decreases. Another benefit of the Internet can be optimized scheduling of production, to meet demand for the product in question (Figure 8.18).

Customers thus might more readily accept higher prices for a product offer online which better meets their needs, even in the face of competition. This tolerance for higher price levels, or diminished price sensitivity, can change due to variations in other factors, such as:

- The extent to which customers are aware of product substitutes and the level of product differentiation in relation to those substitutes, which influence their responses to higher prices for a specific product. Regardless of the value of product characteristics, they alone cannot provide benefits. The company seeks the highest possible value from a transaction, which is accompanied by the overall set of benefits the product can provide.
- The customer's previous attempts to shape an image of the cost of its overall operation. If the price attributed to a particular product changes, to such an extent that it significantly affects the structure (and distribution) of costs in the supply chain, the purchasing behavior of the business will be significantly affected too.
- Any failure by the customer to determine the objective superiority of the product offer over available alternatives. In such a case, the reputation and image of the supplier company, in addition to the price level change, play important roles, by providing the criteria most likely to guide the decision to purchase (or not) from a particular supplier.
- The ease with which a product can be stored. If the product provided by the supplier creates storage challenges, lower price levels are unlikely to drive more purchases, for example.

Figure 8.18 Price and Competition: Differences in the Online Environment

Online Environment and Facilitation of the Pricing Process

The main objective of industrial companies that choose to operate electronically is to reduce the costs involved in completing transactions and searching for appropriate suppliers, as well as reducing procedural complications (e.g., bureaucratic issues) and providing better quality information more quickly. The online environment enables the company to set the highest possible price that any customer considers acceptable, then rapidly shift the price to new levels, as necessary, to prompt further sales. In changing the prices, they must remain competitive, of course, and reflect the competitive conditions.

A feature that supports fluctuations in pricing online is the existence of a price zone within which some variation is tolerated by customers. A prerequisite of this tolerance is a means to differentiate the product relative to available alternatives or substitutes, from the customer's perspective. The more customers consider the product to be differentiated, the more they are willing to tolerate wider variation in the price level. Another element that aids price adjustment processes is the speed at which information is transmitted over the Internet—much faster than occurs in conventional industrial environments. As a result, a supplier company can set higher prices for products in greater demand directly (and vice versa). Auctions and discounts are also relevant tools in this effort. Finally, the Internet can make price differentiation more effective by providing a more complete picture of customers and their purchasing behavior. The resulting market segments are smaller, based on criteria developed by the supplier company and in line with its strategic orientation and the data it has available. With the right strategic moves and adjustments, the price levels achieved in online environments can be adjusted and increased, more so than is possible without the Internet.

Principles Governing Pricing Policy Designs Online

When a company decides to implement a pricing strategy, as part of its online business activities, it must ensure the strategy accords with its overall marketing orientation and the goals set by the marketing department. In particular, the company should guarantee that the skills needed to make the best use of the technology and tools at its disposal exist, as well as that the resources needed to exploit the Internet to implement a pricing policy are available. Such assurances can produce an optimal market segmentation and good decisions regarding how to manage the implementation and timing any strategic changes. Ultimately, it needs an applicable mix of online rates and discounts, bounded by appropriate control systems and checks that monitor customers' responses to and acceptance of changes related to a new pricing policy. With online resources, companies can assess supply-and-demand conditions, then decide whether they need to change their price levels.

If a price change occurs, the organizational structure of the company also needs to be adjusted, to support the altered philosophy signaled by the price level. The structure should make provisions for empowering employees who perform online transactions with responsibilities for pricing-related decisions, as well as granting them an active role in the flexible formulation of prices, assuming of course that the company provides them with sufficient and proper training.

Pricing Implementation in an Online Environment

Regardless of the application context, the difficulties of implementing pricing policies have some similar features. For example, an electronic environment might feature three methods:

- Online auctions: If the customer runs an auction and solicits bids from multiple suppliers, the suppliers can learn more details about customers, with great opportunities for exploiting the Internet as a price implementation tool. With such an approach, it is important to revise the strategic "look" of the supplier company and rearrange its strategic planning priorities. The supplier company should also redesign its production and supply chain processes. Proper, direct, timely, and reliable communication between the customer and supplier can ensure the quality of the information provided to overcome ambiguities and concerns related to contracts.
- Yield management: This dual approach features discounts for customers that are more price sensitive. If customers do not show signs of discomfort following a price change, the company instead follows its predetermined practice. A good understanding of the market and customers is a prerequisite for this approach, which can be achieved with appropriate, detailed segmentation. A series of conditions and characteristics might influence its application; for example, adopting yield management requires the company to address the following considerations:
  - Pricing of products with a short financial, storage, or shelf life.
  - Products with strong seasonal trends in their demand.
  - Differentiations of the perceived value of products across customers that belong to different market segments.
  - Differentiations in customers' sensitivity to fluctuations in pricing.
  - Increased likelihood that products that are not distributed might end up being destroyed.
  - Competition observed between customers who want to buy greater quantities of the product and those who prefer to buy smaller quantities.
  - The need for regular discounts to address competition.
  - Prevailing market conditions that are rapidly changing.
- Bundling: This approach offers a particular price level for groups of products. Bundling is most effective for high profit margin products, so as not to affect the potential of the company to make a profit through price reductions. It can also work well for well-known products, to attract more customers.

9

THE MARKETING MIX: THE INDUSTRIAL PRODUCT

Learning Objectives

- Gain familiarity with the concept and features of industrial products.
- Understand the process and importance of developing new products.
- Outline the factors that lead to success or failure in new product development efforts.
- Explain why effective communication and collaboration across different departments is necessary to ensure integration among those departments.
- Define the product life cycle.
- Detail the features of each stage of the product life cycle and their strategic importance.
- Analyze the product portfolio as a strategic decision-making tool.

Case Study

Meeting the Value Needs of Customers

Many substitute products offer similar functional capabilities, so suppliers have to find novel ways to differentiate their offerings. One way involves social differentiators, a method adopted by Philips Medical Systems (PMS) in its effort to promote its magnetic resonance imaging (MRI) scanning equipment in the Netherlands.

In this market, four categories of buyers seek MRI scanning equipment: academic, teaching, and community hospitals, plus private imaging centers. Across these buying firms, the purchase decision usually involves people in similar roles, such as clinicians, operators, and business managers, who exert varying influences at different stages of the purchasing process, as the customer purchasing framework in Figure 9.1 reveals.

(Continued)

	Radiologist	Referring physician A	Referring physician B	Clinical physician	Technical services	Operator	Board of directors	Supervisory board	Purchasing manager	Department manager
1 Identify benefits of and acquire budget for magnetic resonance imaging scanner	x	x					x	x		x
2 Identify specifications of magnetic resonance imaging scanner	x			x	x	x				x
3 Evaluate alternatives and select supplier of magnetic resonance imaging scanner	x	x		x			x		x	x

Figure 9.1　Stages and Key Decision-Making Stakeholders

| | To whom | | | When | | How | | | | |
	Business responsible	Clinical responsible	Operational responsible	Periodically in time	During the purchase process	Customer magazines	Purchaser meetings	Brochures	White papers	Sales conversations
Energy use	x	x	x		x			x	x	x
Weight	x	x	x		x			x	x	x
Packaging										
Hazardous substances	x	x	x		x			x	x	x
Recycling and disposal	x	x	x		x			x	x	x
Environmental aspects	x	x	x	x	x	x	x	x		x
Proactive safety regulation	x	x	x	x	x	x	x	x	x	x
Health complaints operators	x	x	x		x			x	x	x
Health complaints patients	x	x	x		x			x	x	x

Figure 9.2 Marketing-Related Opportunities: Who, When, and How

Figure 9.2 (Continued)

	To whom			When		How				
	Business responsible	Clinical responsible	Operational responsible	Periodically in time	During the purchase process	Customer magazines	Purchaser meetings	Brochures	White papers	Sales conversations
Availability in different markets										
Accessibility of different patient types	x	x	x	x	x	x		x	x	x
Ethical performance of producer	x	x	x	x		x	x			
Ethical performance of suppliers	x	x	x	x		x	x			
Operator comfort	x	x	x	x	x	x	x	x	x	x
Patient comfort	x	x	x	x	x	x	x	x	x	x
Contribution to science	x	x	x	x	x	x		x	x	x
Increase level of living										
Social aspects	x	x	x	x	x	x	x	x		x
Sustainability aspects	x	x	x	x		x	x			

To appeal to these decision-makers, across stages, as Lindgreen et al. (2009) explain, PMS relied on five social differentiators, based on findings it obtained from focus groups and the characteristics of its MRI scanning equipment offerings:

- Customer health and safety. Taking a proactive approach, PMS designs protections into the equipment's basic usage and maintenance elements; it assumes a duty of care. The complexity of the equipment also means that users must rely on PMS to guarantee safe use.
- Customer/patient comfort. During interactions with scanning equipment, both operators and patients need to feel comfortable, yet their influence and involvement time scales differ. Operators spend all day working with scanners; patients spend far less. But both must be comfortable with using the machinery, to ensure good scan quality and peace of mind.
- Ethical production (material and human capital). PMS seeks ethical suppliers, so that its customers can rest assured that they are working with an ethical producer and supply chain, which reduces their need for monitoring. Unethical practices would be a relevant issue for both customers and patients.
- Product accessibility. Various stakeholders need different forms of availability in different markets, though for many customers, such concerns are distant and not directly relevant.
- Societal benefits. The MRI scanners promise better diagnoses, reduced illness, knowledge development, and employment opportunities. The academic and teaching hospitals in particular seek data to support research efforts; community hospitals and imaging centers also want reassurance that the scanner reflects cutting-edge innovation and contributions to science.

Defining social differentiators for high-tech products is especially useful, because of their strong influence over the purchasing process and the resulting marketing opportunities, as Figure 9.2 notes.

Source

Lindgreen, A., Antioco, M.D.J., Harness, D., and van der Sloot, R. (2009), "Purchasing and marketing of social and environmental sustainability for high-tech medical equipment," *Journal of Business Ethics*, 85(S2), 445-462.

THE INDUSTRIAL PRODUCT

Characteristics of Industrial Products and Offering Superior Value

The approach embraced by a company and all its operations should be defined by the effort to provide appropriate solutions to customers. This operational design also must allow and encourage different units of the company to work together effectively as a team. Finally, resource allocations must be determined carefully and explicitly, to support various activities, including new product development (NPD) processes. Each supplier must deliver product offers that are superior in value to those offered by competitors, which depends on two essential elements: appropriate quality level and appropriate price level.

The quality level in turn is defined by both the product and the services that accompany it. Accordingly, the supplier needs to understand and appreciate its own (industrial) products, with regard to:

1 How the product was created.
2 What the product is.
3 What the product does, and how.
4 What the product offers to end users.
5 What the product might potentially offer to end users.

Proceeding from 1 to 5, the conceptual level for perceiving the product increases, such that the supplier gains more strategic freedom to find creative ways to meet the needs of the market and compete well.

Defining industrial products involves more than just their physical characteristics; value considerations imply and emphasize complex relationships involving multiple factors that inform how the buyer uses the product. Buyers in both consumer and industrial markets search for features that add value to the supplied product. In an industrial environment, the buying company investigates the three types of features in Figure 9.3, which it hopes are available in the product:

- Basic features. These features motivate the buyer to make that particular purchase in the first place, reflecting the key benefits that the buyer wants and seeks in the product.
- Enhanced features. These add-on features differentiate the product from similar, alternative options, such as color, quality, design, style, and other unique features.
- Augmented features. These benefits frame the key features and are available once the buyer purchases a particular product, in the form of after-sales service, spare parts, technical assistance, funding, product distribution/delivery, and so on.

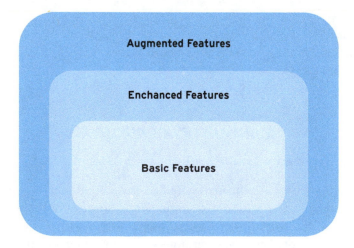

Figure 9.3 Product Features That Influence Customers' Purchase Decision

In industrial markets, high-quality services (especially in the form of augmented features) can strongly shape the perceived value, because customers view the overall package surrounding a particular product offer (Figure 9.4). Such services also tend to require close collaboration among different units and functions within the company.

Perceived value, shaped by the product offer, stems from the following characteristics of the industrial product:

1   Product functionality features. Because they determine the outcome of using the product, functionality features also indicate the utility of the product for end users, according to the extent to which the product addresses their needs. Product functionality can be multilevel, comprised of features that:

   a   Improve the functional performance of the product.
   b   Protect this functional performance from environmental hazards or dangerous situations.
   c   Reduce costs related to sales or operations, without loss of functionality.

2   Technical characteristics. These features reflect the product design and enable it to perform at the desired level, including those that:

   a   Facilitate product distribution, installation, assembly, or integration.
   b   Make it easy to use or incorporate safety features to keep users safe.
   c   Ensure that, in the event of any irregularity, unrelated to product use or customer's functions, no significant damage results.

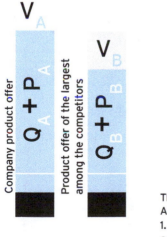

Products A and B
Q_A Quality level of A
Q_B Quality level of B
P_A Price level of A
P_B Price level of B
V_A Customer's perceived value of A
V_B Customer's perceived value of B

The desired outcome: $V_A > V_B$
An optimal combination:
1. High level of quality provided of V_A in relation to V_B
2. Price level selection optimizer of P_A in relation to P_B
It may lead to: $V_A > V_B$

Figure 9.4   Product and Superior Value Offer to the Customer

Product Policy

Products are designed to meet customer needs. Changes in these needs and preferences (Figure 9.5), such as due to the introduction of new technologies, revised government policies, or even product life cycle factors, should lead to changes in the product offers, as well as revised strategies and policies pertaining to the new products. The four categories in Figure 9.6 define the types of product series that form in industrial settings:

- Proprietary products. Provided with preconfigured parameters, designed to meet order fulfillment forecasts.
- Custom-built products. Supplied in some modified form, according to customers' needs and requirements.
- Custom-designed products. Created from scratch, to satisfy a specific set of customers.
- Industrial services. Set of provided services, such as guidance and consultation or operational and maintenance services.

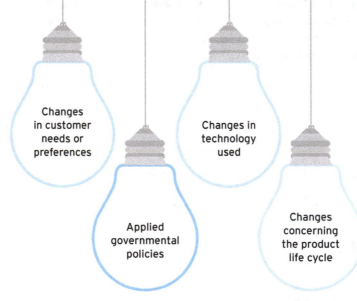

Factors that Influence the Formulation of Product Strategies and Policies

Changes in customer needs or preferences

Changes in technology used

Applied governmental policies

Changes concerning the product life cycle

Figure 9.5 Changes in Product Life Cycles

Figure 9.6 Categories of Industrial Product Series

A product life cycle approach seeks to formulate appropriate product strategies at each stage of its life cycle. In this view, the product (consumer or industrial) proceeds through its "life" over different stages and over time (e.g., introduction, maturity, obsolescence). Each of them has specific, distinct characteristics. Therefore, this approach also provides a way to evaluate the product's impact on firm sales or profitability: the firm tracks trends in the sales volume of its products and the profit margins earned from each sale. In nearly every case, this tracking shows the tendency of the product to lose profit opportunities over time, due to various factors (Figure 9.7), such as buyers' constantly changing needs and preferences, technological developments, competitive moves, and so on. Adding such factors to the assessment then can transform a product life cycle analysis into an assessment of the market life cycle.

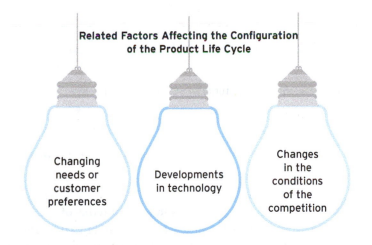

Figure 9.7 Factors Shaping the Product Life Cycle

It may help to identify stages and areas that need special attention, perhaps because they entail changes of particular strategic importance. But because each stage has distinct features and attributes, the formulated strategies must also be differentiated, even as they align to reflect the overall firm strategy.

Product Life Cycle

A common representation of the product life cycle, such as the one in Figure 9.8, comprises five phases: introduction, development, maturity, saturation, and decline.

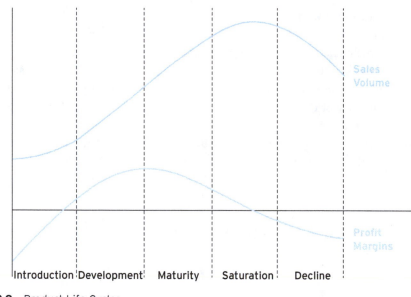

Figure 9.8 Product Life Cycles

Source: Adapted from Webster (1991)

Introduction

When a new product enters the market, it gets evaluated, in terms of whether it can induce significant changes to existing approaches or create new market trends. The supplier works to find customers, informs the public about the product, and builds a distribution network. If it can radically change the market, the supplier might even enjoy a virtual monopoly. Convincing industrial buyers to accept a new product is a very time-consuming process though, because they tend to have well-formed perceptions of the market and the value they expect from a product offer, which create bias against emerging proposals.

Therefore, sales volumes grow but at a slow rate. Profit margins might appear negative at first, due to the costs incurred by the company in developing the product and its market. At the same time, the product price appears high, which can exert deterrent effects on sales. By the end of this stage though, the profit margin should become positive and increase at a faster pace. Such wider acceptance enables the supplier to establish its name in the market, such as through pilot testing offers, which might target distributors operating within the same supply chain. In terms of market structure, we note that it is small in size, but with a growth trend. There are few competitors; as the market starts to grow, customers might be undersupplied.

Development

Assuming a successful introduction, sales volumes start to increase rapidly, and the profit margin starts to increase at a rapidly expanding rate. The primary aim is to build a strong presence in the market, with emphases on design processes, distribution procedures, and service provision, along with an aggressive product promotion strategy. If the number of competitors increases rapidly too, the focal supplier can exploit its price strategy as a countermeasure, leveraging its greater experience and economies of scale.

The larger market also continues to grow, evoking ever more competition and new players in the market. Fluctuations in terms of market adequacy depend on the prevailing conditions and changes in the tide of competition. Focused on the predicted rate of market growth, the supplier aims to match it with growth in its production capacity. It still seeks to build and capture new market share but also works to preserve its existing share, such as by imposing brand-differentiating conditions (even if artificially) and consolidating its positioning in line with customers' preferences. Accordingly, it works to expand its product lines and distribution network. Toward the end of this phase, a turning point in sales volumes occurs, around the same time the profit margin reaches its maximum value, such that it begins to experience a declining growth rate.

Maturity

A further increase in sales, albeit at a slower pace, occurs in the maturity stage, but the heightened competition puts pressure on profit margins. As a result, price reductions, increased promotional and distribution costs, interventions in the product or processes, and added services are likely to arise, which influence and explain the profit margin curve.

Saturation

The pressures from the maturity stage persist here, but in addition, sales volumes have reached their maximum levels and are beginning to decline. The profit margin continues to decrease which might even lead to damaging situations. Across both the maturity and saturation stages, the supplier faces several critical choices, such as whether to pursue a different subset of customers, find new potential buyers of the product, or explore entry into new markets with a modified version of the product offer. The supplier's relationship with agents gains particular importance in this stage. The company should also make preparations to remove the product and introduce a new version into the market.

Also during this period, the number of competitors reaches its peak, such that the market becomes oversupplied, with surplus productive capacity. Through its marketing strategy, the supplier might work to maintain its market share, such as by differentiating the product, but the market keeps growing more fragmented. Distribution is consolidated and becomes more selective during the saturation phase. Competitors are also trying to reduce costs at every level, so significant price drops are possible, leading to greatly diminished profitability at the industry level.

Decline

Finally, the sharp declines in sales volumes and profit margins cause further damage to the circulation of the product, to such an extent that the company must decide whether to revise the product or seek to maximize its profits and leave the product to its obsolescence. An option for industrial companies is to make the (obsolete) product available to other, previously untapped geographic markets, such as countries with a lower level of technological development.

Only a few competitors survive, charging prices that are determined by the cost structure of the least effective remaining supplier. To salvage profit margins, they likely cut marketing and R&D expenditures, as well as the number of intermediaries. In addition to limiting their marketing efforts to just a few market sectors, they slow their productive capacity, reflecting the oversupply of the product in the market.

Summary

Some of these product life cycle features differ for high-tech products, such that when technology changes more quickly, the likelihood of technology depreciation is higher, and the costs associated with R&D are particularly high. But across sectors, it can be helpful to identify life cycle phases for industrial products, even if the difficult, demanding process does not always produce accurate results. That is, identifying the life cycle stage of a product requires taking several factors into account, such as the development conditions of the industry, profits, and sales volumes. Current and emerging trends must also be analyzed, related to the company, the market, the industry, similar industries and products, and even the competitive environment.

Importance of Using the Product Life Cycle Concept

The use of the product life cycle as a strategic planning tool emphasizes the following strategic needs for supplier companies:

- To avoid resting on their laurels in existing conditions and continue seeking to generate ideas for new products. Old and obsolete products can evoke the loss and waste of significant operational resources.
- To develop different marketing strategies, depending on the stage of the product's life cycle at any particular point in time.
- To adopt a long-term perspective in designing products for their entire life spans, during their development and planning phases and when they are introduced to the market.

Industrial Product Portfolio Analysis: The BCG Matrix

The Boston Consulting Group (BCG) proposes a matrix that can address the full range of products that a company can produce, based on a predetermined set of business functions. The functions constantly interact with one another, and at a strategic level, they influence the proportion of the product portfolio that each product represents. In turn, different correlations and combinations of company resources become necessary, as do various kinds of efforts to exploit any window of opportunity, through efficient resource allocation. In this approach, products are not individual elements, existing within the operations of the company, but rather are parts of a wider, integrated system. With this type of analysis, the company can take a long-term perspective on its strategic orientation, while still responding dynamically to any challenges that necessitate strategic adjustments. Accordingly, the company assigns unique roles to different products, seeking to achieve overall strategic goals, whether in the short or long term. Some products are part of the company's core offer; others represent complementary offerings. Some products generate revenue growth directly; others are intended to deliver expected returns over a longer period of time. Defining these operational functions can reflect three axes:

- Attractiveness of the market.
- Position of the company relative to competitors.
- Strengths and weaknesses of the company.

To a certain extent, a BCG analysis aligns with the well-known SWOT (strengths, weaknesses, opportunities, and threats) analysis of a company's environment.

An effective analysis of the product portfolio should produce strategic decisions with regard to how to allocate available resources. The ultimate goal should be an ability to generate cash inflows (and map required cash outflows) through business decisions pertaining to the full range of products that the company provides to the markets it targets. In turn, a four-point (quadratic) matrix emerges, with a vertical dimension related to the market growth rate and a horizontal dimension related to the position the company occupies in the market relative to competitors or its dominance in the market. The two dimensions, represented on the axes, use two gradients to characterize their level, as high or low. That is, the matrix is intersected horizontally by a straight line that defines that value for the vertical dimension, high or low, and it is intersected vertically by another straight line that depicts the relative position of the company in relation to its strongest competitors, high or low. Let's consider the resulting quadrants, as in Figure 9.9, which take four names.

Stars

With their high market growth rate × high level of market dominance, stars enjoy a strong, market-leading position in a market with strong growth; the product is considered very attractive. Despite being a market leader, the company continues to be threatened by potential competition, in terms of the technology used or the rates of acceptance in the market. In addition, observed profits are low, because the costs of maintaining market dominance are high, associated with a sophisticated marketing mix.

In terms of the strategic options available for products in this category, market share attributable to a specific product might increase or persist. The former case requires strategic pricing, innovative distribution, and effective advertising, in ways that make it difficult for new players to enter the industry. The latter case is feasible if the firm invests in market intelligence and responds quickly to changes in the environment, while making selective, appropriate investments in the marketing mix.

Troubled Children

Displaying high market growth rate × low level of market dominance, troubled children products are undergoing a process of development, but they earn only a small market share. To increase their market share, they might invest in advertising and promotion. Often, these products are new to the market. There is a high risk that the product or its technology will not be widely accepted in the market. Losses thus are possible, and large volumes of investment continue to be needed to increase market share. Strong, long-term administrative support might move this product into the star quadrant. Because more than one of the company's products likely falls into this classification, it must identify, evaluate, and choose which products to support over time. Alternatively, it could seek to penetrate a niche market segment.

Cash Cows

With a low market growth rate × high level of market dominance, cash cows aim to reduce their marketing costs by exploiting their market excellence, often by becoming low-cost suppliers. Market conditions tend to support only low growth, but the company produces satisfactory profits and inflows, without much market risk. Relevant strategies in this case include a strategic focus on financial management while maintaining market share. Any market investments require great caution, and any resulting cash inflows should be directed toward troubled products. Cash cows might penetrate specialized markets too, noting their lack of significant future prospects in their existing market. Alternatively, they might withdraw the product if they predict that demand is declining quickly, whether due to the introduction of new technologies or because customers' needs have changed.

Dogs

Finally, because of their low market growth rate × low level of market dominance, along with their high costs, dogs make minimal or no profits, without sufficient cash inflows. The product may be a falling star, but the company continues to invest in it, demanding substantial managerial involvement, regardless of the lack of expectation of profits. Relevant strategies then might aim to maintain the market share for the company, along with whatever cash inflows the product can generate. Changing market segments or adding new ones seems reasonable, but any new product investments should stop. The company tries to use any funds raised to supply products, but it likely encounters strong barriers, unless the product is closely linked to a strong reputation and brand name. Finally, dogs seek some form of recovery, such as through innovative processes, product differentiation, partial reductions, or penetrating more specialized markets.

A healthy business should have products that belong to all of these categories. According to a strategic approach, for example, dogs might be repositioned with a more careful design in a new market segment, or the company might choose to stop supporting them with marketing or else eliminate them from its product range altogether. If the company does not embrace an NPD philosophy, it likely directs its efforts toward troubled children or dogs, thereby recycling the investment required to continue its business. If instead it actively pursues NPD, it needs cash cows and stars to gather sufficient funds to fuel its development processes.

The simplicity of the visualization produced by this method, such that the results are easily comprehensible as decision-making input, make the BCG matrix particularly appealing. It can also be applied to competitors, regarding the positioning of their products. It brings to the fore and emphasizes organizational functions that need attention, whether because they do not have sufficient growth or because they are inherently unable to achieve a leadership position in the market. It is geared toward developing a long-term strategy, and it enables the company to interact dynamically with both the market and competitors.

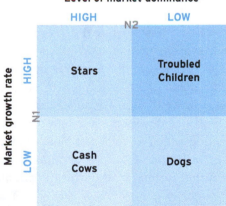

Figure 9.9   BCG Matrix of Market Dominance

Source: Adapted from Henderson (1978)

With regard to NPD, we outline a process: it begins with the conceptualization of a basic product idea, then continues through to the provision of a series of benefits related to its physical characteristics and the services that accompany it. In detail, the NPD process reflects the activation of various actions and mechanisms responsible for the creation of an idea, its evaluation, its proper orientation, and its conversion into a product.

When referring to the potential uses (or applications) of a particular product offer, the company affirms its recognition that it is being called upon to answer key questions related to the different usage characteristics of products and the dimensions of their use. The answers to these questions essentially determine the (potential) uses that must be incorporated into the newly developed product. They are as follows:

- Where is this product intended to be used? This question might pertain to the natural space in which the use of the product will take place, geographical characteristics, the type of operation that accompanies its use, and so on.
- What context determines the use of the product? This question seeks to address whether the specific product is intended to be an intermediate substrate for the application of other components, as well as the extent to which it might interact with other elements (e.g., machinery, equipment).
- When is the product intended to be used? This question seeks to determine the time frame of its potential uses. Elements such as its operating cycle and programming are specified, but so are even simpler concepts, such as daytime or nighttime use or duration of operation.
- Who is going to be using this product? This question refers to the need for the company to know what kind of users will be using the product, which might reflect a user's profile, or else specific types of consumers or end users. It also may refer to a broader approach that investigates the extent to which the end user is some kind of organization or institution or even an entire industry.

These specific questions must be addressed during the design phase; depending on the type of offer and the approach the company takes to design the product offer, at least one of these questions might guide the effort. But what the company must also keep in mind, beyond recognition that estimating the potential uses of its product is of particular importance for its success, is that the (potential) uses can change over time, just as the needs expressed by users change. The company therefore should monitor such shifts continuously and detect, predict, or even direct the emergence of new and different uses for its products.

The features embedded in each (industrial) product offer define the solution provided by a company for a problem that customers face, which might also entail cost reductions that burden the buyer or options to improve its productivity. Therefore, any proposed or provided solution that can satisfy these criteria should find willing buyers and create the conditions for a sale.

Vignette

Platform-Based Business Model Innovation

Traditional marketing scholarship was founded on product innovation strategies. Frameworks featured in countless marketing syllabi, such as the Ansoff or BCG matrix, focus on placing and managing products in markets. Process innovation efforts introduced innovation in terms of delivery mechanisms, such as the moves in retail from direct selling to online marketplaces. Value innovation (Kim & Mauborgne, 1999) instead might not involve any, or only minimal, process or product innovations; it is essentially the identification of how a bundle of existing technologies and processes can be marshaled to target an un- or underexploited market opportunity better.

Business model innovation (Chesbrough, 2010) provides a vocabulary for identifying innovation with minimal product or process innovation. New innovative models, such as the Razor and Blade model used by Gillette, are creatively imitated in other sectors. A blue ocean strategy (Kim & Mauborgne, 2004) is popular as a means to identify new value curves not yet exploited by current providers, including non-competitive strategies, which may not require poaching customers. These examples also represent manifestations of business model innovation.

A consistent feature of business model innovations is the presence of open innovation (Chesbrough, 2007) in core value propositions, which demands a strong business-to-business element in strategizing. Another common element is digital platform-based business models (Bahar et al., 2021), which include successful aggregator approaches, predicated on non-asset ownership strategies: Uber owns no vehicles, and Airbnb owns no properties.

Other examples of aggregator business models appear as insurance comparison sites (Go Compare, Confused.com, Compare the Market), delivery aggregators (Just Eat, Uber Eats, Deliveroo), travel aggregators (Booking.com, Trip Advisor, Expedia), and so forth. They frequently possess little more than a core brand as an asset. Some of the models are disruptive: Airbnb has moved into and seemingly maintained a position in a blue ocean, by establishing supply-side relationships with property owners that would be difficult for market followers to replicate. Unlike a traditional value chain situation, the value created in platform-based business models combines complementor and customer sides of the platform. The emergence of business-to-business considerations in business model innovation, related to open innovation phases and business model performance, helps optimize the relationships of complementors and platform owners. Such marketing efforts must build relationships with asset owners, payment facilitators, digital creators, data analytics companies, search engines, and so forth, to create a unique bundle of complementors that deliver a distinctive value proposition that in turn acts as a disruptive force in the industry. They might consider the placement of their offering on one or more global platforms, according to an exclusivity or multihoming strategy. Thus, business-to-business marketers must determine and, as needed, improve their centrality in any chosen platform ecosystem.

Product Development and Business Culture

To design a new product, including in risky conditions in which success is not guaranteed, a supplier company must navigate a set of decisions that reflect various opportunities that emerge, which the company might exploit by leveraging its strengths, even as it tries to overcome its weaknesses and avoid threats in the external environment. The conditions created by the competitive environment also have an important role (Figure 9.10).

Figure 9.10 Conditions for Product Success

When formulating NPD strategies, there are two key objectives: according to its specific organizational goals, the company must harmonize its product mix, and then it must shape the processes intended for developing product lines, as well as the products themselves.

We can define the NPD process by seven stages (Figure 9.11), which do not follow a strictly linear sequence:

1   New product development strategy. By identifying the strategic conditions that must be met by the product, this stage combines the activities for coming up with the idea, screening and evaluating those ideas, and defining them in accordance with the company's overall strategic orientation. Having positioned the new product strategically, it is necessary to determine the criteria for its success or desired financial performance, as well as the problems the new product needs to solve. This stage increases the percentage of ideas that manage to survive and take the form of an actual product, which in turn improves the way industrial enterprises segment industrial markets.

2   Creation of ideas. Ideas can emerge from multiple sources: business executives and employees, the external environment, the company's partners, or even its customers. Customers are particularly important, especially if the goal is to attain significant financial benefits from the NPD creation. In this stage, appropriate procedures are

identified to collect, structure, and group new ideas together. These processes help integrate ideas into the NPD process. The most popular candidate ideas can be harvested and communicated to appropriate departments, taking into account any possible legal implications that may be implicit.

3   Screening. For early ideas, it is necessary to identify appropriate criteria and procedures to filter these ideas. A kind of clearance of ideas can take place, by rejecting those that appear less interesting and prioritizing others, on the basis of whether they feasibly might be converted into attractive new products. Such processes can be informal or part of the formal organization and standard processes of a company. An audit seeks to evaluate whether an idea justifies the expenditure of business resources. A preliminary check involves if the idea is consistent with the firm's overall strategy and its marketing goals. A second check relates to the availability of the operational resources needed to develop and exploit the idea.

4   Business analysis. This stage entails a more detailed and meaningful evaluation of the NPD ideas, including the investment required, expected sales volume, prices, profit margins, and projected returns on the investment. A marketing analysis and sales forecast study should also take place. Both existing and potential competition inform the attractiveness of the specific proposal too. Finally, the completion of the idea entails pilot-tested production. Then the costs can be reassessed, test marketing can be performed, the price can be determined, and the revenue can be estimated. Customer feedback can also be explored at this point.

5   Development. Scientific staff, engineers, and technicians are recruited in this stage to boost the product. The efficiency and effectiveness of the NPD process depends on information available in the market about customers' needs and reactions, sales staff, distributors, and the requirements set in each stage of the NPD process.

6   Testing. In this stage, the information generated by the NPD process is collected. A first check considers new ideas for products or designs, followed by assessments of different product forms. Once the product is formatted in its likely commercial form, pilot-testing production supplies feedback and quality and cost assessments. The product is then marketed in controlled conditions, with a limited market scope, allowing for careful examination of the remaining elements of the marketing mix and an objective evaluation of the results. At this stage, it is important to address the criteria that determine purchasing behavior in the buying centers of the companies that make up the market.

7   Commercialization and product placement. The company is committed, from a marketing perspective, to commercializing the new product. The marketing plan requires careful identification of the market segments the company will target, a careful definition of the marketing objectives (short and long term), and proper training of sales staff and distributors. The vast range of details that constitute the marketing mix must be determined. At this point, it is important to emphasize placement of the product, as this entails identifying a niche market and emphasizing specific features of the promoted product offer, relative to competitive offers, to establish its unique value. In an industrial setting, the product placement process involves developing a set of services that accompany the product, with advertising and sales promotion playing a secondary (but important) role. A very careful market segmentation analysis is critical.

The whole NPD philosophy constitutes an important element of the overall operation of the company, reflecting the culture, which is expressed through its strategic approaches and choices. To encourage such a culture throughout the company, senior executives must be involved actively in NPD projects; all members of the company must be convinced that creating new products represents a unique and appropriate solution to ensure the company's longevity. An NPD team, devoted solely to this end, should have the necessary freedom and authority to take the required actions. In tandem, there should be a structured, standardized protocol for NPD development.

1. New product development strategy

2. Creation of ideas for the new product

3. Screening

4. Business analysis

5. Development

6. Testing

7. Commercialization and product placement

New Product

Figure 9.11 New Product Development Process

The innovation, to be meaningful and translate into decisions and specific practices, must be in line with the structure of the company and the culture that it embodies. An appropriate business culture is instrumental in nurturing the conditions that allow innovation to thrive. However, culture alone is not enough; the company structure must also be flexible and able to respond appropriately, effectively, and in a timely manner to the challenges and needs that arise. Several organizational features represent catalysts for promoting an innovative culture, as listed in Figure 9.12. The company should display positive attitudes toward approaches that favor change. Decisions should be taken in a decentralized manner. Such companies develop complex structures and functions, often feature informal structures, and try to take advantage of interfacing capabilities at every level. They are characterized by organizational looseness, in terms of the resources they exploit, and they function as open systems.

Creating a corporate culture that fosters innovative thinking

☑ Positive attitude towards change

☑ Decision making

☑ Sufficiently complex structures and functions

☑ Exploitation of informal structures that operate in the business

☑ Ability for effective interface however and wherever this is required

Figure 9.12 Corporate Culture and Innovative Thinking

Success Factors for a New Industrial Product

Success factors consist of the two broad categories in Figure 9.13. The first encompasses four factors associated with the strategy developed by the company:

1   The advantage, perceived by the customer, that the product offers over competitors' product offers. This advantage may relate to the quality, cost effectiveness, or uses and functions of the product. A successful new product must provide better quality than is offered by competitors' products, along with benefits that can be clearly perceived by customers.
2   An equilibrium that balances the needs of the project with the resources and skills available in the company.
3   An equilibrium that balances the project development needs with the resources and capabilities that the R&D department offers (technical synergy).
4   The company's orientation to national borders surrounding its operations. A strategic orientation that fosters cross-border or even global development can increase the success of a new product.

Factors related to the business strategy

Advantages over competing products

Adequacy of marketing resources/skills

Adequacy of R&D resources/capabilities

International orientation

Factors related to the actual process of the development of a new product

Business capabilities in the pre-development base

Level of knowledge of the market/adequacy of marketing capabilities

Level of technical knowledge/adequacy of technical competence

Figure 9.13 Success Factors of New Industrial Products

Source: Adapted from Hutt and Speh (2013)

The second category includes three factors associated with the actual process of developing the new product:

1   The company's competence and predevelopment proficiency, in activities such as preliminary technical and market evaluations, detailed market research, and preliminary business and economic analyses. The ability to complete these activities can increase the chances of success.
2   Knowledge of the market and the capability, knowledge, and proficiency of the marketing department. Key considerations include strong production and use of market knowledge and a good understanding of customer needs. It requires collective in-house marketing capabilities too.
3   Technical knowledge and technical competence, related to the technical demands of the product being developed, complemented by strong management at the technical level, can facilitate transitions between the development stages of the new product and their particular requirements.

Reasons New Industrial Products Fail

Many causes lead to the failure of new industrial product introductions (Figure 9.14), reflecting the substantial risk associated with creating new products in an industrial environment. Any company undertaking an NPD process must be prepared to take on these risks, as well as work to minimize them. To do so, they should engage in careful business planning, at strategic and tactical levels, and develop effective marketing strategies. A good understanding of market opportunities and avoiding the introduction of inadequate products also are options for avoiding potential failure.

A common reason new products fail is their inability to deliver the value and utility that customers expect or that they are designed to deliver. Such an inability does not necessarily mean the product is technically defective, but it implies that the company did not really understand customer needs (whether articulated or not), the conditions surrounding product use, or the interactions with production conditions and processes.

Another reason for failure arises when firms introduce incomplete products. Incomplete products can be product offers that do not possess features that make them useful to customers or that do not deliver what the customer expects. They likely exist when companies have not paid due attention to the proper configuration of the provided services that accompany the specific product offer. Even if this responsibility transfers to intermediaries in the distribution network, the company might not have made the appropriate decisions and choices to prepare them.

A third reason for failure relates to proper training, of both the customer and the company. If staff members of the company trying to market the product lack sufficient acceptance or familiarity with the product, it is unlikely to ever find a suitable market or encouragement for acceptance among customers. The deeper and more fundamental the changes required for new product adoption, the more attention should be devoted to how these demands should be communicated to customers.

Because in industrial settings, all operations of the company must be taken into consideration, another source of product failure might be a failure to align the different functions of the company under a common umbrella. The antidote is an effective design that features joint contribution and collaboration across company units, in the context of cross-sectional NPD process.

Finally, product failure may result if the company does not collect and leverage appropriate, sufficient information about clients. With such information, the company can form a fuller and valid picture of existing market needs, then shape its NPD design and product offers accordingly to maximize customer satisfaction. Failure on this effort implies potential inadequacy of the product, market segmentation processes, or efforts to identify target markets and recognize key purchasing parameters.

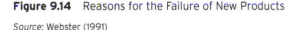

- ☒ Lack of real willingness to take the risk of trying to create a new product

- ☒ Inadequacy of the available product

- ☒ Incorrent estimation of opportunities offered by the market

- ☒ Failure to meet customer expectations in terms of the value or the utility of the new product

- ☒ Failure to provide appropriate training to the customer for the product offered

- ☒ Lack of harmonious collaboration between different operational segments

- ☒ Failure to exploit useful data and information resulting from both the market and the competition

Figure 9.14 Reasons for the Failure of New Products

Source: Webster (1991)

Communication Between Marketing and R&D Departments

The importance of good cooperation across different departments in a company has been noted, especially in industrial environments. Dependence among the different operational departments can promote the success of NPD processes, or it can lead to failure if the company is unable to manage it properly. In particular, two operational departments need to coordinate: marketing and R&D. Through the marketing department, the company comes into contact with customers, gains insights into their needs and desires, and builds specific features into a product offer. The R&D department instead leverages technical know-how and information gathered through marketing processes to construct sought-after features and meet customer expectations, while increasing the chances of success and profit for the company.

When these two functions must collaborate to introduce a new product into the market, a problem arises: balancing the need to focus on customer needs and desires against the technical need to create a product with a superior design that features relevant technical innovations.

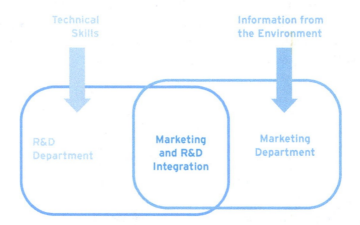

Figure 9.15 Communication Between Marketing and R&D Departments and the Integration of the Two Departments as a Solution

The goal for the company is to establish an interaction between these departments that matches market needs with the company's own technological capabilities, as in Figure 9.15. To do so, it needs to establish behavioral and organizational mechanisms to combine information about the market successfully with provisions for the opportunities that technology offers. Such mechanisms also require each department to recognize diverse capabilities and goals, by understanding the philosophy that drives each department's operations. Shared terms and terminologies about the product concept should be developed, to establish a common language and avoid information loss during the communication process. One potential solution is to integrate the two operating departments, thereby aggregating the capabilities they possess in a way that yields more benefits than either could achieve on their own. This option might also reduce the obstacles that each department faces in contributing to the successful introduction of a new industrial product in the market. Overall, new product success can likely be achieved with a clear market orientation and well-designed programs to manage such projects and exploit the opportunities that arise from the company's flexibility and decision-making.

10

WAREHOUSING IN THE INDUSTRIAL MARKET

Learning Objectives

- Appreciate the significance of warehousing in industrial supply chain management.
- Describe warehousing processes.
- Identify and discuss systems and facilities in warehouses.
- Outline key warehousing decisions in industrial supply chain management.
- Understand Warehousing 4.0 practices and technologies.

Case Study

Flatpacks: Two-Dimensional Furniture?

Return in time for a moment, to 1940s Sweden. A young entrepreneur founded a furniture company and named it to reflect his own name, as well as the farm and village where he was brought up: Ingvar Kamprad, Elmtaryd Agunnaryd (IKEA). Initially, he sold postcards and pens; it took five years until he moved into selling furniture and another seven years before the company began designing its own furniture. Initially, it sold products via mail order, then opened its first store in 1958, largely to showcase the available furniture for customers to peruse. But mail orders, which required freight shipments, were costly to provide.

Around this same time, car ownership was on the rise, and people using those cars for vacations frequently made sure their vehicles had sturdy roof racks. Kamprad looked around

(Continued)

and realized that these customers could collect furniture if it could be transported on their roof racks, such as if it came in flatpacks. Such a packaging design would also allow for more efficient storage for the firm.

The innovation of flatpacks was an initial source of success for the company, but IKEA continued its efforts to keep costs down, such as by working with manufacturers around the globe and seeking innovative designs. A key element underlying flatpacks was the idea that customers could assemble the furniture themselves. Today, the IKEA website contains some 12,000 products, organized according to a system that is based on the type of furniture. Beds take Norwegian place names, sofas refer to Swedish towns, kitchen tables are given names of Finnish sites, rugs often use Danish names, and chairs are male gendered.

The customer still assembles the furniture in many cases, though IKEA's product portfolio today is complemented by assembly and interior design services, and the company has branched out actively to appeal to industrial customers by providing office furniture. That is, even if IKEA continue to design furniture that can be transported in flatpacks, it has worked to add more services to its portfolio, while still maintaining a sustainability commitment, such as by hosting separate websites where customers can buy and sell used furniture.

THE WAREHOUSE IS THE HEART OF ANY SUPPLY CHAIN SYSTEM

Warehousing and warehouses are critical success factors for many businesses, but they also tend to demand large investments and operating costs, including the cost of land, equipment, labor, and so on. But the warehouse is the heart of a logistics system and a supply network. It might serve a single company, a network of companies as a distribution center, or a logistics service provider (and provide storage, transportation, distribution, and so on). The role of warehouses has changed in recent years though: whereas once they provided storage areas for products used or owned by one business, today they tend to function as centers for goods received (e.g., raw materials) from various suppliers, which they then provide to support the production of the company's final products. Furthermore, warehouses might combine products and consolidate shipments from various factories to multiple customers, breaking down massive shipments into smaller loads for each unique customer. Finally, warehouses act as distribution centers for the supply network, such that they can serve as a point of coordination and temporary storage of a business's stocks. Overall, warehouses have five main roles:

1   Production support. Centers unify the goods received (raw materials) from suppliers.
2   Product mixing. Multiple factories ship various products to a central warehouse; each plant produces only part of the total output of the production.
3   Consolidation. Combines products and consolidates shipments from various factories to customers.

4   Break bulk. Receive large loads from a factory, reflecting orders from multiple customers, and break them down into smaller loads to ship to each customer.

5   Cross-docking. Point of coordination and temporary storage of the stock rather than a storage point, such that goods are distributed continuously to customers, for up to 10–15 hours a day.

In general, a warehouse must meet the following needs:

- Maximum possible mechanization and automation of operations.
- Ability to receive delivered goods.
- Optimal use of space and storage facility capabilities.
- Organization with a continuous flow of goods.
- Rational placement of goods.
- Proper storage and preservation.
- Means to find and pick goods quickly to execute orders.
- Tracking of products by code, type, and order.
- Export of goods and preparation for distribution.

The importance of the warehouse is determined by several factors too:

- Stock. The warehouse is the storage area for product stocks. If the company knew market demand in advance, it would have no need to keep any product. The warehouse is related to the inventory and coverage of the space and the corresponding time-to-space gap between the points of production and the point-of-sale/consumption. Timely and efficient supply of the market can be achieved by keeping stocks in warehouses close to demand points.
- Order execution. Some of the most important logistics management tasks take place in warehouses. If the main objective of logistics management is to execute customer orders, the key tasks for the efficient planning, execution, monitoring, and control of those orders all take place in warehouses: product picking, product ordering and shuffling, tagging, order picking and ordering, loading and shipment, returns handling, inventory, and so on. This discussion highlights a second major difference between traditional and today's warehouses: traditionally, the warehouse's operations were labor-intensive (i.e., required heavy lifting and manual effort to load and unload products and collect them to execute orders), but today people with special knowledge and skills are needed to manage complex tasks, using machines, tools, and expensive equipment to perform precision work. Moreover, a warehouse manager is needed to coordinate all the work performed in the warehouse. In addition, warehouse operations today are information-intensive, in the sense that data about the movement of products (e.g., stock levels, storage locations of products, dates of entry and expiry, movements currently being executed or to be executed, incoming and outbound missions, customer and supplier data, staff) are important for smooth business operations.

- Production. Raw materials or semi-finished products are collected and stored in warehouses, for a production unit to manufacture or assemble into finished products. Warehouses are also used for storing and marketing the finished products.

- Economies of scale. In their desire to exploit economies of scale, production units can produce and store large quantities, which reduces production costs. Similarly, commercial businesses can be supplied with large quantities of products and thus achieve reduced market prices.

- Operating costs. The warehouse includes business resources (specialized personnel, premises, electromechanical equipment, information systems and technologies) whose use supports cost-effective implementations of business processes.

- Product seasonality. There are products whose demand (e.g., seasonal goods) or production (e.g., harvesting) refers to a specific season or period of time. Consequently, there is a need to store and dispose of them at the right time.

- Goods prices. The warehouse maintains the required inventory to keep the prices of goods on the market stable. A possible lack of inventory for a given product causes an increase in market prices, or vice versa.

WAREHOUSING MANUFACTURED PRODUCTS

Figure 10.1 shows two standard warehouse designs used for production support, depending on the flow of materials in the warehouse. On the left side, goods received and order execution/dispatch are located on the same side of the warehouse (U-flow); on the right side, goods received and order execution/dispatch are located at different ends of the warehouse (through-flow).

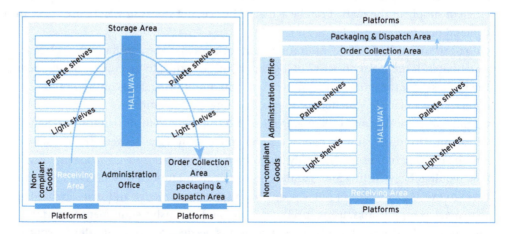

Figure 10.1 Types of Warehouses, by Material Flows

The main warehouse activities are receiving, transfer and putting away of goods, order picking/selection, accumulation/sorting, cross-docking, and shipping.

Receiving

Receiving is the first step in storing goods. It includes unloading goods received from the transport carrier, updating inventory records, initial receipt, checking of documentation, loading and unloading, placement of goods in the receiving area, and inspection for any discrepancies in quality or quantity. If discrepancies exist, the goods are either returned or moved to an area in the warehouse reserved for non-compliant goods, followed by receipt, unpacking/repackaging, and placement of goods in the storage or returns area.

The supplier's documentation (invoice, shipping note) is also checked against either the accompanying note (or list) of expected deliveries that a company's accounting office issues, usually on a daily basis or for each order. This check might take place in the vehicle (if the supplier's consent is required) or in a special demarcated area, such as a temporary storage or pick-up area, located near the warehouse entrance. If a dispute arises, the driver of the vehicle is informed and asked to declare the difference by signing the goods received/shipping note. Differences in the number/amount of goods received might mean:

- Less merchandise arrives than expected, so a credit note is issued by the back office for merchandise that did not arrive.
- More goods arrive than expected with the delivery, whereby the surplus can be received immediately or returned to the supplier.

The supplier is then informed about the incident and its resolution. The internal records of the supplier are updated, to detail the non-compliance event.

Some checks are both qualitative and quantitative. That is, they relate to the quantification of the goods and a comparison with the numbers written on the invoice or shipping note, including control checks for any products, damage to the delivery, damaged goods, and so on. If disputes arise, the same procedure is followed; otherwise, the receipt of the goods is completed with the signature of the accompanying documents.

Another check relates to the decision to apply cross-docking procedures for some goods. In this case, the goods are transported directly to a dispatch area, then labeled and packaged. To make the cross-docking procedure more efficient, the supplier might already have packaged and placed the required labels. If the products have not been transported/received on pallets from suppliers, a number of pallets located outside the warehouse premises, near the pickup area, will likely be used for their subsequent handling and delivery. Otherwise, a usual process of moving and storing the products in main storage areas of the warehouse, according to specific, predetermined inter-handling methods, is applied.

A first step in this task involves examining the receiving documents and labels for the receipt and storage of the products. In the next step, the exact storage location is updated, in coded form. The design of each code is preceded by predefinitions of main or alternate positions, which is the next task.

The storage location generally depends on the individual characteristics of the product (e.g., handling volume, dimensions, weight, consumption order, invoice value). For most small and medium-sized companies, storage systems consist of lightweight (e.g., metal perforated shelves) or pallet shelves. The type of storage systems and warehouse layout dictate the available in-warehouse handling equipment (e.g., pallet truck, forklift). The products that enter the company are recorded, either in a paper file (hard copy) or on a corresponding software application, which informs the inventory update. Finally, documentation of the goods received is sent to the company's accounting offices.

Another kind of goods received involves returns of goods from customers, for various reasons; their handling depends on the policy of each company, but specific steps are needed to return them to the warehouse. The warehouse needs to receive some kind of request or notification from the client company. Then it should undertake quantitative and qualitative testing of the goods. If the quantity on the shipping note is correct, the warehouse, in cooperation with the client, determines whether these products remain suitable for sale or not. If they are deemed unsuitable for resale, they are placed in the non-compliant goods section of the warehouse (or another appropriate place, like an expired goods section).

Transfer and Put Away

Upon acceptance of the delivered quantity and quality and then actual delivery, the product is placed in a specific position in the warehouse. Transfer and put away involves the movement of incoming products to storage locations, through a main aisle. It also includes additional activities such as repackaging from pallets to boxes or units (tertiary to secondary or primary packaging) or physical movements (usually to staging or packaging/shipment areas for cross-docking).

Spatial planning of the products (coding) has already taken place; as mentioned, this element is a basic issue related to storage. The final deliverable is the creation of a table that details the storage space in the warehouse and how it is used, together with the code of the recommended storage locations for each good-related code. For each code, based on demand (quantity and time period), one or more primary or alternative positions (if primary spaces are occupied) can be proposed, at the same level and in the same column or zone. The table also shows spaces that are not recommended or are prohibited for these goods, such as in the case of chemicals or hazardous goods, which require special storage.

Therefore, the process continues by reading the storage space table to find predetermined spaces, then moving the pallets or cartons to those storage locations, placing them accordingly, and updating the goods file (or formal archive that companies use to list the positions, quantities, and movements of goods). Different techniques for installing goods in the warehouse are common, except with regard to a predetermined positioning system: the product should be placed wherever there is free space (informal system) or in the next available position, and goods should be positioned according to the product type. An appropriate method likely combines these rules.

Order Picking/Selection

For many warehouses, order picking/selection is the most critical activity. Picking refers to the process of retrieving products from storage locations and moving them to the shipment area. Warehouse staff execute orders by collecting the right stock-keeping units (SKU), in the right quantity and quality that the customer wants.

Then the order execution process comprises order placement and order processing (collection, dispatch, and loading). First, order placement can be executed in the information system used by the company (enterprise resource planning (ERP), accounting software), manually by the order manager, or electronically through an electronic data interchange (EDI) initiated by the customer. Second, order processing requires checking the inventory to determine if sufficient stock is available to execute the order, assigning the collection work to specific warehouse keepers, and executing this collection. The method adopted to collect orders often determines the degree of competitiveness of a warehouse. Its main objective is to minimize distances and the travel time for the picker. Practices that can enhance this workflow include specifying extra warehouse space for picking; fast picking or forward picking; appropriate techniques and practices that determine the best locations for each product based on speed, physical dimensions, and storage restrictions; and the use (if feasible) of automated systems. Furthermore, there are four main picking methods:

- SKU picking. For a specific order, this simple picking process can take place at any time during the day, without a schedule.
- Batch picking. An employee retrieves products for a group of orders in one shift, one product (line SKU) at a time. When an item appears in more than one order per shift, it is recovered in its entirety once, in a quantity that satisfies all orders.
- Picking in zones (zone picking). Storage areas organized in zones assign one person responsibility for each zone, who then retrieves all the products (line SKU) in that area, for all pending orders. Thus, each employee corresponding to each zone is responsible for one order at a time, and a product recovery plan is issued for each shift.
- Wave picking. This method is similar to discrete order picking, featuring one employee working on one order and one product at a time, but a picking schedule exists to process multiple orders. This method requires coordination between product picking and shipping processes.

A specific objective could be to minimize contact with the handled goods, which might be achieved through the use of conveyor belts that move goods directly from a shelf rather than a forward pickup area. Dynamic or flexible work zones allow for adaptations to work requirements. For example, at peak hours, work zones might be reduced to add more warehouse assistants/pickers to the system, but then in non-peak hours, collection zones may be increased to reduce the number of employees per zone. The benefits of such dynamic zones can be enhanced by an effective warehouse management system. Then in the last step, order dispatch involves gathering the goods at the dispatch site, to be loaded onto a truck that will execute the distribution.

Upon receipt of an order, once the inventory check is completed, an order collection form is issued. This form is not the same as the original order note; it contains additional information, such as the code of collection lists, storage locations, the warehouse keeper in charge, or the type of forklift.

Accumulation/Sorting

In the case of batch picking (as described in the previous section), the items of various orders get collected in a specific area, then grouped by customer. In particular, upon completion of the collection work, the products that form part of an order have been placed in a specific space in the order collection area (packaging zone). This area is delineated clearly; it provides the final checkpoint of products before they are shipped to the customer.

This process is followed by the packaging and labeling of the products. Initially, packaging primarily served to ensure the safe transportation of goods to customers, whether as items that had to be packaged or cartons that had to be palletized. With new developments in the industry though, packaging has evolved into a pivotal service, reflecting specific legal and environmental standards.

Labeling is another important service, required for customs and tax purposes. Details that must be stated on packaging include (1) customer information, (2) content, (3) delivery information, (4) the serial number of the cartons, and (5) information referring to the shipping note. Usually these details get printed on labels by conventional printers and pasted onto the packaging. State-of-the-art technology also offers industrial heat transfer printers that can minimize the use of packages with preprinted information. Necessary details (product code, description, weight) are printed straight onto the packaging, which can help meet fluctuations in demand and limit the stocks of preprinted packaging required.

Cross-Docking

The orders next are packed, placed in the appropriate unit load (e.g., pallet), and shipped to the customer. This process takes place in the packaging and shipping area. Cross-docking is required in special cases when the received products are moved directly to the shipping docks.

Shipping

After picking, orders often must be packed and stacked in the right unit load (main tertiary package unit, such as a pallet), before being shipped. Onboard loading is the final warehouse task. It might be undertaken by warehouse keepers or drivers, together with assistants, subject to the agreement signed between the parties. The goods are already in the consignment area, the driver just conducts a quantitative and qualitative check. If the quantity and quality match the order, the final documents (invoice and shipping note) are issued by the accounting office and signed by both parties. In the case of any discrepancies, these are noted by the driver on a relevant form. Finally, the loading is completed, and the vehicle leaves the warehouse.

Stock Inventory

Another important administrative task involves stock inventory, or recording the stock levels of all products (counting) that exist in the warehouse at a specific point in time. During the inventory count, the accounting stocks (in the accounting records) are compared with the actual physical stocks (in the warehouse). This process helps control the inventory management system over the preceding period, in seeking the smallest possible discrepancy between the accounting and physical inventories, as well as recording stocks, which can be principal assets of a business. (Note: items delivered to a warehouse cease to be the property of the supplier; when moved from the warehouse, they cease to be the company's property.) There are four types of physical inventory that are often undertaken in parallel:

- Annual inventory count, with all stocks in the warehouse physically counted on the balance sheet date.
- Continuous stock taking, with stocks continually counted throughout the year.
- Circular or regular stock taking, during which stocks are counted at regular intervals.
- Inventory sampling, such that randomly selected items are counted.

For example, a combination of circular stock taking (quarterly or biannually) and inventory sampling might be applied to high-traffic items, continuous stock taking for high-value products, and annual inventory counts for all products.

A standard annual physical stock counting process begins with scheduling. The stock taking team is designated, and an implementation schedule is prepared, including the start and end dates and communications with various groups (e.g., staff, suppliers) of their involvement in the inventory count. Each group (usually two people) is assigned specific storage locations to count; a corresponding allocation log table for inventory groups can be prepared for this purpose. The lists of products in these locations, according to the information system, are available as hard copies. The inventory taking also might be based on product type, in which case the system issues lists of locations where the codes being counted each time should appear.

In an inventory based on location, the process requires completing an inventory log. The main areas that need to be filled in are the product and position code, product title and description, unit of measure (e.g., piece, measure, kilogram) or unit load (e.g., pallet, carton, piece), quantity, and comments. The unit value and total value also might be recorded, to support estimates of the inventory cost and value.

If instead the areas to be surveyed organize the inventory process, locations are locked electronically, so no movement of goods can take place, and warehouse keepers begin the process by scanning the stock location code and stored item codes. Upon completion and finalization of these tasks, the records of possible differences provide relevant documentation for correcting the inventory. Any discrepancies between physical and accounting stocks prompt close examinations of the import and export documents of the warehouse items, as well as the overall manner in which they are organized.

In the warehouse area, other tasks also take place, such as cleaning and tidying up, maintenance of equipment and machinery, and administrative practices. But the most important tasks remain inventory and management of available resources.

WAREHOUSING 4.0

The 4th Industrial Revolution (Industry 4.0) for logistics management (Logistics 4.0) reflects the Internet-of-Things, in that it relies on interconnected technologies, including robots, artificial intelligence, intelligent sensors, and flexible production systems, as well as innovative computing practices such as big data analysis, cloud computing, and business intelligence. These solutions mainly involve two functional areas in logistics systems: warehousing and transportation.

Specifically, warehouses gain the capabilities to engage in continuous and real-time monitoring of stocks, automatic replenishment, autonomous identification of materials, and the optimization of daily tasks, such as collection, placement, routing, and so on. Some pertinent examples include the automatic replenishment of stocks using smart boxes and shelves, which rely on sensors or cameras to calculate the number of items remaining and the number needed for a production line, such that if the stock level falls below the level required, a replacement order is placed automatically. The widespread applications of such solutions can dynamically alter the processes and designs of logistics and production systems, to deal efficiently with changes in demand or in the internal and external environment. Demand throughout the chain can then be predicted more accurately, which also informs demand predictions for production capacity, storage, and logistics needs or changes in raw material requirements.

In Table 10.1, we classify these Logistics (Warehouse) 4.0 technologies into four groups:

1   Automation of warehousing processes.
2   Information (real-time) visibility.
3   Optimization of resources.
4   Interconnectivity of resources.

Table 10.1 Warehouse Management Systems: Solutions and Trends

Objectives	Description	Solutions and Trends
Automation of warehousing processes	Enterprise resources operate autonomously by automating logistics processes.	• Robots, cellular transport systems • Pick by voice (voice instructions) • Pick by light • Pick by vision • Embedded systems • Drones
Information (real-time) visibility	Enterprise resources maintain data and useful information. Information is available to the appropriate executives.	• Auto-ID technologies (barcodes, radio frequency identification (RFID), quick response (QR) codes) • Intelligent sensors • Augmented reality and smart glasses • Real-time locating systems • Big data analysis • Business intelligence
Optimization of resources	Enterprise resources operate autonomously by optimizing logistics processes.	• Artificial intelligence • Simulation • Labor management systems
Interconnectivity of resources	Ability to communicate with all available enterprise resources.	• Internet-of-Things • Cloud computing 　○ Software-as-a-service 　○ Infrastructure-as-a-service 　○ Platform-as-a-service • Smartphones and apps

AUTOMATION OF WAREHOUSING PROCESSES

We consider six examples of automated warehousing processes.

Robots and Cellular Transport Systems

Robotics technology effectively enhances warehouse management, because autonomous robotic units can move on grid frames, above storage stacks, and take unit loads (e.g., product bins) from those slots to move them to the picking stations. Robotic moveable rack systems, as an evolution of cellular transport systems, rely on automated, guided vehicles that use autonomous software agents or swarm intelligence.

Pick by Voice

This hands-free technology entails voice instructions, shared through headphones and a microphone, and frees the operator to handle stock items. Thus an order picker can focus entirely on retrieving the required items. It leads to improved picking productivity and accuracy, supports real-time data analysis, and reduces required operator training.

Pick by Light

These systems use specific light and LED displays to direct warehouse operators to product locations for picking. Warehouse staff know which products to pick and how many. In addition to guiding the picker to the exact location, the lights display the precise amounts ordered and require confirmation of each item picked. The main benefits include increased picking productivity, better accountability, and fewer errors.

Pick by Vision

Pick by vision is based on augmented reality technology. Its application requires readers who can scan two-dimensional barcodes or quick response (QR) codes, mounted on a glass frame, then work with the warehouse management system to provide information and directions for collecting orders. The information is displayed on transparent screens, such as smart glasses.

Embedded Systems

Embedded computing solutions help workers enhance their performance, even in harsh environmental conditions, such as very high or low temperatures or when exposed to shocks or vibration. Some solutions feature embedded industrial PC and mobile barcode printers on a lift truck, which can then use specially designed mechanical support and a power convertor.

Drones

Drones perform many warehouse operations, including detection, identification, and tracking of parcels, using their advanced sensors in combination with artificial intelligence, automatic upload of data and results, and synchronization with the warehouse management system. Their autonomous navigation in warehouses and avoidance of obstacles ensures inventory accuracy, reduces operating costs, and increases employee safety. Moreover, drones can work all day, so downtimes or halted operations are reduced; even night stock can be monitored constantly, which should improve inventory management efforts. Another benefit of drones is an autonomous solution: they can count stocks without any human resources, which eliminates the need to count rolling stock or establish guidance infrastructure and also enables faster, cheaper, more accurate inventory replenishment.

INFORMATION (REAL-TIME) VISIBILITY

In this section too, we consider six exemplary technologies.

Auto-ID Technologies

Automatic identification and data capture (Auto-ID) technologies have profound effects on business operations, because they allow for fast, easy downloads and storage of information while it is being created. They include widely used technologies such as magnetic stripes, radio frequency identification (RFID), voice and vision identification, biometrics, and smart cards; of particular relevance for logistics management, especially in warehousing operations, we note the benefits of (1) barcode, (2) QR code, and (3) RFID technologies. All of these technologies work with integrated business management systems like ERP or with specialized business information systems, such as warehouse management systems, providing integrated information and communication technologies solutions that enhance:

- Productivity ("I do more things using or consuming fewer resources").
- Profitability ("I perform my tasks in less time and at less cost").
- Effectiveness ("I perform my tasks reliably and without error while supporting the rest of the company").

Barcode technology is quite mature, since being first introduced in the United States in the late 1960s for industrial use—mainly to meet the needs of large materials handling companies in the automobile industry. Over subsequent decades, it spread widely in retailing, by meeting the needs of supermarkets for faster movement and pricing of goods at the cashiers. Today, barcodes are everywhere, largely having replaced handwritten input or manual data entry into systems. The basic, underlying premise of this specific technology consists of two simple steps:

- A series of information placed on a product allows specific machines to read it automatically and transfer it to a business information system, so that the product is recognizable, and all movements related to that product are recorded.
- Information transmitted by these special readers (e.g., scanners, detectors), usually to a warehouse management system, occurs via cables or in wireless form. The latter is supported by wireless local area networks, through which data can be transmitted from a mobile terminal to a computer system or even the Internet. The collected information then can be used by the warehouse staff to make the right decisions.

The universal product code (UPC-A, UPC-E) and the European article numbering (EAN-8, EAN-13 and EAN-128) are the most popular types of linear or one-dimensional barcodes, because laser beams can read all their information, which is encoded only in width (i.e., perpendicular to the lines).

Two-dimensional codes can encode more data, so QR codes are quickly outpacing one-dimensional barcode labels. The creators named this technology QR to highlight its main feature: It can read the contents encoded in a label really quickly. In addition, this technology offers:

- High character storage capacity (up to 7,089 characters).
- Code resistance to incorrect readings, because the stored information can be maintained at different locations. If some part of this information is destroyed, another part of the same information stored elsewhere can be read.
- The possibility to read it from a variety of applications, on tablets and smartphones.
- Transmission as an SMS or email.
- Ability to encrypt content and ensure its confidentiality.

These possibilities in turn offer many opportunities to support marketing/sales and logistics activities. For example, every operation performed on the logistics circuit (e.g., placing products on shelves, picking them when ordered, loading, confirmation of receipt) can be identified and automated through the use of QR codes.

The general benefits of using barcode technology thus are the speed and accuracy of the data entry process, and the reduced time and cost of such tasks, as well as direct interfaces with business information systems. For warehouses specifically, we note the following main advantages:

- The mature, internationally recognized technology has proven reliability and high productivity, efficiency, and ease of use.
- The standardized technology ensures uniform data collection in a way that is understood and accepted worldwide.
- It increases the speed of import, export, and other movements of products performed in the warehouse, such that it reduces the time needed to gather information.
- It provides accurate information; copying, transcription, and human writing or typing errors completely disappear. When using a handwritten procedure, one mistake occurs for every 300 characters, on average. Using barcodes, one error occurs for every 7,500,000 readings, on average.
- It provides exact knowledge, at any moment in time, about how many and what products (stocks) a company has in its warehouse and their location.
- It provides immediate real-time transfer of information, if required.

Thus, barcodes offer significant financial benefits, reflecting the improved organization and automation of warehouse tasks and operations, along with higher quality and more efficient customer service, such that overall productivity growth should increase.

Newer technologies, such as RFID, add some other components, including:

1   A tag, or transceiver, that receives a signal and then immediately transmits another, different signal.
2   The reader, which consists of the antenna and the control unit.
3   Middleware, acting as the channel of communication between the reading device and the business information system.

The tag contains a microchip that stores data (from a few bits to many Kbytes) and an antenna that receives and responds to transceiver signals. Labels can be read-only, such that they are programmed during their production stage and cannot be altered, or be read-and-write, so their content can be modified. They also might be passive, activated only when found within a radio frequency field transmitted by a reader, or active, with an embedded transceiver and battery, such that they transmit the information on their own. Through the antenna, information gets collected and transmitted to and from labels. The reader is a computer-controlled device that transmits (though the embedded antenna) radio frequency waves to the labels, which must be located within a predetermined radius to be detected and activated. It also contains a control unit that defines its actions (e.g., sending or receiving signals, reading or writing labels). The control unit also communicates with the information system through middleware, functioning like a bridge and translating the commands accordingly.

Because RFID tags store information related to the people or objects that carry them, their practical applications are widespread, across various situations that require object recognition. For example, they can be used on product packaging, in libraries, on credit cards, or even on a badge or identification document such as a passport or driver's license. Another common application pertains to the movement and transportation of products, because RFID can identify products in transport or within the industrial units, whether they are on pallets, in warehouses, or on store shelves. In this way, they progressively are replacing barcode technology.

Overall, the advantages of RFID include their ability to work without direct visual contact, the possibility of multilabel readability, the capacity to encode vast amounts of information, and their operational abilities in adverse environmental conditions (e.g., high temperature, humidity, cold, sunlight, dust). We also note some disadvantages though, which have prevented wider adoption. The disadvantages are (1) technical, in that RFID systems produced by different manufacturers are not necessarily compatible; (2) economic, reflecting the cost of their installation and use; and (3) social, because they might interfere with sensitive personal data.

Intelligent Sensors

Intelligent sensors in warehouses include smart forklifts and safety systems. The sensors of a smart forklift gather evidence of human activity or unmovable objects. These data are analyzed by a control unit, which commands the forklift vehicle to stop or detour to avoid the obstacle. Algorithms inform rapid predictions of potential scenarios and prompt the activation of appropriate reactions. A vehicle can also give priority to certain orders and make decisions about the best sequence and route. Intelligent sensors offer safety benefits, such as by raising an alert when someone is crossing a path or trigging warnings if there is activity in a particular area that has clearance limitations.

Augmented Reality and Smart Glasses

Augmented reality can enrich every object in the warehouse with additional, highly valuable information. Head-mounted displays can be used to place images of both the physical world and virtual objects in the user's field of view. Smart glasses and augmented head-mounted displays allow users to both display and analyze information relevant to their surroundings. These systems aim to optimize most warehousing activities, but especially picking processes.

Real-Time Location Systems

Real-time location systems detect and record, in real-time, the geographical location of various assets in a warehouse, including stock, material handling equipment (e.g., forklifts, trucks), and so on. These solutions can increase warehouse productivity by preventing lost stock and reducing the potential for costly, time-consuming errors, while also increasing safety by preventing collision hazards among moving parts.

Big Data Analysis

The deployment of connected devices in a warehouse such as forklifts, barcode readers, and sensor networks adds a huge number of data sources. Devices like these continuously generate data streams, increasing the velocity of data aggregation and processing. The analysis of all of these unstructured data sources can add intelligence to warehouse activities such as material handling, packaging, and routing.

Business Intelligence

Business intelligence tools allow warehouse staff to see, use, and combine large amounts of data, of different formats and type, from various sources, and integrate them. These tools can also improve internal efficiencies and accountability while saving time and eliminating costs, with metric-driven decision-making and events management.

OPTIMIZATION OF RESOURCES

Warehouse optimization implies increased efficiency and effectiveness, and at the same time minimized errors in terms of equipment usage, warehousing tasks, material flows, and process management. Artificial intelligence, simulation, and labor management systems can be applied to achieve optimization in warehouse facilities.

Artificial Intelligence

Artificial intelligence refers to the paradigm that computer systems can perform independently the tasks that typically have required human intelligence. Applications in warehouse and inventory management include better predictions of market demand, adding intelligence and efficiency into various warehousing processes.

Simulation

Through simulation, a warehouse manager can model and review current practices and warehousing tasks, as well as test potential changes without disturbing the existing warehouse system. The development of what-if scenarios that include different combinations and values for the parameters in the model provide a low-cost, low-risk method to determine the optimal setup for warehousing processes such as receiving, slotting, picking, and distribution, as well as informing other critical decisions, such as schedule and staff optimization, facility layout and design, congestion analysis, and so on.

Labor Management Systems

Labor management technologies can be the basis of stable and efficient labor management, in terms of training and performance measurement.

INTERCONNECTIVITY OF RESOURCES

Network infrastructure in warehouses connects systems, sensors, physical devices, and various warehouse assets/resources in a real-time manner, leading to what was previously referred to as smart warehouses.

Internet-of-Things

Generally, the Internet-of-Things describes the idea that every device (or thing) with an on/off switch is interconnected, as are the people using these devices. In a warehouse, an Internet-of-Things paradigm can connect all the solutions described in the previous sections, such as RFID and other auto-ID and tracking technologies, augmented reality devices, sensors, and so on.

Cloud Computing

Cloud computing achieves scalability and reduced maintenance costs, because the main server and data are located outside the enterprise. A key application is software-as-a-service; for warehouse management, this would enable the company to access the full functionality of its traditional warehouse management system software through the Internet, for a low monthly subscription fee. The platform-as-a-service similarly features a set of tools and services designed to make it easy and quick to code and deploy additional warehouse management system features. Perhaps the most basic category of cloud computing services is infrastructure-as-a-service, such that companies and distribution centers can rent IT infrastructure (servers, virtual machines, storage, networks, operating systems) from a cloud provider, for which they pay based on their usage (e.g., volume of data exchanged). Cloud computing eliminates the need to invest in expensive hardware and software, power and cooling capabilities, and overall infrastructure. Most cloud computing services are on-demand, so even large amounts of computing resources can be made available in minutes, giving businesses a great deal of flexibility. Furthermore, cloud services are scalable; the appropriate resources are available at nearly all times (e.g., more or less computing power, storage, bandwidth), in an accessible location.

Smartphones

Smartphones can leverage the functionality of information systems such as ERP and warehouse management systems. Employees can then gain access to and use these systems remotely. They can also connect to auto-ID technologies (e.g., near field communication, QR codes) to automate various inventory handling tasks.

11

INDUSTRIAL SERVICES

Learning Objectives

- Define the concept of services.
- List the differentiating characteristics between products and services.
- Understand specific questions that must be addressed to implement marketing planning for services.
- Outline the approach adopted to formulate a services marketing mix.
- Connect the basic concept of services with a broader industrial reality.

Case Study

Servitization in Business-to-Business Marketing

In a traditional value chain, services constitute supporting activities, sandwiched between inbound and outbound logistics, such as manufacturing or physical value propositions. With the emergence of servitization as a central concept in business-to-business practice though (Vandermerwe & Rada, 1988), services became a key source of value creation, rather than just value supporting, in an operations model. The term servitization is processual, such that it denotes a transition or change from a previous state to a new state, such as by inculcating greater service provision in an integrated value proposition to make a move away from a traditional product + service model. Service centricity (Raddats et al., 2019) might also imply providing services above and beyond those required to support a physical offering (Baines et al., 2009; Kowalkowski et al., 2017a; Vandermerwe & Rada, 1988), such that services become central to the long-term strategy of even manufacturing firms.

(Continued)

Servitization might also provide an escape from the commoditization trap (Kowalkowski et al., 2017b), especially if this business model innovation combines with digitalization trends (Kohtamäki et al., 2020). Taking a complementary view of servitization and digitization as necessary, strategic co-features, discussions of digital servitization suggest ways to find hidden profit elements in business models, such as through the use of big data to find revenue streams unrelated to the physical product offering.

Adopting servitization in a way that can produce a sufficient return on the investment accordingly requires changes to the culture and capabilities of the business-to-business firm (Kohtamäki et al., 2020). Firms such as IBM, Rolls Royce, and Fujitsu-Siemens have morphed from physical product manufacturers to integrated solutions providers, undergoing significant cultural transformations in the process. The Industry 4.0 agenda (Frank et al., 2019) also challenges the validity of conventional value chain concepts, by promising the removal of geographic constraints on service delivery and reduced reliance on human service staff, as in the context of remote diagnostics.

Other trends are possible too. Reverse servitization (Valtakoski, 2017) implies that a firm that initially focused on providing services later develops tangible product offerings, such as when Google began producing laptops and mobile phones. Deservitization (Kowalkowski et al., 2017a; Valtakoski, 2017) refers to a subsequent retreat from service provision in knowledge-based exchanges, in which an exchange partner has greater knowledge and ability to perform aspects of the service initially provided by the supplier. All these forms of servitization therefore mark reorientations in the relationship between product-oriented value chains and those that include a strong focus on services. As noted, servitization increasingly is synonymous with digital servitization, such that it requires revisions to the process and systems, but also firm-level competences and cultural orientations.

INTRODUCTION TO SERVICES

Marketing, as a science and philosophy, offers a specific perspective on services. We present that perspective in this chapter, by outlining a compact, comprehensive description of the fast-growing, promising service sector, in terms of its relevant impacts, effects, and consequences, all in the context of industrial markets that seek to develop and deliver integrated product offerings.

In many cases, the level of business development in an industry or nation is linked closely with its service development. Furthermore, the customer experience is framed by features that constitute service provision, including checkout queues, behavioral and atmospheric conditions, and daily service functions (e.g., transport, entertainment). Along with the unsurpassed importance of services, the provision of a service remains distinct from the provision of a material good, so it is critical to understand this aspect of the production process. A key question is whether it makes sense to address a service as independent and distinct from a material product, despite their inextricable link.

DISTINCTION OF SERVICES FROM MATERIAL GOODS

An early distinction of outputs reflected whether the production process yielded tangible and visible outcomes, such as materials or natural products, or else intangible features, in the form of services. In this view, services exist and are well recognized, but their value appeared less important or impressive than that of the material product. Thus in services research from the 1940s, we find descriptions of productive sectors of an economy, contrasted with services, which were assigned to a tertiary sector. The primary interest was in how services' particular characteristics could benefit tangible products. Berry (1980) reemphasized the distinction between material products and services by highlighting the existence of physical characteristics and properties in the former, versus intangible features that require processing in the latter; the materiality criterion also highlighted distinctions of elements that can be perceived through a person's own senses.

Yet even at the time, this criterion did not clearly or unambiguously facilitate classifications of offerings into distinct categories. Even after experience with it, people might find it difficult to assign an offering to a product versus service category, especially if its physical and tangible features were not the primary source of the value they obtained from it. Intangible processes are usually involved and have substantial effects on actual consumer experiences.

Shostack's (1977) scale of uncertainty provided a possible solution, by classifying productive and economic activities on a linear axis, depending on which characteristic of the production outcome dominates the other: moving to the left end of the spectrum, the dominant characteristic is the tangible and visible result, as illustrated in Figure 11.1, so material goods would be placed closer to the left. Moving instead to the right, the most prominent feature is intangibility, so offerings labeled as services would be placed closer to that end.

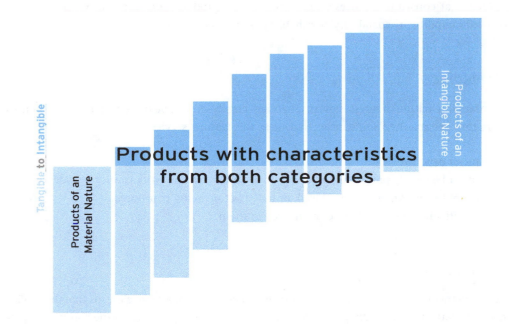

Figure 11.1 Analogy of the Intangibility Scale

Source: Adapted from Shostack (1977)

Applications of the scale of intangibility reveal two important elements: first, the classification of various product offers cannot be sealed or static; it depends on the type and extent to which a dominant feature of intangibility appears. Second, to define the concept of service, we need a more precise approach, capable of capturing more of its facets, characteristics, and parameters, more accurately.

Modern-day mentions of services tend to refer to intangible products, or at least those that are essentially intangible in nature. Their exchange takes place directly, from the producer to the consumer, without any physical transport or storage. The product is consumed almost immediately, at the moment it is produced, which Eiglier and Langeard (1987) refer to as "servuction," by combining "service" and "production." Intangible elements of the product offer may be included but cannot be separated from it (require customer participation, do not require ownership transfer).

Sometimes, the term "services" is used to refer to activities that accompany the sale of a product offer and contribute to the deal or its use. This version implies services that precede the sale or occur after it, such that they operate as added elements to the supplied product but still do not constitute its endogenous characteristics. The American Marketing Association provides the following definition: "activities, benefits, and satisfaction elements that are either provided for sale or provided in connection with the sale of tangible assets."

SPECIAL FEATURES OF SERVICES

Products that constitute services differ from material product categories in four well-known ways: intangibility, inseparability, perishability, and heterogeneity.

Intangibility

The intangible nature of services means that they largely cannot be perceived by human senses before they are acquired and consumed. Due to this feature, services:

- Cannot be stored.
- Cannot be legally protected, because human endeavors and work cannot be patented.
- Cannot be demonstrated, displayed, or tested before being consumed.
- Are difficult to price or have costs applied to them.

Inseparability

The simultaneous production, consumption, and distribution of a service means that the service provider's participation in the production process cannot be separate from the consumer's participation or the interactions of other customers. Therefore, it has the following consequences:

- Customer participation can increase the levels of uncertainty for the customer, but also for the design and implementation of the service.
- Decisions are influenced by the spatial positioning of the production process of the service and choices about the manner in which it will be delivered to the customer.
- The influence of other customers can affect the result, such as by changing the focal customers' emotions or perceptions of the service provided within the space and time it is delivered.
- It is practically impossible to mass-produce a service.

Perishability

Services cannot be stored, unlike material products. This feature can cause problems in relation to the synchronization of supply and demand for a particular service, leading to the following possible situations:

- Demand exceeds supply, which leads to long waiting lists or even a downgrade of the final supplied product.
- Demand is lower than supply, which financially burdens the operations of the service provider, because it is using resources but not earning sufficient returns on them.

Heterogeneity

Finally, heterogeneity refers to the variability that the provided service presents when delivered to different customers, as well as the inability to control this variability completely before the service is delivered to the customer. It can be expressed in two ways:

- Negative heterogeneity, or the degree to which the service provided cannot meet given standards, such as in terms of effectiveness or efficiency.
- Positive heterogeneity, or the degree to which the service provided exceeds given standards and rules to cover and satisfy the customer's special needs.

Heterogeneity also arises because no clearly defined standards or quality controls exist for the production of services, largely because the customer participates in the production of the service. In addition, outcomes depend on the mood and feelings of each employee in charge of service delivery. Finally, it is impossible to ensure that a service will be produced under controlled conditions, unaffected by external forces.

A WIDER CLASSIFICATION OF SERVICES

Continued attempts to conceptualize service according to a modern perspective also have suggested a broad categorization, based on the lack of transfer of ownership, such that a service may fall into one or more of the following categories:

- Rented goods. Customers temporarily acquire the right to use an object, for which no desire or preference to acquire ownership has been expressed.
- Defined space and place rentals. The customer acquires the right to use part of a larger space, such as within a building, vehicle, or area, usually sharing the larger space with other customers.
- Labor and expertise rentals. Customers hire people to do tasks that they themselves cannot complete or that they choose not to do.
- Access to shared physical environments. Customers can lease the right to share the use of physical environments, such as outdoor sites, buildings, or some combination.
- Systems and networks (access and usage). A customer rents the right to gain access to a specific network. Service providers may have a well-developed terminology for access and use, depending on the needs of the customers for whom they are intended.

Alternatively, services could be categorized according to the nature of the processing taking place (tangible or intangible) or the subject matter (persons involved or their data). For example, activities involving material substances can be applied to human beings or their natural property (possessions); activities of an intangible nature can be applied to the minds of individuals or to intangible assets. Figure 11.2 illustrates the correlation network and its four quadrants.

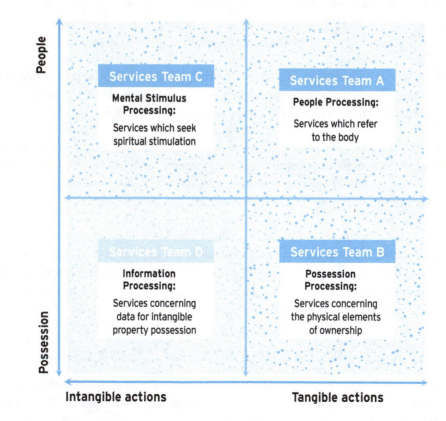

Figure 11.2 A Broad Classification of Services

Sources: Adapted from Lovelock et al. (2009).

People Processing

Services aiming directly at individuals include transportation, accommodations, and other service enhancements. They require the following elements:

- The customer must be present at the physical location where the service is provided. This factor imposes a boundary for the selection of the specific location.
- The customer needs to be actively involved in the service delivery process.
- Administrators need to consider customers' perspectives when designing the process and related products, including financial and non-financial costs (time, physical and mental effort, fear, pain).

Possession Processing

Customer may ask service providers to provide some kind of treatment or facility related to information that they hold. In this case, production and consumption of the service are not necessarily simultaneous, and customer participation becomes limited.

Mental Stimulus Processing

These services, aimed at the minds of customers, can affect and shape attitudes and behaviors. The core provision consists of information-based content, which can take various forms and also be converted into digital or analog, according to the choices made. In this case:

- The customer is not required to be present where the service is provided, as long as the customer can extract the information when exposed to it.
- The customer depends on the service provider, so there is a possibility of exposure to information that is not true. The moral reputation of the provider thus must be strong.
- The service can be stored for future consumption, as well as repeatedly.

Information Processing

Information is the most intangible form of a service, but it might be converted into various forms, with tangible or even permanent natures.

Sometimes, it is difficult to distinguish the latter two categories; they might be combined into a broader category of information-based services too.

ADAPTING THE MARKETING MIX

Just as marketing philosophy can be applied to consumer products, marketing tools, techniques, and practices can be exploited to formulate and implement a comprehensive marketing strategy for companies that provide products and services. Notably, the so-called marketing mix can be relevant, as comprised of the 4Ps of product, price, place, and promotion, perhaps complemented by three more Ps: people, process, and physical evidence.

These elements continue to exert influence even when a company mainly provides a service, but the peculiarities of services require appropriate adaptations to applications of this marketing mix. The overall set of tools used to produce services then reflects appropriate adjustments and variations, designed to ensure that the specifics of the products themselves and of the transactions that include them, as well as the environment in which they take place, are taken into account.

Product

Referring to a service product, this element constitutes a product offer that includes two main components: a main product and secondary services (see Figure 11.3). The main product consists of the benefits leveraged to provide customers with solutions. Then the secondary services encompass a network of additional services that frame the main product and that mainly function to enhance its usage value, as well as consumers' perceived value, and thus to make the overall product offer more attractive to buyers. Choosing an optimal set of secondary services to frame the main product is central to efforts to design a marketing strategy that might give the company a competitive advantage. The services should also make it clear that the product is differentiated from competing products.

The product supplier should devise an ideal way to provide every available service to customers, while also making clear what role the customer plays in the associated service processes. The time requirements for the entire supply process should also be clear. Finally, the product supplier must select a level of supply to provide the customer and design the channels to make that supply available.

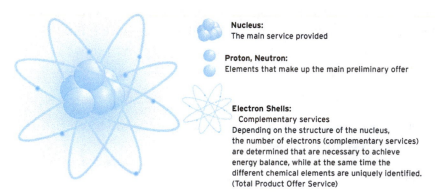

Nucleus:
The main service provided

Proton, Neutron:
Elements that make up the main preliminary offer

Electron Shells:
Complementary services
Depending on the structure of the nucleus, the number of electrons (complementary services) are determined that are necessary to achieve energy balance, while at the same time the different chemical elements are uniquely identified. (Total Product Offer Service)

Figure 11.3 Analogy for the Total Product Offer of a Service

Source: Adapted from Lovelock et al. (2009)

Secondary services can also be divided into two categories (see Figure 11.4) depending on how they affect the supply of the main product. Thus we can distinguish complementary services that aim to either facilitate or improve the provision of the main product. The first category refers to providing information, order-taking, billing, and payment; the second includes the provision of consulting services, hospitality, safekeeping, and the ability to provide exceptional service, usually for specialized requests and problem solving.

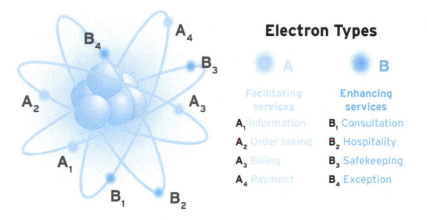

Figure 11.4 Analogy of the Structure of Supplementary Services

Source: Adapted from Lovelock et al. (2009)

Price

The procedure to set prices for services is significantly more complex than for material goods, for which the cost of creating and distributing material goods is very easy to calculate. Not only is the calculation more difficult for the service provider, but from the customer's point of view, it also tends to be difficult to understand how a service is priced. In turn, customers often perceive service purchases as bearing significant risks, or even develop perceptions that the price configuration for a service is unfair or immoral.

The philosophy for building a services pricing strategy in Figure 11.5 is based on three elements: the cost of providing the services, the way customers perceive the value that the company provides them through the specific product offer, and the level of the prices at which the company's competitors provide the same services. First, the cost of providing the service sets a minimum level for the price. Second, the value that the customer assigns to the particular service indicates the maximum price level. Third, competitive pricing for the same or similar versions of the service should influence movements of the price level, in the zone formed by the two extremes.

Figure 11.5 Structure of Strategic Pricing

Source: Adapted from Lovelock et al. (2009) and Siomkos et al. (2017)

Other factors contribute to the pricing decisions, arising from the internal and external environment. For example, the objectives set by the company itself should guide its pricing decisions, as can the company's internal marketing goals. Other elements of the marketing mix might inform the pricing policy too, along with the cost that the company incurs for the overall service provision. Finally, the firm's available and exploitable resources or position in the market are involved in price formation.

Among the external influences, competitors' image or market share, the type and intensity of competition, and the price levels of complementary products or substitutes likely affect the choice of the desired price level. The goals of other intermediaries in distribution channels can also affect prices, as might the broader economic and legal framework in which the company operates, the information that the consumer public has about the provided service, and their purchasing power.

The step-by-step process involved in formulating a pricing policy is illustrated in Figure 11.6. This process allows the company to choose a price level for the product that reflects its goals, such as whether it wants to strengthen its product's position to survive in a competitive context, maximize its profits, achieve desired levels of performance, increase its market share, or strategically respond to competitors' behaviors. This careful process and the pricing policy it establishes can serve the company at various levels.

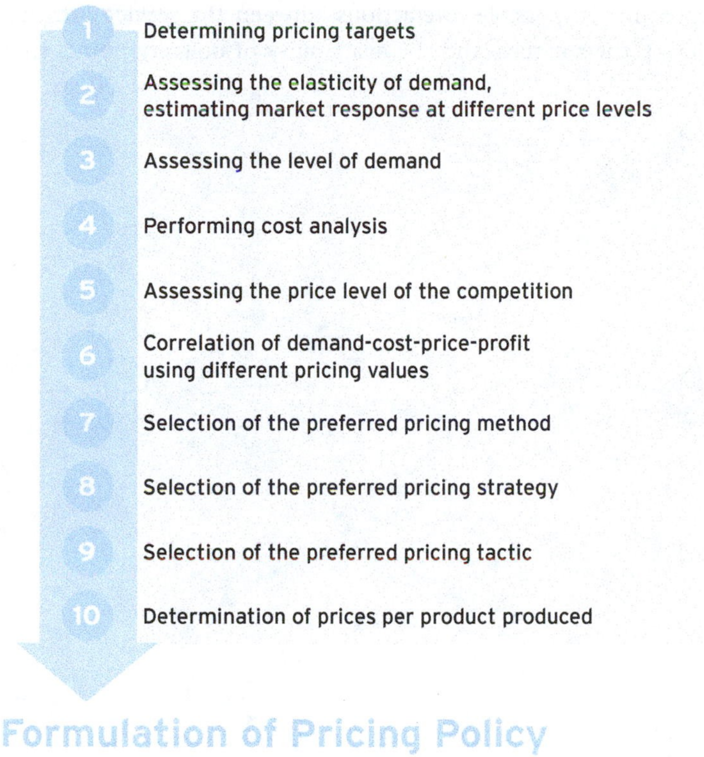

1 Determining pricing targets

2 Assessing the elasticity of demand, estimating market response at different price levels

3 Assessing the level of demand

4 Performing cost analysis

5 Assessing the price level of the competition

6 Correlation of demand-cost-price-profit using different pricing values

7 Selection of the preferred pricing method

8 Selection of the preferred pricing strategy

9 Selection of the preferred pricing tactic

10 Determination of prices per product produced

Formulation of Pricing Policy

Figure 11.6 Steps in the Pricing Process

Source: Adapted from Lymperopoulos and Pantouvakis (2008)

There are three pricing methods traditionally used by companies:

- Pricing based on cost. Here, the price level is determined by adding some certain amount to the cost, so that the sale of each unit produces a profit margin.
- Pricing based on competition. Competitors determine the company's price, such that the price level reflects the average price level found in the market.
- Demand-based pricing. A maximum price level can be set with an effective determination of demand levels. Different types of customers, different demand times for the product, and differences across service points are important differentiation criteria.

Place or Distribution

The distribution of material goods is easily understood and perceived, due to the nature of the products involved. Distribution of services takes on a different character and different dimensions. In particular, possible interactions between the service provider and the customer (Figure 11.7), their nature, and the availability of delivery points shape the choices for distribution.

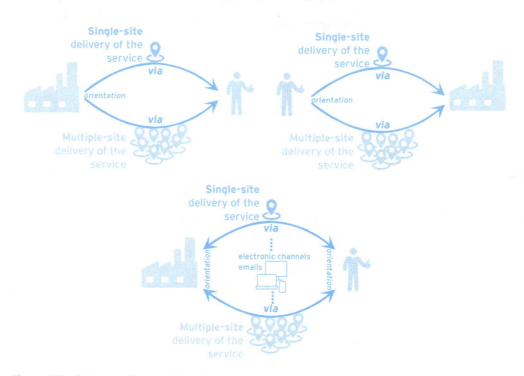

Figure 11.7 Customer Service Interactions

Source: Adapted from Lovelock et al. (2009)

The customer might need to visit the source of the service, so critical factors include the level of comfort and access to the location, as well as the operating hours of the provider. Another option is that the service provider visits the customer, such as when the customer is remote or unable to move voluntarily, as well as when the volume of transactions between companies in the industrial environment is high, such that the service provider prefers to visit the headquarters of its corporate client. A third type of distribution interaction is also possible, when neither the customer or service provider move, because the transactions can be completed remotely, using postal services, telephones, computers and terminals, or digital services.

Figure 11.8 summarizes the reasons why customers tend to choose between these alternative methods of having the service delivered to them.

The choice of delivery mode is often subject to restrictions. Customer comfort might be sought, but the service provider's operating parameters may inevitably reduce this comfort. To overcome such obstacles, service providers might establish multiple, small locations to cover a wider geographical range of customers, or else various installations that offer multiple purposes and utilities.

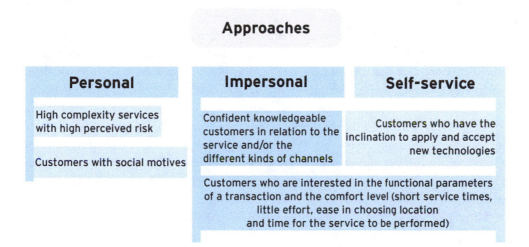

Figure 11.8 Reasons for Choosing Personal Approaches, Impersonal Approaches, or Self-Service Approaches

Finally, the delivery time of the provided service is an important feature. Depending on the type of service, the availability and frequency of delivery may vary, so each company is in a position to decide on the timing of distribution, depending on the needs of the customers it serves, amongst other things.

Promotion or Marketing Communications

Marketing communications promote the product offer to customers; the company that produces and provides the service seeks to explain the benefits that the customer will receive with a purchase and the value that the service will grant the customer, relative to other, similar provisions offered by competitors. This promotion element of the marketing mix not only informs customers but also helps train them, in terms of how to consume and glean the most value from the service, such as by contributing to finding solutions and combining it with other complementary services.

A marketing communications system aims to attract new service customers and maintain relationships with existing customers, while improving this relationship over time, together with the service offer. The service provider can remind and convince customers of the company's performance, relative to competitors, and highlight the special benefits of the solutions it provides. Generally speaking, promotion can help establish a sustainable competitive advantage.

The customer then should be able to understand the content of the services provided: the needs it satisfies, how it does so, the value it provides, and so forth. Customers can also learn about particular features and details that make this service unique or of greater value than services offered by other providers.

Direct contact with service customers is integral to transactions. Both the staff who come in direct contact with the customer and the people who ensure the product is delivered as expected are important elements of the overall process, often representing their own source of differentiation. Marketing communications can demonstrate the company's ability to perform these functions, including the features of the service, and help keep the customer informed about the process required to get the service ready for consumption.

For services in which the customer is actively involved in the production process, marketing communications can be training tools for the customer to achieve the necessary performance level that will improve the overall production capacity of the company. Another type of marketing communications training seeks to achieve a balance in supply and demand. That is, with proper promotion, a provider can influence the time the customer chooses to spend on consuming the provided service, such as evoking increased demand or reducing it with incentives or offers.

The use of easily comprehensible models can help customers give shape to the experience they are likely to have in using the service, which is especially useful when the service is very complex or characterized by a high level of intangibility so that the value of a service and the benefits that the customer can receive will be understood. The utilization of transport creates a complete picture, which the customer can understand, making the necessary correlations in order to comprehend the value that the provider's service product can offer.

In turn, an effective, appropriately planned marketing communications system requires a sufficient level of knowledge and understanding of the service product. The supplier company must carefully research the means it has to ensure its message reaches the targeted part of the market. It must investigate the level of product awareness among customers, then assess the general attitude of the whole market toward the provided service. Finally, the company should select the content, structure, and style of the message it seeks to communicate, based on the budget it can allocate, the timing of the promotional campaign, the goals it aims to achieve, and the ways it plans to evaluate its performance and results. For example, it might answer the following questions:

- Who is the target audience of the company?
- What is the message that the company wants to communicate, and what does it want to achieve with this message?
- How will the message be communicated?
- Where will this communication take place?
- When should this communication take place?

Regarding the first question, three elements need to be emphasized: identifying potential customers, approaching service users, and approaching employees. Then in terms of the goals of marketing communications, the service provider should work to:

- Create an appropriate image for itself and the brand that represents it, which is memorable for the target audience.
- If no prior familiarity exists among this target group, establish conditions to make the brand known to the audience and arouse interest among them.
- Promote the offer as superior to what competitors provide.
- Emphasize the strengths and benefits that arise from using the particular service or brand.
- Define the service appropriately, relative to the services provided by competitors.
- Reduce uncertainty and perceived purchase risk as much as possible for customers, such as by providing comprehensive information or relevant advice.
- Provide appropriate assurances that the service can meet the customer's needs and will address the problems it was intended to solve.
- Offer incentives to encourage customers to try the solution.
- Train customers to become familiar with the procedures involved in the service being provided before using it.
- Explain to customers the best way to use the service to reap its benefits.
- Create appropriate, balanced conditions in supply and demand for the provided service.

Figure 11.9 illustrates the marketing communications mix in greater detail. Individual, personal communications might take place during the delivery process, during the sale or provision of service, as well as through training. The company retains control of these communications, but other messages spread through word of mouth, which usually escapes the company's control. Advertising helps make a service or brand more widely known, by providing information about it or reminding customers about the company and the availability of solutions for their needs. While advertising is a popular solution for consumer goods, in industrial settings, it tends to be implemented less and mostly as a complement to other communication channels. The third element involves public relations, which reflect a company's attempts to arouse public interest in the company, its activities, and its benefits, usually followed by a planned, organized effort to prepare and distribute information and material to the press. With direct marketing, the company instead shares personalized marketing communications with a targeted audience, through tools such as email services, direct postal mail, and telemarketing.

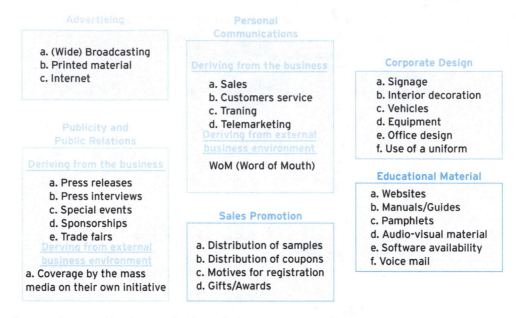

Advertising

a. (Wide) Broadcasting
b. Printed material
c. Internet

Publicity and Public Relations

Deriving from the business

a. Press releases
b. Press interviews
c. Special events
d. Sponsorships
e. Trade fairs

Deriving from external business environment

a. Coverage by the mass media on their own initiative

Personal Communications

Deriving from the business

a. Sales
b. Customers service
c. Traning
d. Telemarketing

Deriving from external business environment

WoM (Word of Mouth)

Sales Promotion

a. Distribution of samples
b. Distribution of coupons
c. Motives for registration
d. Gifts/Awards

Corporate Design

a. Signage
b. Interior decoration
c. Vehicles
d. Equipment
e. Office design
f. Use of a uniform

Educational Material

a. Websites
b. Manuals/Guides
c. Pamphlets
d. Audio-visual material
e. Software availability
f. Voice mail

Figure 11.9 Marketing Communications Mix for Services

Source: Adapted from Lovelock et al. (2009)

Sales promotion is another marketing communications tool that aims to motivate customers to make purchases faster, in larger quantities, or more often. The incentives are determined by considerations of the time, price, and customer category. Like product providers, service providers often use samples, coupons, various discounts, gifts, and contests as promotions.

Personal selling is perhaps the most powerful tool in the marketing communications mix for an enterprise operating in an industrial environment. In face-to-face meetings, the sales representative of the service provider devotes efforts to informing customers and promoting the brand it represents and the services it provides.

Finally, participation in trade fairs enables a company to present its service product offer, while also engaging in personal selling with the interested audience of fair attendees. It is a way for the buyer to approach providers to gather information about new benefits, proposals, or solutions.

Figure 11.10 depicts how buyers might perceive the sources of each element of marketing communications.

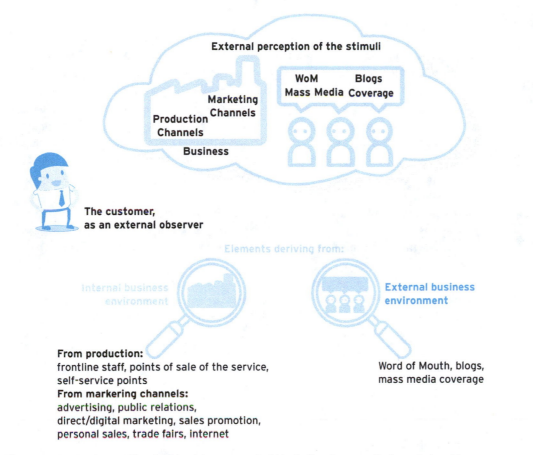

Figure 11.10 Customer View for the Advancement of Marketing Communications Data with a Business, from the Point of View of the Customer

Vignette

Brands Are Affected by Their Context

As business-to-business branding expands into new community and cultural settings, the shifts in societal values, norms, and ethics, as well as market conditions, create relevant implications for marketing mixes. Consider IKEA as an example. The retailer, recognizing growing consumer attention to sustainability questions, created novel marketing campaigns to encourage a perception of its offerings as available for "(Re)Sale," emphasizing both their quality and their sustainability.

(Continued)

The campaign, launched in Denmark in 2019, then expanded in 2020 to wider geographical coverage, and sought to leverage an annual Black Friday shopping tradition to challenge a general perception that it offers form, function, and low prices but not high quality or environmental sustainability. On an eBay-like platform (www.dba.dk), IKEA posted encouragement on private sellers' listings of its furniture to "Buy used, when you're shopping for new on (Black) Friday." The surprising message, discouraging consumers from buying new furniture from the retailer, spread quickly and seeded the notion that its furniture offers such high quality that it can be resold and reused, rather than adding to the problem of "throw away" purchases. At the same time, a new link posted on IKEA's Black Friday (Re)Sale site connected shoppers to the dba.dk site.

The results were substantial and notable. In terms of attention, during the week of the campaign, searches for IKEA increased by 900 percent, and more than 40,000 customers clicked through to visit the dba.dk site. Compared with previous Black Fridays, IKEA sales increased by 170 percent; over the course of the week that the campaign ran, the overall sales increase was 138 percent. Notably, IKEA did not offer any Black Friday discounts during this period. Finally, the brand's sustainability image improved by 24 percent. As this example shows, concrete actions taken by a firm can determine the brand outcomes, in an extremely positive way, if those actions reflect a good understanding and respect for the brand's cultural context.

Sources

Heding, T., Knudtzen, C., and Bjerre, M. (2020), *Brand Management: Mastering Research, Theory and Practise*, London: Routledge.

KreaKom (2019), *Advertising at the Exam*, Copenhagen: The Association of Danish Advertising and Communication Agencies.

People

It is critical to provide services at relevant consumption points, which should be staffed by sales representatives who can ensure that customers receive the service they expect (Figure 11.11).

These sales representatives constitute the "people" element of the marketing mix, though this category might also include other customers who affect the service experience. The appearance and presence of the staff and the quality of the service they provide determine the type of relationship the firm creates with the customer, defines their cooperative efforts, and affects the reputation of the company and its brand. To ensure the necessary level of high-quality support, such that sales representatives exhibit courtesy, friendliness, patience, and willing effort, the company must hire well-qualified staffers, then outline their duties and responsibilities clearly and carefully, as well as providing strong supervisory support.

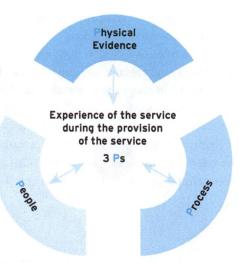

Experience of the service
during the provision
of the service

3 Ps

Figure 11.11 Factors that Determine the Experience when in Contact with the Customer, during the Provision of Service

Source: Based on Booms, B.H. and Bitner, M.J. (1982)

A comprehensive system must exist to plan human resources, the optimal selection of front-line employees, customer service training, and evaluations. The corporate environment also must cultivate a market-oriented culture. In such a culture, a market orientation should be universally accepted by all those involved in the production process. Providing appropriate incentives can encourage the adoption of such conditions. This outcome is only possible if an integrated system has been created and implemented to manage the data and information that emerges from the processes of producing the service itself, the interaction of employees with customers, and applied market research. Staffing must now be executed in accordance with the type of service provided and the level of contact between the employee and the customer. If the service requires a low level of contact, the functions might be automated or standardized, such that they should be treated differently than services that require greater contact.

The customer of a service provider is both a coproducer of the service and its user. Thus, the skills, capabilities, behavior, and experience of customers can affect the service delivery by employees. As users, customers still demand appropriate professionalism and training from the company and its employees, as well as the optimal level of quality in service delivery. More effective communication between the two coproducers of the service can create better conditions for finding good solutions and, ultimately, delivering a high-quality service. However, customers can also be influenced by other customers during the decision-making process and in the post-purchase period.

Process

The production process, as an element of the marketing mix, should offer strong competence and efficiency, in the form of a comprehensive system of activities that shape the service (Figure 11.11).

Such a process signals, to customers, that the company can provide high-quality services, better than competing proposals, which can be a foundation for a competitive advantage. To achieve this high level of quality, the firm's marketing function and production department must share the same orientation, such that they might resolve any philosophical differences through harmonious and effective communication and cooperation. We also can divide the overall production process into: a pre-process, to define the service to be delivered; the main process, including the actual service delivery; and a post-process that includes following up with the customer or asking for reviews. For these three elements to cohere, the structures, procedures, and methods must be designed carefully, then controlled in terms of their performance. Careful planning and scheduling can boost customers' confidence in the process and its underlying systems.

Physical Evidence

The peculiarities related to the nature of services characterize the environment in which the provision of the service takes place, so the physical elements in this environment also constitute part of the marketing mix (Figure 11.11). This element refers to features that contribute to atmospherics, can be perceived by human senses, and shape the image of the service and provider, such as architecture, lighting, brand logos in various material forms that the customer encounters, spatial placements of furniture and equipment, colors, sounds and music, odors and aromas, temperature levels, customer and task flow, and the distribution of departments.

Vignette

The Platform Business Moment

In a platform economy, business exchanges are mediated by digital platforms. On the basis of the relevant technological possibilities, exchanges could take place among private persons (peers); digital matching and evaluation even allowed exchanges among strangers. Such platforms have had various implications for businesses: because peers may share rather than transfer goods or services, companies can be replaced by peers, as self-employed providers. The exchanges also become highly transactional, because suppliers and users are matched algorithmically, without any past or future promise of exchanges.

Sharing represents an extreme form of service, with a focus on use rather than ownership. Following the notion of value-in-use, the sharing economy allows parties to move to a post-ownership era. When suppliers are freelancers or giggers, it challenges what once was considered the essential DNA of industrial, relational exchanges. It also questions the very notion of firms. What was once central to a firm's processes has become distributed among peers who lack any connections among them.

Source

Öberg, C. (2018), "Social and economic ties in the freelance and sharing economies," *Journal of Small Business and Entrepreneurship*, 30(1), 77-96.

SERVICES IN THE INDUSTRIAL MARKET FRAMEWORK

Various interrelationships, consequences, implications, and possibilities arise at the common points that exist between services and industrial marketing. In particular, services must be configured and adapted to meet the distinct requirements and needs of each corporate customer, which in turn demands an appropriate level of prior know-how and specialization, so that the company can provide service solutions of sufficient quality and operate effectively, both in its administration and technical capabilities. The industrial products that accompany provided services tend to be technical and complex, so a service provider must have the ability to train customers in how to use them. Such know-how can differentiate the provider from competitors; a high level of specialization also may be an important operational resource.

Appropriate services diversify the industrial offer too, because they can be customized to meet each customer's needs. For industrial enterprises, even if intangible elements are less evident in the overall solutions provided to customers, services constitute important components of the final product, as well as of the provider's competitive advantage. Intellectual capital also is relevant, as is internal social capital, which refers to relationships within the firm.

Industrial services can take two main forms:

- Maintenance and repair services, such as those related to installations or equipment.
- Consulting services that cover functions such as finance, supply chain management, or marketing.

Such services can be obtained by the customer along with an industrial product, or they might be purchased independently to complete or upgrade a production process.

Providing such services usually affects the cycle of the relationship between the industrial supplier and an industrial buyer (Szmigin, 1993). In industrial markets, each stage of the purchasing decision process emphasizes how the product offer can meet the specific needs of a particular buyer. In addition, perceived quality (according to the buyer) affects both the solutions proposed by the supplier and their relationship. Suppliers can demonstrate their ability to adapt to the customer's needs, as well as highlight their understanding of the problems and needs that arise in the transaction or in their relationship. This understanding of the buyer's needs should contribute to maintaining the relationship and strengthen their commitment, particularly if the relationship is marked by trust, relies on harmonious, effective communication channels, and is founded on mutually acceptable values, along with attractive product offers.

Research has highlighted how customer satisfaction, quality, and perceived value function in industrial markets with regard to maintaining the relationship between suppliers and buyers. For example, some studies link the satisfaction of industrial customers with different benefits, such as functional, emotional, and social benefits. Using these three dimensions to categorize the overall benefits that customers perceive, and noting their interactions in forming the conditions of satisfaction, we can devise effective strategies to achieve higher levels of customer satisfaction.

When industrial suppliers provide services, they also are working to strengthen their brands. The corporate reputation is of paramount importance for industrial service providers.

During a transaction, conditions have already been created to develop a relationship through communication. The nature of this relationship depends on the existence of a framework with a specific logic, even if the product differs from competitive offerings, and those differences enhance its features.

To make this outcome possible, it is imperative that the workforce is properly trained, in terms of the product provided and the operations of the industry, as well as the competitive conditions. Training might outline how sales staff can manage data about potential buyers or optimal sales techniques to encourage a purchase. Communication between the two companies should entail a high level of knowledge sharing, involving product and transaction details. Skilled sales staff can provide more content during the sales process. Other conditions must help potential buyers develop trust in the sales arguments and the company.

An industrial buyer prioritizes the functionality of a sought product. After the sale, as communication between the companies develops, this perceived functionality cannot deviate beyond a permissible limit or from the framework of the agreement. This need can be met by educating and training sales staff, so that they can inform and persuade customers with necessary, accurate details. Complementary informative brochures and consulting services provided by the supplier also represent important promotional efforts.

For manufactured industrial products, the core product is a large-scale construction (machine or building) with great value, which evokes high perceived risk for the buyer and expectations of a long useful lifespan. Consulting, training in the use or implementation of best practices, information about new trends, and financial and quality audits are services the supplier company can provide, based on careful planning, tailored to the needs of each buyer. A similar design should inform services linked to heavy equipment, which also impose high demands on available capital and should promise a long lifespan. Such products might stem from special orders, such that the production process is individually tailored to the needs and requirements of the buyer. The purchase involves great risk, so financial analysis may be essential to define the market; consulting and training services might also frame the usefulness of these products.

Industrial light equipment products, such as tools and office equipment, instead feature lower supply costs, shorter lifespans, and supporting roles in production processes. For example, an appropriately adapted Internet portal offered by the supplier likely represents a valuable service for prospective buyers. The high level of product standardization also allows the firms to automate their operations and devise technological solutions, saving them time, effort, and money: orders can be processed faster, control becomes easier, and the company does not need any additional staff.

In the category of industrial synthetic components or subparts, it is common to find consulting, maintenance, and repair services. The products often need intervention or even replacement, and these services have critical implications for the financial security of the buyer, as well as in assuring compliance with applicable standards.

Industrial products composed of materials and supplies for the processing, maintenance, repair, and operation of other components can also enhance the image of the buyer, so the supplier and the variety of products it has available, on a reliable basis, are very important considerations. Services such as supplier evaluation, consulting, and training can affect the buyer's perception of the value.

Maintenance, repair, and functional products may be consumables involved in the production process. Services such as consulting, information, and quality control may increase the value of the buyer's production process of these items.

In the case of raw materials, the supply chain tends to feature accompanying services, such as rapid and safe transport or appropriate packaging materials. For processed materials, training about specific processing techniques, combined with the ability of the supplier to inform the buyer about relevant benefits and perceived risks, might promote sales.

For the provision of industrial services, staff members should recognize any peculiarities, so that they can persuade prospective buyers of the quality of the offer, despite its intangibility. The procedure adopted to produce an industrial service must be designed carefully, in accordance with strategic planning to enhance the content of the overall product offer and meet the particular requirements of the buyer.

We might also consider industrial services according to the different types of industrial buyers we have identified in another chapter: commercial buyers, institutional buyers, and state buyers. Each category exhibits particular characteristics and needs.

Commercial or industrial buyers make purchases to achieve various goals, which in turn can define subcategories of this group. This more precise classification in turn can suggest which services to offer each type, through which means and methods. For example, users might benefit from an Internet portal that helps keep them informed about issues with the use of the service, troubleshooting, advice, and best practices. Distributors might prefer brochures and training programs. Equipment manufacturers likely need user manuals, as well as specialized advice.

Among institutional buyers, purchasing behavior depends on the extent to which they are subject to, funded, or controlled by government agencies, reflecting the influence of the relevant political environment and legal framework. Employees of these firms tend to be highly educated, specialized, and qualified, and the organizational structures allow for a well-organized market segment (due to their complex nature). Valid, complete, high-quality information is very helpful for all actors involved in these markets. Therefore, hiring and leveraging such staff to disseminate information and execute operations, together with well-designed Internet portals and information systems that include brochures and printed media, can enhance the effectiveness of the purchase process by clarifying the transaction terms and facilitating communications.

Finally, for state or government buyers, the solutions are similar to those for industrial buyers, and the distinct supply procurement process still demands appropriate staffing and staff training, Internet-based points of access to information, and shared knowledge. Furthermore, effective personal sales processes should exploit sales promotions and reliable support services, to encourage stronger relationships in the long run.

The nature and peculiarities of industrial products demand the mobilization of services to ensure the satisfaction of industrial customers and the optimal level of relationship quality. As noted previously, demand in industrial markets derives from demand in consumer markets; it is derivative. The proliferation of the Internet and technological solutions that leverage it (e.g., smartphones with continuous access at high speeds) has boosted customers' ability to create demand for specific products and services. By analogy, with similar tools and technological solutions (e.g., EDI), demand in industrial enterprises can be created and satisfied through the use of complex services that require high levels of knowledge and specialization. The communication and translation of demand from an industrial company to the supplier takes place through communication channels. Some set of potential suppliers likely can meet the same needs, so each company must meet the expectations of the industrial customers better than the others. Therefore, the implemented processes should allow for efficient collaboration and also frame the product offer as appealing, due to the services provided (e.g., transport, installation, maintenance).

Expectations of a supplier and the benefits it can offer, as well as the estimates and predictions that a company makes to respond to the accelerator phenomenon, can determine managerial decisions and the mechanisms it activates to make them. Data analysis, information, and effective communication between companies can enhance planning for both parties, as well as assist in their decision-making process.

Companies operating in industrial markets often encounter high (geographic) concentration of demand. Some companies sell specialized services, based on their ability to provide appropriate know-how and specialization in industrial enterprises.

Modern industrial companies resort to activity that transcends national borders. Therefore, they need to develop processes to meet internationally recognized standards and offer some minimal level of benefits in terms of specifications, quality, and adherence to restrictions. This development has led to the implementation of contemporary developed strategic solutions (e.g., strategic consortiums), as well as mergers and acquisitions. To implement such options, an appropriate infrastructure must be in place to facilitate daily operations and transactions, as well as disseminate decisions efficiently.

To meet particular needs, companies in an industrial environment seek to respond in a timely and reliable manner to changing demands, without compromising their profitability or survival. Thus they need well-designed financial products and corresponding financial tools and facilities. Such companies prefer direct access to capital so they can demonstrate appropriate flexibility in response to changes in demand. That is, another valuable service in industrial markets involves financial products.

The process to achieve a purchase decision is more complicated than in consumer markets. Some specialization usually is required in industrial markets, due to the complexity of the products and the risk for the buyer of investing in an industrial solution. The process tends to be time-consuming. Appropriate software tools can help keep the industrial buyer informed and familiar with the purchase process.

Creating an industrial product with all the necessary technical, structural, and technological features would be a source of competitive advantage. However, as marketing theory explains, it is not enough for the product to satisfy the customer; doing so is only an initial condition for establishing cooperative relationships with customers. The goal is to satisfy the customer with a range of benefits, spanning all facets of the relationship. Services that accompany the focal product and that help it stand out or enhance it thus can improve the overall customer experience in its relationship with the supplier.

Marketing operations in industrial settings primarily focus on communicating with the industrial customer, listening to its needs and problems, and sharing their own corporate culture. This communication is achieved primarily through personal sales, supplemented with promotional tools such as brochures and electronic communication through a properly configured Internet portal. The content of the communication must be coherent, reflecting cooperation among the different operations that form the supplier's business.

The number of customers of each industrial company may be limited, so each customer relationship is valuable. In turn, the company likely wants to provide services to strengthen each relationship and tailor its overall product offer to each customer. One effective way to achieve a competitive advantage is to create parallel service products that accompany the main product or may be offered separately.

Services that might improve the customer experience include technological solutions for adhering to and planning delivery schedules. Technological services and tools that provide know-how, process orders, or enable exchanges of useful information might also be included in solutions. These elements should evoke perceptions of the brand personality too.

The relationship between suppliers and buyers generally is long term: they share ongoing, common experiences related to the conditions that define the relationship and changes taking place in the business environment. For such a relationship to persist, a desire for similar degrees of reciprocity should be present on both sides, which then informs the dependency that develops between them. In addition, both parties need to create effective, shared communication channels and actively share valid information, which may require business resource-sharing processes, such as consulting, transfer of know-how, and training. These efforts should reflect the value and frequency of the transactions between the two companies.

The type of cooperation, the primary product being transacted, and the relationship context all should determine service availability and types. Communication in an industrial environment is direct and personalized; data and information exchanges are complex and may require technical specialization. Purchasing decisions in industrial companies usually are made by groups that serve different functions, each of which may exhibit varying dynamics within the group that in turn influence the terms of each transaction. The supplier should provide appropriate levels of service and information sharing during the sales process, as well as capture and translate the requirements set by the buyer. Factors that inform the buyer's attitude and responses toward sales representatives include the following:

- Personal needs/motivations. They influence how a buyer perceives and translates received signals and accumulated stimuli.
- Organizational needs/goals. They define the conditions, starting with the decision to meet with a salesperson, and the points that a buying manager considers important for the purchase decision. They also might influence the final decision directly.
- Perceived risk. The risk the buyer must accept in the process of making a purchasing decision exerts an influence, and the perception of its magnitude depends on the confidence of decision-makers in their abilities.
- Stage of involvement. Each stage in a purchasing process entails different problems and needs. This differentiation pertains to diverse information needs and the need to access different sources of information. Depending on the stage, important factors arise, which then determine the information needs of each stage.
- Exposure to promotions. Sales representatives can influence buyers by communicating information through personal contacts, which likely shapes the buyer's attitude. In receiving this information, the buyer is likely motivated to strengthen and facilitate commercial processes, and this motivation might be reinforced by other relevant information, such as that communicated through advertising messages.

The operations of the seller, as a provider of information and training or as an intermediary in communication and transaction channels, require this company to design its services in a way that meets any requirements of the transaction, the buyer company, and the person or group responsible for the purchase decision. To identify factors that determine sellers' behavior, we can outline some internal services that should reflect:

- The personal needs of the seller.
- The organizational needs of the seller's employer.
- The trust of the sellers in their own abilities, or degree of their self-confidence.
- The sellers' ability to understand the distribution of responsibilities and power and the limits of their own jurisdiction across different stages of the purchasing process.

The employing company should develop internal processes of control, evaluation, and reward, aligned with the distinct needs of each sales representative, as well as ensuring that it communicates its own needs. Rewards and total sales service designs can boost a salesperson's confidence, as well as clarify the various roles required at each stage of the purchasing process.

The goals of the involved parties for any relationship should be aligned. Their commitment to and support for the relationship, involving appropriate communication and data exchange, can support their long- and short-term goals. As their interdependence grows, so does the need for valid, consistent communication, especially if the relationship leads to the development of a new entity, such as a strategically integrated system.

As mentioned, the buying center of an industrial company consists of members with distinct roles:

- Users. Members of the organization who come in the most direct contact with the outcome of the decision-making process, that is, the purchased product/service.
- Buyers. Actors with ultimate purchasing responsibility.
- Deciders. Actors who choose a specific supplier, product, or brand.
- Influencers. Contributors of information to shape decision criteria.
- Gatekeepers. They control and manage the direction, size, type, and recipients of the information.
- Initiators. Actors responsible for highlighting and determining buying conditions.

Creating services that enable each role to achieve its goals—as if they were internal customers—can enhance the effectiveness of the buying process across every stage. The ability of the company to compose, design, and provide necessary services can evoke superior value for the development of a relationship, allow it to adapt to the needs and requirements of each customer, and create conditions for harmonious, productive cooperation, along with corresponding expectations.

12

MODERN TRENDS AND DEVELOPMENTS IN INDUSTRIAL MARKETING

══ Learning Objectives ══

- Understand the role of technology when implementing a marketing philosophy in an industrial setting.
- Describe how data and information enable the implementation of marketing strategies in an industrial environment.
- Recognize the value of Big Data, as a phenomenon and tool.
- Understand the role of corporate social responsibility in marketing.
- Outline modern trends of marketing implementations in industrial contexts.

Case Study

AI and Programmatic Marketing in Advertising Agencies

The 4th Industrial Revolution, featuring artificial intelligence (AI) and emergent technologies, might make the 7Ps approach to marketing irrelevant (Bag et al., 2021). As a case in point, advertising agency–client relationships traditionally have involved individual human decision-makers at different levels of the advertising process, such as market research, channel and creative strategy, media planning and purchase, and analysis (Qin & Jiang, 2019). But with big data captures, from social media and search engines, firms might rely more on these inputs to gain significant advantages (Bag et al., 2021). Such potential is driving the development of AI-based technologies,

(Continued)

forcing B2B marketers to acknowledge and address the potential of AI for informing marketing practice. In addition to expanding their hardware, B2B firms must possess dynamic capabilities to sense the potential of AI and reconfigure accordingly. For example, advertising agencies might adopt programmatic marketing, which adjusts the positions of advertising and content in real-time to capture value from trending opportunities and capture customer attention at a point of inspiration (Jabbar et al., 2020). To adopt such programmatic marketing, practitioners also need familiarity with two emergent technologies: data management platforms (DMP) and demand-side platforms (DSP) (Chen et al., 2019).

A DMP is designed to deliver enhanced, time-sensitive understanding of potential custom-ers' demographics and psychographics, to identify key customer touchpoints. Building on tra-ditional segmentation techniques, DMPs might include search behaviors and target locations (using GPS technologies) to define programmatic campaigns. A DSP instead allows advertisers to bid for virtual space for online advertisements and content on an online marketplace through mass media owners such as Google (Jabbar et al., 2020).

These opportunities largely depend on analyses of huge data sets, in which humans could not reasonably identify patterns quickly enough to seize the opportunities. Agencies such as IBM Watson, GumGum, and Quantcast offer hyper-targeting tools that rely on AI-based systems. With hyper-targeting, media and creative strategies define which advertisements and content to insert in social media platforms at the moment the target audience's attention is focused there. The potential benefits of AI appear particularly significant for developing content market-ing strategies, often presented in the form of a chat. In addition to early uses of AI for program-matic buying, smart contracts in association with DSPs increasingly define the parameters of a sale, then identify specific placement opportunities (Antonopoulos & Wood, 2018, p. 127). This contractual arrangement fundamentally changes the client-agency relationship, establishes clear communication parameters, and leverages AI to make channel, media placement, and even creative decisions. Furthermore, AI technology is now being used for creative strategy pro-cesses, such as copywriting and message strategy, because it can conduct in-depth analyses of the language that appears in a social media user's posts and identify likely influencers. Agencies increasingly rely on technologies like blockchain to ensure they will be remunerated for their advertising and content placements. Therefore, B2B marketers must acknowledge the potential of AI and its implications for replacing human interventions in buyer–supplier interactions.

DEVELOPMENTS: TECHNOLOGY, INFORMATION, DATABASES, AND DATABASE MARKETING

Technology

Rapid changes and developments in political and economic activity, at varying levels world-wide, strongly influence how companies operate, cope with emerging challenges, develop offer-ings, and undertake production processes. In particular, continued technological developments significantly affect the manufacturing of industrial products. As new technologies emerge, efficiency likely increases, in the processes adopted to produce industrial products, in transactions and communications, and in the development and management of relations between industrial suppliers and buyers.

For example, the global changes brought about by the development and evolution of the Internet, networking technologies, and social media have influenced the operation of industrial enterprises (Figure 12.1). Early in its life, companies began to take advantage of Internet technology, to exploit the reduced communications costs and to make effective use of the available data and information. They also worked to create communication interfaces to facilitate transactions with customers and manage relationships with one another.

Development of mobile telephony

Development of self-service techologies

Development of technological world wide web

Internet  Development of CRM systems

Use of web ports

Configuration of orientation in marketing

Appearance of e-marketplaces

Figure 12.1 Self-Service Technologies

In turn, creating appropriate Internet portals emerged as a need and efficient solution for industrial enterprises to be able to respond to and exploit Internet markets. Their existence and availability worldwide then led to the configuration of virtual e-marketplaces. As more transactions between industrial companies took place in electronic environments, companies began to focus on ways to exploit available information and communication technologies (ICT), to operate more effectively and achieve (and then maintain) competitive advantages.

An electronic marketing orientation represents a new perspective that differs from a traditional marketing orientation, in that it focuses precisely on digital technologies, such as those that support social media. Beyond changes already instituted in the organizational perspectives that companies adopt, social media exert continued influences on the implementation of business strategies in industrial environments.

The evolution of mobile telephony—both the manufacture of smartphone devices and the construction of infrastructure—has brought about rapid developments. Electronic devices with vast functions and Internet access are fundamental features of everyday life, and extensions in their functions and activities continue to emerge. Although this development is particularly noticeable for consumer companies, it exerts an impact on the industrial environment, causing chain reactions in applied strategies and organizational structures.

Growth is observed in so-called self-service technologies in both consumer and industrial environments (Figure 12.1). Customers in industrial environments rely on self-service technologies for different purposes than consumers though; they place more emphasis on service speed, efficiency of the service process, and cost savings—in line with industrial customers' general expectations of transactions with suppliers.

The Role of Technology in Shaping Marketing

The development of Internet portals helps industrial companies achieve their business objectives more effectively, even as they seek to develop appropriate approaches to ensure the efficient implementation of any strategy that relies on such technologies. Internet technologies, including cloud computing, have greatly informed the ways that B2B firms manage their customer relationships. The use of both social media and CRM systems increase both productivity and sales, by making it easier for the company to reach customers and understand their needs and problems better. The Internet also has a positive effect in general on sales management activities. The development and evolution of ICT has brought about significant changes in supply chain management, so B2B companies are both more efficient and more competitive.

Information

Data, Information, and Technology

Applied technological solutions collect, store, and leverage various data and information, transforming them into meaningful, useful forms, in accordance with the principles of a marketing philosophy and the firm's business strategy (Figure 12.2). Marketing data comprise a wide range of unprocessed input that have some promise for enhancing the firm, such as improved product development processes, improved marketing mix elements, or improved characteristics of applied marketing strategies.

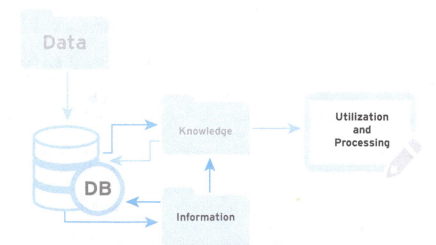

Figure 12.2 Technology and Data-Information-Knowledge Links

Thus marketing data might include customer data, personal profile information, demographic characteristics, and so on. They relate to a target market (e.g., data on needs and preferences as a whole) and should be obtained specifically for a relevant industry, according to its competitive conditions. Alternative product and service offerings, competitors' business skills, and prices charged by competitors thus can be marketing data too. The metrics and indicators used to assess performance in comparison with competitors are marketing data. Furthermore, marketing data come from both sales and transactions—more broadly, from any interactions between two parties involved in a transaction. Data generated by customers, through communication, evaluations, or research, can reveal their preferences and interests. We refer to Figure 12.3.

| Marketing data | Technological solutions | Marketing information | Technological solutions | Dissemination of information | Technological solutions | Making marketing decisions |

Figure 12.3 Data, Information, and Technology in Marketing

Big Data, Databases, and Marketing

Big data arise from the rapid development of technology, especially information technology. The term describes large volumes of complex and variable data that move at such high speeds that the use of highly specialized advanced techniques and technologies is required to extract, store, distribute, manage, and analyze the information they contain (Figure 12.4). Then the appropriate transformation of data into information can facilitate the design of effective strategies for managing this knowledge, with beneficial outcomes at the market research level.

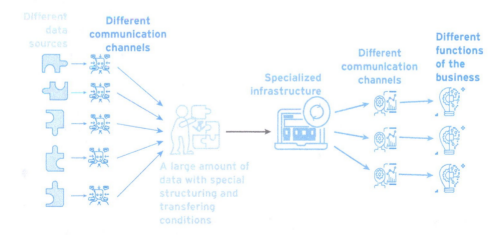

Figure 12.4 Big Data Participation and its Role

Source: © Emerald Publishing, used with permission

A company's ability to manage and transform big data into a useful form significantly determines its ability to achieve its marketing goals. In line with an approach that defines marketing as an information management problem, the value of big data depends on the efforts required for their acquisition and management. First, big data require appropriate organizational and technological infrastructures, to be able to manage large, complex volumes of data. A company with such infrastructures is better positioned in alignment with the goals it has set. Second, by transforming such substantial data into meaningful insights for solving customers' problems and differentiating its product offer, the company maintains a competitive advantage.

Databases and Database Marketing

A database includes data that can be transformed, using appropriate processing, into useful information and knowledge (Figure 12.5). These data, due to technological developments, can be acquired more readily, so databases provide increasing usefulness. When they adopt database marketing practices, companies seek three goals: enhance marketing productivity, create and build relationships with customers, and establish a sustainable competitive advantage. Of these three motives, the first seems more strongly supported, but the other two motives are of equivalent interest.

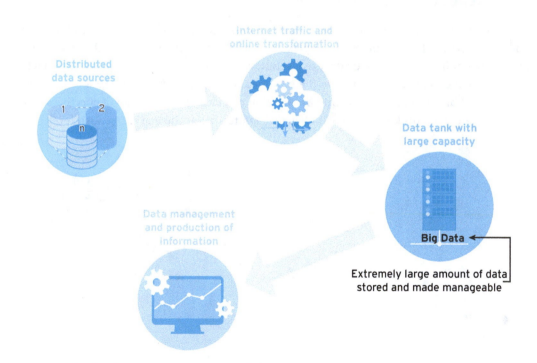

Figure 12.5   The Big Data Concept and the Exploitation of Databases

What characterizes this approach is the ease of measurement of the comprehensibility of the message that the company wants to convey, the immediacy of making contact with the customer, and the results of such an effort. Therefore any metric that is deemed desirable for use can be calculated directly.

Customer relationship marketing has already been discussed. This term can also be used to describe the whole process associated with forming a one-to-one relationship with a customer, such that the relationship adds value to the firm's operations over time. For a relationship to acquire such meaning, the company must be able to understand its relationship with each customer and also how its customers interact with one another. By managing its relationships with customers, the company can reduce marketing costs, increase customer responsiveness, and deliver value throughout the network. Customer relationship management systems can achieve joint satisfaction of supplier and buyer, as well as contribute to organizational performance.

Value Added through the Use of Databases

A company that wants to optimize its management of customer information should pay attention to the strategy it follows on a more general level and apply appropriate standards to ensure a certain level of quality in its data management efforts (Figure 12.6). The company must also include any software application that makes use of both relational and data transactions in the process of developing the customer database (Figures 12.7 and 12.8).

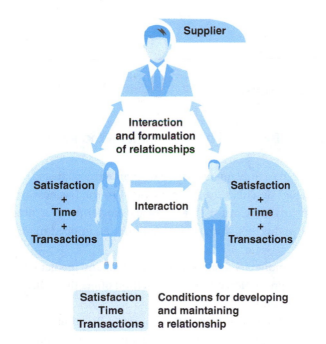

Figure 12.6 Interactions between B2B Suppliers and B2B Buyers

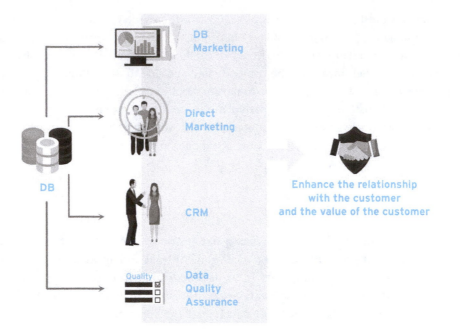

Figure 12.7 Developments in Databases and Value Creation

Figure 12.8 Database and Marketing

Database Marketing Tools: Online Environment and Investments in Digital Solutions

Various tools can be used to implement a database marketing strategy (Figure 12.9). The term "customer lifetime value" describes the value provided to the business over the course of the relationship the company develops with a particular customer over time. This indicator of value constitutes a powerful tool, and using it can offer an applied marketing strategy a specific, desirable goal.

A recency, frequency, monetary analysis helps the company predict which customers might respond positively to its promotion efforts. This method offers flexibility and has been used to implement database marketing.

In a framework of customer communications, a set of communication efforts takes place, designed to approach and appeal to a particular customer. This adaptation effort requires the availability of data stored in a database; it acts to reinforce the company's effort to retain its

Figure 12.9 Database Marketing Tools

Source: Adapted from Hughes (2019)

customers and evoke their commitment, such as by increasing cross- and up-sales and thus the value of the customer, as well as by raising the volume of positive reports ascribed to the brand (reputation). Customer communication thus can be effectively achieved through the maintenance of a database.

The utilization of appended data involves those data that can be attached to existing primary data, such as names and addresses. With this added, useful information about a specific contact, the company can create a clearer marketing profile and use the information more efficiently when implementing marketing strategies and establishing communications with customers. In the case of industrial enterprises, such data may be official business identifiers (brand, trademark) or details about the number of employees or the company's annual sales.

Predictive models use accessible, appended data to anticipate which customers are expected to be lost or which ones are likely to respond to its strategically selected moves.

Relational databases configure the stored data according to a structure that supports the formation of correlations among these data. It also is possible to store a large amount of data about existing or potential customers, offering options for quick and efficient management. The principles underlying relational databases have not changed; their implementation presupposes appropriate training to understand their operations and their optimal utilization.

The ability to identify a customer during a phone call (caller ID), in connection with a marketing database, can give customer service representatives access to a wealth of information about the specific customer, either before answering or during the phone call. Then the representative can engage in personalized communication with customers, giving them a sense of familiarity and appreciation for their needs/problems.

Both the use of the Internet as a resource and the specific solutions for its optimal use (e.g., ability to read cookies, or small files that store information about the profile and activity of each user) suggest how it can replace system operators. Modern technologies used to create websites establish various solutions that facilitate customers' transactions and overall experiences. In the industrial environment in particular, websites may not replace sales operations, but they provide search options; they can render contacts with the supplier more powerful; and they are able to complete some customer orders. The success of database marketing may depend on the existence of such technological solutions and their optimal utilization.

The ability of a company to use available data about its customers, in an automated (or not) fashion, to achieve personalization makes email services and platforms powerful tools for database marketing. Providing email services enriched with greater functionality might establish real-time communication, collaboration, and project management—another facet of those services. Such services can also present offers, along with information about up-to-date developments in the business sector, the industry, or the relationship between the supplier and each buyer, in addition to information that relates particularly to specific transactions.

Companies apply various testing tools and forms of control, then send the content directly to customers. For this process, the impact of the communication effort is measured by the customer response. With advances in technology, companies can accurately assess—through the use of databases—the effects of marketing decisions.

The implementation of loyalty programs can provide customers with continuous incentives to remain committed to the relationship and enhance their desire to maintain this relationship. It is yet another tool whose power has been greatly enhanced by technological advances in databases.

By investing in specialized software packages for data analysis, with multiple uses and possibilities, a company can make the best use of its database marketing. Enhanced analytics and reporting capabilities are two features of this kind of software that make it a powerful tool in the context of database marketing. Another important feature available through specialized software is campaign management. Specific software, connected to the database, can automatically plan activities and make strategic decisions. Such software reduces costs over time, relative to a traditional approach, and often prompts higher response rates from customers.

Shared access to the database for distributed resources (in networks) creates a possibility of interconnections across a network of multiple database users. They can access and edit content. All the departments and operations of the company can have direct access to relevant data, though it may be appropriate to limit such access rights by the hierarchical level of the user in the company.

Another practice involves renting customer lists, rather than companies keeping such information secret. This phenomenon is so powerful that it has led to the creation of an industry that deals with the maintenance, configuration, processing, and economic exploitation of such catalogs.

Services that find and correct inconsistencies in database information shape the data to take the most appropriate form, so that they can be stored, while also ensuring the content is up to date, with valid information and data. They do so in a very short period of time.

Profitability analysis techniques estimate the profitability level of each customer, for specific, predetermined periods of time. With these insights, the company can adapt marketing solutions that apply either as a whole or individually, depending on the situation. Penetration analysis techniques also leverage databases and data analysis software to determine a promotion process for the company and orient the sales staff appropriately.

Cluster coding techniques divide all customers into clusters, or groups with similar characteristics. Combined with penetration analysis, they make it easier for the company to discern who is buying its products or not, which should enhance the company's marketing efforts and sales performance.

Customer segmentation in industrial contexts groups customers in meaningful ways, which is critical in a global economy, across which the relevant information about all existing and potential customers often requires huge storage capacity. To formulate an optimal marketing strategy, the company must divide all of its customers into appropriate segments. Optimal segmentation can inform appropriate marketing strategies for each department and guarantee more effective alignment with its needs.

Marketing through multiple channels recognizes that customers buy through different channels (retail, catalogs, Internet). Therefore, companies seek to take advantage of databases that offer a more complete picture of each customer, along with suggested strategies to distinguish customers and address them personally, at the exact time their presence is perceived in one of the channels. By establishing different customer profiles, the company can find which portion of its customers is responsible for the most revenues and profits. Invoking Pareto's law, 20 percent of customers often are responsible for 80 percent of the company's revenues and profits. Therefore, the company can develop appropriate programs to maintain and improve its relationships with that 20 percent group, even as it also encourages other customers to try to join that category.

The technique of locating the next best product, as used by customer service and sales operations, can configure appropriate actions during customer interactions. The company can identify special features of a particular market segment, as well as differentiation points that indicate where customers come to a purchase decision in a different way, such as when they prefer a competitive product offer (i.e., the next best product).

By placing customers in categories, the company can establish multiple levels of customer status, to understand particular customers and their situation better, then work to encourage customers to move into a higher level (i.e., status). Companies often provide incentives, rewards, and other special benefits to customers at higher status levels.

CONTEMPORARY MARKETING TRENDS IN INDUSTRIAL SETTINGS

Connected Customers and Digital Cultures

Beyond the essential value achieved through an effective firm–customer relationship, a network perspective that acknowledges that customers do not operate independently in any environment in which they and the supplier are active is necessary, because customers are affected by the relationships they develop within networks and the connections they thus acquire (Figure 12.10). In turn, companies must explore and anticipate how their customers are likely to interact. Using advanced technologies and innovative services, interconnected customers complete transactions easily and communicate with one another about their experiences, perceptions of the supplier, and the level of quality associated with the product offer or available services (Figure 12.11). In their social networks, customers also encounter similar stimuli and find additional channels to share their experiences.

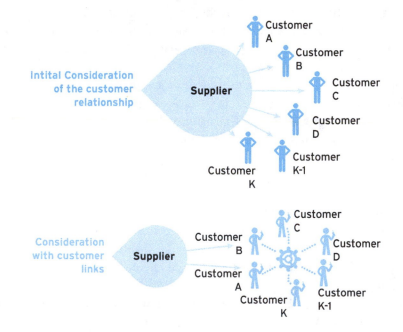

Figure 12.10   Initial Consideration of the Customer Relationship

Source: Adapted from Hughes (2019)

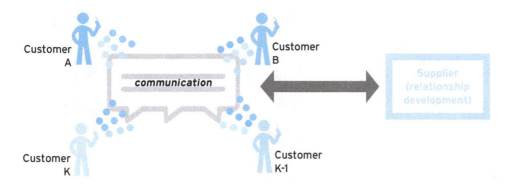

Figure 12.11 Connected Customers

Through these networks and communications, customers can easily discern inconsistencies in the service they receive, compared with that received by other customers. Especially in industrial settings, professional customers are well-informed and stay up-to-date on suppliers' offerings and transactions with other customers, including their competitors.

In turn, suppliers should seek to define each customer's lifetime value in relation to the combined present value of the net contribution that results from purchases made by each customer, together with the net contribution from other customers, because all of them have been affected by one another.

Promotional Channels, Digital Marketing, and Content Marketing

Advances in applied technology and in the application of marketing principles offer new forms of differentiation for companies promoting their offerings in B2B domains (Figure 12.12). In particular, we note shifts in ICT and media channels that have prompted two broad, modern trends in marketing: digital marketing and content marketing. That is, ICT encourage new production processes and applied marketing tools, but they also drive industrial customers to procure the products they need in novel ways. In response, industrial suppliers have had to create appealing digital content, capable of attracting the interest of potential buyers and cultivating relationships with them. It is important to emphasize the organizational processes required to produce appropriate digital content in a timely manner, along with the actual applied practices.

Digital marketing also constitutes a new marketing approach, with its own characteristics and dynamics; its implementation relies on the use of channels such as websites and email, as well as social media, which can effectively promote and manage the company's brand and marketing communications.

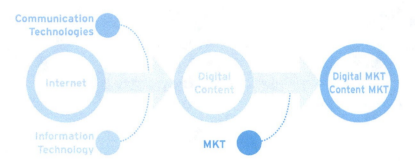

Figure 12.12 Promotional Channels and Modern Times, Differentiated

The Global Economy

The global economy, or new economy, is characterized by the abolition of geographical restrictions, high information transmission speeds, and the availability of a vast volume of information, along with options for controlling its flow, accuracy, and consistency. These elements largely depend on the Internet, because for business operations, it allows for faster, less costly information sharing, reduced search and data costs, and easier (electronic) transactions, as well as improved processes for managing the transportation of products and tracking inventory.

Ongoing growth in e-shopping also relies on the evolution and improvement of supply chain management practices, which have already altered the landscape in which transactions occur, the operations that accompany them, and the ways in which relationships develop between industrial suppliers and industrial buyers. This landscape of the new, global economy features a notable shift of interest in and perceptions of value, related to a firm's ability to manage information and knowledge. At the same time, today's tools and technologies, even in industrial settings, generally have shifted the balance of power in favor of customers.

SOCIAL CONSCIOUSNESS AND ETHICS

Vignette

Sustainability in Industrial Markets

Transportation accounts for much of the environmental harm associated with pollution. In societal efforts to reduce this environmental harm, various pollution taxes, restrictions, and other schemes have sought to force companies to do their best to minimize the effects of their operations on the environment. But is the company level the most appropriate target for allocating responsibility of environmental harms? Consider a few examples.

In a grocery retail chain, with stores across the country, if the retailer decides to take charge of all transportation of products to stores, it can probably create efficient routes, but other companies that deliver to competing stores might suffer less efficient routes, such that the overall harm to the environment increases. In another example, a company located in a sparsely populated area might offer return transports, away from the area, to deliver goods to more populated areas. A company in the sparsely located area then should not be forced to carry the environmental costs of its deliveries, without accounting for how it enables return transports. Finally, reverse flows, such as for empty soft drink bottles, move from consumers (who return the bottles to stores), to the producers (from the stores which return them). Rather than a reverse flow, this may constitute a separate transport system, distinct from the transportation of full bottles to stores.

As these three examples reveal, companies would logically make different decisions if they are solely responsible for the environmental costs of transport, compared with responsibility allocated to the network level, involving the entire retailer chain, other chains, and grocery producers. Consider Figure 12.13.

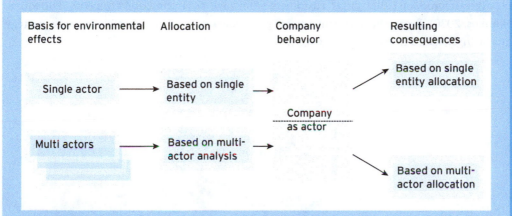

Figure 12.13 Environmental Harm on Company Versus Network Levels

Source: Öberg et al. (2012, p. 248)

An approach that gauges the company's environmental footprint according to not just what it pollutes but also how it functions within a system may suggest new approaches to sustainability that capture environmental harm more holistically.

Source

Öberg, C., Huge-Brodin, M., and Björklund, M. (2012), "Applying a network level in environmental impact assessment," *Journal of Business Research*, 65(2), 247-255.

Green/Environmental/Sustainable Practices in Marketing

A green, environmental, or ecological approach to marketing reflects a new attitude and responsible standard for applying marketing tools strategically, in response to ongoing developments at a global level. Research citing green marketing first started appearing in the early 1980s, followed by the introduction of the term environmental marketing in the middle of that decade. Interest in related topics has increased consistently since then, prompting the American Marketing Association to issue a definition of green marketing that comprises three elements (see www.ama.org):

1   Products that can be described as environmentally safe, mainly from a retail perspective.
2   Marketing processes that minimize negative effects on or improve the quality of the environment, which relates closely to social marketing.
3   Business efforts to produce, promote, package, and retrieve products in response to emerging environmental concerns, according to a wider environmental perspective.

Green marketing also refers to the sale of ecologically safe, recyclable, and biodegradable products (green products) that target customers who have environmental concerns (Fotiadis & Siomkos, 2020). Researchers who investigate green marketing as a responsible business strategy increasingly seek a holistic view (Figure 12.14).

Figure 12.14   Environmental Awareness and B2B Marketing

Five main motives lead companies to adopt green practices: an opportunity, conditions of reciprocal advantage, corporate social responsibility, legislative and competitive pressures, or cost and profit.

Companies might adopt such strategic choices in response to rising costs of raw materials and energy, escalating public pressure, and the promise of increased demand. Consumers' opposition to the new realities of globalization and increased activism by non-governmental organizations also suggest that more evaluations of business performance reflect environmental considerations.

For companies operating in B2B settings, demand for green practices in consumer markets leads to similar demand in industrial markets (derivative demand). If consumer markets demand exhibitions of environmental awareness and precautions, the industrial market in turn must display similar characteristics and concerns. New production process and management system standards, imposed by legal requirements, shape the operating framework.

The raw materials required by industrial firms often raise particularly pressing environmental concerns. Overall, claims of environmental sensitivity require alignment along the entire value chain. It is no longer enough for a product to have green characteristics; the processes that produce it also must be environmentally friendly, avoid creating pollutants or toxic substances, minimize the amount of energy or water required, and reduce waste volumes as much as possible. Similarly, efforts to provide industrial services must take environmental consequences into consideration. Services might be intangible, but they still can create harms for humans or the environment. Industrial enterprises should ensure the diffusion of a coherent environmental philosophy, vertically and horizontally, for both the organizational level and according to a systemic view. In so doing, they can ensure that all the corporate functions meet the requirements of environmental standards, then diffuse that cultural norm throughout their relationships across the supply chain or network. By adopting consistent standards, each actor in the supply chain can establish itself as a safe, green choice for cooperation; by evaluating all its partners and developing relationships with them, each actor also can define its own contributions. Thus, a green marketing philosophy exerts strong influences on supply chain management. Additional research is needed to find ways to link applied green practices to supply chain management in industrial marketing settings as these evolve in contemporary reality.

For industrial enterprises, green marketing strategies can also prompt various innovations that promote competitive advantages. Managing innovation is critical to a firm's culture, organization, and operations, and efforts to infuse this process with environmental values can offer many opportunities for strengthening its competitive position.

Social Marketing, Socially Responsible Marketing, Marketing Ethics, and Fair Trade

Traditional marketing practices primarily seek to influence (improve) performance indicators for the company, but social marketing instead puts social interests in a central position, with a particular emphasis on customer satisfaction (Figure 12.15). The goal thus is to meet customers' needs and desires, resolve their problems, and develop strong relationships with them while also achieving superior value by adopting and exhibiting behaviors that benefit individuals and community groups, in support of the general social well-being (International Social Marketing Association, European Social Marketing Association, Australian Association of Social Marketing).

As a related but distinct philosophy, socially responsible marketing involves an extension of corporate social responsibility to marketing; it tends to include considerations of overconsumption and the risk of environmental destruction caused by firms' operations. It proposes that marketing practices should not be solely for profit but instead must promote and encourage the use of social and moral value, to ensure the enterprise contributes to the well-being of society as a whole. In applying an operational corporate social responsibility model, as in Figure 12.16, we identify four distinct levels of activity, from the base to the top: economic activities, legal activities, ethical activities, and charitable activities. This ladder is similar to the pyramid of Maslow's (1943) needs, such that to rise to a higher level, the lower-level conditions must be met first.

Figure 12.15   Ethical Values and B2B Marketing

Figure 12.16   Corporate Social Responsibility Ladder

Source: Adapted from Ferrell and Hartline (2011)

Morality is relevant to social responsibility; however, something considered moral by an individual, society as a whole, or a business does not necessarily represent a moral element for someone or something else. Therefore, socially responsible behavior is not a guarantee of ethical conduct. Ethics in applied practices (Encyclopedia.com, n.d.) imply the company's conscientious application of some sense of justice in the decision-making processes involved in marketing, leading to marketing behaviors that ultimately appear morally correct.

Fair trade is an institutional and economic approach, designed to create better (fairer, more equitable) conditions in trade transactions, involving producers in underdeveloped and developing countries. It often involves setting higher selling prices, while also providing support for implementing stringent, standardized social and environmental parameters, along with sustainable development conditions. In B2B markets, regulations, standards, and ethical values can encourage fair trade, as well as connect companies with one another, such that they can share data and usable information to inform their marketing strategy in relation to environmental/social/ethical business practices.

Impacts of Moral, Social, and Environmental Conscientiousness on B2B Practices

Commonly accepted standards for organizing the company's operations and management and for interacting with the environment in which the company operates (involving customers, partners, and the wider community) can encourage healthy cooperative relationships that

Figure 12.17 Awareness and Ethics in Industrial Business

deliver significant value and facilitate both effective communication and mutual trust. Trust and mutual commitment must exist for a relationship of an industrial supplier and industrial buyer to take root; these developments in turn can benefit from displays of ethical values in their approach to their relationship. For example, communication is easier if the parties share common values and perspectives on ethical business operations, cooperation, and environmental risks. These shared values can enhance overall supply chain management, with added value for B2B operations.

The adoption and implementation of conscientious, well-planned, well-oriented activities should enhance the value of industrial products and services, through interactions of industrial enterprises. That is, services and production or supply processes imbued with ethical values satisfy demands for environmental protection and societal benefits, so they promote value in the supplier–buyer relationship and in the wider industry in which they operate (Figure 12.17).

The actions adopted by industrial enterprises are influenced by their reputations, acceptance by target audiences, and the power of their brand name. Decisions and subsequent actions can complement the profile the company displays to the public, and the brand name might reflect these choices as integral to its identity. Derivative demand can also help industrial enterprises identify deeper, broader needs in the market, often depicted as consumer trends. Then they can leverage these trends to adjust their organizational structures, facilities, equipment, production and communication processes, or strategic orientation.

Systems Theory and Interfunctional Integration

Systems Theory

The study of systems is a relatively recent trend (von Bertalanffy, 1968). Systems theory refers to the study of systems by integrating different views, as provided by distinct scientific approaches, in an effort to identify principles that might be applied universally, across systems and scientific contexts (Figure 12.18). It encompasses several pertinent concepts and principles. For example, systems theory requires identifying the system to be studied as a complex set of interconnected, interdependent elements, whether found in nature or produced through artificial means. The system is also defined by its space and time, along with the level at which it interacts with environmental elements. The structure and purpose of its existence and operation complement the profile and description of a system; its function reflects how all its elements constitute the overall entity. At the system level, the function might differ in various ways from the functions of its individual component parts, so the system represents a different entity than the simple sum of its parts (Turner, 2017). The level of synergies among the parts still determines how the system as a whole interacts with the environment though, and such interactions can be subject to continuous change (Andreae, 2011). We might also distinguish dynamic, active systems from static, passive systems, such that the former imply ongoing interactions of behaviors and processes, and the latter lack such interactions and instead operate as passive recipients of exogenous effects.

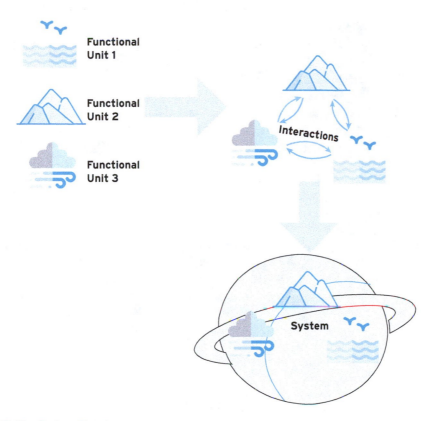

Figure 12.18 System Structure

Complex Systems

Many forms of systems can be identified and created; so-called complex systems consist of multiple components that interact, usually in complex and multifaceted ways (Figure 12.19). The study of such systems is difficult, due to the interdependencies among their components, behaviors, and so forth, which also makes them difficult to integrate into regular operating environments. Complex systems feature non-linear behaviors, hidden components, self-organizational features, often chaotic conditions, an ability to adapt depending on changing (internal or external) characteristics, and feedback loops that allow for causal conditions to inform their operations. In efforts to understand the emergence and operations of complex systems, a systemic approach to problem-solving processes has been conceptualized in previous research. It integrates individual functions performed by different components of such a system, along with the interactions of these different functions, to predict and determine the overall operation and behavior of the system, including in interaction with the environment.

The ecosystem of a business environment consists of many complex systems; in other terms, this ecosystem can be called a company. Every company constitutes a complex system, and its systemic approach to resolving business issues or making changes to respond to altered conditions reflects its existing applied structures.

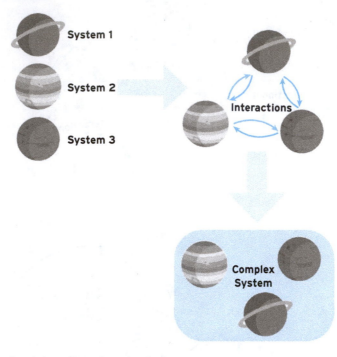

Figure 12.19 System Interactions, Complex Systems

It is important for a company to develop the ability to manage its information and knowledge to be able to address buyers' needs. The ability to develop interactions over time depends on how firms manage knowledge elements. As Powell and Swart (2010) suggest, in highlighting the importance of knowledge management systems, knowledge co-creation requires input from both sides of a relationship.

Perceiving the company as a complex system is both a management method and a goal. First, this perspective can contribute to the strategic planning of the company, as well as the implementation and dissemination of the strategic plan. Second, it can lead to an appropriate culture, in line with the logic of knowledge management, while also altering the organizational structure to allow such a culture to prevail. A systemic approach does not stop at the business level. Market structures, the contemporary logic of transactions that include services, and the process of value creation might also be subject to the principles of systems theory. In environments that feature high mobility, frequent and intense changes, and peculiarities (e.g., high-tech markets), a systemic approach is particularly beneficial. Such firms likely pursue strong capabilities for individual business functions such as R&D or marketing, but such individual developments cannot guarantee the successful and effective exploitation of these skills. Instead, a systemic view is needed to exploit individual skills in a way that guarantees the effective functioning of the whole.

Conceptualizing Function within a Company

A function refers to the process or sequence of activities that takes place repeatedly (in a way that can be characterized as routine) in an effort to carry out the main mission of a company. As a concept, function can be understood according to the role assigned to each part of the company, which together constitute the business's operation. These activities start in response to some specific event; they aim to produce a specific result. But each business operation produces a different result, which may or may not be discernible or integrated (as a feature) into the final product.

A broad distinction of business functions refers to core and support functions (Figure 12.20). First, core functions generate revenue for the company, such as the production of products or services directed toward the target market. The operations within this category shape the image and main activity of the company. The company largely defines its core functions for itself, in accordance with its environment. Second, support functions are operations that facilitate the core functions and enhance the company's productive activity. Their outcomes apply to internal recipients or customers within the company. These functions include supply chain management, ICT, data processing, database services, administrative and managerial support, engineering, and technical services. In some cases, companies seek to outsource such support functions and hire external providers with relevant resources, know-how, and expertise, such that they can provide those services more efficiently than the company could internally.

Although this classification is helpful, it requires the crucial recognition that it does not signal a value assessment; core and support functions do not imply greater or lesser value due to their assignment to either category. All the business operations involved in producing the final product and service are important and essential to meeting the company's promises (Figure 12.21). The purpose of a company is to harmonize these functions and create conditions in which their interactions (as complex systems) lead to a better, more efficient operation of the whole business, still in interaction with other systems (companies).

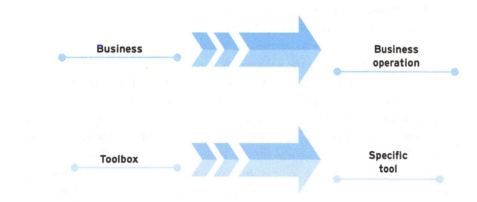

Figure 12.20 Ratios for Business Operation

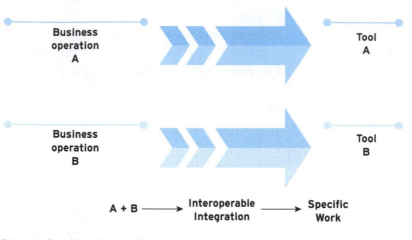

Figure 12.21 Interfunctional Integration

Interfunctional Integration

The need to integrate different functions is clear; it supports a symbiotic form of interaction across two or more entities that yields benefits to the overall company that are greater than the benefits that each entity could achieve on its own. In practice, interfunctional integration also manifests systems theory. A single entity results, in which different operations work together to achieve goals, or more precisely, the same overriding goal: to provide a superior product offer and ensure customer satisfaction. With this common goal, integrated business functions can coexist and collaborate, despite their unique perceptions, philosophies, scientific foundations, specializations, techniques, tools, perspectives, and approaches.

Transformation and Change through Interfunctional Integration

Integrating different functions demands carefully planned actions and designs, strong management commitment, and a business culture that accepts that changes need to take place. Relevant efforts also need to identify potential barriers to interfunctional integration, according to a systemic approach. The culture, way of thinking, codes, priorities, and perceptions among different operations often differ, as do the goals set by operational departments. They tend to communicate using different terminology, which may prevent them from reaching a shared understanding. In some cases, this difference is relatively minor (e.g., marketing and sales), but in others, the gap is difficult to bridge (e.g., marketing and R&D). Even when these elements align across departments, it is necessary to ensure their alignment with the features of the overall business entity. Thus, integration is both critically important and very difficult.

The experience of managers and executives is relevant in this effort; if these top-level actors have accumulated experience with multiple functions, they likely can establish and drive a successful integration effort. With such experience, they gain a deeper understanding of bilateral processes across functions, so they can help all the parties anticipate and understand differences in terms or conditions and encourage clear, harmonious, efficient communication.

Such communication in turn is critical to integration; it requires adequate procedures (in terms of time and content) and mutual understanding. A suitable platform can be beneficial, which collects necessary data and features appropriate technological and communication infrastructures to facilitate efficient data management. The quality of communication among integrated functions also tends to reflect executives' personalities (Fotiadis, 2018).

The departments might disagree about the best approach for the company, and to resolve these disagreements, they must learn to stop regarding themselves as individual entities and instead embrace a view in which they are parts of a set of integrated entities. In support of that effort, the operational staff also need a complete picture of their role, duties, and unique abilities and value for the company overall. Any integration effort should clearly identify expectations about each function's and each employee's responsibilities and roles, which then may limit the potential for conflicts. At the same time, conflicts can evoke productive, creative dialogue, so they should not be discouraged completely, as long as the company's culture and management ensure that they remain productive.

Different applications of the concepts of specialization and integration might appear to reflect a spectrum:

- Specialization can exploit the skills and competencies available in a particular function more efficiently and ensure the achievement of its objectives.
- Specialization can alienate each function from its surrounding conditions. Achieving specialized goals also might not contribute to objectives of the overall company, or at least to the preferred degree.
- Interfunctional integration elides the distinct character or personality of each function, and it might reduce some of the benefits of specialized knowledge or expertise.
- Interfunctional integration increases opportunities and abilities to adopt a systemic response to problems, by creating effective synergies. With a well-balanced match of different functions, the company might produce better innovations and thus attain a strong competitive advantage.

Coopetition: Competition through Cooperation

Coopetition is a neologism, reflecting the hybrid combination of cooperation with competition. The term emerged from the evolution of corporate strategy theories and applied practices, in response to ongoing changes in the environment, as firms sought to address their competitive contexts. A coopetitive perspective and approach entails the following features (Figure 12.22):

- Interdependence between companies that creates economic value and establishes the field for distributing that economic value. Mutual benefits should accrue to cooperating companies, but they are not necessarily fairly distributed, depending on competitive pressures and their potential to undermine cooperation.
- Stable coopetition requires at least the partial convergence of each company's interests in the survival of the other.

The concept of coopetition also reflects game theory, a scientific discipline that applies mathematical models to strategies, with an assumption of rational decision-making. In addition to logic and computer science fields, game theory can inform a wide range of behavioral relationships and decision-making processes adopted by humans and animals, as well as computers.

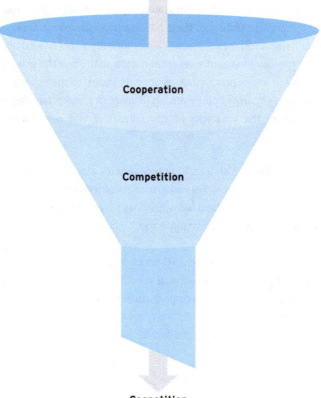

Cooperation

Competition

Coopetition

Figure 12.22 Constituents of Coopetition

Coopetition within a company involves different operational departments, whether the people working in them or the operational units more generally. It can also include different companies. These latter relationships, assuming some partial convergence of interests, seek greater value than is available to each coopeting company on its own. For example, companies might jointly devote their resources to gaining knowledge or conducting research into new product development, within the same or proximal markets. They still compete for the market share created by such information and innovation efforts, as well as for control over the resulting knowledge capital.

Coopetition thus can affect not only the accumulation of knowledge but also the behaviors involved in disseminating and distributing it. Together with a systemic approach to strategic design and the strategic integration of various functions, a firm's strategic choice to engage in coopetition can shape the wider enterprise landscape, prompting structural and operational changes. The connections across these approaches are evident, with combined implications for executives and firms that adopt such a philosophy to drive decision-making and actions.

Emotional Intelligence in Modern Industrial Marketing

Emotional intelligence (EI) refers to a person's ability to recognize the emotions that they experience, as well as those exhibited by others. With greater EI, a person can distinguish among different emotions, then use that information to anticipate, understand, guide, and even manipulate one's own and others' thoughts and behaviors. The ability to manage one's own emotions and adapt to the environment can facilitate goal achievement, too (Figure 12.23). Among the various models of EI, a prominent one combines elements based on ability (ability EI) with elements based on personality characteristics (trait EI).

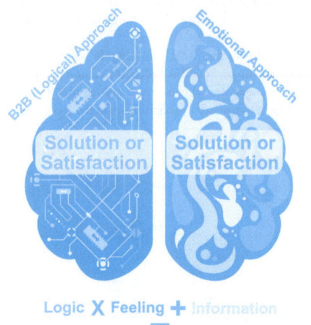

Figure 12.23 Business-to-Business Logical Approach

The former elements include individual behavioral dispositions and abilities, as perceived by the self or others. To measure them, the individual requires relevant information, based on self-perception. The latter elements entail how people's personalities inform their ability to process relevant information and relate it to emotion, then use those insights to function appropriately in a social environment.

Considering these insights, EI seems like a valuable tool for companies; for example, marketing and communications often seek to influence customers' emotional perceptions. In industrial settings in particular, suppliers might refer to emotional connections with consumers, to encourage derivative demand. But EI can also be extremely relevant for various interactions with buying companies, such as in purchasing negotiations and the development of trusting relationships. Personal sales efforts also often feature two conflicting demands: to complete a sale immediately so the employer earns profits but also to establish customer satisfaction and long-term relationship viability. Therefore, each salesperson's EI is extremely influential. For example, to communicate the value of its offering to customers, salespeople must identify and empathize with the needs and problems of those buyers, some of which can entail emotional reactions, such as stress. With strong EI, salespeople can adapt their approaches during the sales process to appeal particularly to each buyer. Furthermore, emotions inform every stage of the purchase decision process, though they vary across those stages. Because different emotions influence buyers' tendencies to take action or make a purchase, supplier representatives must be able to adjust as needed to reflect and accommodate the dynamic emotional experiences of industrial buyers.

In summary, EI is relevant for industrial marketing, in terms of not just derived demand but also with regard to its influences on the purchase decision process undertaken by industrial buyers. Therefore, we argue that EI constitutes another tool, skill, and attribute that can enhance the performance of industrial suppliers, as well as the quality of the relationships they cultivate with their buyers.

13

INDUSTRIAL MARKETING IN A HIGH-TECH CONTEXT

Learning Objectives

- Detail and explain the specific characteristics and demands of high-tech marketing.
- Outline the connection between high-tech marketing and industrial marketing.
- Learn strategic approaches for marketing in a high-tech environment.

Case Study

New Companies Entering Established Industrial Markets

New firms, particularly those that introduce new technologies with the aim to disrupt current operations in industrial markets, often struggle to reach their intended customers, for several reasons. First, customers' acceptance of new technology tends to be slow, especially when such adoption would require them to invest in new, complementary technologies or knowledge. Second, new firms generally lack any existing relationships with customers or insights into how to navigate the marketplace. Third, of particular importance in industrial markets, the existing market consists of well-established or nested firms that raise network barriers to the new entrants.

A study involving five university spin-offs (that is, firms that have their origin in research carried out at a university), from Sweden and Taiwan, sought to determine how new firms can carve out a position for themselves in industrial markets. The study identified three roles for university spin-offs (see also Table 13.1):

1   Resource mediator. This spin-off attempts to access and adapt to existing resources and parties in the industrial market, such as by proposing a novel service to enhance existing

(Continued)

products. This solution does not challenge deliveries by existing suppliers. The main challenge is to convince customers of the value of the solution.

2   Resource re-combiner. Also relies on existing resources and parties, but in this case, the spin-off aims to link previously unconnected resources and parties and establish bridges across them, in a way that requires those parties to make some adjustments. For example, a new product coating might be introduced by a resource re-combiner, which requires current manufacturers to adopt a new procedure.

3   Resource renewer. Finally, this spin-off attempts to replace resources in the market. Introducing a digital solution that can replace an analog solution, for example, requires customers, as well as other parties in the supply chain, to adapt to the new solution. The company that has been selling the analog solution might even be forced out of the market, if the resource renewer succeeds.

For new firms, the easiest route is to adapt and become a mediator, because in this role, it does not challenge the existing market structure, even if it still requires acceptance by parties in that structure.

Table 13.1   University Spin-Off Roles

Role	Resource mediator	Resource re-combiner	Resource renewer
Resource interactions	Present resources are connected through the spin-off.	Resource recombination in specific relationships between spin-off and business parties.	Resource replacement on the network level.
Main resource interfaces	Business relationships and business units.	Products and facilities.	Products, facilities, business units, and business relationships.
Direction of adaptation	Spin-off adapts, other parties continue as before.	Mutual adaptations between spin-off and business party.	Replacement of resources on a network level.

Source

Aaboen, L., Laage-Hellman, J., Lind, F., Öberg, C., and Shih, T. (2016), "Exploring the roles of university spin-offs in business networks," *Industrial Marketing Management*, 59, 157-166.

DEFINITION OF HIGH TECHNOLOGY AND DETERMINATION THROUGH KNOWLEDGE ATTRIBUTES

High Technology: Definitions and Features

There are many definitions of high technology (Figure 13.1). For example, one definition of the high-tech industry could be that high technology concerns designing, developing, and introducing new products and/or innovative manufacturing processes, and that such processes apply scientific and technical knowledge. Also, high-tech could be regarded as technology that is related to leadership share in the concerned field. It is the technology which instinctively leads from its emergence in the laboratory to its practical application. It implies processes or sciences characterized by progressive development, typically with a short, fluid life cycle. Yet another definition implies that high-tech refers to a branch of industry devoted to research, such as computers, biotechnology, pharmaceuticals, chemistry, and aerospace. In turn, high-tech products can be defined as those that result from turbulent, volatile technologies and that induce significant changes in the behavior of at least one member of a market. Marketing managers instead define the high-tech field according to the features that constitute the relevant products, such as their rapid development and replacement. Moore's Law (named after Intel's founder) asserts that the number of transistors per memory circuit should double every 18 months. Economists' definitions tend to emphasize measures of innovative inputs relative to outflows of innovative products and industrial development. Perhaps the most straightforward way to classify high-tech products is to use standard industrial classification (SIC) codes that indicate high-tech industries.

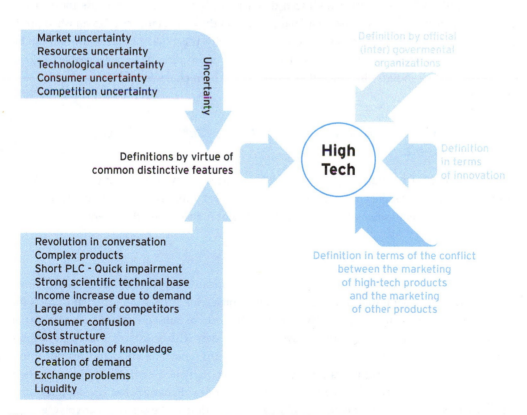

Figure 13.1 Summary of Approaches for Defining High Technology

The varied definitions of high technology can be grouped largely into two categories, as in Figure 13.1: how official government sources and global organizations define it, and how researchers do so. We consider the first category, the high-tech industry, which is categorized according to specific criteria, such as the number of technical staff, the volume of research conducted, development plans, and the number of standards introduced. For example, the US Department of Labor Statistics ranks industrial sectors by employment ratios in R&D departments. The Organization for Economic Co-operation and Development (OECD) uses a similar rationale, defining high-tech firms by the proportion of their expenditures in R&D, according to the added value of each specific industry. The US National Science Foundation also examines the intensity or proportion of R&D expenses to net sales (National Science Foundation 1973, 1983, and 1996).

Such measures create inherent ambiguities though. For example, the broad definition used by the Labor Statistics Service allows some industries that market products that have been modified only marginally (e.g., cigarette industry) to be classified as high-tech, alongside other industries that have featured remarkable technological leaps. Furthermore, this classification might fail to recognize industries that achieve most of their production volume through standardized processes with relatively unskilled labor as high-tech, even if they achieve high-tech outputs, as in the example of computer manufacturers that produce components on a mass scale, using production routines and minimal technical staff. Alternatively, a high proportion of scientific-to-technical staff may justify a high-tech designation, but the firm might use most of the knowledge it acquires to make just marginal changes to the characteristics of established products in slow-growing, mature markets (Mohr, 2001). Finally, this type of broad definition can be short-sighted and ignore the emergence of new products or processes by knowledgeable workers, simply because the industry in which they work has not been characterized as high-tech.

Definition Based on Knowledge Attributes: Common Features of High-Tech Markets

A high-tech market generally features complex products, many competing companies, consumer confusion, and rapid change (see Figure 13.2). It also implies processes that rely on high-tech features. We detail some other common features of high-tech markets here.

Cost per Unit

The cost structure of high-tech markets reflects the significant value that results from the know-how or knowledge that is manifested in the product or service. Therefore, production costs for the first unit are very high relative to reproduction costs of subsequent units. In industrial markets, featuring large-scale, complex system businesses, with substantial strategic importance, different companies exhibit idiosyncratic demands, characteristics, and relationships; the interaction between suppliers and buyers acquires particular complexity, because their optimal use of the systems that constitute their operations demands that the supplier offer substantial expertise in relation to its offerings. Transaction processes often involve groups rather than individuals, and these buying centers seek broad-based solutions. The size and value of transactions also creates more risk for buyers. Such factors motivate companies to seek out well-respected suppliers, to ensure the product offerings will be legitimate and acceptable.

Increased Profits Due to Demand

Network externalities, or the bandwagon effect, imply greater value of a product offering due to expanded adoption by consumers. In other words, the usefulness of a product/innovation is a function of the number of its users. Once a supplier gains a critical mass of market share, its product value increases sharply.

Exchange Issues

When knowledge represents much of the value offered, exchanges between buyers and sellers become transactions of intellectual property. Exchange problems arise if it is difficult to assess the value of the knowledge, especially novel forms or insight that are embedded in people and organizational routines.

Dissemination of Knowledge

Synergies emerge during the creation and transmission of knowledge, which increase the existing pool of knowledge further. Quite simply, each innovation creates conditions that help a larger number of innovations thrive, building knowledge on the basis of knowledge that already exists. Knowledge transfer is a relevant theme here; it involves the use and creation of value on the basis of organizational knowledge.

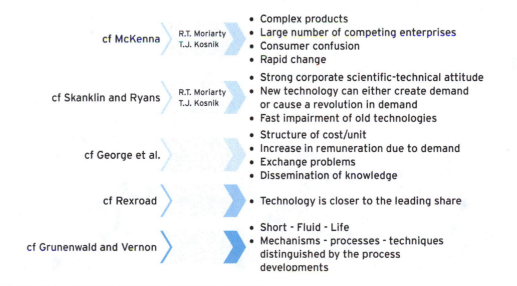

Figure 13.2 Common Features of High-Tech Markets

Marketing Strategies for High-Tech Markets

High-tech environments feature market and technological uncertainty, as well as competitive volatility. Operating in a B2B market involves more complex decision-making about products and solutions than is required of consumer firms. Therefore, marketing strategies for high-tech B2B markets must also differ. One approach leverages both the level of technology exhibited by the product and consumers' perceptions of the innovative offering to market a new high-tech product according to the altered benefits it offers, its technological capabilities, and its usage or consumption standards.

In support of these efforts, suppliers need a long-term orientation, especially if their goal is to establish technologies that link them with their buyers, distributors, and end customers, such as EDI or radio frequency identification (RFID) systems. Unlike consumer technologies or products, these buyer–seller, system-level technologies involve multiple stakeholders that must decide to adopt and implement them and that also prefer and enter into different collaborations. In turn, they can facilitate inter-firm coordination and the efficient movement of information or products across organizational boundaries.

Vignette

Customers as Innovators

Innovation literature increasingly recognizes the participative role of customers. Rather than passive recipients of innovations pushed by the supplier, customers as innovators can be active in all the phases of an innovation process: search, select, implement, and capture. They might provide feedback on early ideas or finalized prototypes; they might even develop a new offering for the supplier. Such customer participation also implies that the phases of the innovation process become less orderly or clearly distinguished.

Consider an example of the customer as innovator. This customer describes how she would prefer to use a new product, as well as where and how she wants to be able to buy it. On the basis of this input, the supplier solicits further insights and input on its emerging ideas, design offerings, and manufacturing process, to match those preferences. A possible classification of the roles of customers as innovators might define them by their consumption activities: traditional (buying and using), added (helps develop a product, provides input while buying or using), or transferred (stops buying and using and instead develops innovations for others). In this view, an added role implies developing innovations for one's own benefit, whereas the transferred role shares these benefits with other customers.

Source

Öberg, C. (2010a), "Customer roles in innovations," *International Journal of Innovation Management*, 14(6), 989-1011.

Uncertainty in High-Tech Markets

High-tech products require substantial resources and R&D investments, but they also create substantial market and technological uncertainty (Figure 13.3), due to the rapid rate of technological change and the lack of relevant prior experience among adopters. Many high-tech companies thus seek greater contributions from their marketing departments, to communicate effectively about the intense technological complexity, knowledge intensity, and systemic approaches that characterize high-tech products.

Market uncertainty can be synonymous with the degree or extent to which customer needs can be met by the technology; this perspective reflects a customer orientation, focused on understanding and satisfying consumers' needs. But potential customers in high-tech markets often cannot articulate their needs, and five key questions lead to market uncertainty:

1   What needs will be met by the new technology? Consumers likely do not fully understand which of their needs can be addressed by a novel technology.
2   How will needs change in the future? Even if the needs are clear, they will likely undergo rapid, unexpected changes, due to a chain reaction of rapid changes in the wider environment.
3   Will the market adopt the industry's standards? Products that meet customers' needs must have some degree of compatibility with complementary products.
4   How fast will the new technology spread? The spread is extremely difficult to predict.
5   How big is the potential market? The potential size of the market is also difficult to predict.

These issues can also be summarized by the acronym FUD, referring to the fear, uncertainty, and doubt that can overwhelm customers, due to their need to consider which problems the new technology might solve and how well it can do so. Due to their FUD, customers often are slow to adopt innovations and may require substantial training, education, and information about the innovation. Then they need post-purchase confirmation and empowerment, to reduce any doubt after the purchase. High levels of uncertainty mark high-tech B2B settings especially, due to the unpredictable business environment and unspecified market goals (Yang & Gabrielsson, 2017). Moreover, marketing decisions by a company can influence the existing market, rather than decisions solely being shaped by changes to the market.

In a sense, technological innovation represents a process for reducing uncertainty by gathering and processing information; here, uncertainty is the difference between the information required to complete a specific purpose and the information already available in the company's knowledge stores. Information in this context comprises verbal, codified knowledge, such as (1) facts, truths, or principles; (2) understanding as a natural consequence of experience; (3) practices; (4) ideas or processes that have been certified as valid, based on previous investigations; and (5) findings from relevant research. The process of technological innovation therefore encompasses actions required to process information and thus reduce uncertainty.

Technological uncertainty also reflects five key factors:

- Whether the new product will work as expected, due to a lack of certainty and information about the functional performance of the product.
- Whether the product will be available at a predetermined delivery time or subject to delays by producers, which is often the rule rather than the exception.
- Whether the supplier can meet post-purchase product needs if problems arise (service), related to a lack of experience in the market that has not been able to test the product as much as it has mature technologies, leaving open questions about whether maintenance problems will be addressed quickly and efficiently.
- The potential existence of side effects of the product or service.
- Whether the new technology will make existing technology in use obsolete.

Consider the information systems market where post-sales service and its strong effects on the decision-making behavior of potential consumers are important. Service and maintenance offerings also strongly influence the purchasing costs in information system markets and the reputation of the supplier. Negative experiences for buyers of information systems include untimely or incomplete provision of support, as well as excessive, problematic financial and business consequences.

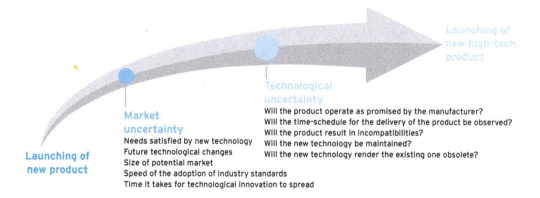

Figure 13.3 Uncertainty in Launching of New High-Tech Product

The combination of technological uncertainty and market uncertainty can be shown as in the matrix in Figure 13.4.

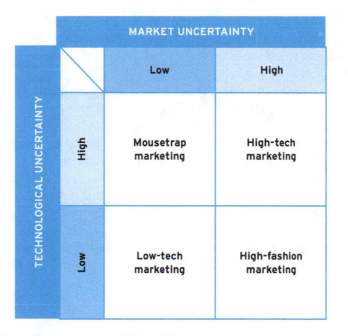

Figure 13.4 Matrix of Technological and Market Uncertainty

Source: Adapted from Rangan and Bartus (1995) and Mohr (2001)

The matrix in Figure 13.4 in turn can be used to juxtapose high-tech marketing against three other types. Low degrees of both market and technological uncertainty imply uses of mature technology to address relatively well-known needs. When high technological uncertainty combines with low market uncertainty, a new technology arises to satisfy an existing need, of which the consumer is aware. If high market uncertainty exists together with low technological uncertainty, the technology might be changing slowly, but consumer needs are difficult to predict. Finally, high degrees of both types of uncertainty should activate high-tech marketing.

Beyond the well-established notions of market and technological uncertainty, a third form might be relevant: competitive uncertainty, based on the intensity of competition in the market and changes that take place in it, in terms of who competitors are, what products they offer, and which tools they adopt to compete in the market. Because competitors often target the same market segment, with similar product offerings, greater uncertainty can undermine a focal organization's innovation success or its very survival. If a business is uncertain about its customers and about alternative technologies, it likely is uncertain about its competitive position in the industry too.

Jakkie Mohr (2001) identifies three sources of intense competition that increase the degree of uncertainty (Figure 13.5):

1   Unknown identity of potential future competitors. High-tech markets tend to be relatively inaccessible and inhospitable, because new technologies get introduced and commercialized by entirely new companies that have not necessarily operated in this space previously.

2   Outsiders that introduce unfamiliar tactics. Some competitive tactics may be well-known in other fields of activity, but in a high-tech field, entrants that seek to use these unfamiliar methods create confusion among existing players. If the new players can change the rules of the game, they will alter the market profile for all actors.

3   New products, platforms, or options for satisfying consumer needs. An example clarifies this source: in 2000, the PC industry confronted new information devices that could access the Internet. Hewlett-Packard decided to focus simultaneously on PCs and information devices, putting it in an uncertain and challenging position.

The intersection of these three sources of uncertainty defines the area where high technology exists. In this sense, the simultaneous coexistence of all three factors establishes its uniqueness.

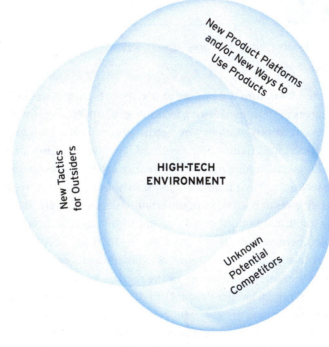

Figure 13.5   Sources of Intense Competition That Increase Uncertainty

Source: Mohr (2001); Adapted from Gadbois (2000)

Nevertheless, all organizations must work to reduce uncertainty, whether related to competition, technology, or the market, if they are to develop successful innovations. A primary means to do so is to obtain information about each source of uncertainty. The degree to which a business allocates its human, financial, and technological resources efficiently is highly correlated with its innovative success, but these same resources must also be devoted to efforts to reduce uncertainty. In a sense, this logic implies a fourth form of uncertainty: resource uncertainty. Greater competitive, technology, and market uncertainty likely produces more uncertainty about the kind and size of resources the business needs. We depict these correlations in Figure 13.6 and summarize this discussion in Figure 13.7.

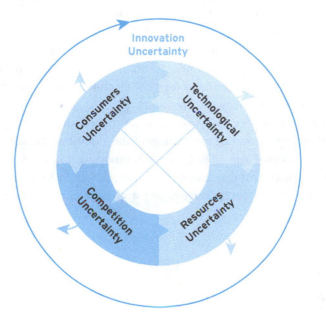

Figure 13.6 Sources of Uncertainty

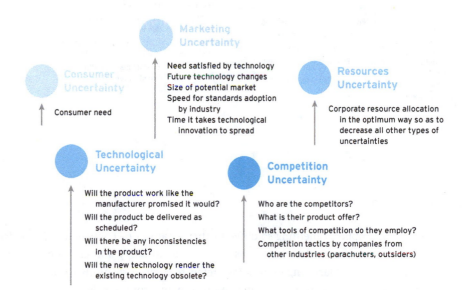

Figure 13.7 Summary of Types of Uncertainties in High-Technology Markets

Innovation

A high-tech product might also be defined by the quality of the innovation that underlies it. Higher quality can induce changes in the market and make other products obsolete, so a sustainable competitive advantage can be established by continuous, high-quality innovations that leverage dynamic organizational, technological, and marketing capabilities. In terms of our discussion in this chapter, high technology is related, directly or indirectly, with innovation, in that innovation is an outcome of high technology, and high technology offers a natural environment for creating innovations. In other words, high technology becomes the vehicle, tool, or medium through which an innovation is developed. Even if the conception of an innovation is not guided by high technology, high technology eventually will play a role in its development and transformation into a product.

To establish a reference point for understanding innovative offerings, we might use a dual classification of innovation types, reflecting the intensity of the innovation introduced, namely, radical and incremental innovations (Figure 13.8). Companies' innovative capabilities depend on the intellectual assets and knowledge that they possess, as well as their ability to deploy them; the innovation process represents one of the most complex and knowledge-intensive business processes.

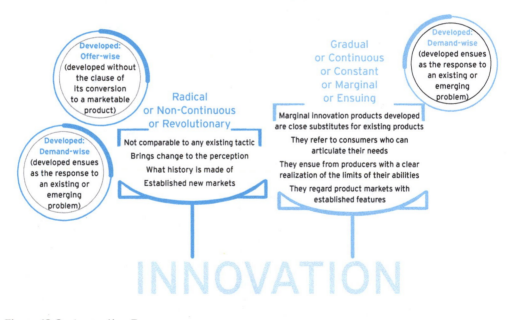

Figure 13.8 Innovation Types

Radical innovation implies something so different that it cannot be compared to any existing practice or perception in use. Such innovations use high technology and create new markets, based on novel perceptions. Marketing terminology refers to them as disruptive; other synonyms include revolutionary or non-continuous innovation. On the supply side, these innovations emerge from companies that are seeking to commercialize their R&D results; their marketing departments must find a way to convert the radical idea into a marketable product. Such efforts generally do not include any pre-existing ideas of usefulness or depend on possible applications, even if some radical innovations represent clear responses to existing or emerging needs. But whether radical innovations are products of scientific research that find useful applications (supply side) or constitute more complete, modern, or effective solutions to (existing or emerging) problems, they create new markets. In this sense, radical innovations have the potential to destroy business assets: hard-earned customers desert a company they have been collaborating with so far, as soon as an innovation by another company increases the value for them. Then prior high-cost investments and skills become devalued, and the company loses its competitive advantage. But on the flipside, that radically innovative product is a source of competitive advantage for the company that introduces it, with potentially substantial, positive, and lasting results.

Incremental or gradual innovation instead emerges over time, as an extension or marginal evolution of existing methods, practices, and offerings. The emergent products that result are close substitutes for existing ones, and both consumers and producers recognize the products' capabilities and limitations. The markets for incremental innovations usually contain products with clearly defined characteristics and consumers who can describe their needs, so the innovations mostly derive from the demand side.

Of course, these simplified descriptions refer to "pure" cases, in which the innovation can be clearly classified, and there are no discrepancies in the views of consumers and producers regarding what type of innovation it is. But more realistically, innovations can be assigned to the matrix in Figure 13.9, reflecting combinations based on the divergent views of customers and producers. For example, if companies perceive the innovation as radical, but customers see it as incremental, we can define the product as delusionary; the reverse case implies the introduction of shadow products.

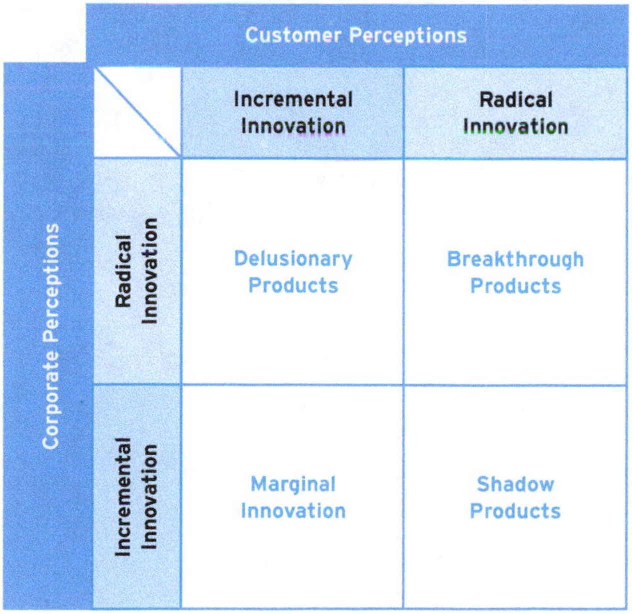

		Customer Perceptions	
		Incremental Innovation	**Radical Innovation**
Corporate Perceptions	**Radical Innovation**	Delusionary Products	Breakthrough Products
	Incremental Innovation	Marginal Innovation	Shadow Products

Figure 13.9 Matrix of Corporate and Customer Perceptions of Innovations

Source: Adapted from Rangan and Bartus (1995) and Mohr (2001)

Although this matrix can be insightful, it does not offer a comprehensive framework for understanding which organizational factors affect the type of innovation produced. For example, the size of the supplier might be an antecedent of radical innovation, but the way the company is organized might be more important, because radical innovation requires high levels of autonomy. Information flows and organizational memory also affect a supplier's innovative propensity.

We thus might adopt an approach, similar to the consideration of uncertainty, and define innovation according to the extent to which it encompasses technology and market dimensions. The technology dimension pertains to the extent to which technology involved in a new product is different from previous technologies. A technological innovation is any product, process, or entity whose development requires the innovator to invest human, financial, and technical resources to acquire new or unknown technologies or combine already known technologies in a novel way. Then the market dimension refers to the extent to which the new product meets the key needs of consumers, better than existing products, as might be measured by their willingness to pay for an innovation. The combination of these dimensions in turn suggests four types of product innovation:

1   Marginal product innovation. Combination of low technological differentiation and a relatively small contribution toward satisfying consumer needs.
2   Market revolution. The technology differs only marginally, but the resulting product evokes significantly more customer satisfaction than existing products.
3   Technology revolution. The technology adopted is fundamentally different from others currently in use; the resulting product does not improve consumer satisfaction levels though.
4   Radical innovation. At high levels for both dimensions, customers gain substantial value and pleasure from the use of this very novel technology.

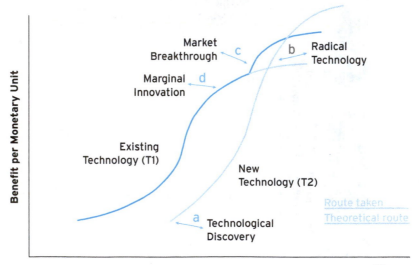

Figure 13.10   Dynamic View of Innovation

The four types of innovation then can be linked by S-curves, as in Figure 13.10. Following these curves, a given technology (e.g., T1) initially improves consumer satisfaction at an increasing rate when the technology is newly introduced, but during its maturation phase, the satisfaction rate decreases, and its slope changes. Over the lifespan of T1, a new technology also emerges (T2). Upon its introduction, it has a disadvantage relative to T1 in terms of the satisfaction it can offer customers; this stage signals a technology revolution. Over time, and as a result of intensive research, T2 begins to increase the satisfaction it offers with its products at an increasing rate, which erases the positive slope. In the next phase, it fully outperforms T1; at this point, the product and its technology enters the realm of radical innovation. But T1 users, threatened by T2, make efforts to improve the benefits offered by T1, potentially evoking marginal innovation or market revolutions. Nevertheless, the marginal improvements move at a much slower rate than for T2, so T1 is fatally replaced by T2, which becomes the dominant technology. Over time of course, T2 will also become obsolete, following the same cycle.

The Chasm

Another school of thought sees innovation as a process of bridging the information gap, regarding users' needs, with opportunities based on technology. Innovators trap, connect, and exploit pools of knowledge to address customers' uncertainties, needs, and requirements. But another chasm arises, related to the distance and difficulty associated with developing high-tech, innovative offerings into profitable, lucrative products in a stable market. Depending on their attitudes toward innovations, customers fall on either side of the chasm: visionaries or pragmatists/realists. Visionaries (also known as early adopters) jump at the chance to adopt a new technology (and pay a correspondingly high price); pragmatists instead take their time but also constitute the critical mass of the market. The transition between them is, at best, difficult.

Thus the chasm also represents the gap between markets for technology products (Figure 13.11). The first, early market, consisting of early adopters, appeals to them with its rapid evolution of product advantages. The second, mass market includes buyers who want to reduce their risk but still reap the benefits of the new technology, without having to experience the growing pains of its early iterations. A factor that makes this gap more chaotic is the inherent differences of these two groups of buyers, based on the degree of annoyance and risk they are willing to tolerate.

For software users, for example, annoyance is likely if a new product reveals itself as incompatible with their operating system. The chasm depends on the degree of tolerance they have for such problems. Early adopters still appreciate the psychological benefits they gain from being first, which outweigh the annoyance costs that their choice entails. In contrast, the critical mass of pragmatists calculates a different cost–benefit assessment, such that the annoyance cost of adopting the new technology is too high, exceeding any benefits, and they require additional benefits, as might result from wider market adoption. These potential adopters might also consider switching costs, which result from their earlier commitments to other, existing high-tech products.

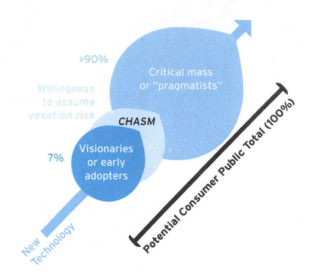

Figure 13.11 The Chasm

As a result of this chasm, many high-tech companies never succeed in extending beyond a niche market of early adopters. That is, even if a product appeals to early adopters, which represents an initial market victory, doing so demands enormous effort, such that the innovative firm might not have sufficient resources remaining to cross the chasm. This crossing requires a transformation of its existing marketing habits and the adoption of new ones, such as educating novice customers about the product in user-friendly language. Many high-tech companies find such forms of communication extremely difficult. They might also struggle to understand the mass market of pragmatists, such that they cannot effectively predict whether, when, and by how much they will adopt, at what rate, so they cannot estimate the size of the potential market to gauge if the effort is even worthwhile. But such predictions are invaluable, even if executives largely recognize that new product forecasts are invariably wrong, due to the difficulty of forecasting both the life cycles of high-tech products and customer adoption.

One option, reflecting a broader understanding of how markets behave when undergoing change, would be to pursue strong relationships with customers, as a means of facilitating the transition and minimizing the chasm. A relationship acts as an impediment of sorts, capable of reducing the distracting, detrimental effects of the chasm. Even high-tech, innovative companies are subject to Leavitt's transition from the sales era to the marketing era, requiring a customer-oriented perspective.

In this light, the chasm and its implications reflect market reactions to change; in the case of high-tech products, the dynamic nature of the markets, which make it difficult to predict market size or when a critical mass of buyers will adopt, creates greater insecurity for businesses. In addition, network effects, dominant designs, and technological standards increase the complexity of identifying, implementing, and evaluating marketing strategies for high-tech innovations.

Vignette

Radical Innovation: Dealing with Uncertainties

The issues that confront suppliers dealing with radical innovation are numerous and varied: they must figure out what the innovations consist of, how to access the technology, what suitable production processes are required, and how much risk they are willing to accept to use the innovation to develop something new. Then suppliers need to help their customers understand and adopt new thoughtworlds. Such efforts might require them to search for ideas beyond their normal scope of business, such as checking with other industry sectors for solutions. But even the evaluations of these solutions differ from previous efforts, and their implementation may challenge existing operations. Therefore, even if the innovation represents an improvement over past offerings, customers might not perceive its value, and they also might not be willing to give up their existing thoughtworlds and processes.

Therefore, many suppliers try to overcome customer resistance to change by designing new solutions that resemble past offerings in some way. An electric car looks very similar to a gas-powered version. A revolutionary new pen probably would take the same shape as conventional ballpoint pens. This design approach is a way to get over the first hurdle in new product adoption: getting customers to understand what the product is supposed to do.

Source

Bessant, J., Öberg, C., and Trifilova, A. (2014), "Framing problems in radical innovation," *Industrial Marketing Management*, 43(8), 1284-1292.

BUSINESS CULTURE AND STRATEGIES FOR HIGH-TECHNOLOGY BUSINESSES

Strategic Challenges and Approaches

Core Capabilities Become Core Rigidities

Due to the volatile, tumultuous, turbulent changes in high-tech settings, at both the market and technology levels, many companies focus strongly on developing new products. Then a conflict of interest develops, between innovation efforts and the firm's previously established advantages, such that it seeks to both establish new core advantages and maintain existing ones, even if they require separate efforts. New products thus create a visible arena of conflict, between the undeniable need for innovation and the urgent need to maintain a core set of competitive advantages. In turn, another paradox emerges, because the firm's existing core skills simultaneously favor and hinder its innovation. That is, a business's capabilities are unique (core) only if they can differentiate the business strategically. In marketing literature, various authors have defined core capabilities as distinct skills, sources of development, or invisible capital (assets).

But in addition to this view of the role and relationship of innovation with core competencies as competitive or in conflict, another view describes them as complementary. According to this perspective, competitive success depends on gradual innovations created through the exploitation of carefully constructed, unique, core capabilities, but those skills and abilities also create incumbent inertia in the face of environmental change. Another approach refers to coopetition, defined as simultaneous cooperation and competition, as an effective innovation strategy in high-tech industries, where short product life cycles, technology convergence, and high R&D costs encourage such approaches.

At any stage of a company's life, its unique skills evolve, together with the paradox of their simultaneous operation as catalysts for or brakes on the development of innovative (high-tech) new products. Therefore, it may be helpful to consider the nature of innovations and the components that constitute them, as well as the mechanisms that transform them into obstacles to change or innovation, as outlined in Figure 13.12.

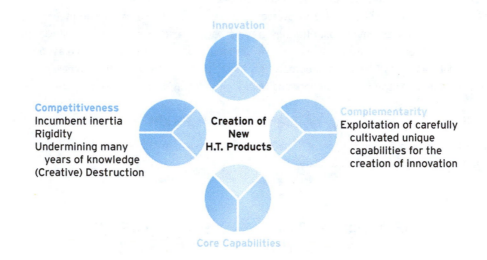

Figure 13.12 Correlation of Innovation and Core Capabilities

The dimensions of core capabilities identified in prior literature include being unique, distinct, difficult to imitate, and superior to competitors; such studies also suggest ways that firms can cultivate core capabilities. This set of differentiated skills, supplementary capital, and processes provides a basis for competitive opportunities and sustainable advantage in a particular business, and the totality of knowledge that it represents differentiates the business, according to four elements:

- Employees' knowledge and skills.
- Knowledge and skills integrated into techniques and technical systems, as a result of years of accumulation, coding, and structuring of knowledge held by employees.

- Management systems that establish official and unofficial ways to create and manage knowledge.
- Combinations of the previous three dimensions, related to the value the business assigns to the content and structure of knowledge.

To understand how NPD interacts with core capabilities, and highlight both competitive and complementary perspectives, we can focus on the transition from positive to negative impacts, as it occurs in each organizational dimension.

Knowledge and Skills

If a skill is part of a core capability, it implies the firm has superior technical and professional abilities in relation to that skill, along with the corresponding knowledge background. The idiosyncrasies of high-tech industrial markets also create distinct information processing patterns. High-tech companies increasingly focus on technology commercialization to maintain their competitive advantage. High-tech start-ups that adopt a global perspective from the moment of their creation are also characterized by substantial knowledge that enables them to accelerate their international growth and overcome traditional resource constraints.

The knowledge management discipline has developed in parallel with this global, knowledge-based economy, shifting the emphasis from traditional factors of production (e.g., capital, land, labor) to knowledge. It also features two main perspectives, centered on outcomes (creation, retention, and transfer of knowledge) or on the context (units, relationships among units, knowledge properties). Systematic and effective knowledge management is necessary to avoid knowledge fragmentation and losses of organizational learning. The ability to convert knowledge and information into marketable products and services depends on the type and quality of market relationships that a company can establish. The quality of the company's knowledge tank is directly proportional to the qualifications of the best (elite) employees. Effective knowledge management in turn is a critical determinant of organizations' sustainable, strategic competitive advantages. For example, total quality management can be a useful strategy for fostering learning and increasing a company's competitive advantage.

Learning and Knowledge Transfers

Continuous learning enables companies to overcome path dependency, gain new insights, and reduce the risks of falling into competency traps, all of which can enhance innovation and NPD. The effectiveness of learning for innovation also depends on its interaction with the external environment. Strong learning abilities can stimulate innovation capabilities that support competitive advantages even in turbulent environments. At a basic level, organizational knowledge creation and learning is also embedded in the technology commercialization process. The knowledge economy is characterized by economic globalization, technological advances in industrial and scientific domains, and the progressive primacy of knowledge-intensive and technology-based industrial markets.

The problem—the incompatibility of creating an innovative (high-tech) product with existing core capabilities—starts from a realization: no matter how big a company is, its resources are finite. If the company assigns more resources to retaining staff who support its competitive advantage, it cannot allocate those resources to other operational investments, for example. In turn, a chasm might emerge between the requirements of the environment and the company's existing core capabilities. The marketing department can function as a connective bridge over the chasm, by listening to the needs of consumers and transforming those needs into input to be shared with operational departments (mainly R&D), which can then pursue the creation of products that meet those needs. In high-tech firms, the most esteemed staff are often engineers and scientists, so the marketing department might not receive sufficient attention or resources, which would hinder its ability to bridge the chasm. Ignoring the marketing department disrupts the necessary flow of information.

Because core advantages tend to be renewed and developed in the same direction, marketing executives generally do not regard jobs in high-tech companies as very attractive; they anticipate that their role will be largely ignored. A myopic focus on the existing core competence eventually turns the competence into an obstacle that deters future NPD. This myopia is difficult to recognize internally though, because it is linked to the firm's existing superiority. But for things to stay as they are (superiority), changes are needed (upgrading, innovation).

Tools of the Job

Systems, processes, and tools in general allow for the application of the knowledge and skills of the staff and the firm, ideally in a simple and quickly accessible form. In turn, they can contribute to competitive advantages, if they are created, applied, and enriched by specialized, skilled staff. For example, the sales function of B2B organizations has changed dramatically, largely due to the introduction of information systems. However, some skills and processes contained in these tools can be devalued. Designers of new products may not understand whether and how other systems affect their new products, or where incompatibilities arise. At this subtle turning point, the tools might change, from advantages to obstacles.

Administrative Systems

Effective administrative systems comprise a mixture of unusual skill sets and promote beneficial behaviors that competing companies cannot mimic. Motivation systems that encourage innovative activities are essential and critical features of such systems. However, they can also become tightly sealed or entrenched, preventing the pursuit of opportunities that the systems do not define as necessary or significant. Among industrial organizations, both supplier and customer companies function like professional organizations, staffed by highly qualified personnel at all levels.

Value

The value assigned to the content and the creation of knowledge, as determined by business leaders and integrated into the administrative practices, affects the products under development.

Clearly, (new) products receive tremendous input from core capabilities. Unique abilities could give birth to new products and processes, because creative potential is focused on discovering new opportunities for the application of accumulated knowledge. If NPD requires skills that traditionally have received less weight or respect in the firm, the company's own history becomes an obstruction. For example, the lack of prestige assigned to less technical or non-dominant functions may become a cyclically redundant process that limits their potential contributions to NPD and thus the functional integration and unification processes that often encourage innovation. Consider for example the following issues:

- Who goes to whom. Lower ranking executives usually visit higher ranking ones, which reinforces established prestige but also limits the ability of the higher-prestige executives to learn about work performed among the lower ranking operational departments.
- Self-fulfilling prophecies. Expectations about people's roles and status can lead to their realization, in a sort of Pygmalion effect: one party's expectations of the other affect the latter's actual performance, either positively or negatively.
- Reliability of information sources, which is directly affected by the prestige of the source.
- Differences in the specific vocabulary/terminology used by each group.

Although core capabilities are essential components of success, they can easily transform into obstructive factors for NPD (Figure 13.13). When market conditions change, firms must re-evaluate their unique capabilities too. Routines, procedures, preferences for sources of information, and an entrenched view of the market—all factors related to unique skills—can become obstacles to the recognition of new opportunities, so they must be re-evaluated and re-examined continually.

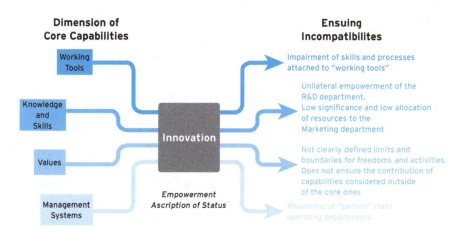

Figure 13.13 Incompatibilities between Core Capabilities and Innovation

Strategic Recommendations to Avoid the Transformation of Core Benefits into Core Rigidities

Cannibalism

Creative destruction or cannibalism can prevent a high-tech company from falling victim to the obstacles involved in the transformation of core capabilities. In a marketing or sales sense, cannibalism refers to a decrease in the sales volumes of a manufactured product, due to replacement sales of a new product from the same company. Most marketers regard cannibalism as something to avoid and an unintended, detrimental consequence of NPD. But cannibalism can also offer a legitimate tool to promote radical product innovation and encourage the long-term viability and success of the company. We propose that cannibalism has a multidimensional structure, with two forms: cannibalism of capital and cannibalism of organizational routines. Capital is tangible, including production lines or equipment; routines are intangible and pertain to things like knowledge, expertise, or access to distribution channels. The success of a new technology may prove destructive in terms of the firm's capital investments in its previous technology. Cannibalism of its organizational routines, including established procedures used to carry out its day-to-day operations and activities, may also stem from their incompatibility with a new technology.

Capital and routines thus offer critical explanatory variables for why companies often are reluctant to cannibalize or creatively destroy. Leading companies in a market usually adopt a skeptical reluctance to embrace or promote radical innovations, due to their well-established investments in capabilities to cover and serve the existing markets. But a company that accepts some cannibalism can adjust and reduce the real or potential value of its investments. A willingness to cannibalize one's own products can allow a company to move forward, by leveraging internal markets, product champions, and a future focus, all of which establish a framework for compensatory benefits of creative self-destruction. To achieve these benefits, a company must compare the benefits of creative destruction, in terms of a future market focus and the company's internal markets, against the costs of destruction for its existing investments in capital and routines.

Cannibalism is especially important for high-tech companies, due to its impact on innovation (Figure 13.14). A willingness to cannibalize might even function as a driving force of innovation, as depicted by S-type technology curves. When a new (T2) technology is in its infancy, the firm can either continue to promote its current technology (T1) or shift to T2. A company that continues to rely on T1 likely has made large-scale, specialized investments in it, so by persisting with T1, it can continue to capitalize on those specialized investments. Changing to T2 requires new investments in the new technology, probably leaving prior investments in T1 obsolete. A company that is reluctant to cannibalize continues using T1 indefinitely, which might allow it to maintain an impression of success, but ultimately, it must confront the realization that the obsolete technology is in decline. By continuing to invest in T1, the firm falls behind in adopting and understanding T2, which otherwise might have contributed to a facilitative environment for radical innovation and NPD. Whereas ongoing commitment to an old technology ultimately can cause a company's decline, a willingness to cannibalize existing technology encourages members of the staff to gain familiarity with and work on new technologies, including radical innovations. Such an atmosphere is more likely to lead to innovation, and it suggests the company's determination to be the first to bring it to the market.

Leaders in a market often are reluctant to cannibalize their specialized investments until it is too late—a tendency that is understandable. Specialized investments lose value once they are no longer implemented, and leaders in high-tech markets by definition make many specialized investments, such as result from their long-term trials and the employment of senior executives who have linked their career with the trajectory of the company and devoted their painstaking and time-consuming efforts to its success along that current path. These strong professional and personal bonds may lead to somewhat irrational or at least less than optimal decisions.

The history of innovation also shows that a new innovation like T2 is rarely introduced to the market by the leaders or administrators of T1; rather, it comes from some other entity, often from outside the focal industry. Late entrants also tend to overtake pioneers in various markets, because they can exploit the innovator's NPD efforts, then overtake it with improved products.

According to the cross-elasticity of demand theory, the percentage change in the price of product A might depend on the percentage change in the price of product B, depending on whether those products are independent, supplementary, or substitutes. If they are perfect substitutes, a reduction in the price of product A reduces the quantity demanded of product B, *ceteris paribus*. In reality though, other factors nearly always inform this link, including not just price but also the physical characteristics of the product, its advantages, or alternative ways of promoting it. From the perspective of this economic theory then, income earned through cannibalism is redistributed, because some of it came from income that would have been earned with the substitute product. In turn, economists propose that profit losses due to cannibalized products should be accounted for as part of the costs of the new product.

Another perspective on cannibalism classifies it as either expected (planned) or unexpected, as might result from poor management of the NPD process. The planned type is a legitimate and even necessary solution for businesses, as an alternative to losing customers who choose to turn to other suppliers by changing their offering and ensuring those customers continue to buy from them, even if they buy different products.

Especially in high-tech environments, the need for cannibalism often arises because high-tech products compete for a specific, short time period as the cutting-edge technology, then are promptly replaced by newer versions. Thus, in high-tech markets, the benefits of economies of scale or experience curves diminish, even to the point of non-existence, and each milestone achieved is rapidly devalued. Whether a company wants to cannibalize or not, its cutting-edge high-tech product will become devalued by time $t + \ldots$. Instead of letting competitors steal market share, by ignoring new developments or insisting on maintaining investments in the current technology, a successful company will overcome and devalue its existing cutting-edge technology on its own, leading to the next version. Doing so requires recognition of the harsh reality that the value of their specialized investments disappears and they must become cannibals to retain or even gain more market share. If the company does not cannibalize, it will lose out to competitors that have introduced the next cutting-edge technology.

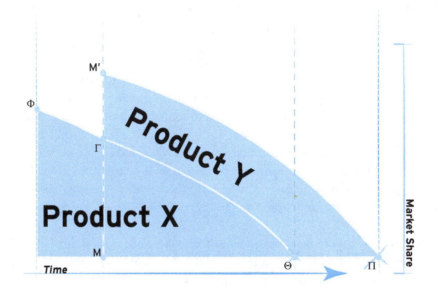

Figure 13.14   Differential Advantage of Cannibalism

Corporate Imagination

Another strategic tactic to avoid core benefits from becoming significant obstacles involves corporate imagination and creativity. Many companies whose success relies on innovative NPD use the percentage of the contribution of innovation as an indication of success. We define corporate imagination as an ability to create a vision for the future, including markets that do not yet exist, beyond the rigidity of prevailing conditions. When companies can imagine, define, and build new markets, they can compete more effectively, beyond just reducing production costs and so forth. For such efforts, corporate imagination is a necessary prerequisite, because the company strives to create a new competitive space, which means the opportunities that it pursues must move beyond the limits of current markets, to exploit some significant new benefit, create a new competitive space, or reshape an existing one. However, implementing the outcomes of corporate imagination also demands the existence of a logical process for identifying and exploring the novel competitive spaces, then consolidating control and dominance over the emerging market opportunities. Corporate imagination consists of the four main components depicted in Figure 13.15.

Figure 13.15 Components of Corporate Imagination

Companies operating in high-tech, knowledge-based industrial markets should rely on their own internal resources but also develop external relationships and networks to complement their knowledge domains and develop innovations faster and more effectively. Seller–buyer and interorganizational network interactions are essential for NPD in technology-based industrial markets. An emerging innovation management strategy, known as collaborative or open innovation, entails knowledge management efforts that pursue innovation, knowledge, and intellectual capital exploration, retention, and exploitation both within and outside the company's boundaries.

A stumbling block to corporate imagination, similar to that we described previously, is the often myopic perspective on emerging opportunities, relative to exploiting current markets. Shifting focus to exploiting potential opportunities is likely to affect existing profits, and if the company finds this risk sufficiently problematic, it may halt its efforts to develop the corporate imagination and ignore future opportunities.

Furthermore, corporate imagination often is most successful when it involves the decomposition of a product into its functional features, then a reorganization of these features in a way that gives rise to the discovery of a new product that can satisfy needs that have not been sufficiently covered. Awareness of market needs is rare enough; the number of companies with the corporate imagination capacities to transform these needs into new products is tiny.

Change in Yield/Price Ratio

To some extent, a strategic approach that prefers marginal changes to existing products is understandable, because it may enable the firm to continue to serve existing customers by offering them easy-to-understand, readily adoptable improvements to the technologies they already use. But given finite resources, firms need to invest time, money, and effort in new products that address new situations, which entail different performance assumptions. In S curves, marginal changes in products and their underlying technologies offer short-term benefits, and the utility they offer customers has less influence than would a new technology.

According to Moore's law, every 18 months or so, marginal improvements in technology lead to a reduction by half of any given technology's performance. However, this law seemingly may be approaching its natural limit. The marginal cost of improving existing technology also continues to grow as that technology approaches the natural end of its functional life, so the need to develop new technology proactively is great. Executives often assume the yield/price ratio is linear, which may discourage the pursuit of radical innovation. However, the Ministry of International Trade and Industry of Japan has invested $30 million in the radical innovation of neural networks and quantum physics, in an effort to change the current status of the yield/price ratio. Companies that refuse to challenge the yield/price ratio use an existing product as the sole starting point for their NPD process.

New technologies are often introduced by "paratroopers" who parachute in from external sectors (Cooper & Schendel, 1976). They are able to sneak in due to the myopia that makes it difficult for existing companies to envision and create new, advanced technologies. This voluntary blindness is widespread; resistance to change can be excused by cost justifications and dedication to already devalued products, then reinforced by ignorance or underestimations of the threat of new technologies coming from unfamiliar, innovative paratrooper firms.

Escape from Market Tyranny

Market tyranny results from a myopic view, adopted by many established companies, focused only on producing specialized solutions for customers using the current technology. This view precludes any possibility of those needs being addressed in radically different ways. Such market tyranny then creates a space for paratroopers to enter, from outside the existing, tyrannized market. These new entrants challenge the rules of the game and propose new technology.

Array of Benefits

Regard the business as a benefit bundle, which constitutes the best way to expand the opportunities horizon of the business. If executives cannot see beyond the limits of the current market they serve, they will miss out on opportunities that result from combining the available skills across different parts of their business. Therefore, they should propose investigating the transparent boundaries that lie between the products of their companies.

Empathic Planning

As an expression of corporate imagination, some companies try to guide and encourage consumers to articulate their unrealized needs. Technical superiority is useless if it does not fulfill consumers' needs. To embrace such a customer-oriented approach, the company also should establish multifunctional teams and procedures to inform customers about emerging technological possibilities. Using this concept, we might categorize companies as those that:

1   Ask customers what they want and attract repeat followers. Many companies have become so familiar and reliant on certain marketing approaches that they recognize effective combinations of features for new products. However, such an approach is limited to insights based on currently available market data.

2   Push customers, even if just temporarily, in new directions they did not want to go. Especially in high-tech environments, even if the goal is to be close to the customer and listen to their wishes, many customers cannot articulate their needs in relation to truly innovative new products. Therefore, they need feasible guidance, so that they can experiment with new products, moving beyond the limits of their prior experiences and ability to envision alternative options.

3   Facilitate and guide customers to go where they want, even if the customers did not consciously realize that desire. This empathetic design approach demands both conventional marketing knowledge and deep insights into potential needs arising from customers' expectations and lifestyles, using techniques borrowed from anthropology and information gathered by monitoring consumer behavior in a particular environment. Such techniques can reveal needs and problems that consumers are dealing with but that they do not consider as problems that might be solved.

Although some of these approaches are somewhat novel, they still require some input from traditional marketing research methods. Innovations that can reshape markets or industry boundaries, by creating new competitive spaces, tend to arise if a firm can replace its conventional view of customer service or products with a matrix of customer needs and its own operational features.

Missionary Marketing

Creating markets and entering them before competitors is risky; the desired new market might not emerge, or it might take longer than expected (Figure 13.16). Initial entrants have an imperfect ability to understand the situation and make accurate, quick decisions. Even careful market research related to new products remains frequently inaccurate, leading to under- or overestimates of emerging opportunities. To minimize this risk, a company might prefer to be a follower, rather than enter the new market first, waiting until it feels confident its product offer has superior value relative to the pioneer's. This method enables the firm to avoid first-mover problems, but it also cannot enjoy first-mover advantages. Pioneers in a market often gain a rapid leadership position, and if it can address the challenges of entering a new market, it likely will consolidate this competitively superior leadership position, effectively barring the entry of competitors.

In contrast, if the company determines to gain a clear understanding of the market as soon as possible, it might undertake a series of low-cost, fast-paced market excursions to map the new market, in an approach known as missionary marketing. With a sequence of successive efforts, the firm seeks to anticipate the direction the market will take, in terms of the specific combination of functional product features that offer value to customers, as well as its distance from a current market (e.g., technical and other difficulties to be overcome, right combination of price and performance). Speed is of the essence, so even as the company pursues deep insights into price and performance demands, it simultaneously reorganizes and reshapes its product offer. In turn, through missionary marketing, the company increases the number of market opportunities, niches, and product combinations that it explores, thus acquiring more market knowledge that it can exploit in its NPD.

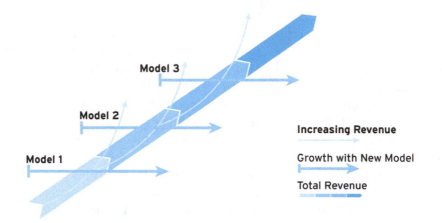

Figure 13.16   Missionary Marketing Incursions

Vignette

Technology-Mindset Interaction in New Product Development

In foundational B2B marketing discourses, innovation often pertains primarily to new product development. But B2B marketers also need to consider value propositions, beyond exploiting novel technologies or proposing new physical products that stem from business model innovation. Ringberg et al. (2019) suggest that marketers' first priority should be to establish mindset determinism in a way that orients the entire firm toward innovation, rather than remaining satisfied with incremental innovations based on existing technologies and operations.

Consider Kodak, once one of the most valuable brands in the world, which failed to embrace digital technology, despite having been involved in its conception, and instead chose to maintain its focus on existing markets and customers for traditional cameras and film. This decision likely led to the brand's collapse (Lucas & Goh, 2009); we argue that it also represents an example of a managerial mindset determinism, including a myopic view of end users and a refusal to pursue innovation with potentially complementary actors such as mobile phone manufacturers and social media platforms.

Other B2B firms have evolved successfully though, such as HS Markit. With a radical mindset toward innovation, a careful evolution process, and a thoughtful acquisition strategy, it both developed and acquired dynamic capabilities to shift from expertise in handling microfilm and hard-copy data to a world-leading data analytics and solutions firm. Yet it also is telling that many influential firms in the new economy began as start-ups, rather than evolving out of the old economy. DocuSign spotted an opportunity in the legal industry for platform-facilitated, secure signature authentication and contract facilitation, and it now leads this specialized but global market.

Exploratory innovation—rather than incremental, exploitative innovation (Jansen et al., 2005)—can occur through the exploration of new disruptive technology but also as a result of a radical mindset innovation by individual members of a firm. For the firm to exploit the identified opportunities fully though, such a mindset must also be embedded in the firm's leadership. According to Ringberg et al. (2019, p. 104), radical mindset innovation "springs from managers' sensemaking of new business models and the creative use of existing artifacts, such as technology" (Figure 13.17). It requires a shift, from a reliance on ordinary capabilities to the development of dynamic leadership capabilities that enable the firm to sense, seize, and reconfigure to exploit opportunities (Schoemaker et al., 2018). Many of the most dominant firms in the new economy (e.g., Facebook, Amazon, eBay) emerged from both an initial radical mindset by their founders and an active effort to leverage technological innovations, which produced innovative business models. Ringberg et al. (2019) also propose two routes to radical innovation: exploitation or exploration of technology or else radical mindset innovation. If they seek to achieve new product development, B2B marketers must address both the mindset of key decision-makers in the firm and the technologies that can be created by product and technological specialists.

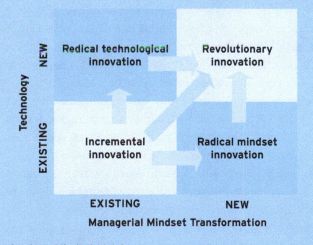

Figure 13.17 Technology Mindset Matrix

Source: Ringberg et al. (2019, p. 104)

Innovative Culture in High-Tech Enterprises

Even if companies pursue innovation, they also engage in bureaucratic processes, which tend to filter out potential new products, based on the application of formalized plans and procedures. This process tends to appear analytical and logical, and it conflicts with the non-linear, unexpected elements that define innovation. Therefore, instead of a step-by-step filtering process, innovation should be subjected to an internal environment, stemming from a broader business process that favors innovation and an entrepreneurial spirit. Several corporate features can help establish an innovation-friendly climate:

1   The company recognizes a need in the market, due to its organizational strategy.
2   The initial roles and responsibilities of key players are not defined precisely but instead emerge and are clarified as strategies evolve.
3   The process of filtering ideas relies on unofficial bodies with access to the skills of engineers and marketing executives, not official administrative procedures.
4   Communication takes place less through prescribed organizational channels and more through informal channels.
5   Commitment to the idea is reinforced by product champions.

Executives who create, define, or adopt an innovation, and are willing to take significant risks to achieve it, are product champions. Often referred to as mavericks or crusaders, they break the rules to transform companies and take risks. Due to their strong commitment, they work tirelessly, behind the scenes, to secure resources for implementing the ideas. In turn, as a result of their strong motives, aggressive claims, technical skills, and market knowledge, they remain unaffected by any resistance to cannibalism at the organizational level. A creative organizational culture promotes their influence, and top management should actively support them.

A climate of innovation might also be encouraged by relevant incentives and time allocations. Some companies share some percentage of the potential profits of an innovation with the employees responsible for it, but they should avoid punishing ideas that fail. Failure is a necessary part of the creative process and often the basis for subsequent, greater success.

Creating such a climate is difficult, especially for large organizations, so some firms designate a separate team to work on innovative ideas, even moving the team to a different physical location. The idea underlying this tactic is that innovations result from going against the organization, not adopting its staid approach. But separating the innovation team can create problems too. For a company that wants to become and remain truly innovative, mechanisms must be added to allow for expansive creativity, even within the daily routines and functional processes of the company. That is, an innovative culture must be able to flourish without special protection mechanisms. Nor is shifting innovation-related organizational skills to separate spaces in line with the protection of new ventures. Such "orphan" groups might suffer from creative isolation, as well as a lack of access for sharing and promoting their new ideas to the company hierarchy. Still, even if the ideal would be to create the conditions for innovation throughout all the processes of the organization, a large, well-established, bureaucratic firm might require such an approach to ensure its survival as it attempts to change its conditions to become more broadly creative.

Composition of Strategic Approaches/Cultural Approaches

Figure 13.18 depicts processes by which competitive core advantages transform into disadvantages: the P1 and P2 curves both exhibit positive slopes at first, which become negative after peaks (at max P1 and max P2). These curves represent an implicit series of eight steps related to core advantages in high-tech markets:

1 From point O (dividing line between core competencies/basic rigidities) to point A, P1 has a positive slope. The product exerts an impact on the market, which is made up of innovators. The small slope reflects the limited suitability of core competencies for meeting the needs that the technology seeks to cover. In addition, the factors that constitute the main components of the three uncertainty factors (fear, uncertainty, and doubt, cf. Moore, 1995 and 1999) have not been completely clarified.

2 From point A to point B, the curve breaks, depicting the chasm that results from uncertainty in high-tech markets; it is the distance between early customers (visionaries, early adopters) and pragmatist customers who represent the critical number or share needed to ensure the success of the product/technology. This chasm is also an indicator of the chances of the technology's success. The three types of uncertainty define the discontinuity. Failure to overcome them produces a negative slope. Transition speed to pragmatist customers is also relevant, because this variable informs uncertainties. Therefore, firms prefer to make the distance from A to B as small as possible (reflecting three groups of uncertainty) and the transition across this gap as short as possible (achieved with core capabilities).

3 Moving from point B to max P1, core capabilities should evoke positive results once the chasm has been overcome. The P1 slope is more positive due to spiraling adoption (increasing benefits at increasing rate) of technology/core capabilities and their positively correlated sizes.

4 Points I and K in the positive part (B-Max P1) of P1 represent missionary marketing. The introduction of marginal improvements and the estimation of the public's response (feedback), along with assessments of proposed improvements facilitated by core capabilities help the firm approach good strategic fit between the technology and the need it aims to satisfy, through more efficient exploitation of core capabilities.

5 After this max point, decline occurs, as a result of a myopic view of needs satisfaction (market tyranny), involving only current needs and the same technology. The magnitude of the slope is proportional to the slope of the S1 technology curve. If max P1 corresponds to max S1 (the natural limit of technology), the negative slope of P1 thereafter will be sharper, because core advantages weaken at a rapidly increasing rate

due to the rapid technological devaluation of S1. If max P1 corresponds to an ascending part of the S1 curve though, the core capabilities will tend to decrease (S2 technology is in its infancy) but at a slower rate, because S1 has not yet reached its natural limit.

6   From point H to point Z, all core capabilities have become core rigidities in the constantly changing, dynamic, unstable environments, preventing further innovative growth over time. The core capabilities reflect consistent preferences for existing and known technologies, routines, practices, norms, values, culture, and prestige, so they consolidate a specific view, used improperly to assess new events too. Leveraging its old (successful) recipe for success, the firm tries to translate signals, ideas, and facts into implementable, useful, acceptable innovations. But this effort, in a dynamic environment, represents a form of voluntary blindness and ultimately leads to negative performance outcomes.

7   Regarding points N and Θ, the former is located in the ascending part of the P curve, while Θ is in the descending part. They represent a potential transition, for the new S2 technology and the P2 curve. If N is projected at some point on P2 before the P2 gap (in the presence of a new core competencies framework), the company restarts the course, encounters the P2 gap, and has also destroyed its core capabilities while P1 was still increasing (positive slope). As the first company to introduce the new technology though, it can reap the advantages of being first to market (assuming it bridges the P2 gap). If N instead is projected at a point on P2 after the chasm, it still exploits its core competencies for P1, does not need to bridge the chasm (and also is not forged by it), and loses the first-mover advantage. As a follower though, it might learn to adapt the technology and take advantage of feedback on the competitor's actions. Regarding Θ, depending on its promotion in P2, the company probably becomes a "me-too" follower, for which the transition to a new core skills framework might be easier, because conditions will have matured (P1 is in decline). Finally, a transition from any point of P1 to P2 presupposes the destruction of existing (P1) core capabilities, to a degree proportional to the distance of P1 from the horizontal axis. A perfect distance is possible, such that the course continues along the entire length of P1 (or as long as there are positive financial results or clear reasons), in parallel with a restructuring of core competencies along the course of P2. Such an ideal development minimizes risk and enables both sustainable leadership and development.

8   Point M, or the intersection of P1 and P2, indicates that the new technology has been introduced and largely replaced the old one. To the right of point M, the difference between the old and new framework of core capabilities is increasing, due to the simultaneous presence of a negative slope in P1 and a positive slope in P2.

Finally, for P2, the preceding analysis and comparison exists relative to some P3. However, its max is higher than that of P1 because (even given the positive magnitude of the effect of the core capabilities) the new S2 technology offers better performance than S1. Thus, based on their multiplier (spiraling) relationship, the performance of the (new) core competencies increases. Finally, the S-curves represent well-known technology curves; the lines parallel with the time axis show the technological and physical limits beyond which a technology cannot be improved, even marginally. We also note a mismatch of the chasm with the discontinuity in S, because the technology might be abandoned in response to the factors that add to the uncertainty of the technology.

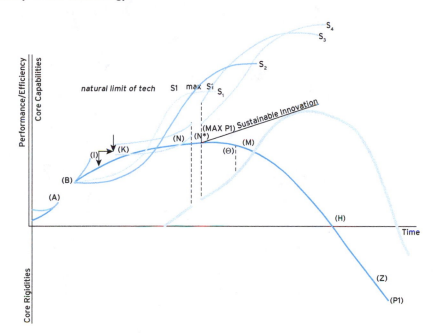

Figure 13.18 Composition of Strategic Approaches/Cultural Approaches

BIBLIOGRAPHY

Aaboen, L., Laage-Hellman, J., Lind, F., Öberg, C., and Shih, T. (2016), "Exploring the roles of university spin-offs in business networks," *Industrial Marketing Management*, 59, 157–166.

Abell, D.F. (1980), *Defining the Business: The Starting Point of Strategic Planning*, Englewood Cliffs, NJ: Prentice Hall.

Abernathy, W.J., and Utterback, J.M. (1978), "Patterns of industrial innovation," *Technology Review*, 64(7), 40–47.

Abratt, R., and Pitt, L.F. (1985), "Pricing practices in two industries," *Industrial Marketing Management*, 14(4), 301–306.

Achillas, C., Aidonis, D., Bochtis, D., and Folinas, D. (2018), *Green Supply Chain Management*, 1st edition, Abingdon: Routledge.

Age, L.J. (2011), "Business maneuvering: A model of B2B selling processes," *Management Decision*, 49(9), 1574–1591.

Albernathy, J.W., and Wayne, K. (1974), "Limits of the learning curve," *Harvard Business Review*, 52(5), 109–119.

Alegre, J., and Chiva, R. (2008), "Assessing the impact of organizational learning capability on product innovation performance: An empirical test," *Technovation*, 28(6), 315–326.

Allen, P. (1977), "Psychology of the buying decision," *Purchasing and Supply Management*, December, 10–12.

American Marketing Association (2022). Definition of advertising. Retrieved 8 July 2022 from www.ama.org/topics/advertising/.

Ames, B.C. (1968), "Marketing planning for industrial products," *Harvard Business Review*, 46(5), 100–111.

Ames, B.C. (1970), "Trappings vs trappings substance in industrial marketing," *Harvard Business Review*, 48(4), 93–102.

Anderson, E., Chu, W., and Weitz, B. (1987), "Industrial purchasing: An empirical exploration of the buyclass framework," *Journal of Marketing*, 51(3), 71–86.

Anderson, H.B. (1988), *Professional Sales Management*, 2nd edition, Columbus, OH: McGraw-Hill International Editions.

Anderson, J.C., and Narus, J.A. (1990), "A model of distributor firm and manufacturer firm working partnerships," *Journal of Marketing*, 54(1), 42–58.

Anderson, J.C., and Narus, J.A. (1999), *Business Market Management: Understanding, Creating, and Delivering Value*, Upper Saddle River, NJ: Pearson Prentice Hall.

Anderson, J.C., Narus, J.A., and Narayandas, D. (2009), *Business Market Management: Understanding, Creating and Delivering Value*, 3rd edition, Upper Saddle River, NJ: Prentice Hall.

Andreae, D. (2011), "General systems theory: Contributions to social work theory and practice—Social work treatment," *Interlocking Theoretical Approaches*, 5, 242–254.

Ansoff, I., and McDonnell, E. (1990), *Implanting Strategic Management*, 2nd edition, Hemel Hempstead: Prentice Hall International (UK).

Antonopoulos, A.M., and Wood, G. (2018), *Mastering Ethereum: Building Smart Contracts and DApps*, Sebastopol: O'Reilly Media.

Asoko Insight (2021), *Uganda's Floriculture Industry*. Retrieved 2 August 2021 from www.asokoin-sight.com/content/market-insights/uganda-floriculture-industry.

Athaide, G.A., and Zhang, J.Q. (2011), "The determinants of seller–buyer interactions during new product development in technology-based industrial markets," *Journal of Product Innovation Management*, 28(s1), 146–158.

Avlonitis, G., and Indounas, K. (2004), "The impact of market structure on pricing objectives of service firms," *Journal of Product and Brand Management*, 13(5), 343–358.

Avlonitis, G.J., and Karayanni, D.A. (2000), "The impact of Internet use on business-to-business marketing: Examples from American and European companies," *Industrial Marketing Management*, 29(5), 441–459.

Avlonitis, G.J., and Panagopoulos, N.G. (2005), "Antecedents and consequences of CRM technology acceptance in the sales force," *Industrial Marketing Management*, 34(4, Special Issue), 355–368.

Avlonitis, G., Dimitriadis, S., and Intounas, K. (2015), *Strategic Industrial Marketing*, Athens: Rosili Publications.

Avlonitis, G., Gounaris, S., and Papavasileiou, N. (2008), *Industrial Market Marketing and Sales Management*, Patras: Hellenic Open University—EAP.

Avlonitis, I.G. (2001), *Strategic Industrial Marketing*, 2nd edition, Athens: Stamouli Publications.

Avlonitis, I.G., and Gounaris, S. (1999), *Marketing I: Industrial Marketing*, Patras: Hellenic Open University—EAP.

Avlonitis, I.G., and Stathakopoulos, M.B. (1997), *Effective Organization and Sales Management*, Athens: Stamouli Publications.

Avlonitis, V., Frandsen, T., Hsuan, J., and Karlsson, C. (2014), *Driving Competitiveness through Servitization*, Copenhagen: CBS Competitiveness Platform.

Backhaus, K. (2003), *Industriegütermarketing, 7, erweiterte und überarbeitete Auflage*. München: Verlag Franz Vahlen GmbH.

Bae, J., Lund-Thomsen, P., and Lindgreen, A. (2021), "Global value and supplier perceptions of corporate social responsibility: A case study of garment manufacturers in Myanmar," *Global Networks*, 21(4), 653–680.

Bag, S., Gupta, S., Kumar, A., and Sivarajah, U. (2021), "An integrated artificial intelligence framework for knowledge creation and B2B marketing rational decision making for improving firm performance," *Industrial Marketing Management*, 92, 178–189.

Bahar, V.S., Nenonen, S., and Starr, R.G. (2021), "From channel integration to platform integration: Capabilities required in hospitality," *Industrial Marketing Management*, 94, 19–40.

Baines, T.S., Lightfoot, H.W., Benedettini, O., and Kay, J.M. (2009), "The servitization of manufacturing: A review of literature and reflection on future challenges," *Journal of Manufacturing Technology Management*, 20(5), 547–567.

Baker, N.R., Winkofsky, E.P., Langmeyer, L., and Sweeney, D.J. (1980), "Idea generations: A procrustean bed of variables, hypotheses, and implications," in B.V. Dean and J.L. Goldhar (eds.), *TIMS Studies in the Management Sciences*, Vol. 15, Amsterdam: North-Holland Publishing.

Balliaris, G.P. (2001), *Introduction to Marketing*, 3rd edition, Athens: Stamouli Publications.

Ballou, R. (1999), *Business Logistics Management: Planning, Organizing, and Controlling the Supply Chain*, New York: Prentice Hall.

Baltas, G. (2004–2005), *Sales Promotion, Notes*, Athens: Athens University of Economics and Business.

Becker, M.C., and Lillemark, M. (2006), "Marketing/R&D integration in the pharmaceutical industry," *Research Policy*, 35(1), 105–120.

Behnam, T., and Walleigh, R. (1997), "Defining next generation products: An inside look," *Harvard Business Review*, 75(6), 116–124.

Beldoch, M. (1964), *Sensitivity to Expression of Emotional Meaning in Three Modes of Communication: The Communication of Emotional Meaning*, New York: McGraw-Hill.

Bellizzi, J.A. (1981), "Organizational size and buying influences," *Industrial Marketing Management*, 10(1), 17–21.

Berry, L.L. (1980), "Services marketing is different," *Business*, 30(3), 24–29.

Bert, G.S.J. (1972), *Integrated Marketing*, London: Pelican Books.

Bessant, J., Öberg, C., and Trifilova, A. (2014), "Framing problems in radical innovation," *Industrial Marketing Management*, 43(8), 1284–1292.

Beswick, C.A., and Cravens, D.W. (1977), "A multistage decision model for salesforce management," *Journal of Marketing Research*, 14(2), 135–144.

Beverland, M.B., and Lindgreen, A. (2007), "Implementing market orientation in industrial firms: A multiple case study," *Industrial Marketing Management*, 36(4), 430–442.

Beverland, M., Lindgreen, A., Napoli, J., Roberts, J., and Merrilees, B. (2007), "Multiple roles of brands in business-to-business services," *Journal of Business & Industrial Marketing*, 22(6), 410–417.

Beverland, M., Napoli, J., and Lindgreen, A. (2007), "Industrial global brand leadership: A capabilities view," *Industrial Marketing Management*, 36(8), 1084–1093.

Biemans, W.G., Brencic Maja, M., and Malshe, A. (2010), "Marketing–sales interface configurations in B2B firms," *Industrial Marketing Management*, 39(2), 183–194.

Bjerre, M. (2021), Interview with Henrik Larsen, CPO, A.P. Møller-Mærsk Group.

Bjerre, M., and Jensen, P.A. (2017), *The Danish Customer-Centricity Index*, Copenhagen: Confederation of Danish Industry.

Bjerre, M., and Ulrich, T. (2021), *Sales Governance: The Future of Sales Management*, Copenhagen: The Value Footprint.

Bjerre, M., Johansen-Duus, H., and Ulrich, T. (2019), *Virksomheder kan sælge mere, hvis de gør som et Tour de France-hold*. Retrieved 16 June 2022 from https://videnskab.dk/forskerzonen/kultur-samfund/virksomheder-kan-saelge-mere-hvis-de-goer-som-et-tour-de-france-hold.

Blattberg, R.C., Kim, B.D., and Neslin, S.A. (2008), "Why database marketing?," in *Database Marketing*. New York: Springer.

Blois, K.J. (1970), "The effect of subjective factors, on customer/supplier relations in industrial marketing," *European Journal of Marketing*, 4(1), 18–21.

Blois, K.J. (1977), "Large customers and their suppliers," *European Journal of Marketing*, 11(4), 281–290.

Blois, K.J., and Ivens, B. (2006), "Measuring relational norms: Some methodological issues," *European Journal of Marketing*, 40(3/4), 352–365.

Bollinger, A.S., and Smith, R.D. (2001), "Managing organizational knowledge as a strategic asset," *Journal of Knowledge Management*, 5(1), 8–18.

Bonfield, M.E.H., and Speh, T.W. (1977), "Purchasing's role in industry," *Journal of Purchasing and Materials Management*, 13(1), 10–17.

Bonoma, T.V. (1979), "A general theory of interaction applied to sales management," in R.P. Bagozzi (ed.), *Sales Management: New Developments from Behavioral and Decision Model Research*, Cambridge, MA: Marketing Science Institute.

Bonoma, T.V., and Johnson, W.J. (1978), "The social psychology of industrial buying and selling," *Industrial Marketing Management*, 7(4), 213–223.

Booms, B.H., and Bitner, M.J. (1982), "Marketing services by managing the environment," *Cornell Hospitality Quarterly*, 23(1), 35–40.

Booz, E., Allen, J. and Hamilton, C. (1968), *Management of New Products*, New York: Booz, Allen and Hamilton.

Booz, E., Allen, J. and Hamilton, C. (1982), *New Product Management for the 1980s*, New York: Booz, Allen and Hamilton.

Borg, E.A. (2009), "The marketing of innovations in high-technology companies: A network approach," *European Journal of Marketing*, 43(3–4), 364–370.

Boulding, W., Morgan, R., and Staelin, R. (1997), "Pulling the plug to stop the new product drain," *Journal of Marketing Research*, 34(1), 164–176.

Bourne, F.S. (1959), "Group influence in marketing and public relations," in R. Likert and S. Hayes (eds.), *Some Applications of Behavioral Research*, New York: UNESCO Publications.

Bowersox, D., Closs, D., Cooper, M., and Bowersox, J. (2009), *Supply Chain Logistics Management*, New York: McGraw-Hill.

Brandenburger, A.M., and Nalebuff, B.J. (1997), *Co-opetition*, New York: Currency Doubleday.

Brandenburger, A.M., and Stuart Jr., H.W. (1996), "Value-based business strategy," *Journal of Economics & Management Strategy*, 5(1), 5–24.

Brennan, R., and Croft, R. (2012), "The use of social media in B2B marketing and branding: An exploratory study," *Journal of Customer Behaviour*, 11(2), 101–115.

Brennan, R., and Turnbull, P. (1995), "Adaptations in buyer–seller relationships," *Proceedings of the 11th Annual IMP International Conference*, Manchester, 7–9 September.

Brennan, R., Canning, L., and McDowell, R. (2014), *Business-to-Business Marketing*, 3rd edition, Los Angeles, CA: SAGE Publications.

Brettel, M., Heinemann, F., Engelen, A., and Neubauer, S. (2011), "Cross-functional integration of R&D, marketing, and manufacturing in radical and incremental product innovations and its effects on project effectiveness and efficiency," *Journal of Product Innovation Management*, 28(2), 251–269.

Brockner, J., and Rubin, J.Z. (1985), *Entrapment in Escalating Conflicts: A social-psychological Analysis*, New York: Springer Verlag.

Brown, W., and Jaques, E. (1964), *Product Analysis Pricing*, London: Heinemann.

Bruhn, M., Schoenmueller, V., and Schäfer, D.B. (2012), "Are social media replacing traditional media in terms of brand equity creation?," *Management Research Review*, 35(9), 770–790.

Bryan Jean, R.J., Sinkovics, R.R., and Kim, D. (2008), "Information technology and organizational performance within international business to business relationships: A review and an integrated conceptual framework," *International Marketing Review*, 25(5), 563–583.

Bukhari, S.S. (2011), "GM and its impact on consumer behavior," *European Journal of Business and Management*, 3(4), 375–383.

Bunn, M.D. (1993), "Taxonomy of buying decision approaches," *Journal of Marketing*, 57, 38–56.

Bunn, M.D., Butaney, G.T., and Huffman, N.P. (2001), "An empirical model of professional buyers' search effort," *Journal of Business-to-Business Marketing*, 8(4), 55–81.

Burgelman, R.A. (1983), "Corporate entrepreneurship and strategic management: Insights from a process study," *Management Science*, 29(12), 1349–1364.

Burrows, P. (2000), "Computers and chips," *Business Week*, 10 January, 92–93.

Cady, J.F. (1982), "Reasonable rules and rules of reason: Vertical restrictions on distributors," *Journal of Marketing*, 46(3), 27–37.

Candi, M., and Kahn, K.B. (2016), "Functional, emotional, and social benefits of new B2B services," *Industrial Marketing Management*, 57, 177–184.

Capon, N., and Glazer, R. (1987), "Marketing and technology: A strategic coalignment," *The Journal of Marketing*, 51(3), 1–14.

Cardozo, R. (1983), "Modeling organizational buying as a sequence of decisions," *Industrial Marketing Management*, 12, 75.

Carroll, A.B. (1991), "The pyramid of corporate social responsibility: Toward the moral management of organizational stakeholders," *Business Horizons*, 34(4), 39–48.

Cavusgil, S.T., Yeoh, P.L., and Mitri, M. (1995), "Selecting foreign distributors: An expert systems approach," *Industrial Marketing Management*, 24(4), 297–304.

CGTN (2020), Uganda's flower sector to grow as China's appetite for cut flowers increases. Available at: https://www.youtube.com/watch?v=9oPxrL_45Ns.

Chamblee, R., and Sandler, D. (1992), "Business-to-business advertising: Which layout style works best," *Journal of Advertising Research*, 32, 39–46.

Chan, F.T.S. (2003), "Interactive selection model for supplier selection process: An analytical hierarchy process approach," *International Journal of Production Research*, 42(21), 4457–4474.

Chan, H.K., He, H., and Wang, W.Y. (2012), "Green marketing and its impact on supply chain management in industrial markets," *Industrial Marketing Management*, 41(4), 557–562.

Chandy, R.K., and Tellis, G.J. (1998), "Organizing for radical product innovation: The overlooked role of willingness to cannibalize," *Journal of Marketing Research*, 35(4), 474–487.

Channon, D. (1982), "Industrial structure," *Long Range Planning*, 15(5), 78–93.

Charter, M. (1992), *Greener Marketing: A Responsible Approach to Business*, Sheffield: Greenleaf Publishing.

Chen, G., Xie, P., Dong, J., and Wang, T. (2019), "Understanding programmatic creative: The role of AI," *Journal of Advertising*, 48(4), 347–355.

Chesbrough, H. (2007), "Why companies should have open business models," *MIT Sloan Management Review*, 48(2), 22–28.

Chesbrough, H. (2010), "Business model innovation: Opportunities and barriers," *Long Range Planning*, 43(2–3), 354–363.

Chisnall, P.M. (1985), *Marketing: A Behavioural Analysis*, Maidenhead: McGraw-Hill.

Chisnall, P.M. (1989), *Strategic Industrial Marketing*, Hemel Hempstead: Prentice Hall.

Chisnall, P.M. (1995), *Strategic Business Marketing*, 3rd edition, Englewood Cliffs, NJ: Prentice Hall.

Chopra, S., and Meindi, P. (2001), *Supply Chain Management: Strategy, Planning and Operation*, Englewood Cliffs, NJ: Prentice Hall.

Christopher, M. (2015), *Logistics & Supply Chain Management*, 5th edition, Harlow: Pearson Education.

Churchill, G.A., and Iacobucci, D. (2006), *Marketing Research: Methodological Foundation*, New York: Dryden Press.

Churchman, C.W. (1968), *The Systems Approach*, New York: Delacorte Press.

Clark, C. (1940), *The Conditions of Economic Progress*, London: Macmillan.

Clark, K.B. (1985), "The interaction of design hierarchies and market concepts in technological evolution," *Research Policy*, 14, 235–251.

Clarke III, I., and Flaherty, T.B. (2003), "Web-based B2B portals," *Industrial Marketing Management*, 32(1), 15–23.

Coe, J.M. (2004), "The integration of direct marketing and field sales to form a new B2B sales coverage model," *Journal of Interactive Marketing*, 18(2), 62–74.

Cooke, E.F. (1986), "What is business and industrial marketing?," *Journal of Business and Industrial Marketing*, 1(1), 9–17.

Cooper, A.C., and Schendel, D. (1976), "Strategic responses to technological threats," *Business Horizons*, 19(1), 61–69.

Cooper, R.C., and Kapian, R.S. (1991), "Profit priorities from activity-based costing," *Harvard Business Review*, 69(3), 130–135.

Cooper, R.G., and Kleinschmidt, E.J. (1986), "An investigation into the new product process," *Journal of Product Innovation Management*, 3, 71–85.

Copeland, M.T. (1924), *Principles of Merchandising*, Chicago, IL: A.W. Shaw.

Corey, E.R. (1976), *Industrial Marketing: Cases and Concepts*, 2nd edition, Englewood Cliffs, NJ: Prentice Hall International.

Corey, E.R., Cespedes, F.V., and Kasturi Rangan, V. (1989), *Going to Market: Distribution Systems for Industrial Products*, Boston, MA: Harvard Business School Press.

Cova, B., and Salle, R. (2008), "The industrial/consumer marketing dichotomy revisited," *Journal of Business and Industrial Marketing*, 23(1), 3–11.

Coviello, N.E., and Brodie, R.J. (2001), "Contemporary marketing practices of consumer and business-to-business firms: How different are they?," *Journal of Business and Industrial Marketing*, 16(5), 382–401.

Cunningham, M.T., and Roberts, D.A. (1974), "The role of customer service in industrial marketing," *European Journal of Marketing*, 8(1), 15–28.

Cunningham, M.T., and Turnbull, P.W. (1983), "Interorganizational personal contact patterns," in H. Hakansson (ed.), *International Marketing and Purchasing of Industrial Goods: An Interaction Approach*, Chichester: Wiley.

Cutler, B.D., and Javalgi, R.G. (1994), "Comparison of business-to-business advertising: The United States and the United Kingdom," *Industrial Marketing Management*, 23(2), 117–124.

Dagnino, G.B. (2009), "Coopetition strategy: A new kind of interfirm dynamics for value creation," in G.B. Dagnino and E. Rosso (eds.), *Coopetition Strategy*, Abingdon: Routledge.

Damanpour, F. (1991), "Organizational innovation: A meta-analysis of effects of determinants and moderators," *Academy of Management Journal*, 34(3), 555–590.

Davenport, T.H., Harris, J.G., and Kohli, A.K. (2001), "How do they know their customers so well?," *MIT Sloan Management Review*, 42(2), 20.

De Meyer, A. (1985), "The flow of technological innovation in an R+D department," *Research Policy*, 14, 315–328.

Dean, A., and Kretschmer, M. (2007), "Can ideas be capital? Factors of production in the postindustrial economy: A review and critique," *Academy of Management Review*, 32(2), 573–594.

Dean, J. (1948) "Cost structures of enterprises and break-even charts," *The American Economic Review*, 38(2), 153–164.

Dempsey, W., Bushman, A.F., and Plank, R.E. (1980), "Personal inducement of industrial buyers," *Industrial Marketing Management*, 9, 281–289.

Deshpande, R., and Webster Jr, F.E. (1989), "Organizational culture and marketing: Defining the research agenda," *The Journal of Marketing*, 53(1), 3–15.

Despres, C., and Hiltrop, J. (1995), "Human resource management in the knowledge age," *Employee Relations*, 17(1), 9–23.

Diamantopoulos, D. (1991), "Pricing theory and evidence: A literature review," in M.J. Baker (ed.), *Perspectives on Marketing Management*, Sussex: John Wiley & Sons.

Dibb, S., Simkin, L., Pride, W., and Ferell, O.C. (2019), *Marketing Concepts & Strategies*, 8th edition, New York: Cengage Learning EMEA.

Dichter, E. (1966), "How word-of-mouth advertising works," *Harvard Business Review*, 44(6), 147–166.

Dimitriadis, S., and Baltas, G. (2003), *E-Commerce and Marketing*, Athens: Rosili Publications.

Dowling, G.R. (2004), *The Art and Science of Marketing*, Oxford: Oxford University Press.

Doyle, P., Woodside, A.G., and Michell, P. (1979), "Organizational buying in new task and rebuy situations," *Industrial Marketing Management*, 8, 7–11.

Drucker, P.E. (1985a), *Innovation and Entrepreneurship*, London: Heinemann.

Drucker, P.E. (1985b), "The discipline of innovation," *Harvard Business Review*, 63 (May-June), 67–73.

DSV (2020) *DSV Introduces Fast China-Europe Road Freight*. Retrieved 16 June 2022 from www.dsv.com/en/about-dsv/press/news/com/2020/10/dsv-introduces-fast-china-europe-road-freight.

DSV (n.d.) *DSV Silkway Express—Try Our Alternative to Air Freight*. Retrieved 16 June 2022 from www.dsv.com/en/our-solutions/modes-of-transport/road-transport/dsv-silkway-express.

Duncan, R.D. (1972), "Characteristics of organizational environments and perceived environmental uncertainty," *Administrative Science Quarterly*, 17, 313–327.

Dwyer, F., and Tanner, J. (2002), *Business Marketing*, 2nd edition, Boston, MA: McGraw-Hill.

Dwyer, F.R., Schurr, P.H., and Oh, S. (1987), "Developing buyer–seller relationships," *Journal of Marketing*, 51(2), 11–27.

Eatwell, J., Milgate, M., and Newman, P. (eds.) (1987), *The New Palgrave: A Dictionary of Economics*, Basingstoke, New York: Palgrave Macmillan.

Encyclopedia.com (n.d.) "Ethics in marketing," in *Encyclopedia of Business and Finance*, 2nd edition. Retrieved 17 September 2019 from www.encyclopedia.com/finance/finance-and-accounting-magazines/ethics-marketing.

Eiglier, P., and Langeard, E. (1987), *Servuction, le Marketing des Services*, Paris: McGraw-Hill.

Ellinger, A.E. (2000), "Improving marketing/logistics cross-functional collaboration in the supply chain," *Industrial Marketing Management*, 29(1), 85–96.

Emden, Z., Calantone, R.J., and Droge, C. (2006), "Collaborating for new product development: Selecting the partner with maximum potential to create value," *Journal of Product Innovation Management*, 23(4), 330–341.

Emery, F.E., and Trist, E.L. (1965), "The causal texture of organizational environments," *Human Relations*, 18, 21–32.

Ettlie, J.E., Bridges, W.P., and O'Keefe, R.D. (1984), "Organization strategy and structural differences for radical versus incremental innovation," *Management Science*, 30(6), 682–695.

Eurostat (2013), *Glossary: Business Functions—Statistics Explained*. Retrieved 16 June 2022 from https://ec.europa.eu/eurostat/statistics-explained/index.php/Glossary:Business_functions.

Farmer, D.H., and MacMillan, K. (1976), "Voluntary collaboration vs disloyalty to suppliers," *Journal of Purchasing and Materials Management*, 12(4), 3–8.

Fern, E.F., and Brown, J.R. (1984), "The industrial/consumer marketing dichotomy: A case of insufficient justification," *Journal of Marketing*, 48 (Spring), 68–77.

Ferrell, O.C., and Hartline, M.D. (2011), *Marketing Strategy*, 5th edition, Melbourne: Cengage Learning Australia.

Fill, C., and Fill, K.E. (2005), *Business to Business Marketing: Relationships, Systems and Communications*, 4th edition, Englewood Cliffs, NJ: Prentice Hall.

Flynn, B., Huo, B., and Zhao, X. (2010), "The impact of supply chain integration on performance: A contingency and configuration approach," *Journal of Operations Management*, 28(1), 58–71.

Folinas, D. (2013), *Outsourcing Management for Supply Chain Operations and Logistics Service*, New York: IGI Global.

Folinas, D., and Fotiadis, T. (2017), *Marketing and Supply Chain Management: A Systemic Approach*, Abingdon: Routledge.

Folinas, D., Manthou, V., Sigala, M., and Vlachopoulou, V. (2004), "e-Volution of supply chain: Cases and best practices," *Internet Research: Electronic Networking Applications and Policy*, 14(4), 274–283.

Fontana, E., Öberg, C., and Poblete, L. (2021), "Nominated procurement and the indirect control of nominated sub-suppliers: Evidence from the Sri Lankan apparel supply chain," *Journal of Business Research*, 127, 179–192.

Ford, D., Berthon, P., Brown, S., Gadde, L.-E., Håkansson, H., Naudé, P., et al. (2002), *The Business Marketing Course: Managing in Complex Networks*, Chichester: John Wiley & Sons.

Foster, R. (1986), *Innovation: The Attacker's Advantage*, New York: Summit Books.

Fotiadis, T. (2000) "Marketing and MIS maintenance," *2nd International Conference of Neural Parallel and Scientific Computations*, Atlanta, GA, 7–10 August.

Fotiadis, T. (2006), "Integration of marketing and R&D in high-tech enterprises: Concept-signifiance-barriers," *The Cyprus Journal of Sciences*, 4, 129.

Fotiadis, T. (2018), *Strategic Marketing for High Technology Products: An Integrated Approach*, London: Routledge.

Fotiadis, T., and Siomkos, G. (2020), *Industrial Marketing*, 1st edition, Nicosia: Broken Hill.

Fraj, E., Martínez, E., and Matute, J. (2013), "Green marketing in B2B organisations: An empirical analysis from the natural-resource-based view of the firm," *Journal of Business & Industrial Marketing*, 28(5), 396–410.

Frank, A.G., Mendes, G.H., Ayala, N.F., and Ghezzi, A. (2019), "Servitization and Industry 4.0 convergence in the digital transformation of product firms: A business model innovation perspective," *Technological Forecasting and Social Change*, 141, 341–351.

Frazier, G.L., Spekman, R.E., and O'Neal, C.R. (1988), "Just-in-time exchange relationships in industrial markets," *Journal of Marketing*, 52(4), 52–67.

Friedman, M. (1979a), *An Excerpt from an Interview with Phil Donahue*. Retrieved 16 June 2022 from https://youtu.be/RWsx1X8PV_A.

Friedman, M. (1979b), "The social responsibility of business is to increase profit," in T.L. Beauchamp and N. Bowie (eds.), *Ethical Theory and Business*, Englewood Cliffs, NJ: Prentice Hall.

Friedman, M. (2007), "The social responsibility of business is to increase its profits", in W.C. Zimmerli, M. Holzinger, and K Richter (eds.), *Corporate Ethics and Corporate Governance*, Berlin: Springer.

Friedman, M., and Friedman, R. (1990), *Free to Choose: A Personal Statement*, New York: Mariner Books.

Frishammar, J., Lichtenthaler, U., and Rundquist, J. (2012), "Identifying technology commercialization opportunities: The importance of integrating product development knowledge," *Journal of Product Innovation Management*, 29(4), 573–589.

Gadbois, R. (2000), *High Technology Marketing, High Tech vs Low Tech*, Berkeley, CA: Haas School of Business.

Galbraith, C.S., DeNoble, A.F., and Ehrlich, S.B. (2012), "Predicting the commercialization progress of early-stage technologies: An ex-ante analysis," *IEEE Transactions on Engineering Management*, 59(2), 213–225.

Galbraith, J. (1973), *Designing Complex Organizations*, Reading, MA: Addison-Wesley.

Gardner, D. (1990), "Are high technology products really different?" *Faculty* Working Paper #90-1706, University of Illinois at Urbana-Champaign.

Gardner, D.M., Johnson, F., Lee, M., and Wilkinson, I. (2000), "A contingency approach to marketing high technology products," *European Journal of Marketing*, 34(9/10), 1053–1077.

gCaptain (2018), "Maersk announces latest step in business integration strategy," *gCaptain*, 19 September. Retrieved 16 June 2022 from https://gcaptain.com/maersk-announces-latest-step-in-business-integration-strategy.

Gerbner, G. (1956), "Towards a general model of communication," *Audio-Visual Communication Review*, 4(3), 171–199.

George, J., Weiss, A., and Dutta, S. (1999), "Marketing in technology intensive markets: Towards a conceptual framework," *Journal of Marketing*, 63, 78–91.

Geroski, P., Machin, S., and Van Reenen, J. (1993), "The profitability of innovating firms," *The RAND Journal of Economics*, 24(2), 198–211.

Ghemawat, P. (1991), "Market incumbency and technological inertia," *Marketing Science*, 10(2), 161–171.

Ghingold, M. (1986), "Testing the Buygrid buying process model," *Journal of Purchasing and Materials Management*, 22(Winter), 30–36.

Ghingold, M., and Wilson, D.T. (1998), "Buying center research and business marketing practice: Meeting the challenge of dynamic marketing," *Journal of Business and Industrial Marketing*, 13(2), 96–108.

Ghobadi, S., and D'Ambra, J. (2012), "Knowledge sharing in cross-functional teams: A coopetitive model," *Journal of Knowledge Management*, 16(2), 285–301.

Glaser, E.M., Abelson, H.H., and Garrison, K.N. (1983), *Putting Knowledge to Use: Facilitating the Diffusion of Knowledge and the Implementation of Planned Change*, Hoboken, NJ: Jossey-Bass.

Glazer, R. (1991), "Marketing in an information-intensive environment: Strategic implications of knowledge as an asset," *Journal of Marketing*, 55, 1–19.

Gnyawali, D.R., and Park, B.-J. (2009), "Co-opetition and technological innovation in small and medium-sized enterprises: A multilevel conceptual model," *Journal of Small Business Management*, 47(3), 308–330.

Golder, P.N., and Tellis, G.J. (1993), "Pioneer advantage: Marketing logic or marketing legend?," *Journal of Marketing Research*, 30(2), 158–170.

Goleman, D. (1995), *Emotional Intelligence*, London: Bloomsbury.

Gonzales-Zapatero, C. (2015), "Determinants of functional integration during new product development: the purchasing-marketing link," *Industrial Marketing Management*, 52(January), 47–59.

Gounaris, S. (2012), *Marketing Services*, 2nd edition, Athens: Rosili Publications.

Graham, D., Manikas, I., and Folinas, D. (2013), *E-Logistics and E-Supply Chain Management: Applications for Evolving Business*, New York: IGI Global.

Grewal, D., Levy, M., Leonidou, L., and Fotiadis, T. (2022), *Marketing*, 1st Greek edition, Athens: Kritiki Publishing.

Griffin, A., and Hauser, J. (1996), "Integrating R&D and marketing: A review and analysis of the literature," *Journal of Product Innovation Management*, 13(3), 191–215.

Grishikashvili, K., Dibb, S., and Meadows, M. (2014), "Investigation into big data impact on digital marketing," *Journal of Communication and Media Technologies*, 4(October), 26–37.

Grunenwald, J.P., and Vernon, T.T. (1988), "Pricing decision making for high-technology products and services," *Journal of Business & Industrial Marketing*, 3(1), 61–70.

Guenzi, P., and Troilo, G. (2006), "Developing marketing capabilities for customer value creation through marketing–sales integration," *Industrial Marketing Management*, 35(8), 974–988.

Guiltinan, J.P. (1987), "The price bundling of services: A normative framework," *Journal of Marketing*, 51(2), 74–85.

Guirdham, M. (1972), *Marketing: The Management of Distribution Channels*, Oxford: Pergamon Press.

Gulati, R. (1998), "Alliances and networks on JSTOR," *Strategic Management Journal*, 19(4), 293–317.

Habibi, F., Hamilton, C.A., Valos, M.J., and Callaghan, M. (2015), "E-marketing orientation and social media implementation in B2B marketing," *European Business Review*, 27(6), 638–655.

Hadlock, P., Hecker, D., and Gannon, J. (1991), "High technology employment: Another view," *Monthly Labor Review*, 114, 26.

Hamel, G. (1997), "Killer strategies that make shareholders rich," *Fortune*, 135(12), 70–84.

Hamel, G., and Prahalad, C.K. (1990), "Corporate imagination and expeditionary marketing," *Harvard Business Review*, 69(4), 81–92.

Hannan, M.T., and Freeman, J. (1997), "The population ecology of organization," *American Journal of Sociology*, 82(5), 929–964.

Hardy, K.G., and Magrath, A.J. (1988), *Marketing Channel Management: Strategic Planning and Tactics*, Glenview, IL: Scott Foresman and Co.

Hart, S.H. (1978), *Business to Business Marketing Communications*, 6th edition, London: Kogan.

Hart, S.H., Moncrief, W.C., and Parasuraman, A. (1989), "An empirical investigation of salespeople's performance, effort and selling method during a sales contest," *Journal of the Academy of Marketing Science*, 17(1), 29–39.

Hatzichronoglou, T. (1997), "Revision of the high technology sector and product classification," OECD STI Working Paper, No. 1997/02, OECD Publishing: Paris.

Hayes, R.H. (1985), "Strategic planning forward—reverse?," *Harvard Business Review*, 63(6), 111–119.

Heding, T., Knudtzen, C., and Bjerre, M. (2020), *Brand Management: Mastering Research, Theory and Practise*, London: Routledge.

Heffernan, T., O'Neill, G., Travaglione, T., and Droulers, M. (2008), "Relationship marketing: The impact of emotional intelligence and trust on bank performance," *International Journal of Bank Marketing*, 26(3), 183–199.

Helander, A., and Möller, K. (2007), "System supplier's customer strategy," *Industrial Marketing Management*, 36(6), 719–730.

Hellman, K. (2005), "Strategy driven B2B promotions," *Journal of Business and Industrial Marketing*, 20(1), 4–11.

Henderson B. D. (1979), "The product portfolio: Growth Share Matrix of the Boston Consulting Group," in H. Mintzberg and J.B. Quinn (eds.), *The Strategy Process: Concepts, Contexts, Cases*, Essex: Pearson. 678–680.

Henderson, S. (1978), *Psychological Principles of Marketing and Consumer Behavior*, New York: Lexington Books.

Herbst, U., and Merz, M.A. (2011), "The industrial brand personality scale: Building strong business-to-business brands," *Industrial Marketing Management*, 40(7), 1072–1081.

Herzberg, F., Mausner, B., and Snyderman, B.B. (1959), *The Motivation to Work*, New York: Wiley and Sons.

Heyes, R.H., Wheelright, S.C. and Clark, K.B. (1988), *Dynamic Manufacturing: Creating the Learning Organization*, New York: Free Press.

Hingley, M.K., Lindgreen, A., and Beverland, M.B. (2010), "Barriers to network innovation in UK ethnic fresh produce supply," *Entrepreneurship and Regional Development*, 22(1), 77–96.

Hingley, M.K., Lindgreen, A., and Grant, D.B. (2015) "Intermediaries in power-laden retail supply chains: An opportunity to improve buyer–supplier relationships and collaboration," *Industrial Marketing Management*, 50, 78–84.

Hingley, M.K., Lindgreen, A., Grant, D.B., and Kane, C. (2011), "Using fourth-party logistics management to improve horizontal collaboration among grocery retailers," *Supply Chain Management: An International Journal*, 16(5), 316–327.

Hinterhuber, A. (2004), "Towards value based pricing: An integrative framework for decision making," *Industrial Marketing Management*, 33(8), 765–778.

Hlavacek, J.D., and McQuistion, T.J. (1983), "Industrial distributors: When, who and how?," *Harvard Business Review*, 61(1), 96–101.

Holland, C.P., and Naude, P. (2004), "The metamorphosis of marketing into an information-handling problem," *Journal of Business & Industrial Marketing*, 19(3), 167–177.

Holliman, G., and Rowley, J. (2014), "Business to business digital content marketing: Marketers' perceptions of best practice," *Journal of Research in Interactive Marketing*, 8(4), 269–293.

Homburg, C., and Kuester, S. (2001), "Towards an improved understanding of industrial buying behavior: Determinants of the number of suppliers," *Journal of Business-to-Business Marketing*, 8(2), 5–29.

Homburg, C., Jensen, O., and Krohmer, H. (2008), "Configurations of marketing and sales: A taxonomy," *Journal of Marketing*, 72(March), 133–154.

Hoque, A.Y., and Lohse, G.L. (1999), "An information search cost perspective for designing interfaces for electronic commerce," *Journal of Marketing Research*, 36(3), 387–394.

Hovland, C.I., and Weiss, W. (1951), "The influence of source credibility on communication effectiveness," *Public Opinion Quarterly*, 15(Winter), 635–650.

Hovland, C.I., Janis, I., and Kelley, H.H. (1953), *Communication and Persuasion: Psychological Studies of Opinion Change*, New Haven, CT: Yale University Press.

Howard, J.A., and Sheth, J.N. (1969), *The Theory of Buyer Behavior*, New York: John Wiley and Sons.

Hughes, A.M. (2019), *The 24 Essential Database Marketing Techniques*. Retrieved 7 September 2020 from www.dbmarketing.com/articles/Featured.htm.

Hung, A., Parker, A.M., and Yoong, J. (2009), "Defining and measuring financial literacy," *SSRN Electronic Journal*. http://dx.doi.org/10.2139/ssrn.1498674

Hunt, S., and Nevin, R.J. (1974), "Power in a channel of distribution: Sources and consequences," *Journal of Marketing Research*, 11(2), 186–193.

Hunter, G.K., Bunn, M.D., and Perrault Jr., W.D. (2006), "Interrelationships among key aspects of the organizational procurement process," *International Journal of Research in Marketing*, 23, 155–170.

Hutt, M.D., and Speh, T.W. (1992), *Business Marketing Management: A Strategic View of Industrial and Organizational Markets*, 4th edition, Orlando, FL: The Dryden Press.

Hutt, M.D., and Speh, T.W. (2013), *Business Marketing Management: B2B*, 11th international edition, Boston, MA: Cengage Learning.

Hutt, M.D., Reingen, P.H., and Ronchetto Jr., J.R. (1988), "Tracing emergent processes in marketing strategy formation," *The Journal of Marketing*, 52(1), 4–19.

Hutton, P. (1991), "Corporate image," in K. Sutherland (ed.), *Researching Business Markets*, London: Kogan Page.

ICCMI June 22–24, 2016 Heraklion, Greece (p.327).

Industrial Marketing Research Association (IMRA) (1969), *Regulations*, Lichfield: IMRA Publications.

Ingram, T.N., LaForge, R.W., and Avila, R.A. (2008), *Professional Selling: A Trust-Based Approach*, 3rd edition, Mason: Thomson, South-Western.

Ingram, T.N., LaForge, R.W., and Leigh, T.W. (2002), "Selling in the new millennium," *Industrial Marketing Management*, 31(7), 559–567.

International Chamber of Commerce (2020a), *Handbook on Transport*, Paris: International Chamber of Commerce.

International Chamber of Commerce (2020b), *Incoterms® 2020*. Retrieved 16 June 2022 from https://iccwbo.org/resources-for-business/incoterms-rules/incoterms-2020/.

Jabbar, A., Akhtar, P., and Dani, S. (2020), "Real-time big data processing for instantaneous marketing decisions: A problematization approach," *Industrial Marketing Management*, 90, 558–569.

Jackson, B.B. (1985), *Winning and Keeping Industrial Customers*, Lexington, MA: Lexington Books.

Jaffe, A.B. (1996), "Trends and patterns in research and development expenditures in the United States," *Proceedings of the National Academy of Sciences of the United States of America*, 93(23), 12658–12663.

Jakson Jr., D.W., Keith, J.E., and Burdick, R.K. (1984), "Purchasing agents' perceptions of industrial buying center influence," *Journal of Marketing*, 48(Fall), 75–83.

Jansen, J.J., Volberda, H.W., and Van Den Bosch, F.A. (2005), "Exploratory innovation, exploitative innovation, and ambidexterity: The impact of environmental and organizational antecedents," *Schmalenbach Business Review*, 57, 351–363.

Järvinen, J., and Taiminen, H. (2016), "Harnessing marketing automation for B2B content marketing," *Industrial Marketing Management*, 54, 164–175.

Jasimuddin, S.M. (2008), "A holistic view of knowledge management strategy," *Journal of Knowledge Management*, 12(2), 57–66.

Jauch, L.R., and Kraft, K.L. (1986), "Strategic management of uncertainty," *Academy of Management Review*, 11(4), 777–790.

John, G., Weiss, A.M., and Dutta, S. (1999), "Marketing in technology-intensive markets: Towards a conceptual framework," *The Journal of Marketing*, 63(4), 78–91.

Johnson, E.M., Kurtz, D.L., and Scheving, E.E. (1994), *Sales Management Concepts, Practices and Cases*, 2nd edition, Columbus, OH: McGraw-Hill.

Johnston, W.J., and Bonoma, T.V. (1981), "The buying center: Structure and interaction patterns," *Journal of Marketing*, 45(2), 143–156.

Johnston, W.J., and Lewin, J.E. (1996), "Organizational buying behavior: Toward an integrative framework," *Journal of Business Research*, 35(1), 8–10.

Jones, E.E., and Thibaut, J.W. (1958), "Interaction goals as bases of inference in interpersonal perception," in R. Tagiuri and R.L. Petrullo (eds.), *Person Perception and Interpersonal Behavior*, Stanford, CA: Stanford University Press.

Kahn, K.B, and McDonough, E.F. (1997), "An empirical study of the relationships among co-location, integration, performance, and satisfaction," *Journal of Product Innovation Management*, 14, 161–178.

Kalwani, M.U., and Narayandas, N. (1995), "Long-term manufacturer-supplier relationships: Do they pay off for supplier firms?" *Journal of Marketing*, 59(1), 1–16.

Kannan, G., and Haq, A.N. (2007), "Analysis of interactions of criteria and sub-criteria for the selection of supplier in the built-in-order supply chain environment," *International Journal of Production Research*, 45(17), 3831–3852.

Kaplan, S., and Sawhney, M. (2000), "E-hubs: The new B2B marketplaces," *Harvard Business Review*, 78(3), 97.

Katz, D., and Kahn, R.L. (1966), *The Social Psychology of Organizations*, New York: Wiley.

Katz, E., and Lazarsfeld, P.F. (1955), *Personal Influence,* Glencoe, IL: The Free Press.

Kemp, E.A., Borders, A.L., Anaza, N.A., and Johnston, W.J. (2018), "The heart in organizational buying: Marketers' understanding of emotions and decision-making of buyers," *Journal of Business & Industrial Marketing*, 33(1), 19–28.

Kerin, R.A., Harvey, M.G., and Rothe, J.T. (1978), "Cannibalism and new product development," *Business Horizons*, 21(5), 25–31.

Ketteringham, J.M., and White, J.R. (1984), "Making technology work for business," in R.B. Lamb (ed.), *Competitive Strategic Management*, Englewood Cliffs, NJ: Prentice Hall.

Kian Chong, W., Shafaghi, M., Woollaston, C., and Lui, V. (2010), "B2B e-marketplace: An e-marketing framework for B2B commerce," *Marketing Intelligence & Planning*, 28(3), 310–329.

Kim, W.C., and Mauborgne, R. (1999), "Strategy, value innovation, and the knowledge economy," *MIT Sloan Management Review*, 40(3), 41–54.

Kim, W.C., and Mauborgne, R. (2004), *Blue Ocean Strategy: How to Create Uncontested Market Space and Make the Competition Irrelevant*, Brighton, MA: Harvard Business Review Press.

Kirchner, W.K., and Dunnette, M.D. (1959), "How salesmen and technical men differ in describing themselves," *Personnel Journal*, 37(April), 418–419.

Kleindorfer, P.R., Singhal, K., and Wassenhove, L.N.V. (2005), "Sustainable operations management," *Production and Operations Management*, 14(4), 482–492.

Kleinschmidt, E.J., and Cooper, R.G. (1991), "The impact of product innovativeness on performance," *Journal of Product Innovation Management*, 8(4), 240–251.

Kohtamäki, M., Parida, V., Patel, P.C., and Gebauer, H. (2020), "The relationship between digitalization and servitization: The role of servitization in capturing the financial potential of digitalization," *Technological Forecasting and Social Change*, 151, 119804.

Kokmotos, E.D., Konstantoglou, A., Fotiadis, T.A., and Folinas, D. (2016), "Marketing: Evolution in green," *4th International Conference on Contemporary Marketing Issues*, June 22–24, Heraklion.

Kotler, O., and Armstrong, G. (2013), *Principles of Marketing*, 15th edition, Englewood Cliffs, NJ: Prentice Hall.

Kotler, P. (1986), *Principles of Marketing*, Englewood Cliffs, NJ: Prentice Hall.

Kotler, P. (1991), *Marketing Management: Analysis, Planning and Control*, Englewood Cliffs, NJ: Prentice Hall.

Kotler, P. (2000), *Marketing Management*, 10th edition, Englewood Cliffs, NJ: Prentice Hall.

Kotler, P., and Armstrong, G. (2010) *Principles of Marketing*, 13th edition, Upper Saddle, NJ: Prentice Hall.

Kotler, P., and Pfoertsch, W. (2006), *B2B Brand Management*, Cham: Springer International Publishing.

Kotler, P., Armstrong, G., Saunders, J., and Wong, V. (2001), *Principles of Marketing*, 9th edition, Englewood Cliffs, NJ: Prentice Hall.

Kowalkowski, C., Gebauer, H., Kamp, B., and Parry, G. (2017a), "Servitization and deservitization: Overview, concepts, and definitions," *Industrial Marketing Management*, 60, 4–10.

Kowalkowski, C., Gebauer, H., and Oliva, R. (2017b), "Service growth in product firms: Past, present, and future," *Industrial Marketing Management*, 60, 82–88.

KreaKom (2019), *Advertising at the Exam*, Copenhagen: The Association of Danish Advertising and Communication Agencies.

Krugman, H.H. (1988), "Point of view: Limits of attention to advertising," *Journal of Advertising Research*, 28(5), 47–50.

Kubacki, K., Rundle-Thiele, S., Lahtinen, V., and Parkinson, J. (2015), "A systematic review assessing the extent of social marketing principle use in interventions targeting children (2000–2014)," *Young Consumers*, 16(2), 141–158.

Kumar, N., Stern, L.W., and Achrol, R.S. (1992), "Assessing reseller performance from the perspective of the supplier," *Journal of Marketing Research*, 29(2), 238–253.

Kurian, G.T. (2013), *The AMA Dictionary of Business and Management*, New York: American Management Association.

Lambert, D., Emmelhainz, M., and Gardner, J. (1999), "Building successful logistics partnerships," *Journal of Business Logistics*, 20(1), 118–165.

Landis, S. (2013), "Beware the cannibal in your product line," *Harvard Business Review*. Available at: https://hbr.org/2013/06/beware-the-cannibal-in-your-pr

Lanzilloti, R.F. (1958), "Pricing objectives in large companies," *American Economic Review*, 48(5), 921–940.

Lasswell, H.D. (1950), *Politics: Who Gets What, When, How*, New York: Peter Smith.

Lazarsfeld, B.B., and Gaudet, H. (1944), *The People's Choice*, New York: Duell, Sloan, and Pearce.

Leavitt, H.J. (1964), "Applied organization change in industry: Structural, technical, and human approaches," in W.W. Cooper, H.J. Leavitt, and M.D. Shelley II (eds.), *New Perspectives in Organization Research*, New York: John Wiley & Sons.

Lee, J., and Qualls, W.J. (2010), "A dynamic process of buyer-seller technology adoption," *Journal of Business and Industrial Marketing*, 25(3), 220–228.

Leenders, M.R., Harold, E.F., and Wilbur, B. (1995), *Purchasing and Materials Management*, Burr Ridge, IL: Irwin.

Lehtimäki, T., Simula, H., and Salo, J. (2009), "Applying knowledge management to project marketing in a demanding technology transfer project: Convincing the industrial customer over the knowledge gap," *Industrial Marketing Management*, 38(2), 228–236.

Leonard, M. (2021), "Maersk pursues M&A for end-to-end logistics, moves to 'larger targets'," *Supply Chain Dive*, 12 May. Retrieved 16 June 2022 from www.supplychaindive.com/news/maersk-mergers-acquisition-ocean-shipping-logistics/600027.

Leonard-Barton, D. (1992), "Core capabilities and core rigidities: A paradox in managing new product development," *Strategic Management Journal*, 13(S1), 111–125.

Leonard-Barton, D., and Rayport, J.F. (1997), "Spark innovation through empathic design," *Harvard Business Review*, 75(6), 102–113.

Leonidou, L.C. (2004), "Industrial manufacturer-customer relationships: The discriminating role of the buying situation," *Industrial Marketing Management*, 33, 731–742.

Leonidou, L.C. (2005), "Industrial buyers' influence strategies: Buying situation differences," *Journal of Business & Industrial Marketing*, 20(1), 33–42.

Levitt, T. (1965), *Industrial Purchasing Behavior: A Study of Communication Effects*, Boston, MA: Harvard University Press.

Lewin, J.E., and Donthu, N. (2005), "The influence of purchase situations on buying center structure and investment: A select meta-analysis of organizational buying behavior research," *Journal of Business Research*, 58(October), 1381–1390.

Lichtenthal, J.D. (1998), "Business-to-business marketing in the 21st century," *Journal of Business-to-Business Marketing*, 12, 1–5.

Lichtenthaler, U., and Lichtenthaler, E. (2009), "A capability-based framework for open innovation: Complementing absorptive capacity," *Journal of Management Studies*, 46(8), 1315–1338.

Lieberman, M.B., and Montgomery, D.B. (1988), "First-mover advantages," *Strategic Management Journal*, 9(S1), 41–58.

Lilien, G.L. (1987), "Business marketing: Present and future," *Industrial Marketing and Purchasing*, 2(3), 3–21.

Lilien, G.L., and Wong, M.A. (1984), "An exploratory investigation of the structure of the buying center in the metalworking industry," *Journal of Marketing Research*, 21(February), 1–11.

Lilien, G.L., Silk, A.J., Choffray, J.-M., and Rao, M. (1976), "Industrial advertising effects and budgeting practices," *Journal of Marketing*, 40(1), 16–24.

Lindgreen, A. (2008), *Managing Market Relationships: Methodological and Empirical Insights*, Aldershot: Gower Publishing.

Lindgreen, A. (2009), *Fate Chooses Your Transactions; You Choose Your Market Relations*, inaugural lecture, Hull Business School, Hull.

Lindgreen, A., and Wynstra, F. (2005), "Value in business markets: What do we know? Where are we going?" *Industrial Marketing Management*, 34(7), 732–748.

Lindgreen, A., Antioco, M.D.J., Harness, D., and van der Sloot, R. (2009), "Purchasing and marketing of social and environmental sustainability for high-tech medical equipment," *Journal of Business Ethics*, 85(S2), 445–462.

Lindgreen, A., Palmer, R., Vanhamme, J., and Wouters, J.P.M. (2006), "A relationship-management assessment tool: Questioning, identifying, and prioritizing critical aspects of customer relationships," *Industrial Marketing Management*, 35(1), 57–71.

Lindgreen, A., Vanhamme, J., Raaij, E., and Johnston, W.J. (2013), "Go configure: The mix of purchasing practices to choose for your supply base," *California Management Review*, 55(2), 72–96.

Lipkin, R. (1996), "Fit for a king," *Science News*, 18 May, 316–317.

Loebecke, C., Van Fenema, P.C., and Powell, P. (1999), "Coopetition and knowledge transfer," *ACM SIGMIS Database: The DATABASE for Advances in Information Systems*, 30(2), 14–25.

Lohtia, R., Johnston, W.J., and Aab, L. (1995), "Business to business advertising: What are the dimensions of an effective print ad," *Industrial Marketing Management*, 24(5), 369–378.

Lopes de Sousa Jabbour, A.B., Jabbour, C.J.C., Hingley, M., Vilalta-Perdomo, E.L., Ramsden, G., and Twigg, D. (2020) "Sustainability of supply chains in the wake of the coronavirus (COVID-19/SARS-CoV-2) pandemic: Lessons and trends," *Modern Supply Chain Research and Applications*, 2(3), 117–122.

Lovelock, C., Wirtz, J., and Chew, P. (2009), *Essentials of Services Marketing*, Upper Saddle River, NJ: Prentice Hall.

Lucas Jr., H.C., and Goh, J.M. (2009), "Disruptive technology: How Kodak missed the digital photography revolution, *Journal of Strategic Information Systems*, 18(1), 46–55.

Luhmann, N. (2017), "Systems theory," in A. Marinopoulou (ed.), *Critical Theory and Epistemology: The Politics of Modern Thought and Science*, Manchester University Press: Manchester. 111–138.

Luker Jr., W., and Lyons, D. (1997), "Employment shifts in high technology industries 1988–1996," *Monthly Labor Review*, June, 12–25.

Lymperopoulos, K., and Pantouvakis, A. (2008), *Marketing Services*, 2nd edition, Patras: Hellenic Open University.

Lynch, J., and De Chernatony, L. (2007), "Winning hearts and minds: Business-to-business branding and the role of the salesperson," *Journal of Marketing Management*, 23(1–2), 123–135.

Ma, C., Yang, Z., Yao, Z., Fisher, G., and Fang, E.E. (2012), "The effect of strategic alliance resource accumulation and process characteristics on new product success: Exploration of international high-tech strategic alliances in China," *Industrial Marketing Management*, 41(3), 469–480.

MacTavich, R., and Maitland, A. (1980), *Industrial Marketing*, London: The McMillan Press.

Madhavaram, S., and Hunt, S.D. (2017), "Customizing business-to-business (B2B) professional services: The role of intellectual capital and internal social capital," *Journal of Business Research*, 74, 38–46.

Maersk Annual Report (2019), AP Möller – Maersk A/S, Copenhagen.

Magrath, A.J., and Hardy, K.G. (1988), "A strategic framework for diagnosing manufacturer-reseller conflict," Working Paper, Report No. 88-101, Cambridge, MA: Marketing Science Institute.

Maritime Gateway (2021), "Maersk accelerates transformation to integrated service," *Maritime Gateway*, 12 May. Retrieved 16 June 2022 from www.maritimegateway.com/maersk-accelerates-transformation-to-integrated-service/.

Marquis, D.G. (1982), "The anatomy of successful innovations," in M.L. Tushman and W.L. Moore (eds.), *Readings in the Management of Innovation*, Boston, MA: Pitman.

Marrian, J. (1968), "Marketing characteristics of industrial goods and buyers," in A. Wilson (ed.), *The Marketing of Industrial Products*, London: Hutchinson.

Martínez-Costa, M., and Jiménez-Jiménez, D. (2008), "Are companies that implement TQM better learning organisations? An empirical study," *Total Quality Management & Business Excellence*, 19(11), 1101–1115.

Maslow, A.H. (1943), "A theory of human motivation," *Psychological Review*, 50(4), 370.

Mason, C.H., and Milne, G.R. (1994), "An approach for identifying cannibalization within product line extensions and multi-brand strategies," *Journal of Business Research*, 31(2–3), 163–170.

Mason, J.L. (1965), "The low prestige of personal selling," *Journal of Marketing*, 29, 7–10.

Mathur, U.C. (2008), *Business to Business Marketing*, New Delhi: New Age International Publishers.

Mattson, M.R. (1988), "How to determine the composition and influence of a buying centre," *Industrial Marketing Management*, 17, 200–214.

Mayer, D., and Greenberg, H. (1964), "What makes a good salesman," *Harvard Business Review*, 42(4), 119–125.

McDade, S., Oliva, T.A., and Thomas, E. (2010), "Forecasting organizational adoption of high-technology product innovations separated by impact: Are traditional macro-level diffusion models appropriate?," *Industrial Marketing Management*, 39(2), 298–307.

McKenna, R. (1985), *The Regis Touch*, Reading, MA: Addison-Wesley.

McKenna, R. (1991), *Relationship Marketing: Successful Strategies for the Age of the Consumer*. Boston, MA: Addison-Wesley.

McQuiston, D.H., and Dickson, P.R. (1991), "The effect of perceived personal consequences on participation and influence in organizational buying," *Journal of Business Research*, 23(2), 159–177.

McTavish, R. (1966), "The marketing channels of office machinery," *Journal of Management Studies*, 3(1), 85–95.

McTavish, R., and Maitland, A. (1980), *Industrial Marketing*, Basingstoke: McMillan Publishers.

McWilliams, R.D., Naumanna, E., and Scott, S. (1992), "Determining buying center size," *Industrial Marketing Management*, 21(February), 43–49.

Milliken, F.J. (1987), "Three types of perceived uncertainty about the environment state, effect and response uncertainty," *Academy of Management Review*, 12(1), 133–143.

Misirlakis, N., and Kyriakos, S. (1994), *Practical Guide to Industrial Marketing*, Athens: S. Barberopoulos Publications.

Mitchell, V.W. (1995), "Organizational risk perception and reduction: A literature review," *British Journal of Management*, 6, 115–133.

Moenaert, R.K., and Souder, W.E. (1990), "An information transfer model for integrating marketing and R&D personnel in new product development projects," *Journal of Product Innovation Management*, 7(2), 91–107.

Mohr, J. (2001), *Marketing of High Technology Products and Innovations*, Upper Saddle River, NJ: Prentice Hall.

Mohr, J., Sengupta, S., and Slater, S. (2009), *Marketing of High-Technology Products and Innovations*, 3rd edition, Upper Saddle River, NJ: Prentice Hall Business Publishing.

Molinari, L.K., Abratt, R., and Dion, P. (2008), "Satisfaction, quality and value and effects on repurchase and positive word-of-mouth behavioral intentions in a B2B services context," *Journal of Services Marketing*, 22(5), 363–373.

Mollenkopf, D., Gibson, A., and Ozanne, L. (2000), "The integration of marketing and logistics functions: An empirical examination of New Zealand firms," *Journal of Business Logistics*, 21(2), 89.

Moncrief, W.C. (1986), "Selling activity and sales position taxonomies for industrial sales forces," *Journal of Marketing Research*, 23, 261–270.

Moncrief, W.C., and Marshall, G.W. (2005), "The evolution of the 7 steps of selling," *Industrial Marketing Management*, 34(1), 13–22.

Moon, J., and Tikoo, S. (2002), "Buying decision approaches of organizational buyers and users," *Journal of Business Research*, 55(4), 293–299.

Moon, M.A., and Armstrong, G.M. (1994), "Selling teams: A conceptual framework and research agenda," *Journal of Personal Selling and Sales Management*, 14(Winter), 17–30.

Moore, G.A. (1995), *Moore, Inside the Tornado*, New York: Harper Business.

Moore, G.A. (1999), *Crossing the Chasm: Marketing and Selling Technology Products to Mainstream Customers*, New York: Harper Collins.

Morgan, R.M., and Hunt, S.D. (1994), "The commitment-trust theory of relationship marketing," *Journal of Marketing*, 58(July), 20–38.

Morgendagens Salg (2020), Results from the research project. Retrieved 16 June 2022 from www.morgendagenssalg.dk.

Moriarty, R.T., and Kosnik, T.J. (1987), *High-Tech vs. Low-Tech Marketing*, Boston, MA: Harvard Business School.

Moriarty, R.T., and Kosnik, T.J. (1989), "High-tech marketing: Concepts, continuity, and change," *MIT Sloan Management Review*, 30(4), 7.

Moriarty, R.T., and Swartz, G.S. (1989), "Automation and marketing to boost sales and marketing," *Harvard Business Review*, 67(1), 100–108.

Morrill, J.E. (1970), "Industrial advertising pays off," *Harvard Business Review*, 48(2), 4–14.

Mukerjee, H.S. (2009), *Industrial Marketing*, Noida: Excel Books.

Murphy, P.E., and Enis, B.M. (1986), "Classifying products strategically," *Journal of Marketing*, 50(July), 24–42.

Murphy, P.E., Laczniak, G.R., and Wood, G. (2007), "An ethical basis for relationship marketing: A virtue ethics perspective," *European Journal of Marketing*, 41(1/2), 37–57.

Myerson, R. (1991), *Game Theory: Analysis of Conflict*, Boston, MA: Harvard University Press.

Nagle, T.T. (1987), *The Strategy and Tactics of Pricing*, Englewood Cliffs, NJ: Prentice Hall.

Narasimhan, R., Talluri, S., and Mendez, D. (2001), "Supplier evaluation and rationalization via data envelopment analysis: An empirical examination," *The Journal of Supply Chain Management*, 37(3), 28–37.

Narus, J.A., and Anderson, J.C. (1986), "Turn your industrial distributors into partners," *Harvard Business Review*, 64(2), 66–71.

Narver, J.C., and Slater, S.F. (1990), "The effect of a market orientation on business profitability," *Journal of Marketing*, 54(4), 20–35.

National Science Foundation (1973), *Barriers to Innovation in Industry*, Washington, DC: NSF, Productivity Improvement Research Section.

National Science Foundation (1983), *The Process of Technological Innovation: Reviewing the Literature*, Washington, DC: NSF, Productivity Improvement Research Section.

National Science Foundation (1996), *Science and Engineering Indicators*, Washington, DC: NSF, Productivity Improvement Research Section.

Nault, B.R., and Vandenbosch, M.B. (1996), "Eating your own lunch: Protection through preemption," *Organization Science*, 7(3), 342–358.

Neale, M.R., and Corkindale, D.R. (1998), "Co-developing products: Involving customer earlier and more deeply," *Long Range Planning*, 31(3), 418–425.

Newall, J. (1977), "Industrial buyer behavior," *European Journal of Marketing*, 2, 3.

Newvision (2020), *Uganda's Flower Exports Exceed sh200b*. Retrieved 2 August 2021 from www.newvision.co.ug/news/1516644/uganda-flower-exports-exceed-sh200b.

O'Leary-Kelly, S.W., and Flores, B.E. (2002), "The integration of manufacturing and marketing/sales decisions: Impact on organizational performance," *Journal of Operations Management*, 20(3), 221–240.

Öberg, C. (2010a), "Customer roles in innovations," *International Journal of Innovation Management*, 14(6), 989–1011.

Öberg, C. (2010b), "What happened with the grandiose plans? Strategic plans and network realities in B2B interaction," *Industrial Marketing Management*, 39, 963–974.

Öberg, C. (2018), "Social and economic ties in the freelance and sharing economies," *Journal of Small Business and Entrepreneurship*, 30(1), 77–96.

Öberg, C., and Graham, G. (2016), "How smart cities will change supply chain management: A technical viewpoint," *Production Planning & Control*, 27(6), 529–538.

Öberg, C., and Shams, T. (2019), "On the verge of disruption: Rethinking position and role—The case of additive manufacturing," *Journal of Business and Industrial Marketing*, 34(5), 1093–1105.

Öberg, C., Huge-Brodin, M., and Björklund, M. (2012), "Applying a network level in environmental impact assessment," *Journal of Business Research*, 65(2), 247–255.

Öberg, C., Shih, T., and Chou, H.-H. (2016), "Network strategies and effects in an interactive context," *Industrial Marketing Management*, 52, 117–127.

Olins, W. (1989), *Corporate Identity: Making Business Strategy Visible*, London: Thames and Hudson.

Olson, E.M., Walker Jr., O.C., and Ruekert, R.W. (1995), "Organizing for effective new product development: The moderating role of product innovativeness," *The Journal of Marketing*, 59(1), 48–62.

Oviatt, B.M., and McDougall, P.P. (1994), "Toward a theory of international new ventures," *Journal of International Business Studies*, 25(1), 45–64.

Palmer, A. (2005), *Principles of Services Marketing*, 4th edition, London: McGraw-Hill.

Pantouvakis, A.M., Siomkos, G.I., and Christou, E.S., (2015), *Marketing*, Athens: Livanis Publications.

Papavassiliou, N., and Baltas, G. (2003a), *Retail & Wholesale Marketing*, Athens: Rosili Publications.

Papavassiliou, N., and Baltas, G. (2003b), *Distribution Network & Logistics Management*, Athens: Rosili Publications.

Papavassiliou, N., and Indounas, K. (2005), *The Business Pricing Strategy*, Athens: Stamoulis Publications.

Patrinos, D.U. (2009), *Industrial Marketing*, 2nd edition, Athens: Hellenic Publications.

Patti, C.H. (1977), "Buyer information sources in the capital equipment industry," *Industrial Marketing Management*, 6(4), 259–264.

Patty, C.R. (1982), *Managing Salespeople*, 2nd edition, New York: Reston Publishing Company.

Pavitt, K. (1991), "Key characteristics of the large innovating firm," *British Journal of Management*, 32, 41–50.

Perreault, W.D., Cannon, J.P., and McCarthy, E.J. (2012), *Basic Marketing, A Marketing Strategy Planning Approach*, Chicago, IL: McGraw-Hill, Irwin.

Petrides, K.V., and Furnham, A. (2001), "Trait emotional intelligence: Psychometric investigation with reference to established trait taxonomies," *European Journal of Personality*, 15(6), 425–448.

Petroni, A., and Braglia, M. (2000), "Vendor selection using principal component analysis," *The Journal of Supply Chain Management*, 36(1), 63–69.

Pinckot, G. (2000), *Intrapreaneuring: Why you Don't Have to Leave the Corporation to Become an Entrepreneur*, San Francisco, CA: Barrett-Koehler Publishing.

Politz, A. (1960), "The dilemma of creative advertising," *Journal of Marketing*, 25(2), 1–6.

Porter, M.E. (1980), *Competitive Strategy: Techniques for Analyzing Industries and Competitors*, New York: The Free Press.

Porter, M.E. (1982), "The technological dimension of competitive strategy," Working Paper HBS 82–119, Boston, MA: Harvard Business School.

Powell, E. (1981), "Truth, politics and persuasion," *Advertising Quarterly*, 67(Spring), 12.

Powell, J.H., and Swart, J. (2010), "Mapping the values in B2B relationships: A systemic, knowledge-based perspective," *Industrial Marketing Management*, 39(3), 437–449.

Prahalad, C.K., and Hamel, G. (1990) "The core competence of the corporation," *Harvard Business Review*, 68(5), 79–91.

Pujari, D. (2004), "Self-service with a smile? Self-service technology (SST) encounters among Canadian business-to-business," *International Journal of Service Industry Management*, 15(2), 200–219.

Puri, S.J. (1993), "Where industrial sales training is weak," *Industrial Marketing Management*, 22(2), 101–108.

Puto, C.P., Patton III, W.E., and King, R.H. (1985), "Risk handling strategies in industrial vendor selection decisions," *Journal of Marketing*, 49(Winter), 89–98.

Qin, X., and Jiang, Z. (2019), "The impact of AI on the advertising process: The Chinese experience," *Journal of Advertising*, 48(4), 338–346.

Quinn, J.B. (1985), "Managing innovation: Controlled chaos," *Harvard Business Review*, 63(3), 73–84.

Quinn, R., and Cameron, K. (1988), "Organizational paradox and transformation," in R. Quinn and K. Cameron (eds.), *Paradox and Transformation*, Cambridge, MA: Ballinger Publishing.

Raddats, C., and Easingwood, C. (2010), "Services growth options for B2B product-centric businesses," *Industrial Marketing Management*, 39(8), 1334–1345.

Raddats, C., Kowalkowski, C., Benedettini, O., Burton, J., and Gebauer, H. (2019), "Servitization: A contemporary thematic review of four major research streams," *Industrial Marketing Management*, 83, 207–223.

Rangan, V.K., and Bartus, K. (1995), "New product commercialisation: Common mistakes," in V.K. Rangan, B.P. Shapiro, and R.T. Moriarity (eds.), *Business Marketing Strategy*, Chicago, IL: Irwin.

Rao, V.R. (1984), "Pricing research in marketing: The state of the art," *The Journal of Business*, 57(1), s39–s60.

Rau, P.A. (1987), "Awareness advertising and international market segmentation," *International Journal of Advertising*, 6(4), 313–321.

Rauyruen, P., Miller, K.E., and Groth, M. (2009), "B2B services: Linking service loyalty and brand equity," *Journal of Services Marketing*, 23(3), 175–186.

Ray, M.L. (1974), "Marketing communications and the hierarchy of effects," in P. Clarke (ed.), *New Models for Communications Research*, Beverly Hills, CA: Sage.

Ray, M.L. (1982), *Advertising and Communication Management*, Englewood Cliffs, NJ: Prentice Hall.

Reeder, R.R., Brierty, E.G., and Reeder, B.H. (1987), *Industrial Marketing: Analysis, Planning and Control*, Upper Saddle River, NJ: Prentice Hall.

Rexroad, R.A. (1983), *High Technology Marketing Management*, New York: Ronald Press.

Ringberg, T., Reihlen, M., and Rydén, P. (2019), "The technology-mindset interactions: Leading to incremental, radical or revolutionary innovations," *Industrial Marketing Management*, 79, 102–113.

Risley, G. (1972), *Modern Industrial Marketing*, New York: McGraw-Hill.

Robertson, T.S. (1967), "The process of innovation and the diffusion of innovation," *Journal of Marketing*, 31(January), 14–19.

Robinson, P.J., and Stidsen, B. (1967), *Personal Selling in a Modern Perspective*, Boston, MA: Allyn & Bacon.

Robinson, P.J., Faris, C.W., and Wind, Y. (1967), *Industrial Buying and Creative Marketing*, Boston, MA: Allyn and Bacon.

Rodriguez, M., Peterson, R.M., and Ajjan, H. (2015), "CRM/social media technology: impact on customer orientation process and organizational sales performance," in K. Kubacki (ed.), *Ideas in Marketing: Finding the New and Polishing the Old*, Cham: Springer.

Rogers, E.M. (1995), *Diffusion of Innovation*, 4th edition, New York: Free Press.

Rosen, D.E., Schroeder, J.E., and Purinton, E.F. (1988), "Marketing high tech products: Lessons in customer focus from the marketplace," *Journal of Consumer and Market Research*, 98(6), 6–16.

Rosenberg, L.J. (1977), "Job performance in the industrial sales force," *Industrial Marketing Management*, 6(1), 99–102.

Rosenbloom, B. (1987), *Marketing Channels: A Management View*, Orlando, FL: The Dryden Press.

Ross, E.B. (1984), "Making money with proactive pricing," *Harvard Business Review*, 62(6), 145–155.

Rothwell, R., and Robertson, A.B. (1973), "The role of communications in technological innovation," *Research Policy*, 2(3), 204–225.

Rouziès, D., Anderson, E., Kohli, A.K., Michaels, R.E., Weitz, B.A., and Zoltners, A.A. (2005), "Sales and marketing integration: A proposed framework," *Journal of Personal Selling & Sales Management*, 25(2), 113–122.

Rowley, J. (2008), "Understanding digital content marketing," *Journal of Marketing Management*, 24(5–6), 517–540.

Roy, S., and Sivakumar, K. (2007), "The role of information technology adoption in the globalization of business buying behavior: A conceptual model and research propositions," *Journal of Business and Industrial Marketing*, 22(4), 220–227.

Rozell, E.J., Pettijohn, C.E., and Parker, R.S. (2004), "Customer-oriented selling: Exploring the roles of emotional intelligence and organizational commitment," *Psychology & Marketing*, 21(6), 405–424.

Rubenstein, A.H., Chakrabarti, A.K., O' Keefe, R.D., Souder, W.E., and Young, H.C. (1976), "Factors influencing innovation success at project level," *Research Management*, 19(3), 15–20.

Saavedra, C.A. (2016), *The Marketing Challenge for Industrial Companies: Advanced Concepts and Practices*, Cham: Springer International.

Salovey, P., Mayer, J., and Caruso, D. (2004), "Emotional intelligence: Theory, findings, and implications," *Psychological Inquiry*, 15(3), 197–215.

Samli, A.C., and Wills, J. (1986), "Strategies for marketing computers and related products," *Industrial Marketing Management*, 15(1), 23–32.

Sarin, S., and Mohr, J.J. (2008), "An introduction to the special issue on marketing of high-technology products, services and innovations," *Industrial Marketing Management*, 37(6), 626–628.

Sarkis, J., and Talluri, S. (2002), "A model for strategic supplier selection," *The Journal of Supply Chain Management*, 38(1), 18–28.

Schillewaert, N., Ahearne, M.J., Frambach, R.T., and Moenaert, R.K. (2005), "The adoption of information technology in the sales force," *Industrial Marketing Management*, 34(4, Special Issue), 323–336.

Schilling, M.A., and Hill, C.W.L. (1998), "Managing the new product development process: Strategic imperatives," *Academy of Management Executive*, 12(3), 67–81.

Schindler, R.M. (2012), *Pricing Strategies: A Marketing Approach*, Thousand Oaks, CA: Sage Publications.

Schoemaker, P.J., Heaton, S., and Teece, D. (2018), "Innovation, dynamic capabilities, and leadership," *California Management Review*, 61(1), 15–42.

Schumpeter, J. (1942), *Capitalism, Socialism and Democracy*, New York: Harper.

Seymour, D.T. (ed.) (1989), *The Pricing Decision: A Strategic Planner for Marketing Professionals*, Chicago, IL: Probus Publishing Co.

Shaltoni, A.M., and West, D.C. (2010), "The measurement of e-marketing orientation (EMO) in business-to-business markets," *Industrial Marketing Management*, 39(7), 1097–1102.

Shanklin, W., and Ryans, J. (1982), *Essentials of Marketing High Technology*, Lexington, MA: Lexington Books.

Shanklin, W., and Ryans, J. (1984a), "Organizing for high tech marketing," *Harvard Business Review*, 62, 164–171.

Shanklin, W., and Ryans, J. (1984b), *Marketing High Technology*, Lexington, MA: Lexington Books.

Shanklin, W., and Ryans, J. (1987) *Essentials of Marketing High Technology*, Lexington, MA: DC Health.

Shapiro, B.P. (1974), "Build marketing strength into industrial selling," *Harvard Business Review*, 50, 30–46.

Shapiro, B.P. (1977a), *Industrial Product Policy: Managing the Existing Product Line*, Cambridge, MA: Marketing Science Institute.

Shapiro, B.P. (1977b), "Improve distribution with your promotional mix," *Harvard Business Review*, 55(2), 115–123.

Shapiro, B.P., and Jackson, B.B. (1978), "Industrial pricing to meet customer needs," *Harvard Business Review*, 56(6), 119–127.

Shapiro, R.D., and Heskett, J.L. (1985), *Logistics Strategy*, St. Paul, MN: West.

Sharma, A. (2002), "Trends in Internet-based business-to-business marketing," *Industrial Marketing Management*, 31(2), 77–84.

Sharma, A., and Mehrotra, A. (2007), "Choosing an optimal mix in multichannel environments," *Industrial Marketing Management*, 36(January), 21–28.

Shibutani, T. (1962), "Reference groups and social control," *in* A.M. Rose (ed.), *Human Behavior and Social Processes: An Interactionist Approach*, Boston, MA: Houghton Mifflin, 128–147.

Shipley, D., and Kiely, J. (1988), "Motivation and dissatisfaction of industrial salespeople: How relevant is Herzberg's theory?," *European Journal of Marketing*, 22(1), 35–43.

Shipley, D., and Prinja, S. (1988), "The services and supplier choice influences of industrial distributors," *The Service Industries Journal*, 8(2), 176–187.

Shipley, D.D. (1981), "Pricing objectives in British manufacturing industry," *Journal of Industrial Economics*, 29(4), 429–443.

Shipley, D.D., and Jobber, D. (2001), "Integrative pricing via the pricing wheel," *Industrial Marketing Management*, 21(3), 301–314.

Shipley, D.L., Arnett, J.D., Arnett, W.A., Baumel, S.D., Bhavnani, A., Chou, C.J., Nelson, D.L., Soha, M., Yamada, D.H., and Tolerant Systems, Inc. (1989), "Distributed multiprocess transaction processing system and method," US Patent, 4, 819, 159.

Shostack, G.L. (1977), "Breaking free from product marketing," *Journal of Marketing*, 41(2), 73–80.

Siebert, J.C. (1970), "Advertising and selling objectives for industrial markets," in T.C. Koram and R.W. Hill (eds.), *New Ideas in Industrial Marketing*, London: Staples Press.

Siegel, M. (1998), "Do computers slow us down?," *Fortune*, 30 March, 34–38.

Siems, T.F. (2001), "B2B e-commerce: Why the new economy lives," *Southwest Economy*, July/August, 1–5.

Simchi-Levi, D., Kaminsky, P., and Simchi-Levi, E. (2003), *Designing and Managing the Supply Chain: Concepts, Strategies, and Case Studies*, New York: McGraw Hill Professional.

Simkin, L. (2000), "Marketing is marketing—maybe!," *Marketing Intelligence Planning*, 18(3), 154–158.

Singh, R., and Koshy, A. (2010), "Determinants of B2B salesperson's performance and effectiveness: A review and synthesis of literature," *Journal of Business and Industrial Marketing*, 25(7), 535–545.

Siomkos, G., and Fotiadis, Th. (2020), *Industrial Marketing*, 1st edition, Nicosia: Broken Hill Publishers.

Siomkos, G., Tsiamis, I., and Fotiadis, T. (2017), *High Tech and Industrial Product Marketing*, Athens: Livani Publications.

Sirkin, H.L., Hemerling, J.W., and Bhattacharya, A.K. (2008), *Globality: Competing with Everyone from Everywhere for Everything*, New York: Business Plus.

Skankin, W.L., and Ryans, J.K. (1984), "Organizing for high-tech marketing," *Harvard Business Review*, 62(6), 164–171.

Slater, S.F., and Narver, J.C. (2000), "The positive effect of a market orientation on business profitability: A balanced replication," *Journal of Business Research*, 48, 69–73.

Smith, D., and Bard, M. (1989), "Everything you always wanted to know about industrial buying behavior, but were afraid to ask-in case it made the research too expensive," *Journal of the Market Research Society*, 31(3), 307–330.

Song, L.Z., and Song, M. (2010), "The role of information technologies in enhancing R&D–marketing integration: An empirical investigation," *Journal of Product Innovation Management*, 27(3), 382–401.

Souder, W.E., and Moenaert, R.K. (1992), "Integrating marketing and R&D project personnel within innovation projects: An information uncertainty model," *Journal of Management Studies*, 29(4), 485–512.

Spekman, R.E. (1979), "Organizational boundary behavior: A conceptual framework for investigating the industrial salesperson," in R.P. Bagozzi (ed.), *Sales Management: New Developments from Behavioral and Decision Model Research*, Report No. 79–107, Cambridge, MA: Marketing Science Institute.

Spekman, R.E. (1988), "Strategic supplier selection: Understanding long-term buyer relationships," *Business Horizons*, 31(4), 75–81.

Stank, T.P., Daugherty, P.J., and Ellinger, A.E. (1999), "Marketing/logistics integration and firm performance," *The International Journal of Logistics Management*, 10(1), 11–24.

Stanton, W.J. (1978), *Fundamentals of Marketing*, Kogakusha: McGraw-Hill.

Stanton, W.J., and Futrell, C.C. (1987), *Fundamentals of Marketing*, New York: McGraw-Hill.

Stephenson, P.R. (1969), "Identifying determinants of retail patronage," *The Journal of Marketing*, 33(3), 57–61.

Stern, L.W., and Sturdivant, F.D. (1987) "Customer driven distribution system," *Harvard Business Review*, 65(4), 34–41.

Stern, L.W., El-Ansary, A.I., and Brown, J.R. (1989), *Management Marketing Channels*, Englewood Cliffs, NJ: Prentice Hall.

Stremersch, S., Wuyts, S., and Frambach, R.T. (2001), "The purchasing of full-service contracts," *Industrial Marketing Management*, 30(1), 1–12.

Swink, M., and Song, M. (2007), "Effects of marketing-manufacturing integration on new product development time and competitive advantage," *Journal of Operations Management*, 25(1), 203–217.

Szmigin, I.T. (1993), "Managing quality in business-to-business services," *European Journal of Marketing*, 27(1), 2–21.

Taiminen, H.M., and Karjaluoto, H. (2015), "The usage of digital marketing channels in SMEs," *Journal of Small Business and Enterprise Development*, 22(4), 633–651.

Takeuchi, H., and Nonaka, I. (1986), "The new product development game," *Harvard Business Review*, 64(1), 137–146.

Tech American Foundation (2004), *Demystifying Big Data-IBM*. Retrieved 15 February 2014 from www-304.ibm.com/industries/publicsector/fileserve?contentid=239170.

Technology, Innovation and Regional Economic Development (TIRED) (1982), Washington, DC: US Congress, Office of Technology Assessment, September 9.

Teece, D.J., Pisano, G., and Shuen, A. (1990), "Firm capabilities, resources and the concept of strategy," Consortium on Competitiveness and Cooperation Working Paper # 90-9, Berkeley, CA: University of California at Berkeley, Center for Research in Management.

Teller, C., Alexander, A., and Floh, A. (2015), "Competition and cooperation in retail and service agglomerations: The case of the high street," *Industrial Marketing Management*, 52(January), 6–17.

Theron, E., Terblanche, N.S., and Boshoff, C. (2008), "The antecedents of relationship commitment in the management of relationships in business-to-business (B2B) financial services," *Journal of Marketing Management*, 24(9–10), 997–1010.

Tomaras, P.A. (2009), *Industrial Marketing*, Athens: Tomaras Petros.

Tompkins, J.A., White, J.A., Bozer, Y.A., Frazelle, E.H., and Tanchoco, J.M.A. (2003), *Facilities Planning*, New York, NJ: John Wiley & Sons.

Toon, M., Morgan, R., Lindgreen, A., Vanhamme, J., and Hingley, M.K. (2016), "Processes and integration in the interaction of purchasing and marketing: Considering synergy and symbiosis," *Industrial Marketing Management*, 52(February), 74–81.

Toon, M., Robson, M.J., and Morgan, R.E. (2012), "A value-in-process analysis of relationship interactions in non-equity alliances," *Industrial Marketing Management*, 41(January), 186–196.

Tretyak, O., Tsybina, E., and Rebiazina, V. (2013), "Managing portfolios of interconnected customers: Evidence from Russian B2B market," *Journal of Business & Industrial Marketing*, 28(3), 229–239.

Turnbull, P.W. (1974), "The allocation of resources to marketing communications in industrial markets," *Industrial Marketing Management*, 3(5), 297–310.

Turner, F.J. (ed.) (2017), *Social Work Treatment: Interlocking Theoretical Approaches*, Oxford: Oxford University Press.

Tushman, M.L., and Anderson, P. (1986), "Technological discontinuities and organizational environments," *Administrative Science Quarterly*, 31(3), 439–465.

Utterback, J. (1994), *Mastering the Dynamics of Innovation*, Boston, MA: Harvard Business School Press.

Utterback, J.M. (1971), "The process of technological innovation within the firm," *Academy of Management Journal*, 14(1), 75–88.

Vaccaro, V.L. (2009), "B2B green marketing and innovation theory for competitive advantage," *Journal of Systems and Information Technology*, 11(4), 315–330.

Valtakoski, A. (2017), "Explaining servitization failure and deservitization: A knowledge-based perspective," *Industrial Marketing Management*, 60, 138–150.

Vandermerwe, S., and Rada, J. (1988), "Servitization of business: Adding value by adding services," *European Management Journal*, 6(4), 314–324.

Vargo, S.L., and Lusch, R.F. (2011), "It's all B2B… and beyond: Toward a systems perspective of the market," *Industrial Marketing Management*, 40(2), 181–187.

Verma, R., and Pullman, M.E. (1998), "An analysis of the supplier selection process," *Omega*, 26(6), 739–750.

Veryzer Jr., R.W. (1998), "Key factors affecting customer evaluation of discontinuous new products," *Journal of Product Innovation Management*, 15(2), 136–150.

Viio, P., and Grönroos, C. (2015), "How buyer–seller relationship orientation affects adaptation of sales processes to the buying process," *Industrial Marketing Management*, 52(January), 37–46.

von Bertalanffy, L. (1968), *General System Theory: Foundations, Development*, New York: George Braziller.

von Hippel, E. (1986), "Lead users: A source of novel product concepts," *Management Science*, 32(July): 791–805.

Vroom, V. (1964), *Work and Motivation*, New York: Wiley and Sons.

Wagner, S.M., and Eggert, A. (2015), "Co-management of purchasing and marketing: Why, when and how?," *Industrial Marketing Management*, 52, 2.

Weber, C.A., Current, J.R., and Benton, W.C. (1991), "Vendor selection criteria and methods," *European Journal of Operational Research*, 50(1), 2–18.

Webster Jr., F.E. (1968), "Interpersonal communication and salesman effectiveness," *Journal of Marketing*, 32(3), 7–13.

Webster Jr., F.E. (1970), "Informal communication in industrial markets," *Journal of Marketing Research*, 7, 186–189.

Webster Jr., F.E. (1974), *Marketing Communication: Modern Promotional Strategy*, New York: The Ronald Press Co.

Webster Jr., F.E. (1975), "Perceptions of the industrial distributor," *Industrial Marketing Management*, 4, 257–264.

Webster Jr., F.E. (1976), "The role of the industrial distributor in marketing strategy," *Journal of Marketing*, 40(1), 10–16.

Webster Jr., F.E. (1978), "Management science in industrial marketing," *Journal of Marketing*, 42(1), 21–27.

Webster Jr., F.E. (1983), *Field Sales Management*, New York: John Wiley & Sons.

Webster Jr., F.E. (1984), *Industrial Marketing Strategy*, 2nd edition, Hoboken, NJ: Wiley & Sons.

Webster Jr., F.E. (1988), "The rediscovery of the marketing concept," *Business Horizons*, 31(3), 29–39.

Webster Jr., F.E. (1991), *Industrial Marketing Strategy*, 3rd edition, Hoboken, NJ: Wiley & Sons.

Webster Jr., F.E., and Wind, Y. (1972a), "A general model of organizational buying behavior," *Journal of Marketing*, 36(2), 12–19.

Webster Jr., F.E., and Wind, Y. (1972b), *Organizational Buying Behavior*, Englewood Cliffs, NJ: Prentice Hall.

Weinberg, B.D., and Berger, P.D. (2011), "Connected customer lifetime value: The impact of social media," *Journal of Direct, Data and Digital Marketing Practice*, 12(4), 328–344.

Weiss, A.M., and Heide, J.B. (1993), "The nature of organizational search in high technology markets," *Journal of Marketing Research*, 30(May), 230–233.

Wengler, S., Ehret, M., and Saab, S. (2006), "Implementation of key account management: Who, Why and How? An exploratory study on the current implementation of key account management programs," *Industrial Marketing Management*, 35(1), 103–112.

Widing, R.E.I., and Talarzyk, W.W. (1993), "Electronic information systems for consumers: An evaluation of computer-assisted formats in multiple decision environments," *Journal of Marketing Research*, 30(2), 125.

Wiersema, F. (2013), "The B2B agenda: The current state of B2B marketing and a look ahead," *Industrial Marketing Management*, 42, 470–488.

Wilcox, J.B., Howell, R.D., Kuzdrall, P., and Britney, R. (1987), "Price quantity discounts: Some implications for buyers and sellers," *The Journal of Marketing*, 51(3), 60–70.

Williamson, N.C. (1983), "A method for determining the causes of salesperson turnover," *Journal of Personal Selling and Sales Management*, 3(1), 26–35.

Wilson, D. (1999), *Organizational Marketing*, London: International Thompson.

Wilson, D.F. (2000), "Why divide consumer and organizational buyer behavior?," *European Journal of Marketing*, 34(7), 780–796.

Wilson, E., and Woodside, A. (2001), "Executive and consumer decision processes: Increasing useful sensemaking by identifying similarities and departures," *Journal of Business & Industrial Marketing*, 16(5), 401–414.

Wind, J., and Mahajan, V. (1997), "Editorial: Issues and opportunities in new product development: An introduction to the special issue," *Journal of Marketing Research*, 34(1), 1–12.

Wind, Y. (1970), "Industrial source loyalty," *Journal of Marketing Research*, 7(November), 450–457.

Wind, Y. (2005), "Marketing as an engine of business growth: A cross-functional perspective," *Journal of Business Research*, 58(7), 863–873.

Wind, Y., and Claycamp, H.J. (1976), "Planning product line strategy: A matrix approach," *Journal of Marketing*, 40(1), 2–9.

Woodside, A.G., Liakko, T., and Vuori, R. (1999), "Organizational buying of capital equipment involving persons across several authority levels," *Journal of Business and Industrial Marketing*, 14(1), 30–48.

Worcester, R. (1973), *Consumer Market Research Handbook*, Maidenhead: McGraw-Hill.

Worcester, R. (1986), "Corporate image research," in R. Worcester and J. Downham (eds.), *Consumer Market Research Handbook*, 3rd edition, Amsterdam: Elsevier on behalf of ESOMAR.

Wright, R. (2004), *Business-to-Business Marketing: A Step-by-Step Guide*, London: Pearson.

Xu, Y., Yen, D.C., Lin, B., and Chou, D.C. (2002), "Adopting customer relationship management technology," *Industrial Management & Data Systems*, 102(8), 442–452.

Yang, M., and Gabrielsson, P. (2017), "Entrepreneurial marketing of international high-tech business-to-business new ventures: A decision-making process perspective," *Industrial Marketing Management*, 64, 147–160.

Yu, C.S., and Tao, Y.H. (2009), "Understanding business-level innovation technology adoption," *Technovation*, 29(2), 92–109.

Yuan, L., and Chen, X. (2015), "Managerial learning and new product innovativeness in high-tech industries: Curvilinear effect and the role of multilevel institutional support," *Industrial Marketing Management*, 50, 51–59.

Zahay, D. (2008), "Successful B2B customer database management," *Journal of Business & Industrial Marketing*, 23(4), 264–272.

Zeynep Ata, U., and Toker, A. (2012), "The effect of customer relationship management adoption in business-to-business markets," *Journal of Business & Industrial Marketing*, 27(6), 497–507.

Zhang, S., and Markman, A.B. (1998), "Overcoming the early entrant advantage: The role of alignable and nonalignable differences," *Journal of Marketing Research*, 35(4), 413–426.

Ziggers, G.W., and Henseler, J. (2015), "The reinforcing effect of a firm's customer orientation and supply base orientation on performance," *Industrial Marketing Management*, 52(January), 18–26.

INDEX